WHEN A REAL LION MEETS
A REAL MASTER

WHEN A REAL LION MEETS
A REAL MASTER

SWAMI SWATANTRA SARJANO

OSHO WORLD FOUNDATION

NIYOGI
BOOKS

Published by:

NIYOGI BOOKS

D-78, Okhla Industrial Area, Phase-I
New Delhi-110 020, INDIA
Tel: 91-11-26816301, 49327000
Fax: 91-11-26810483, 26813830
email: niyogibooks@gmail.com
website: www.niyogibooksindia.com

In collaboration with

Osho World Foundation

C-5/44, Safdarjung Development Area
New Delhi-110016
Tel: 91-11-26862898, 26964533
Email: contact@oshoworld.com
Website: www.oshoworld.com

Compiled and Edited by: Ma Anand Bhagawati
Further Editing by: Ma Anand Vandana

Co-ordination: Ma Prem Naina

Cover Design and Layout: Osho World Foundation

Photographs of Osho: Osho World Foundation

ISBN: 978-93-85285-36-3

Publication: 2016

Printed at: Niyogi Offset Pvt. Ltd., New Delhi, India

This book is dedicated with gratitude to

Mai -

The only woman on earth

Who never said no to me.

CONTENTS

Introduction

It has been more than twenty years that I wanted to write this book, a book about the ineffable and mysterious relationship that exists between a disciple and his Master. After starting several times, I always dropped the whole idea and forgot my noble intentions, and for a very simple reason, and that is the inadequacy and poverty of our language.

Let's say the truth about this: it is very difficult to communicate with a written language, much more than with an oral transmission, because when you talk, you have the help of your expressions, the tonality of your voice, the movement of your hands, the laughter that you can have between a sentence and the next, while writing is a 'cold medium', as acutely pointed out by Marshall McLuhan and fully subscribed to by Osho, my Master.

You can look for yourself: when you have an extraordinary experience, out of the blue, don't you usually say, "I have become speechless," or "I had no words…?" And you don't even need to go that far away, because you just have to think about the first time you have kissed someone's lips: have you later told everybody, or did you try to explain to your partner how beautiful it was? No, because normally we have no words to describe the experiences that have touched us deeply, and we don't even try to find them!

I would have loved to narrate my thirty years with an enlightened Master, but the project was a little embarrassing to say the least, because I didn't really know which language to use, which metaphors, which literary artifices. At a certain point I had adventured towards a sumptuous 'Phenomenology of Enlightenment', just to make all those secondhand intellectuals that I used to hang out with before meeting Osho happy, but then I simply gave up, because it was not reaching anywhere and it was not possible to explain deeply what I was trying to convey.

I even tried with 'mystical language', comparing the Master to a light on the path, to a silent oracle, to a modern Jesus Christ – but much more articulated – defining him as 'far superior than Buddha!', but they were all terms that made me laugh; therefore you can imagine how much they would make the readers laugh!

I have tried in every possible and impossible way to narrate this experience, to communicate in which way a Master works on his disciple – and how this person defends himself but I have always failed. I admit this openly and with no shame, but one day I said to myself, "And what about if we let the Master himself tell the whole story?"

In fact, during all these years the Master did nothing else than seduce me, hit me, flatter me, caress me, giving me some heavy slaps – metaphorically speaking – just to lift me up a minute later, maybe just in order to hit me again with another

Zen stick, followed inevitably by another caress, a kiss, a twinkle of his eyes, then another hit…and all this for thirty years and more!

I then decided to collect all the answers the Master had given me during our relationship, and even those discourses when he suddenly would bring up my name, just to give me a pat on the head or to hit me again with one of his fatidic hammerings, and offer all this to you.

I'm presenting his words on a plate made of bamboo leaves, hoping that this will help you understand much better than I could write myself what this

'exemplary relationship' between Master and disciple is made of, and how it works. I call it 'exemplary' because, in spite of my effort to put myself down, out of ancient modesty and healthy realism, I finally realized that my relationship with Osho has been quite 'special', hence exemplary.

I always refused the assumption that my Master could possibly love one of his disciples more than he would love any other one, because I was perceiving him as pure love, indiscriminate, choiceless, and most of all total towards all and everyone, and yet Osho seemed truly to have a special affair with this Sarjano, and he was showing an inexplicable sympathy towards this crazy Italian and an even more inexplicable perseverance in hitting him.

Sometimes I would say to myself that I probably reminded him of his childhood, perhaps he had some friend resembling me or he himself had been very similar to me, because we both grew up – even if in different circumstances – without a solid father figure to break our balls and teach us all the bullshit that usually fathers teach their children. Moreover, we both used to spend our days by the river – which were two different rivers, but we all know anyway that it is always the same river – and we swam in those dangerous waters, or we jumped into the river from some trees, or we were chasing the snakes to place them in our pockets and scare our friends later, on the way home.

There are many points we have in common about our childhood, and even where our adolescence is concerned, from the enchantments of the river to a premature passion for philosophy and the great questions of life. In fact at the age of twelve I was reading La Nausée by Jean Paul Sartre, while Osho was reading the scriptures of Buddha and the chants of Mahavira – to each of us his own way of searching, but the fact remains that both of us had started to search for their inner truth very early.

Perhaps, as the Master had repeated many times, we have been together in some past life too, but what matters is that this turbulent Italian has been the person to whom the Master has spoken more often during his holy career, amongst his disciples – and he was not only the one that had posed the largest number of questions but even the ones that got more answers! I would have loved to publish the words of the Master to his disciple just like this, with no comment, one after the other, but some close friends begged me to narrate at least briefly, in my own way, what was happening to me and to the Commune during the days when Osho was addressing me with those words. So I surrendered and I did just that.

I have kept the narration in the third person for two reasons: firstly because it feels much better in this way and secondly because I simply want to be a witness, someone who just watches and then tells you what he has seen! Besides the joke (and who is joking?), what I'm trying to say is that in the end I decided to limit my personal story to a minimum, and to report only the most significant moments of it; hence I must have forgotten many people who were very dear to me, just to let the Master himself speak more, with his infinite simplicity and his infinite love.

His style of expression has been represented here as faithfully as is possible, with all repetitions and all reiterations, because I certainly do not wish to get another stick from him! Once, during my job of translating one of his books from English to Italian, I had started to cut a little here and there, to erase all his repetitions, the most redundant sentences, and even modifying lightly – but only for the peace of mind of the reader – his more risky statements! Osho got to know about it – I can't even imagine how – and he slammed me openly, saying that Sarjano was trying to make his words more digestible!

A friend helped me track that discourse which was given some time during 1980, and I'm giving you the most salient parts so that you can have a little taste of how things were functioning in this place!

"Just the other day I received a note from Arup (one of his secretaries) that 'Sarjano is translating your book into Italian, but he changes many things. He drops few things, he adds few things from his own knowledge.' Of course he is trying to do some good work; his intention is good! He wants to make it more logical, more intellectual, more sophisticated. And I am a little wild type of man! He wants to trim me here and there. You look at my beard! If Sarjano is allowed he will trim it like Nikolai Lenin, but then it will not be my beard. He is trying to make it more appealing. There is no doubt about his intentions, but these are the intentions which have always destroyed.

When he was told my message that he has to do exactly as it is: 'Don't try to improve upon it. Leave it as it is. Raw, wild, illogical, paradoxical, contradictory, repetitive, whatsoever it is, leave it as it is!' It is so difficult for him. He said, 'Then I will not translate. I would rather like cleaning work.'

You see how the mind works? He is not ready to listen to me; he would rather like to do cleaning work. Otherwise he has to be allowed to interpolate, to change, to color things according to his idea.

Now, whatsoever you will do you will do wrong, because what I am saying is from a totally different plane and what you will be doing will be a totally different effort – it won't belong to my plane, it won't belong to my dimension. It may be scholarly, but I am not a scholar. It may be knowledgeable, but I am not a knowledgeable person.

Knowledgeable people have their own ways. Just small things they will do...

For example, I had said that Saraha is the founder of Tibetan Buddhism. Now, no scholar will say so decisively. Only a madman can say so decisively because you have to give proofs, you have to give footnotes and you have to make a big appendix in which you have to give proofs. I never give any proofs, I never give any footnotes, I never give you any sources from where. I know only one source, the Akashic records!

So just to make it more appealing, more digestible, he had changed it just a little, not much, that 'Saraha can be said to be the founder of Tibetan Tantra, Tibetan Buddhism.' '… can be said…' Now this is a scholarly way, a legal way, but it destroys the whole beauty of it. It destroys its whole certainty, its decisiveness, its hammer-like quality. And hammers are not supposed to be digestible!

Sarjano, it is not a spaghetti! He is a good cook and makes beautiful spaghetti. I don't know anything about spaghetti, but I know Saraha is the founder of Tibetan Buddhism. And I will not give any proof about it. I don't believe in proofs; I simply know. I know Saraha; it is a personal friendship with Saraha. Even if the historians prove something else, I won't listen. I won't pay any attention to them, because I know Saraha."

Tao: The Golden Gate Vol. 2, Ch 4, Q 1, Excerpt

This is just a little taste of what is waiting for you, besides being a good excuse in order to justify the repetitions of my Master!

Try to understand this simple thing: when he was speaking to his disciples he was not reading a written discourse, neither was he thinking about the posterity that one day would read his words; he was just chatting with a few thousand friends that had come to listen to him. Hence it's natural that his elocutions are repetitive and fragmented by long pauses and infinite repetitions, because – I repeat it – his intention was not to make a nice book but to manage to communicate to some thick heads like ours his simple truth!

I hope that this will help you understand the journey a little better – the journey towards oneself, I mean, the journey to come back home, in the eternity that created us, and where, like it or not, we will all come back to one day, each of us with their own timing of course!

To find a living Master can be of immense value for your growth. But you don't have to worry about finding a Master, because it is not the disciple who chooses the Master (and how can he – with which criteria?) but it is rather the Master who chooses his disciples. It will be sufficient then that you prepare yourself and get ready to start your inner journey.

For this purpose it will be useless you start searching for Osho because he is no longer in his body, dead, and alive only in the hearts of his true disciples. For the rest, the organization that carries his name is nowadays in the hands of a little group of common delinquents who are destroying unopposed his entire heritage. But even if these miserable people step on everything, or even cancel the name of Osho from the earth, they will never be able to cancel Osho from my soul, and that's enough, more than enough!

And for those who are deaf to the call, I have here a little invocation written by Ronald D. Laing as the conclusion of his famous book The Politics of Experience. I offer it to you with all my heart:

"If I could turn you on
If I could drive you out
Of your wretched mind
If I could tell you
I would let you know..."

Have a good trip, my fellow traveler!

Swami Swatantra Sarjano

CHAPTER 01

Exodus and Arrival

During the mid-seventies he lived in Sicily, in the beautiful commune he had created with his life partner Silvia, a young schoolteacher who had dropped her assignment five years before to devote herself to another, much more interesting mission – the project to create the very first 'Alternative Commune' in Italy.

They had chosen Sicily for this experiment, because at that time it was still a quiet and uncontaminated place, wild and beautiful, with a rich and generous nature, besides being beset by the notorious generosity of its inhabitants.

During a long visit to this island, after the euphoria of '68 and its wind of revolution, they had come across an old castle facing the ocean, which seemed to have been uninhabited since a long time, but it was still so beautiful and in such great condition that they decided to enquire about the owner and if he would possibly rent the place to them.

The only person they could spot was a farmer called Antonino who was taking care of the fields surrounding the castle, and they asked him if he knew the owner and if he would be ready to rent out the castle. Antonino told them that the property had been deserted since twenty years, but they could visit the owner in Palermo, the nearby city, and ask him if he wanted to rent it out. He also warned them that this man was a sort of bureaucrat, a very respectable person, and that it would be unlikely for him to rent his castle to a bunch of hippies!

"No problem," they said, "we know how to appear appropriate!" And so, the very next morning they both dressed up in proper and straight clothes – he even managed to hide his long hair under a respectable hat – and set off. He introduced himself as a journalist working in Rome, while Silvia presented herself as a schoolteacher, and told the owner that they both loved the idea to have a countryside retreat for their holidays, a perfect place like the castle they had admired in Cala Rossa (Red Bay).

The owner of course believed what they said, and agreed to sign a five year contract, for the modest amount of what would be today the equivalent of 25 US Dollars a month!

The very next day they returned to Cala Rossa, and started the big feat of cleaning this place that had been abandoned for such a long time. After a few days, when everything was clean and shining, they began calling their friends all over the world, telling them that they had finally found the magic place that could give birth to their dream, a libertarian commune, and invited everybody to join the project as soon as they could manage.

After only a few days the first of their friends arrived, and within a few weeks the new commune was already housing more than twenty people. They started living together, dancing and singing together, sharing all they had together, and for five years lived a marvelous life, full of love, caring, solidarity, and a very intimate feeling of brotherhood and sisterhood.

Meanwhile Antonino, the farmer they had initially met, had become almost part of the family because he was still single and didn't have a girl-friend. His only job was to take care of the property, and now he also took care of all of these freaks like an unexpected angel, to the point that he was always available for their needs. He slept in one of the stables near the house, getting up early in the morning to light the fire, a task he would repeat in the evening mainly for the purpose of roasting the fish that his fishermen friends would drop every day in the courtyard. There was a huge well around which everybody gathered in the evening to eat the delicious fish cooked on the embers by Antonino himself, singing and dancing, drinking the local wine (that too provided by our angel) and having a lot of fun…

After five years of this life, a silent undercover train for Pune started operating, completely without his knowledge or any information about it, but this train took away nearly half of his friends in just a couple of years, and without him being aware of their destination!

The first *desaparecido* turned out to be a guy named Marco Salghetti, also called 'The Engineer', because he had in fact a PhD in engineering, but had left the family business long ago, because in reality he wanted to be a carpenter.

At the beginning of his new career, Marco had found for himself a small studio in Trastevere in the center of Rome, but when he got to know about the birth of this commune, he joined it immediately and placed his roots in the castle, where he could work with his beloved wood all day, without anybody breaking their balls about it. After two or three years that Marco had been living happily there, he saw him one day packing all his stuff, as if he were leaving for a long trip.

"I'm going to India," he explained simply.

"India…how come you are going to India?"

"A friend has invited me, and I couldn't just say no!"

"I didn't know that you have friends in India," said he.

"I didn't know either!" Marco replied in a weird and vaguely mysterious tone, and in no time he had gone forever.

He didn't receive any news for nearly three years about this guy, and one day a woman who was a successful therapist and occasional resident of the commune, left for India too, and without saying a word to anybody.

After a few months came the turn of Andrea Valcarenghi, his companion of a thousand political battles and metropolitan adventures during the sixties – he too disappeared quietly to mysterious India, and then Stefano and Patrizia, a couple who had been living in the commune from its very beginning left as well, without leaving any trace whatsoever!

This entire story was becoming truly disquieting, because in less than two years almost half of the commune seemed to have run away to India, and without giving explanations to anybody, not even to him! Furious but in vain he would ask, "But where the fuck are you going? Why in hell are you all going to India?"

Finally someone answered that he was going there "to meditate", or "to find myself ", to which he answered angrily: "But what do you want to meditate for? Why don't you meditate instead over my dick, which is much better! Then you say that you are going to find yourself, without knowing that wherever you go, you are going to find always the same piece of shit! We have to stay here, we have to create our revolution right here, we have to change this society before this society changes us, and you are just a coward, that's what you are, an escapist, one that runs away from life, from his responsibilities…"

He was that kind of guy in those years, and he just couldn't believe why all his friends were moving to India, which is a huge country, and god knows where precisely all these people were going to. Finally one day he came to know, with great surprise, that all his friends had traveled to the same place, to the same small Indian city! The place was called Pune, or Puna, as the Italians used to pronounce it, and it hosted the ashram of a certain Osho (at that time Bhagwan Shree Rajneesh), a guy he had never heard of before.

He managed to find a couple of books by this Osho, which – according to him – had been translated into a horrible Italian, but when he started to read, he found that they were really interesting and tremendously insightful. These books were practically a collection of the discourses that this spiritual master was imparting every morning from eight to nine thirty, and from seven to nine in the evening.

His discourses on specific sutras alternated with questions from the disciples, followed by his sagacious answers that were often punctuated by jokes so brutal and vulgar that most likely nobody dared to repeat them, not even in the army!

At first glance this Osho seemed to him a sort of 'organic intellectual', well informed on any subject and with a remarkable sense of humor, and more than anything else, he was definitely a great provocateur, something that he liked very much; yet all this wasn't throwing any light on why all his friends had gone to place themselves at the feet of this guy.

He was thinking and mumbling every day about this incredible story, without ever being capable of finding an answer to his questions, and he was more and more intrigued by this strange sequence of events, until Terry, his English girlfriend for the last five years, told him one day: "Listen, let's get it over with! I just bought two return tickets to Bombay, because I wanted to surprise you one of these days and take you to Pune, so you can finally stop frying your brain over this subject! It seems that you are always thinking about this story, so let's go there to have a look for ourselves!"

They left the very next week, and as soon as they arrived in Bombay, they jumped in a taxi directly at the airport, without wasting time for rest or to refresh themselves a little, and asked the driver to take them straight to Pune. After a four hour drive, he could not resist his curiosity, and even before looking for a hotel, he decided to go directly to this famous ashram, which the driver obviously knew quite well; ten minutes later they were dropped with their entire luggage in front of the big wooden entrance gates.

Just as they had unloaded their stuff, Marco, the first *desaparecido*, the one who had started that massive exodus towards India, came out of the gate and saw them. He held in his hands a small plate with several pieces of cake, which he offered to both very coolly, saying, "Ah, it's good that you came in time for my little celebration, 'cause I've been waiting for you since a long time!"

"What are we celebrating?" he asked without understanding what his friend Marco was talking about.

"We are celebrating my sannyas birthday, because today it is three years that I have been initiated into sannyas, and usually here we celebrate this date, as this is the day of our real birth. I am so happy that you have finally arrived, and now I can cross out your name from my little list!"

"Forget it," he answered with a laugh. "We have come here just for a couple of weeks, only to see what has happened to you and all the others, and why you never unglue yourselves from this place!"

"Is that so?" replied Marco, who was now going by the name of 'Ashish'. "Now you will see how many people are going to come here to see what has happened to YOU!" He thought that this was a nice punch, but nothing else, because to him this locale really didn't look like a place where he would want to live, but he decided to have at least a quick look, and entered the premises.

At that time the rules to enter were very simple, not like nowadays where one needs twenty legal papers with stamps and more just to step inside! Then it was sufficient that you put your signature in the guestbook and you were inside, so he and Terry went in and were immediately welcomed by hordes of kids of all ages; they had just finished their school lessons and were now invading the ashram with all their vivacity and playfulness. He looked at them, and realized instantly that these children were the most free, natural, spontaneous kids that he had ever seen in his life, with the exception perhaps of those in his commune. He suddenly had the absolute sensation to have ended up in a 'different' place, a place that must have for sure some qualities, because children do not pretend, and they are just who they are, and if they were so free and natural here, that meant at least that this place must be very healthy and truly 'libertarian'.

He was so overwhelmed by the impetuous energy of these kids, that after a minute he got rid of his leather jacket, of his boots and even of his jeans, because he had decided to tie a simple lungi around his waist, just to be free to play with them!

Later they went to stay at the Blue Diamond, a five star hotel very close to the ashram, but he could hardly sleep the whole night out of excitement, because the next morning he would see this guy that everybody was calling Osho, and he was curious to the max!

The next morning he started walking at the first light of the dawn along the path of Koregaon Park, until he arrived in front of the ashram gate. Disciples were entering in large numbers, and he estimated that there must have been at least a few thousand people there. He entered the hall – then called 'Buddha Hall' – which hosted all the meditations and the Master's daily discourses, and realized that it was already full of people; hence he took a seat among the last rows and, sitting on the marble floor, he thought that next time he would have to bring a cushion, like everybody else.

Gradually, from a small podium at the center of the hall, sweet music expanded its notes into the air, to receive the arrival of the Master. The music went on for at least ten minutes when suddenly Osho appeared on the podium at the end of the hall, where only a comfortable chair was situated, and nothing else. He raised his hands near to his face in a silent *namaste*, rotating slowly, slowly, for 180 degrees, to give his blessings to everybody present.

In that moment he was literally hit by the most incredible and intense experience of his life, because out of the blue, as fulgurated on the way to Damascus, he remembered *everything!*

He remembered that in his past lives he had been in India many times, even with Jesus after he had pretended to die on Golgatha and then resurrected to escape unseen to Kashmir, where he lived to the respectable age of 98 years; and if you don't know this story, make a little trip to Kashmir, where you can see his grave, the grave of Jesus of Nazareth. He remembered that he had been with Osho many times before in other past lives, and that he had walked on many paths with him.

Looking around the hall, he had the impression of seeing only familiar faces, somehow, as if he had found again his fellow-travelers, as if he had finally joined again with his tribe, as if he had finally come home.

That morning, almost as if Osho had been waiting for him, he started to talk about the masses that he compared to the camels, and of those few individuals that are rebellious, which he called 'lions'…

It was the first time that he was listening to his words, and he discovered immediately that his words were almost as sweet as his silence!

> *…Man is not born perfect. He is born incomplete. He is born as a process. He is born on the way, as a pilgrim. That is his agony and his ecstasy too – agony because he cannot rest, he has to go ahead, he has always to go ahead. He has to seek and search and explore; he has to become, because his being arises only through becoming. Becoming is his being. He can only be if he is on the move.*
>
> *Evolution is intrinsic to man's nature, evolution is his very soul. And those who take themselves for granted remain unfulfilled; those who think they are born complete remain unevolved. Then the seed remains the seed, never becomes a tree, and never knows the joys of spring and the sunshine and the rain, and the ecstasy of bursting into millions of flowers.*

That explosion is the fulfillment, that explosion is what God is all about – exploding into millions of flowers. When the potential becomes the actual, only then is man fulfilled. Man is born as a potential; that is unique to man. All other animals are born complete; they are born as they are going to die. There is no evolution between their birth and their death: they move on the same plane, they never go through any transformation. No radical change in their life ever happens. They move horizontally, the vertical never penetrates them.

Or, we can use the metaphors used by Friedrich Nietzsche. He says that man's life can be divided into three successive metamorphoses of the spirit. The first he calls 'the camel', the second he calls 'the lion', the third he calls 'the child'. These are very pregnant metaphors: the camel, the lion and the child.

Each human being has to draw upon and assimilate the cultural heritage of his society – his culture, his religion, and his people. He has to assimilate all that the past makes available. He has to assimilate the past; this is what Nietzsche calls the camel stage. The camel has the power of storing up in his body enormous amounts of food and water for his arduous journey across the desert. And the same is the situation of the human individual; you have to pass across a desert,

you have to assimilate the whole past. And remember, just memorizing is not going to help…assimilation. And also remember, the person who memorizes the past memorizes only because he cannot assimilate. If you assimilate the past you are free from the past. You can use it, but it cannot use you. You possess it, but it does not possess you.

When you have assimilated food you need not remember it. It does not exist separate from you: it has become your blood, your bone, your marrow; it has become you…

This Nietzsche calls the camel stage, but don't be stuck there. One has to move. The camel is the larva, the camel is a hoarder. But if you are stuck at that state and always remain a camel, then you will not know the beauties and the benedictions of life. Then you will never know God. You will remain stuck with the past. The camel can assimilate the past but cannot use it.

In the course of his personal development the time comes when the camel has to become the lion. The lion proceeds to tear apart the huge monster known as 'thou shall not'. The lion in man roars against all authority.

The lion is a reaction, a rebellion against the camel. The individual now discovers his own inner light as the ultimate source of all authentic values. He becomes aware of his primary obligation to his own inner creativity, to his inmost hidden potential. A few remain stuck at the stage of the lion: they go on roaring and roaring and become exhausted in their roaring.

It is good to become a lion, but one has still to take one more jump – and that jump is to become the child. Now, each of you has been a child. But those who know, they say the first childhood is a false childhood. It is like first teeth: they only look like teeth but they are of no use, they have to fall out. Then the real teeth are born. The first childhood is a false childhood; the second childhood is the real childhood. That second childhood is called the 'stage of the child' or the 'stage of the sage' – it means the same. Unless a man becomes utterly innocent, free from the past, so free that he is not even against the past.... Remember it; the person who is still against the past is not REALLY *free. He still has some grudges, some complaints, some wounds. The camel still haunts, the shadow of the camel still follows. The lion is there but still afraid somehow of the camel, fearful that it may come back.*

When the fear of the camel is completely gone, the roaring of the lion stops. Then the song of the child is born.

I would like you to go into these three stages very deeply and very penetratingly, because they are of immense value.

The stage of the camel, assimilation, is just like a child in the womb who does nothing but assimilate – just eats the mother, gets bigger and bigger, is getting ready for the final plunge to move into the world. Right now there is no other work for the child: for nine months in the mother's womb he eats and sleeps, sleeps and eats. He goes on sleeping and eating; these are the only two functions. Even after the child is born, for months he will be just doing that – eating and sleeping. Slowly, slowly, sleeping will become less and less and eating will also become less and less. He is ready, he is ready to become an individual – and the moment the child becomes ready to be an individual, disobedience enters in. The child starts saying no, yes-saying by and by disappears. Obedience dies, disobedience is born.

The state of the camel is the state of assimilation. The camel does not know how to say no. The camel is not acquainted with the no. He has not heard the word and he has not tasted the joys of saying no. He only knows yes. His yes cannot be very deep, because without knowing no your yes cannot be very deep; it has to remain superficial. The man who has not known no, how can he really know yes? His yes will be impotent. The camel's yes is impotent. The camel does not know what is happening; he only goes on saying yes because that is the only word that he has been taught. Obedience, belief – these are the characteristics of the stage called 'camel'. Adam was in this state before he ate the fruit of the Tree of Knowledge, and each human being passes through this state.

The child does not yet know himself as separate. Adam, before he ate the fruit, was part of God. He was in the womb, he was obedient, a yea-sayer, but he was not independent. Independence enters only through the door of no; through the door of yes, only dependence. So in this stage of the camel, there is dependence, helplessness. The other is more important than your own being: God is more important, father is more important, mother is more important, society is more important, the priest is more important, the politician is more important. Except you, everybody is important; the other is important, you are still not there. It is a very unconscious state. The majority of the people are stuck there; they remain camels. Almost ninety-nine percent of people remain camels.

This is a very sad state of affairs – that ninety-nine percent of human beings remain as larvae. That's why there is so much misery and no joy. And you can go on searching for joy but you will not find it, because joy is not given there – outside.

Unless you become a child and the third stage is attained, unless you become a butterfly, you will not be able to know joy. Joy is not something given outside; it is a vision that grows inside you. It is possible only in the third stage.

The first stage is of misery and the third stage is of bliss, and between the two is the state of the lion, which is sometimes miserable and sometimes pleasant, sometimes painful and sometimes pleasurable.

At the stage of the camel you are parrots. You are just memories, nothing else. Your whole life consists of beliefs given to you by others. This is where you will find the Christians and the Mohammedans and the Hindus and the Jainas and the Buddhists. Go into the churches and the temples and the mosques and you will find great gatherings of camels. You will not find a single human being. They go on repeating, parrot-like.

The camel lives in the magic of believing. It works. It can work miracles. But the camel remains a camel; growth is missing.

The people praying in the temples and the churches are under the influence of belief. They don't know what God is, they have never felt anything like that; they only believe. Their magic of belief goes on doing certain things to them, but that is all make-believe, a kind of dream-world. They are not out of the unconscious, out of their sleep. And remember, I am not saying that this stage is not necessary; it is necessary, but once it is complete one has to jump out of it. One is not here to remain a camel forever...

In the first stage everybody has to be a camel, yea-saying, believing whatsoever is given, assimilating, digesting, but this is only the beginning of the journey, this is not the end.

The second stage is difficult. The first stage the society gives you; that's why there are millions of camels and very few lions. The society leaves you when you have become a perfect camel. Beyond that, the society cannot do anything. It is there that the work of the society ends – at the school, the college, the university. It leaves you a perfect camel with a certificate.

A lion you have to become on your own, remember it. If you don't decide to become a lion, you will never become a lion. That risk has to be taken by the individual. That is a gamble. That is very dangerous too, because by becoming a lion you will annoy all the camels around you, and the camels are peace-loving animals; they are always ready to compromise. They don't want to be disturbed, they don't want any new thing to happen in the world, because all new things disturb. They are against the revolutionaries and the rebellious and not about great things, mind you – not about Socrates and Christ; they are bringing great revolutions – the camels are so afraid of small things that you will be surprised.

The camels are simply against anything new; it does not matter what. Hence the lions are not welcome. The society creates every kind of difficulty for the lions. The camels are afraid of these people. They disturb their convenience, they disturb their sleep, and they create worry. They create a desire in the camels to become lions – that is the real problem.

Why is Jesus crucified? His very presence... and many camels start dreaming of becoming lions, and that disturbs their sleep, and that disturbs their ordinary, mundane life.

Why is Buddha stoned? Why is Mahavir not allowed to enter cities? Why is Mansur beheaded? These people disturb; they disturb sleep, they go on roaring. Buddha has called his sermons 'The Lion's Roar'.

The first, the state of the camel, is given by the society. The second state has to be attained by the individual. In attaining it, you become an individual, you become unique. You are no more a conformist; you are no more part of a tradition. The cocoon is dropped: you become a caterpillar, you start moving.

The state of the lion has these characteristics: independence, no-saying, disobedience, rebellion against the other – against authority, against dogma, against scripture, against the church, against political power, against the state. The lion is against everything! He wants to shatter everything and create the whole world anew, closer to the heart's desire. He has great dreams and utopias in his mind. He looks mad to the camels, because the camels live in the past and the lion starts living in the future. A great gap arises. The lion heralds the future, and the future can come only if the past is destroyed. The new can enter into existence only if the old ceases to exist and creates space for the new. The old has to die for the new to be. So there is a constant fight between the lion and the camel, and camels are the majority. The lion happens once in a while; the lion is an exception – and the exception only proves the rule. Disbelief is his characteristic, doubt is his characteristic.

Adam eats the fruit of the Tree of Knowledge: the mind is born, the self becomes a defined phenomenon. The camel is non-egoistic, the lion is very egoistic. The camel knows nothing of the ego; the lion knows only the ego. That's why you will always find revolutionaries; rebellious people – poets, painters, musicians – are all very egoistic. They are bohemians. They live their life, they do their thing. They don't care a bit about others. Let the others go to hell! They are no more a part of any structure, they become free from structures. The movement, the lion's roar, is bound to be egoistic. They need a great ego to go into this.

In the East you will find more camels, in the West you will find more lions. That's why in the East to surrender seems so easy. For the Western mind surrender seems so difficult. But one thing has to be remembered: the Eastern mind finds it very easy to surrender; that's why his surrender is not of much value. He's already surrendered. He does not know how to say no, that's why he says yes. When a Western mind surrenders it is very difficult. It is a struggle for the Western mind to surrender, but when the Western mind surrenders there is great transformation, because the surrender has been hard, arduous, an uphill task. In the East the surrender is cheap; in the West it is costly. Only a few courageous people can afford it.

The East surrenders because there is no more possibility of becoming a lion. It feels very comfortable, easy to surrender, to become part of a mob, a mass. The West has created the ego. The West has paid more attention to the lion – doubt, disbelief, and ego – but whenever the Western mind surrenders, there is really great transformation.

The Eastern mind surrenders, remains the camel. If the Western mind surrenders there is a possibility for the child to be born. When the lion surrenders he becomes the child; when the camel surrenders he remains the camel.

So I may appear paradoxical to you, but if you understand what I am saying it will not be very difficult and the paradox will not really look like a paradox. Each individual has to be taught the ego before he will be able to drop it. Each individual has to come to a very crystallized ego; only then is the dropping of any help, otherwise not.

The first state, of the camel, is unconscious. The second state, of the lion, is subconscious – a little higher than the unconscious. A few glimpses of the conscious have started coming in. The sun is rising, and a few rays are entering into the dark room where you are asleep. The unconscious is no more unconscious. Something is stirred in the unconscious; it has become subconscious. But remember, the change is not very great – from the camel to the lion – as it is going to be from the lion to the child. The change is a kind of reversion. The camel starts standing on its head and becomes the lion. The camel says yes, the lion says no. The camel obeys, the lion disobeys. The camel is positive, the lion is negative. It is to be understood that the camel has been saying yes so much and must have been denying the no, hence the no goes on accumulating, and a point comes where the no wants to take revenge on the yes, the denied part wants to take revenge. Then the whole wheel turns – the camel turns upside-down and becomes the lion.

The difference between the camel and the lion is big, but both exist on the same plane. The cocoon is static at one place; the caterpillar starts moving, but on the same earth. Movement is born but the plane is the same. The first thing is given by the society: your being a camel is a gift of the society. Your being a lion will be a gift that you give to yourself. Unless you love yourself you will not be able to do it. Unless you want to become an individual, unique in your own right, unless you take the risk of going against the current, you will not be able to become a lion.

But if you understand the mechanism...in the very heart of the camel the lion is created. Again and again, saying yes and denying no, no goes on accumulating. And one day comes when one is fed-up with saying yes; just for a change one wants to say no. One is fed-up with the positive, the taste of it becomes monotonous; just for a change one wants to taste no.

That's how the camel, for the first time, starts having dreams of the lion. And once you have tasted the no, the doubt, the disbelief, you can never be a camel again, because it brings such liberty, such freedom.

The majority is stuck at the camel stage; the minority is stuck at the lion stage. The majority means the masses, and the minority means the intelligentsia. The artist, the poet, the painter, the musician, the thinker, the philosopher, the revolutionary – they are stuck at the second stage. They are far better than the camels, but the goal is not yet complete. They have not come home. The third stage is the child.

Listen attentively: the first stage is given by the society, the second is given by the individual to himself. The third is possible only if the caterpillar comes close to a butterfly; otherwise it is not possible. How will the caterpillar ever think that he can fly on his own, that he can become a winged thing? It is not possible! It is impossible to think of it! It will be absurd, illogical. The caterpillar knows how to move, but to fly is just absurd.

I have heard about butterflies teaching caterpillars that they can fly, and they object and say, "No. It may be possible for you, but it is not possible for us. You are a butterfly, we are only caterpillars! We only know how to crawl." And one who knows only how to crawl, how can he imagine flying? That is a different dimension, an altogether different dimension – the vertical dimension.

From the camel to the lion, it is evolution. From the lion to the child, it is revolution. A Master is needed at that stage. The society can make you a camel, you yourself can make yourself a lion, but you will need a Master – a Buddha, a Christ, a Rumi – you will need a butterfly that has wings. Only with a winged phenomenon will you be able to start dreaming about wings. How can you dream about something that you have not known at all? If you approach them with sympathy and love, you will be able to have a few glimpses of their inner sky. And once you have seen that inner sky you will start dreaming about it. A great longing will arise in you: how to become a winged phenomenon?

That is the infection that comes from the Master to the disciple. The third phenomenon happens through the Master. 'The child' means creativity, interdependence.

In the first stage, the camel was dependence; the second stage was independence. But in innocence one comes to know that neither is there dependence and neither is there independence. Existence is interdependence – all are dependent on each other. It is all one.

The sense of the whole is born: no I, no thou, no fixation with yes or no, no obsession either to say yes always or to say no always; more fluidity, more spontaneity; neither obedience nor disobedience, but spontaneity. Responsibility is born. One responds to existence – does not react out of the past, and does not react out of the future.

The camel lives in the past, the lion lives in the future, the child lives in the present, here-now. The camel is pre-mind, the lion is mind, and the child is post-mind. The camel is pre-self, the lion is self, and the child is post-self. That's the meaning of the state of no-mind. Sufis call it fana *- the ego is gone, the other too. They are both together; you cannot have one without the other. I-thou are part of one energy; they both disappear.*

The child simply is –ineffable, indefinable, a mystery, a wonder. The camel has memory, the lion has knowledgeability and the child has wisdom. The camel is either Christian, Hindu or Mohammedan – theist. The lion is atheist. And the child is religious – neither theist nor atheist, neither Hindu nor Mohammedan nor Christian nor communist; just a simple religiousness, the quality of love and innocence.

Adam eats the fruit, becomes a lion. Adam, before eating the fruit from the Tree of Knowledge, is the camel. And when Adam has vomited the fruit, dropped knowledge, he is the child. That child means Christ. Christ says again and again to his disciples, "Repent!" The word 'repent' in Hebrew means return, go back. The Garden of Eden is still waiting for you. Vomit this apple of knowledge and the doors will be opened unto you.

The camel is Adam before eating the fruit, the lion is Adam after eating the fruit, and the child is Adam become Christ, returning back home. Buddha calls it nirvana, *Jesus calls it the Kingdom of God. You can call it anything you like:* Tao, dhamma, moksha. *Words don't mean much there; it is a wordless silence, a thoughtless innocence.*

The camel cannot understand 'the nowhere'. The camel can understand only a certain visible source. He lives in the visible. He can understand the book, he cannot understand the heart. He can understand the theories about God but he cannot understand God Himself.

Doubt is a privilege. Until and unless you have been assimilating you will not be able to become the lion. Until you learn to say no, to doubt is a privilege. It is a higher stage than belief, because any coward can go with belief. For saying no and for creating doubt, courage is needed. It is almost always so: the so-called theists are on a lesser, a lower spiritual plane than the atheist. The atheist is on a slightly higher plane, although he denies. He is the lion.

The camels are camels. They are more interested in possessing knowledge than becoming knowledge. They are more interested in the containers than in the content. The camel is interested in quantity, not in quality.

Remember, the concern of the camel is quantity, the concern of the lion is quality, and the child goes beyond duality. He is not concerned with either quality or quantity. He transcends all dualities.

The last thing:

Because there are millions of camels, many Masters have spoken in the language of the camels – Mohammed, Moses, and people like that. They have spoken in the language of the camels so the camels could understand. There is compassion in it, but there is danger too that the camels remain camels.

A few Masters have chosen to speak the language of the lion – people like Christ or Buddha. As far as the expression is concerned it is better than that of Moses and Mohammed, but it will not be understood by the masses; that's a problem. The camels will not be able to absorb it.

Jesus was killed because the camels were very angry. He was speaking a different language, utterly unintelligible. It looked like nonsense to them. This man was mad! Just think, in a world full of camels, a lion comes and starts talking – no camel will understand. When Jesus was killed, the disciples that he had, those twelve apostles, were camels. He was a child talking the language of the lion, they were camels; they created Christianity. And once the camels created Christianity it became a world religion.

The child has no language of its own. Innocence is wordless. Hence, the child has to speak the language of a lion out of necessity. That is the closest that he can come to expressing himself.

It happened in Buddha's time. Buddha talked in the language of the lions. The country was in such a state that there were many lions available. It was at a climax, at a peak. It was not a dark valley; it was a very sunlit peak. For thousands of years in the past India had been searching and working on truth and what it is and how to attain it. Many people understood Buddha. Buddha's disciples were not camels, they were lions. Jesus' disciples were camels. Jesus was a child talking in the language of the lion. When Buddha died, his followers were very, very stubborn. They wouldn't compromise with the camels. They were bribed, they were persuaded, but they wouldn't compromise. They continued to roar. Buddhism was uprooted from India; the camels finally destroyed it.

You can gather great masses around you if you speak the language of the camel. You can gather intelligentsia around you if you speak in the language of the lion.

Krishnamurti gathers intelligentsia around himself – he speaks the language of the lion. Lao Tzu or Ramana, they speak the language of the child. Nobody understands them, but they are not killed, remember; they are not crucified either. Nobody understands them, nobody follows them, and nobody bothers about them. They are thought to be good people, poets, a little eccentric, crazy. People can sometimes go to them, it is beautiful to be around them, but they don't create any stir in the world. Lao Tzu comes and disappears, leaves no trace. Ramana came and disappeared, left no trace behind.

These are the three languages: I speak all the languages! So you will find camels and lions and children, all kinds of people, around me. Hence, I look very contradictory. I can't be consistent: when I talk to a camel I talk his language, when I talk to a lion I roar, and when a child comes to me, I laugh, smile, and sit silently with him.

This experiment has never been done before: nobody has spoken all three languages, because it is troublesome. One language is good because one remains consistent. With me you can never be certain, you will always remain confused. But I use confusion also as a device. If the camel is confused, he will start growing into a lion – because unless he is utterly confused he will never grow. If the lion is confused he will start growing into a child, because you grow only when you are very confused. When you see no point in being where you are, you start growing higher and you start looking for higher peaks – maybe from there a greater vision, a bigger vision is available. I confuse you as a device. I will confuse the camels, I will confuse the lions; and children cannot be confused, they will understand. They will be able to understand that my contradictions are not contradictions at all – because I am speaking three languages, that's why they only appear to be…

My message is not in my words but in the pauses in-between. My message is not in what I say but in what I am. My message is not reducible to theories and systems. Either you can live it with me, or you miss it. It is an alive phenomenon. Once I am gone you will start looking into books, and you will be annoyed, and you will be angry with me, because you will feel you have missed.

While I am here, be nourished by me, get drunk with me, and be absorbed. Abandon yourself into this mystery that is being revealed to you, and then there will be the possibility that you will not die in your larva, that you will become a caterpillar, and finally you will be metamorphosed into a butterfly.

Grow wings! Dream great dreams of growing wings! You have the potential. You are the seed; a great, great phenomenon is possible through you. And only when you have bloomed will you know what God is, what truth is.

Wisdom of the Sands Vol. 1, Ch 4

As soon as he went back to his hotel, he immediately got pen and paper and wrote his first letter to Osho – without ever imagining that this was going to be the first of a long, long series! The letter read:

When a real lion meets a real Master he recognizes him…and he decides to be defeated, and decides to have his ego broken, because he knows that this is the path and will lead him to more ease. Now, I'm afraid that it is still my ego deciding for me. Please explain.

Carlo, the decision to take sannyas has to be of the ego. But it is a decision to commit suicide. These two things have to be understood.

When a man decides to commit suicide, life is deciding for death, in favor of death. When a man commits suicide, what happens? He has lived and found something is lacking in life, it is not worth living; he moves in the opposite direction, of death. He searches for death.

The same happens in sannyas too: it is the ego deciding to take sannyas. Sannyas means the suicide of the ego.

The ego has lived and found only agonies. The ego has searched, groped in the dark, and never has anything happened to it, only tension, anguish, misery. The ego has lived through hell. The ego is hell!

Jean-Paul Sartre says, "The other is hell" – that is absolutely wrong. The ego is hell! Not the other, but the I is the hell. And when you have felt this in the very guts of your being

– in your bones, in your blood, in your marrow – when the ego has utterly failed you, the ego decides to commit suicide. That's what sannyas is.

But once you take sannyas a totally different world, a totally different vision, starts in your being. You start living egolessly, and suddenly you are surprised. It is not life that was wrong, it was the ego that was wrong. Life is immensely fulfilling, it is SHEER *joy, it is made of the stuff called bliss. It was ego that was a barrier and was not allowing you to live. Once you surrender, even for a moment if the window opens in that surrender.... And that's what sannyas is, initiation is looking into the eyes of the Master : for a moment you disappear. For a moment you start seeing through the eyes of the Master. For a moment you are not separate, you vibrate with the Master. You take his color, you take his vibration, you pulsate with him, you breathe with him. It is a single moment, but in that single moment you have come across the gap from where the door opens, and you can see a totally different world. The same world, but yet in a totally different perspective.*

This is initiation – looking through the Master's eyes. You have looked through your eyes and you have not found anything. Now you close your eyes and you look through the eyes of the Master. This is obedience, this is surrender. This is trying to put aside your past patterns, and learning of something new. It is an unlearning process, unlearning as far as the ego and its ways are concerned, and a learning process as far as the ways of non-ego are concerned.

The Master is one who has no ego. The disciple is one who has come to understand that the ego and its ways are false, they lead only into cul-de-sacs. The disciple is one who is ready to drop the ego and wants to know, "How to drop it?" He has suffered long with it, he has carried the burden long. Now he's tired of it! He wants to be unburdened. He does not know how to put it away, how to throw it away. He has been clinging to it for so long that he has forgotten that it can be put aside. He comes to a man who has put his ego aside, looks into those eyes, starts trembling in a new way. A new streaming energy is felt, and suddenly a link is broken between the ego and you.

This is what initiation is. It is just a beginning certainly, much will have to be done later on; but if you have taken one step, half the journey is complete. Yes, I say half the journey is complete, because the first step is the most difficult step. All other steps are going to be the same, repetition of the same step again and again.

Carlo's question is significant.

He says, "When a real lion meets a real Master he recognizes him..."

That is true. Camels cannot recognize a Master. The camels have to be persuaded.

And sometimes a camel comes to me and I persuade really hard.

Just a few days ago, I was persuading a woman really hard. I could see that she could become a lion, but she persists to remain a camel. I could see the potential, that just in a single step she could become a lion. Ordinarily I don't persuade too much, because persuading a person too much for sannyas can become a barrier. The person can start thinking that he or she is so important, that's why I am persuading. That feeling of importance can enhance the ego. But when I see that somebody is just on the verge, a push IS needed. I go out of my way to give a push. But it is always moving into the unknown. One never knows how the person is going to react.

I persuaded her. She became a sannyasin, but missed the point. While looking into my eyes, she was not looking into my eyes. She was still afraid, she was clinging to the camel. A great opportunity was given to her, she missed it. I have given her a message that she can drop sannyas, because really it has not happened. She wants to remain a camel, so let her be happy as a camel. A camel cannot recognize, a camel is blind. The camel is the larva, a stagnant pool.

But a lion can recognize. That's why almost always it happens that those who have any kind of courage in them immediately take the jump into sannyas. Not that they will not have to face the world, not that they will not have problems – they will have problems, but that is secondary. Those problems can be tackled, that world can be faced. But when a moment arises when one has to take the risk, the lion takes the risk. The lion recognizes the Master.

The camel cannot recognize, the camel has to be persuaded, goaded into sannyas. The lion can recognize and accept sannyas, ask for it, take the jump on his own accord. And in that very jump the lion starts moving to the third stage: the child.

In surrender you become a child; you become soft, feminine, you allow the Master to penetrate you deeply. You allow the Master to make you pregnant, you become pregnant with the divine. And the state of child is really a state of pregnancy. You die and you are born anew as a child, out of your own womb.

It is the greatest miracle in the world – man being born out of his own womb. But the decision is going to be of the ego. Just as suicide is the decision of life, sannyas is the decision of the ego. But once you have decided the ego starts disappearing, the ego has committed suicide. In fact, sannyas and suicide are very similar. Suicide is a false sannyas, sannyas is a real suicide – because in suicide only the body dies and you will be born again. In sannyas the ego dies, and if you work it out totally, you may not be born again.

Wisdom of the Sands Vol. 1, Ch 6, Q 7

He was certainly a lion, even the Master had said so, and what do lions do, they jump! He then wrote a letter to Osho, telling him that he wanted to be initiated into sannyas straight away, but the Master suggested for him to do first some therapy groups, and to wait at least for a couple of weeks. He asked him to do first the Centering Group, then the Intensive Enlightenment Group, and finally the Tantra Group, and to ask for sannyas later!

Unfortunately this kind of inner revolution was not happening to his girlfriend Terry, who even tried to take sannyas later, but it was only a nice gesture from her side, as she wanted to be closer to him even in this adventure…

Poor Terry, after the two weeks previously scheduled, he had already decided that he was not going to leave this place anymore, so she would have to go back to Italy on her own. That made him a little sad, because Terry had been living all these years with the fear that he would quit one day for a more beautiful girl than her, because, even being a famous actress, she was not fully aware of her beauty, but how could she have ever imagined that she would be dumped for an old man with a beard!

He saw her leaving without shedding even a tear, because he had dropped everything from his past life, and Terry alas was part of his past, since she didn't manage to fit with the ashram. But he was bound to be consoled very soon – on the day she left he had already started his first group, Centering.

He realized immediately that he wouldn't have to wait for the Tantra Group to give vent to his sexual energy, because already during the Centering one could breathe in that aura of extreme freedom of communication for which the ashram was rightly famous! In fact, every time the participants would all go together to have a shower, there was inevitably some little romance going on, or some little adventure, or a "quickie" to be consumed in ten minutes…

The big shower and toilet building contained twenty cubicles lined up along all the walls, plus a couple of small rooms with a door and a lock, hence whoever wanted to be alone could enter into one of them and even look the door with the key. So it then would happen that if he liked one of the girls in the group, he simply twinkled at her while she was having her shower with everybody else, and if she would answer in the same fashion, they would run into one of those little rooms, lock the door with the key, and start fucking like two rabbits, which means very quickly, because after ten minutes they were supposed to be back in their group!

The Centering Group lasted for five days; it was very amusing and full of surprises, with a lot of little games to be played in order to awake a little of your awareness, or at least to show to you just how unaware you are.

Prasad, the leader of this group, was a real angel, perhaps the most beautiful person he had ever met in the ashram, who showed infinite patience in his effort to awaken, at least a little bit, more than one hundred people at the time.

One of the games he liked most consisted of partnering up two groups of people; the two groups were then told to stand opposite each other and at the two opposite sides of the room. From that moment on they were supposed to always keep eye contact with their partner, and to start advancing towards him or her, and – here is the trick – they had to move in slow motion, the slowest movements they could manage. Once in front of their partner, they were invited to bow down in *namaste*, and to tell their partner as if in a mirror: "Welcome, welcome to yourself !"

After that, they had to depart from their original partner in any way they preferred, but always in slow motion; at this point everybody was hugging each other slowly, slowly, and for a long time, and then they would move forward and repeat the same ritual with the next person they were going to meet.

There were huge mirrors on all the walls and once everybody had met everyone else, the next instructions were to look at yourself in one of the mirrors, then start moving towards your own image, always very, very slowly, and once you arrived just in front of the mirror, bow once more with the gesture of *namaste*, repeating again, but this time to yourself, "Welcome, welcome to yourself !"

The result was such that in the end, saying these words to themselves, anyone could see how almost everybody was crying copiously in that moment, and without any control!

Lastly, the group was residential in the sense that all participants left the room only in the morning and in the evening to attend Osho's discourses, and then they would go back to their group room to eat the food that was being served, and finally everyone would go to sleep. Naturally during the night there was a continuous back and forth of couples looking for each other, and once found they would caress each other, make love, and all this without even sharing their name!

After the beautiful experience of the Centering Group, he immediately joined the second group, the Intensive Enlightenment, which was truly something incredibly hard for him! The group was scheduled for three days only, but it was spent in total isolation from the rest of the world; you were not supposed to leave the group room at all for these three days, and in addition you had to remain in complete silence all the time!

For a big mouth like him it seemed an almost impossible task, but he decided to throw himself totally into it with all his heart, because if Osho had given him this group, it certainly meant that there must be some gift for him there, hidden in some corner!

The present was indeed there, and it would become clear on the last day...

but how to describe it?

He had never been in silence for three days in his entire life, and this event was triggering a silent explosion:

Suddenly there was no Time anymore.

Suddenly there was no Space anymore.

Suddenly there were no more Divisions.

Suddenly there was no Life and Death anymore.

Suddenly everything was One.

Suddenly he had returned to the Source....

Yes, but how to tell you?

How to find the words to say it?

And if we leave it as a mystery, where does he belong to?

The only thing he could remember was a sweet sense of being finally at home....

That journey was over, and now another journey was about to start.

***

CHAPTER 02

The Death of Carlo Silvestro

When the day of his initiation came, he decided to buy just a very simple orange robe, because contrary to his habits, he didn't want to be noticed, or to exhibit one of his phantasmagoric costumes.

While he was waiting for the darshan to start, he had only one idea in his mind, and that was that in a few minutes Carlo Silvestro would be dead and buried; he would have a new name, and he would have to start his life from scratch!

It was an incredible sensation and in the end very similar to his decision to commit suicide when he was sixteen, with the only difference that on this occasion he was feeling very calm and totally relaxed, ready for everything, whatever the price would be.

Wasn't he a real lion that had decided to surrender totally to a Spiritual Master?

When finally they called his name, Carlo, a name that he would hear for the last time in his life, he stood up and went to place himself in front of Osho. The Master looked at him in silence for a long, long time, and then he said:

> *Swatantra means freedom, Sarjano means creativity. Freedom is true only if it creates. Creativity is the indication of a true freedom, and creation is true only if it comes out of freedom. Creativity without freedom is not true creativity; it is imitation, it is borrowed. It can be very skillful, it can be technically perfect, but something essential will be missing in it: the soul will be missing.*
>
> *There are creative people who are not free, who have not known the freedom of no-mind. They simply go on repeating; all that they do is more or less a new combination of old things. The wine is old, the bottles new. Maybe there are mixtures of many wines – something from here, something from there. It appears as if it is new; it is not. It is only a combination, it is not a creation; it is a composition, not a creation.*
>
> *There are people who are free but not creative; their freedom is dead. There are people who sit in the Himalayan caves and have known something of the silence, of the interior, but they are not creative; their freedom is not true. They are also imitating the state of no-mind. They are sitting like a Buddha practicing a posture. It is only a gesture, there is nothing behind it. Sitting in their Himalayan caves they are simply vegetating.*
>
> *So to me these two words are of immense value, and they go together; in fact they cannot exist separately. They are like yin-yang, day-night, summer-winter, the positive and*

the negative; they are always together. Whenever one is there, the other must be there somewhere, has to be there. Seeking one, one finds both; losing one, one loses both. So let this be my message for you.

Feel at home – this is your home! Forget, the past, let it simply disappear. From this moment think anew, feel anew. This is your second birth, and without the second the first is incomplete. The second is the true birth, but one has to be very receptive to allow it to happen. Immense changes are on the way; just be receptive and every day things will be happening.

A great energy is being released here; those who can be receptive are fortunate. If somebody misses, it is only he who is responsible. If he remains closed there is no way to penetrate him. The spiritual energy cannot be aggressive energy; it cannot even knock on your door. It simply waits like sunlight: if you open the door it comes in; if you don't open the door it does not knock, it does not force. It is not like wind in that it knocks and tries to enter. It is like sunlight: it simply waits there, it has infinite patience. And only those who are capable of opening up to it are benefited. Then there is great celebration, great rejoicing happens inside. For the first time one knows what life is.

So just be open, and allow things to happen.

Don't Bite My Finger, Look Where I'm Pointing

Meanwhile he was looking into the Master's eyes, and he was full of the most fantastic expectations, imagining that within a minute he would be overwhelmed by an ocean of love, that he would feel a tremendous wave of compassion, that the energy of the Master would have transported him immediately into heaven…but the more he looked into his eyes, the more he realized that there was nothing in front of him, only an abysmal emptiness!

There was no love, there was no compassion, there was no sympathy, there were no celestial trumpets…there was only a fucking nothing!

There was only a bottomless abyss that was opening its arms in front of him, inviting him with a deadly song, because in that moment he had the absolute certainty that if he had jumped into this abyss, he would have disappeared forever, he would have disappeared from earth, vanished into the deepest abysses of nothingness.

He jumped, without thinking twice…and he disappeared completely!

How can one explain such an experience?

How can one narrate his own death?

For an instant he disappeared into the *nothingness* represented by the Master, and in that moment he became one with him, and he came to know forever and ever what a real Master is.

There are experiences in life that you simply cannot describe, because either you know it and you have lived them, or to talk about it is useless, it's only hot air!

There are experiences that once told became simply trivial and mundane, and moreover cannot be communicated in any way; hence I'm not even trying to describe how I died and how I resurrected.

Let's say the whole truth about it: only those who have met a Spiritual Master in their life will be capable of understanding, while for everybody else it will be only a mythological story, a fairy tale, if not great bullshit! Hence, we are not going to talk about it, but we will just say that in that moment Carlo Silvestro had died forever, and from his ashes Sarjano was born – period! The only thing worth saying about this 'phenomenon' is that he was no more. "He had gone" – as we usually say.

He was invited to let go in this emptiness, in this state of no-mind of the Master, looking *through his eyes*, and he had accepted the invitation just to die, just to resurrect later and find out that he was no longer the same person.

At the end of the darshan, Osho asked him if he wanted to do some more therapy groups, an offer he gently declined, telling him that his desire was to start working in the Commune very soon, that he wanted to serve him, that he was not the parasitic type, and finally that all these therapies had only the result of breaking his balls!

Osho laughed at his expression 'breaking my balls' and told him that he could very well understand, and that if he wanted to start working in the ashram, he already had his blessings!

A week after having been initiated into sannyas, he decided that since he was not going to do any more therapy groups, he could as well start working somewhere, because he always liked the idea of being useful wherever he was, especially in this place that had already become his new home.

In those days, many of the Italian sannyasins had recognized him as the guy who used to cook at every big alternative gathering that was happening in Italy, like the Rock Festival and all these kinds of events, and the rumor finally reached the ears of Deeksha, the big Italian mama in charge of the kitchen. One day she sent somebody to call him, and once he was in front of her she told him how much she had heard about him, and how he had been cooking at all these big gatherings, so she wanted to propose to him to cook for the ashram.

"Well, right now I wouldn't like a steady job," he answered, "because I'm still doing a lot of meditations, plus I'm going to each and every group in Buddha Hall, and all in all I'm having a rather busy day!"

"Listen, why don't you cook us something good one of these days, one of those things that you know best, just to try at least once, then we'll see…."

The proposal sounded acceptable to him and he promised that as soon he would find the ingredients to cook what he had in mind, he would inform her and come to her kitchen to do it.

He had a friend in the ashram, an Italian, who was shocked and surprised by the fact that with all those buffalos around, and with all this buffalo milk, there has never been anybody who decided to make some good mozzarella out of it! He took this issue so much to heart that as soon as he went back to Italy, he spent a month in Sicily, just to learn from the local artisans how to make the delicious mozzarella he had eaten there so many times, and in the end he became such an expert that he could do it by himself. All he had to do now was to bring the cultures and the bacteria from Italy in order to create this white delicacy.

He went to visit this guy who meanwhile had started a little production of his creation for the ashram, and asked him if he could make 50 kilos of mozzarella for the next day, because he had in mind to make at least 500 portions of 'Melanzane alla Parmigiana'!

The guy promised to provide these fifty kilos of mozzarella around twelve noon the next day, mainly because this was a great humanitarian project, so at this point all he had to do was to find one hundred kilos of juicy eggplants, plus around one hundreds kilos of tomatoes, and get from the ashram gardeners a good quantity of basil plants, which are absolutely necessary for this creation.

The next morning, long before the mozzarella would be delivered, he was in the kitchen to prepare the tomato sauce, to cut and fry the eggplants, and when finally the white treasure arrived, he started to compose, layer upon layer, his little masterpiece...

In the afternoon at five o'clock sharp when the canteen was to open, there were more than five hundred portions of succulent Eggplant Parmesan on the counter and he could finally head towards home, because he was very tired after all this work, but also very satisfied about what he had done.

There were two ways to leave the canteen, one coming out from the back of the kitchen, without crossing the eating area were people had their meal, and another one that followed a path parallel to the canteen. He decided to take this second path while leaving, because he was curious to see the faces of the people while they were eating his little masterpiece. The scene he saw in front of him was simply incredible and fascinating at the same time, and in fact there were hundreds of people having a portion of his eggplants in front of them, and they were all eating it with an openly visible pleasure, feeding each other, letting out some big satisfactory "Oooohhhh," licking their fingers, establishing these eggplants as an unprecedented success.

The scene was so touching and so unexpected that he couldn't manage to hold back his tears, and while he was crying silently behind a tree, he decided in that moment that he would have to cook for the ashram *every day*, because he didn't have the heart to deprive his friends of the pleasure they had just tasted; moreover he already had a few other little things in mind that he could prepare with no effort, all things that nobody had ever eaten before, with the exception perhaps of the Italians living in the commune.

He thought that all these people had never eaten *gnocchi* in their life, and surely never *polenta*, and neither the Neapolitan-style tomato sauce like his mom used to make...and there were so many other things that he could cook here...and slowly, slowly he was determined to do it all!

Meanwhile, he was keeping on practicing at least three meditations a day in Buddha Hall, namely the Kundalini Meditation, because he liked very much the idea of shaking his sexual energy every day. He then attended every night the Music Group where he could dance wildly like a dervish, and finally a meditation that was offered every day from 10 to 11am called Sufi Dance, which was his absolute favorite among all the meditations.

This meditation was led by Ma Aneeta who, according to him, was a true Sufi wing of the Master, while the music was provided by Swami Anubhava and Friends, and it was very pleasant and deliciously rhythmic. During this meditation, all participants were singing not only religious songs from all over the world, but also those belonging to every possible religious tradition, with the result that they might first sing a "Shree Ram – Jay Ram"…to move after a while to "Shalom Ala'Hem" in perfect Hebrew tradition, followed by a Muslim chant like "La Ilaha Allahu".

All these chants were sung while performing some specific dance, of which Aneeta was showing the correct steps to everybody and practicing them for a minute with Anubhava, so that in the end everybody could sing and dance simultaneously! He used to get totally lost in these movements and songs, as if he knew them all to perfection, perhaps from some past life, and he was giving himself to this ecstasy with total abandon, until after a few months he had become such a regular feature that Aneeta would recognize him and even show him off as an example to the other participants whenever they would become lethargic, with low energy and low passion.

At this point Aneeta would stop the meditation, call him to the center of Buddha Hall, close to her, and then she would ask everybody to simply imitate Sarjano: "Let him guide you for the next five minutes, and just do *everything* he does, as if he were your leader!"

Too bad that during one of these demonstrations his *lungi* fell down, leaving him in the middle of the hall totally naked, while everybody was looking at him, and at the same time they were looking at Aneeta, trying to understand if they had to imitate even *this*, and before Aneeta realized what was going on, a dozen people had removed their *lungis* too, and they were now dancing as naked as they were born!

"Stop, stop please!" shouted our leader immediately, and then she asked somebody to tie Sarjano's *lungi* properly, so that it would stay up, and finally the meditation could continue among everyone's laughter.

One day, after he had been working in the kitchen for about a month he was called by the secretary of Osho, that she had a message for him from the Master. When he sat in front of her, she told him simply that Osho had expressed the wish that he, Sarjano, should write a book about his sannyasin adventure!

He thought immediately that this guy must have good eyes, but how in hell did he get to know that he was a good writer? Did he have his informers, or was he reading in people's hearts like in an open book? He would never get an answer to this, but he started immediately to write the first pages; he instantly thought that this was a very good idea, since now Pune and the ashram were on everybody's lips, and that perhaps once the book would be finished he could find a publisher, and that without having to leave the ashram or go to Italy!

He was writing usually during the night, before going to sleep, and he managed almost every night to write at least a couple of pages. He calculated that with this rhythm it would take about six months to complete the book, but there was no hurry, and he could easily relax and continue with calm, without thinking of any deadline.

One day he had been unexpectedly invited to a darshan and Osho had called him to sit in front of him. Without understanding why, once he was sitting at his feet, the Master asked him to come closer, much closer, until he was almost in physical contact with him. He thought that maybe Osho wanted to slap him, because lately he had become more and more irreverent, but the Master looked at him with a great smile, then placed one of his feet in his hands and said simply: *"Touch me!"*

To him it seemed just incredible that Osho could know his innermost hidden secret, which was in fact the desire to touch him, at least once in his life, because he was really that type of person who believes only in what he can touch! He had always dreamed of touching him, at least for a moment, and now the Master had placed his foot in his hands!

He grabbed this poor foot like a madman and started to kiss it, caress it and squeeze it as if some sort of miracle was happening to him, until the Master, maybe concerned that he would reduce his foot to a pulp, helped him stand up and told him simply: *Good Sarjano, this is good!*

The next day Osho narrated this event during discourse the next day:

> *When Vivekananda reached Ramakrishna, he asked this question: "Can you prove to me that God exists?" And Ramakrishna said, "I cannot prove that God exists, but I can make you know. Are you ready? This very moment!"*
>
> *Vivekananda was shaken to his very roots. The man was standing there and asking, "Are you ready? This very moment I can show God to you! But there is no proof."*
>
> *Vivekananda had not expected this. He had seen many other philosophers before; he was expecting something like that Ramakrishna would give a few proofs, would argue for God, would destroy the proofs that say God does not exist. He had never come across a man of real knowledge; this was the first time.*
>
> *His throat went dry, he could not utter a single word, he was simply dumb. For a moment everything stopped. And Ramakrishna touched his chest with his feet and he fell into deep ecstasy. When he came back he was trembling. What he had seen was impossible to believe – he had fallen out of the mind for a moment. That touch of Ramakrishna's feet: for a moment he had fallen out of the mind.*
>
> *Just the same happened last night. Sarjano was there – and Vivekananda must have been in exactly the same situation as Sarjano was last night – and I told him to hold my feet in his hands for a moment, and it happened. For a moment he slipped out of the mind.*

The impact of no-mind, if you are ready, can take you into a state of no-mind. And there is knowing. Knowing is not through the mind, it is always through the no-mind; it is not through the knower, it is only when the knower is not.

Take It Easy, Vol. 2, Ch 7, Excerpt

Naturally he was very grateful for this, but just one week later the first hit from the Master came suddenly (how else!) and right on top of his skull. He was answering a question to one Devabhakta, who had asked him something about gratitude…

Just a few days before, I talked about Sarjano. One evening he came, and he was in such a beautiful state that I gave my feet into his hands and he had a beautiful satori. A door opened – for a moment he was transported. For one day he remained in great ecstasy. But the next day the ego started coming in, playing games with him.

In fact to be grateful to the master is very difficult. If you can simply be in a state of forgiving the master, that is more than can be expected. If you can forgive the master, that is enough! That's all that I expect from you. It is very difficult to forgive the master…

After just twenty-four hours, Sarjano started going mad. He started writing ugly letters to me as a revenge, because "How do you dare? Who are you to give me this experience?" – not exactly in those words. He started pretending to be my friend, no more a disciple, because he is enlightened. That small window that opened created great ego in him. He started using abusive words towards me. So what to say about gratefulness? He started thinking that he is now no more a disciple, just a friend – he has attained to the same state, so why should he be a disciple anymore?

And in a subtle way the ego started being violent. His letters became more and more ugly and nasty. And all the time meanwhile he must have been thinking that he was just being Zen-ish. It is not so easy to be Zen-ish.

Many times it happens that I have to resist the temptation of giving you a glimpse. Many times I see that you are just on the verge – just a small push, and you will have a great experience. But if I see that the ego is lingering behind, if I give you the push and you attain to some experience the ego will immediately jump on it, will take possession if it, will drive you berserk.

I have to wait, I have to wait long. Slowly, slowly, that door has to be opened – you may not be able to absorb the light, so much light, suddenly. That's what happened to Sarjano.

Forget all about gratitude. If you can forgive me, that is enough, more than I expect from you. When you become enlightened, please forgive me.

Take It Easy Vol. 2, Ch 9, Q 1, Excerpt

He wrote Osho another letter:

I have begun to feel that there is another way to miss the point: rather than being too serious (which I carefully avoid) I have become too silly. I decided that I am too intelligent to take life seriously, so I moved to the opposite side of the pendulum. I had been feeling quite comfortable and different in that space, but now I'm feeling very, very confused. The only thing I can see is that I am still missing the point.

Please help me.

Sarjano, that's how the mind functions – it moves from one extreme to another. That is the mind's way to avoid change; that is the mind's trickery, deception. And it is really a very subtle deception, because it seems such a great change. When you move from one polarity to another, naturally it seems such a great change. What change can be more great than this?

You were eating too much, and then you start fasting. Naturally you think this is a great change. But the mind has deceived you. Whether you eat more or you fast, you remain obsessed with eating. You have not changed. Your concentration is still on food – you are still thinking of food, fantasizing about food. On the surface you have moved so much, it seems a one-hundred-and-eighty-degree turn: you were eating too much and now you are fasting. You were running after women continuously, chasing – and now whenever a woman passes by, you simply close your eyes and say, "Hare Ram, Hare Ram..." You think you have changed! You are the same, you have just moved to the opposite polarity. The mind has deceived you – you are still obsessed by women, you are still thinking of the woman, you are obsessed.

But this has been happening – and not only with you, Sarjano. Millions have been deceived by this cleverness of the mind. People move to the monasteries. There are monasteries where no woman has ever been allowed in, for thousands of years – not even a small girl has ever been allowed in. But the people who live in these monasteries continuously think of women and nothing else. They can't think of anything else; their whole mind becomes possessed by the thought of feminine energy. And these are the people who think that they have changed. They have not changed.

Mind's greatest and most clever trick is, when you want to change, when you insist on change, it goes from one polarity to another. It says, "Look – what more do you want? I give you all."

Sarjano is an intellectual author. He must have been very serious; authors are serious people. Then, listening to me, trying to understand me, coming closer to me – and he is in love with me – something started happening. He had a small satori experience, and that day he decided, "No more seriousness." He moved to the opposite pole, he became silly. He started writing very silly letters to me. And he must have been thinking that he is turning Zen...

Then when I said that this is stupid, naturally he became confused. Now where to go? Seriousness was wrong, now silliness is wrong – now where to go? I have closed both the doors. That is one of the devices. I would like you to be exactly in the middle – neither serious nor silly, neither for money nor against money, neither obsessed with eating nor obsessed with fasting. I would like you to be just in the middle.

Buddha has called his way 'the middle path' – majjhim nikaya. *And that is one of the most important things to be understood: when you are exactly in the middle, you transcend the polarity. The exact middle is the transcendence point. Then you are no longer serious and no longer silly; then you are simply conscious. Then all modes disappear, patterns disappear; then one is simply aware.*

I can understand your confusion, Sarjano. First I closed one door, the door of seriousness. You immediately turned to another door, the door of silliness. Now I have closed that door too. Naturally you are feeling suffocated – where to go? You cannot go to the first, you cannot go to the second, and there is no other door. And I know it, there is no other door.

Now be just exactly in the middle. And if you can come to that balance which I mean by saying 'exactly the middle' you will be surprised: all doors disappear, you are transported into another world. You are no more in the mind. Mind means excess, mind means exaggeration.

I have heard:

An old maid married a farmer. The first night produced no sexual activity, and none occurred for over a year.

One day as she was watching the farmer plowing in a distant field, he threw down the plow and came running into the house. He rushed up to her, tore off her clothes, and laid her right on the living-room floor.

Things seemed promising at that point, but about a year went by with no more sex. Again, one day as she was watching him with the plowing, he threw down the plow and came running towards the house.

Rather than have all her clothes torn off again, she undressed and found a comfortable place to lie down on the floor.

The farmer burst in, took one look at her and shouted, "Get up, you sex fiend, the barn is on fire!"

These people who live in polarities… One year fasting, and then this mad love- making. One year of no anger, and then a murder. One year of living in celibacy, and then you are bound to fall into indulgence. And the indulgence will come like a revenge – it can't be natural. Your life will move like a pendulum, you will always

remain torn apart. And then indulgence will again take you into celibacy – and it is a vicious circle, it can go on forever.

You have dropped seriousness, there is no need to choose silliness. That is the same thing! Now you are just standing on your head.

And Zen can give that feeling to many people. There is a kind of Zen becoming prevalent in the West which is not real Zen, it is just another extreme. People enjoy it just because of the extremity of it.

For example, you have always heard that Jesus is God and Jesus has to be worshipped. And Jesus has not to be even thought of as human, he is born of a virgin. He lived a superhuman life – all those miracles are just to prove that. For twenty centuries, the whole effort of Christian theology has been this, to prove that Jesus is divine, is not human.

People have become tired in the West – tired of Jesus, tired of the Virgin Mary, tired of the miracles, tired of this superhuman bombastic exaggeration. Then suddenly they come across Zen statements. A master says, "If you meet Buddha on the way, kill him immediately." This looks beautiful, far-out. That's what people are really hankering to do. Enough! – twenty centuries of worship, one is fed up. One would like to kill Jesus.

That's what Friedrich Nietzsche did when he declared, "God is dead." What he was saying was, "Enough! We have heard about you enough. Now it is time: we want to get rid of you."

So when you come across Zen statements like "If you meet the Buddha on the way, kill him immediately," it is such a relief. But you don't know who said this. The man who said this had been worshipping Buddha for thirty years. And the day he said it, that day he had also worshipped in the morning. And after he said it, by the evening he was worshipping again. The disciples who had heard him say this could not believe it – and when they saw him worshipping again they asked, "What are you doing? Just today you said, 'If you meet Buddha on the way, kill him.' Now why are you worshipping?"

And he said, "Because I love him. And because he even allows himself to be killed, my love grows more. He does not want me to cling to him, because that will become a barrier. He wants me to drop him too. Hence my gratitude is even more.

But if you just see the statement taken out of its context, it becomes silly. You hear of a Zen master just hitting a disciple on the head with his staff and a great satori happens. Now these stories are becoming very prevalent in the West. And people think this is beautiful – just a single hit. But you don't know; the man had been meditating for twenty-six years. That was the last thing, he was ready for it.

Those hits from the master have to be deserved – one has to be worthy of them, one has to be capable of receiving them.

Zen masters use words for Buddha which no other tradition has ever used. And that is possible only because their love is tremendous.

It is said that when Buddha was born he declared: "There is no one higher than me, above or below." And Ikkyu is reported to have said, "If I had been there I would have killed this guy immediately and thrown him to the dogs."

And Ikkyu was worshipping Buddha, morning and evening, with tears in his eyes – dancing around his statue, bringing flowers for him. If you don't know Ikkyu's whole context you will miss the point. He is saying it out of great love – his love is so great that it can be said. He is not offending Buddha. Buddha will understand – he will smile, he will know.

But Ikkyu is not being silly. He is neither serious nor silly, he is simply spontaneous. When he feels like worshipping he worships. When he feels like throwing him out he throws him out too...

He used to live in a hut, and there was no Buddha statue there. A few soldiers were passing by and they stayed the night in Ikkyu's hut. And they saw the man, and the beauty of the man – he was a Buddha himself.

And they said, "You look so much like a Buddha, and yet you don't have a Buddha statue here? We have a picture – we will present it to you." But Ikkyu said, "Take your picture with you, because the place is already much too crowded. Don't you see? It is such a small hut, we both cannot live here! Only one can live here."

But they could not understand. They laughed, and they still said, "You keep this picture, this will not take much space." So he kept it. He hung the picture on a pole and told Buddha, "Now be here. And don't ask for any reverence from me and don't ask for any worship. I am not going to take care of you, and I am not asking any favours from you! This place is already much too crowded, and you know it! But if you insist, be here."

And next morning, he is worshipping. Tears in his eyes...

Now, to understand this man is difficult, difficult because we don't know the spontaneity. That moment was that moment, this moment is this moment. And he is so one with Buddha, he can throw all formalities to the wind.

But if you throw the formalities to the wind – knowingly, with effort, deliberately, just so that you don't look serious – you have missed the point.

Now, Sarjano, you have tried to be serious, you have tried to be silly. Please don't try anything anymore: just be. Just be natural, as you are. And sometimes you will be silly and sometimes you will be serious – it is okay. Just be simple, don't try to be anything in particular. If you try to be anything in particular you will go on missing the point. If you don't try to be anything in particular, you have got it.

Take It Easy Vol. 2, Ch 13, Q 5

Finally the day came when he had to leave the commune and go to Italy. He had been at the ashram for more than one year, and Osho had sent him a message, suggesting to him to go back to Italy, to finish all his things, to publish his book, and then to move to Pune for good; hence he was getting ready to leave wholeheartedly.

But before leaving he would have a darshan with the Master, a darshan that was given to everyone leaving and to everyone just arrived, and in fact this one was called a 'leaving darshan'. He wrote him a short note, telling him that he was about to leave, and asked him to talk to him about 'acceptance', during their short meeting.

He wrote to him that lately he was continuously judging himself, and he didn't manage to accept himself as usual, hence he was asking right now to tell him what to do about this problem. He explained also that when he was in front of him all his problems were gone, totally dissolved, hence he would not be able to ask him any questions while in front of him, so to please remember what his problem is!

That evening, when his name was called and he went to sit in front of Osho, the Master asked him instantly:

And what is your problem? Can you kindly remind me?

He looked at the Master hopelessly, because he just didn't have the energy to answer. What problem, where is this problem, if in this moment there is only an immense peace? He swallowed a big sigh, and then, with tremendous effort he managed to whisper just a few words: "It's…it's that I don't accept myself fully…"

Oh yes, now I remember… the Master said laughing, then continued:

Mm mm…I don't see that that is the problem; the problem is something else. And the mind is very clever : it always creates a false problem to protect the real problem so you become engaged with the false problem. And because it is false it can never be solved, so you become occupied and the real problem remains. It is a device. It has to always be remembered, that the mind cannot give you the right diagnosis – it always gives you the wrong diagnosis; hence the need of a master.

Because if you listen to your mind, the mind will tell you "This is the problem" and because you know nothing except your mind, you will believe it! People never doubt their minds, that's the problem. They doubt everything else – they never doubt their minds, and their whole life becomes a mess. The beginning of spiritual life is the doubt about your own mind.

That is the function of a master – to create a doubt against your mind. This is another aspect of the same thing; to create trust in the master means to create doubt in your own mind. If you believe in your mind, you cannot trust the master; if you disbelieve your mind, then only can you trust the master.

It is not the real problem. You are receptive; the problem is that you cannot accept yourself as you are. You have great ideas about how you should be; you have ideals about how you should be. And because of those ideals you remain in a kind of anxiety, because you are always falling short. Now this is a very vicious circle: first you make a great ideal…. The great ideal means it is as far away from you as possible, that's why it is great. You put it as high as you can – it is the ultimate in your imagination, you cannot imagine beyond it. It is the Everest, it is far away in the clouds, and then suddenly you look at yourself and now you are crawling on the earth, in the dust. So the gap between you and the ideal becomes so big, it creates anxiety, anguish, sadness, a kind of meaninglessness, futility, despair. It is because of the ideal.

Those ideals have to be destroyed; they have to be dropped. That's what I mean by accepting yourself totally. You are the way you are, and this is the only way you can be; there is no other way. So not even a small lurking desire to be somebody else has to be allowed, because that very desire will create despair; it will condemn you. You will always be comparing and you will always feel inadequate. That's the misery that you create.

My basic teaching is: accept yourself in toto. Nothing is missing, all is as it should be. Everyone is already perfect. Perfection has not to be achieved; it is already there. The moment you accept yourself, it is revealed. If you don't accept yourself, you go on chasing shadows, mirages, faraway mirages. And they only look beautiful when you are very far away from them. The closer you come, the more you find that there is nothing, only sand; it was a mirage. Then you create another mirage. And this is how people waste their whole life.

Just accept yourself as you are. Don't condemn; nothing has to be condemned, nothing has to be judged. There is no way to judge, no way to compare, because each person is unique. There has never been a man like you and there will never be again, so you are alone; comparison is not possible. And this is the way God wants you to be, that's why you are this way. Now don't fight with God, and don't try to improve upon yourself, otherwise you will create a mess. That's how people have created a mess out of their lives.

So this is my message to you: in the days that you will be there, accept yourself. It will be hard, very hard, because the idealistic mind is always there and watching and saying 'What are you doing? This is not the right thing to do! You are not supposed to do it. You have to become a great man. You have to become a Buddha or a Christ – and what are you doing, Sarjano? This does not look like a Buddha. You are behaving like a fool. Are you mad?'

Accept yourself. In that acceptance is Buddhahood. And when will you be back?

While saying these words, Osho made a gesture with his arms as if to collect something, while he was totally melting in a cloud of peace, finding himself prostrate at his feet, incapable of the slightest movement.

Good Sarjano, this is good…

The phantom of Sarjano stood up painfully, stretched his arms towards Osho, receiving something white, a feather, a gift, and then he fell down again weeping softly, "Grazie…grazie…grazie…"

Very good, Sarjano! Bring it always with you, and every time that some ideal comes into your mind, just wear this robe and you will feel like a Buddha!

The Tongue-Tip Taste of Tao, Ch 8

It was time to get up and go back to his place, moving like an amoeba, a leaf, a cloud carried by the wind, slowly finding control of his legs and of a body which had abandoned him completely. Finally he sensed some delicate weight on his arm, then saw a white something…he touched it and touched it again, while his heart jumped in his throat and he was about to explode incredulously, and he absolutely couldn't believe it, but the more he touched and looked carefully, he finally realized that inevitably this is just the case: Osho had placed one of his white robes in his arms!

Fare you well my last gift, fare you well oh my Master, fare you well Eternal Smile. Nobody to thank, his light and heavy robe in his arms…

Once back to his seat, all his friends gathered around to hug him, to pat his shoulders, repeating all together: "Hey, the Master has been asking you to translate his book into Italian! Now you are 'The Translator of God'! He didn't quite understand what they were saying, but he was happy anyhow for all the attentions his friends were showering on him, until somebody noticed his disconcertedness and explained to him what Osho had actually said:

"The Master said at the end that when you'll be back, you will start to translate his book into Italian…" – and he knew so little English that he hadn't understood what the Master had just told him!

He thought once more that his Master had really good eyes and a very good nose too, because it seemed he knew about his complaints about the poor translations, and now he had thrown them at him, who didn't speak English well enough for such a job. But, and here comes his tremendous sagacity, he had understood that the real question was not to know perfect English, because with a good dictionary even an illiterate person can translate his books, but the real question was to know the Italian language, and about this, in all modesty, he had no doubts to be the one who knew Italian better than anybody else in the whole ashram. He thus decided that while in Italy he would buy a good dictionary, and once back in Pune he would start his new job, being 'Translator of God'. Because he liked this definition so much, he immediately thought to make some funny business cards – 'Sarjano, Translator of God', just like this, to irritate a few people!

***

CHAPTER 03

Short Trip To Italy and Return To Pune

When he landed in Rome without having informed anybody of his arrival, he found that someone was waiting for him at the airport where his plane had landed just before midnight. There, waiting at the exit, was Terry, who in some mysterious way had got to know about his arrival!

He was so surprised to see her there, that he was suddenly overwhelmed by an uncontainable wave of love for this woman, who was still waiting for him after more than one year that they hadn't seen each other and, surrendering to an impulse that he couldn't contain, he threw himself at her feet, until Terry helped him to get up and hugged him for an eternity; meanwhile several hundred people had stopped walking, staring at the whole scene with open mouths!

Let's face it, the scene was quite something: there was this guy who looked just like a modern version of Jesus Christ, dressed in a long orange robe reaching the floor, prostrated at the feet of a beautiful blond girl who a few people had already seen in some movies! Many of those people were even looking around trying to spot some cameras, because they were probably thinking they were in front of a movie scene! To tell you the truth, it looked like a movie to him too, a movie he had loved immensely when he was younger, called 'Le Repos du Guerrier', directed by Roger Vadim, starring Brigitte Bardot, Michel Serrault and Robert Hossein.

The movie narrates the story of a man who commits suicide; a woman inadvertently enters his hotel room, mistaking it for her room, and when she sees this man on the floor, surrounded by several empty containers of sleeping pills, she realizes immediately that the man has committed suicide, calls an ambulance and the guy gets saved in time.

When the man comes back to his senses, he understands that this woman has saved him from a certain death; he therefore decides instantly to give his life to her, puts it literally in her hands, telling her that from now on she will have to direct his life – taking him around, feeding him, helping him even to breathe, because from this very moment his life belongs to her, she who had saved him without even asking for his permission!

He felt like in a sort of remake of this movie, and he loved this role too much, without saying that he was very touched by it!

Outside the airport a taxi was already waiting for them, so they jumped in and went to Silvia's house. Once they arrived, he found out that when Terry had come back to Italy, she was diagnosed with having contracted an ugly hepatitis while in India; hence she had to spend a few weeks in hospital and then went to Silvia's house for her convalescence. Now she was back in full shape and looked like the usual Terry, and moreover she had just starred in a big "historical erotic" movie called 'Caligula', directed by the famous Italian director Tinto Brass, a movie starring Malcolm McDowell, Helen Mirren, Peter O'Toole, and other international stars.

They made love all night, and the next morning they decided to go to Sicily straight away, in order to "finish all his things," as the Master had told him to; Terry bought two tickets and they flew towards their magic castle.

At Villa Fassino there were only a half dozen die-hards left, who so far had no intentions to travel to India, and neither to vacate the house! He spoke with them, saying that he had come to close down the castle and give it back to the owners, hoping that these people would give him some money as goodwill for his departure, He also informed them of the fact that this process would take perhaps a few months, as he himself didn't want to go to the owners but wait until they would come forward with an offer. So those people could relax for now, take it easy.

Before he was to leave for India again, the owner of the castle had sold the entire property, lemon trees included, to a group of a local Mafiosi, and these people had already come a few times to the castle to tell him to vacate the premises as soon as possible. As he was not the type to accept anybody's impositions, not even from the Sicilian Mafia, he simply answered that he would leave only when he felt like it, and warned them not to make any strange moves, or try to damage them or their property in any way. He explained there were more than twenty people who participated in the '68 revolution, and they all had expertise in making Molotov cocktails:

"If anything happens to any of us, and I mean *anything*, you'd better know that we are going to bomb all the petrol pumps that you own around here!"

Strangely enough, these Mafiosi bowed and left, and after that came just a couple more times to offer some money if he was ready to quit with his group of friends. In the past he had always refused these offers, but now he was hoping that as they knew he had returned, they would come to make him a new offer. He had to wait for nearly a month, and then they finally came to visit him and repeated their eternal song: "When are you going to vacate the space?"

This time he answered that if they would make him a good offer he would accept it and be gone forever; the Mafiosi discussed this a little amongst themselves and then offered him ten million Lira if he was ready to leave in ten days. He thought that this was a quite convenient offer, because this amount of money was even more than what they had paid as rent in seven years; hence he didn't waste any time in bargaining, and with a simple shaking of hands the whole transaction was over once and for all. The next day he asked everybody not to waste time and start packing, because in less than two weeks they all had to be out of there for good.

In those days he spent a lot of time with Antonino, the angel of the castle and his best friend in the whole of Sicily, because he knew that most likely he would not see him again, yet he didn't want to say anything about it, because he knew that Antonino would be devastated if he knew that neither he, nor anybody else would ever come back there.

Poor Antonino in fact was literally being torn apart, and just like a neglected lover, the next year, seeing that indeed nobody was coming back, he committed suicide, and there wasn't any blond heroine to save him…

This beautiful man had been living nearly eight years with this band of hippies, long-haired, alternative people, taking care of all of them like an angel, and now his life had no meaning anymore, no reason to be; hence he finished it all by hanging himself from the ceiling. He was glad that the news reached him only after he had returned to Pune, so he could just cry about his sad demise, pray for him, promising that he would never forget him, and as you can see, he kept his promise…

Once they left Sicily, instead of going back to Rome, he and Terry flew to Milan, where he wanted to meet a couple of publishers seemingly interested in his book, even if according to him the book had a title a little embarrassing, because it was called in fact 'The Orange Enchantment' and this bizarre title – if not too obvious – had been chosen by nobody else than the Master in person.

The story went like this: when he had almost completed his book, he was so happy that he decided to write a letter to Osho, telling him that the book was almost finalised, and that now it was time to find an appropriate title for it, and then, just to have some fun – because he loved to share some jokes with his Master – he proposed a series of titles, one more crazy and awkward than the next, pretending that he was inspired directly by the books of the Master himself, hence in homage to his book 'Hammer on the Rock' he was now proposing 'Hammer on the Prick'!

Not only that, he continued with another inspiration, this time by a book called 'Get Out of Your Own Way', which in his interpretation had become 'Get Out of Your Own Way, the Bus Is Coming' or even from a sacred text called 'Come Follow Me!' he made up a little variation that says 'Come Follow Me, I'll Take You For a Beer' – and other insanities of the kind, and in the end he proposed as a title the top of ridiculous lyricism, a category that he had just invented for the occasion, that sounded like 'The Orange Enchantment' which translated into Italian would become 'L'Incanto D'Arancio'!

Osho, probably in order to hit an idiot who was taking the liberty of joking with him in such a way, answered simply:

'The Orange Enchantment' is the title that I have chosen for your book.

He even wrote to him later that he had just been kidding, that he had been proposing the titles just for fun, but the Master was adamant and insisted, until finally he had to accept this awkward title!

The first editor he went to see turned out to be the last one too, because he was the editor of 'The New Leftism'; he was very open and friendly, and the memories of an ex-militant on a pilgrimage to Pune was according to him a very good book, and moreover it was coming out in the right moment, since Pune and the ashram were on everybody's lips.

It was too bad that this Savelli, to remain in the theme of '68 and to sell some more copies, added to that title, already ridiculous by itself, a sub-title even more pathetic and according to him risible, namely 'The conversion and the trip to Pune of a militant in crisis'.

At this point he had quit the house in Sicily, he had published his book, he had even made some money that he intended to give as a donation to the ashram: what else was he to stay in Italy for?

He had come only three months before, and now he was ready to go back to Pune, even if this time he was very sad about leaving Terry, because he had the feeling that he would never see her again.

Silvia meanwhile was promising and vowing that she would come to Pune very soon with Bill, the young actor of The Living Theatre who had become her companion. He asked her to promise solemnly to bring Amore with her too, because by now he was eight years old and he would be immensely happy to quit both Italy and his school to join him in India. He then kissed everybody and left.

Back to Pune

He had been away for less than four months, yet when he came back to Pune he saw a lot of changes. The first one was that he discovered that somebody had taken down the little house by the river where he had been living, hence he had to search immediately for another place to stay; he could not sleep in the ashram with his previous girlfriend anymore, since she had launched herself – second surprise – into a love affair with Ashish, the old 'engineer'...you definitely couldn't trust anybody in those days!

Naturally it didn't take much time before someone else came to console him, namely Satya Bharti, the wife of that particular Chaitanya who was leading most of the meditations in Buddha Hall, who had lost her head – so to say – over him.

Since coming back to Pune, he had written to Osho only once, and one word only, and his letter said,

Beloved Master, YES!

Sarjano, this simple word "yes" contains all the religions of the world. It contains trust, it contains love, it contains surrender. It contains all the prayers that have ever been done, are being done, and will ever be done. If you can say yes with the totality of your heart, you have said all that can be said. To say yes to existence is to be religious, to say no is to be irreligious.

That's my definition of the atheist and the theist. The atheist is not one who denies God, and the theist is not one who believes in God – not necessarily so, because we have seen great theists who never believed in any God. We have known Buddha, Mahavira, Adinatha: we have known tremendously enlightened people who never talked about God. But they also talked about yes; they had to talk about yes.

God can be dropped as an unnecessary hypothesis, but yes cannot be dropped. Yes is the very spirit of God. And yes can exist without God, but God cannot exist without yes. God is only the body, yes is the soul.

There are people who believe in God and yet I will call them atheists, because their belief has no yes behind it. Their belief is bogus, their belief is formal; their belief is given by others, it is borrowed. Their parents, priests and teachers have taught them that God is; they have made them so much afraid that they cannot even question the existence of God.

And they have given them promises of great things if they believe in God. There will be great rewards in heaven if you believe, and great punishments in hell if you don't believe.

Fear and greed have been exploited. The priest has behaved with you almost like the psychologist behaves with the rats upon which he goes on experimenting. The rats in psychological experiments are controlled by punishment and reward. Reward them, and they start learning the thing for which they are rewarded; punish them, and they start unlearning the thing for which they are punished.

The priests have behaved with men as if men are rats. Psychologists are not the first to dehumanize humanity; priests were the pioneers. First the priests behaved with men as if they were rats, now the psychologists are behaving with rats as if they are men. But the process is the same, the technique exactly the same.

There are people who are theists – believers in God, churchgoers, worshippers – and yet in their hearts there is no yes; in their hearts there is doubt. On the surface they behave religiously, deep down they are suspicious. And it is the depth that determines you. It is not what you do that is decisive; it is what you feel at the deepest core of your being that determines you, that creates you. And there are atheists who go on saying there is no God, but they are not in any way different from the believers. Their disbelief has as much doubt in it as the belief of the believers.

In Soviet Russia, in China, and in other red countries, disbelief is the belief; not to believe is to be a conformist, to believe is to be a revolutionary. The state goes on teaching that there is no God. If people are taught continuously, conditioned continuously, they become whatsoever they are conditioned for. It is a kind of mass hypnosis.

Theists, atheists, both are victims. The really religious person has nothing to do with the Bible or the Koran or the Bhagavad Gita. The really religious person has a deep communion with existence. He can say yes to a rose flower, he can say yes to the stars, he can say yes to people, he can say yes to his own being, to his own desires. He can say yes to whatsoever life brings to him; he is a yea-sayer.

And in this yea-saying is contained the essential prayer.

The last words of Jesus on earth were: "Thy kingdom come, thy will be done. Amen."

Do you know this word amen, what it means? It simply means "Yes, Lord, yes. Let thy will be done. Don't listen to what I say, I am ignorant. Don't listen to what I desire; my desires are stupid – bound to be so. Go on doing whatsoever you feel right – go on doing it in spite of me." That is the meaning of the word amen.

Mohammedans also end their prayer with amin *– it is the same word.*

Sarjano, your question is tremendously significant. First, it is not a question, hence it is significant. It is a declaration, it is a dedication, it is surrender, it is trust.

You say, "Beloved Osho, YES!"

This is the beginning of real sannyas. If you can say yes with totality, with no strings attached to it, with no conditions, with no desire for any reward, if you can simply enjoy saying yes, if it is your dance, your song, then it is prayer. And all prayers reach God – whether God is mentioned or not, whether you believe in God or not. All prayers reach God. To reach him, a prayer has only to be an authentic prayer.

But I would like to tell you that your yes should not only be a prayer. It should become your very lifestyle; it should become your flavor, your fragrance. Down the ages, religions have been teaching people life-negation, life-condemnation. Down the ages, religions have been telling you that you are sinners, that your bodies are the houses of sin, that you have to destroy your life in order to praise the Lord, that you have to renounce the world to be able to be accepted by the Lord. This is all holy cow dung, utter nonsense.

Life-affirmation, not life-negation, is religion – because God is life, and there is no other God. God is the green of the trees and the red of the trees and the gold of the trees. God is all over the place. Only God is. To deny life means to deny God, to condemn life means to condemn God, to renounce life means you are thinking yourself wiser than God.

God has given you this life, this tremendously valuable gift, and you cannot even appreciate it. You cannot welcome it, you cannot feel any gratitude for it. On the contrary, you are complaining and complaining and complaining. Your heart is full of grudges, not gratitude.

But this is what you have been taught by the priests down the ages. Priests have lived on it; this has been their basic strategy to exploit people.

If life is lived in its totality, the priest is not needed at all. If you are already okay as you are, if life is beautiful as it is, what is the need for a priest? What is the need of a mediator between you and God? You are directly in contact with God: you are living in

God, breathing in God, God is pulsating in you. The priest will be utterly useless, and so will be all his mumbo jumbo, his religion and scriptures. He can be significant only if he can create a rift between you and God. First the rift has to be created, then he can come and can tell you, "Now I am here, I can bridge the rift." But first the rift has to be there, only then can it be bridged.

And of course, you have to pay for it. When the priest does such great work bridging the rift, you have to pay for it. And in fact deep down, he is not interested in bridging it. He will only pretend that he is bridging it; the rift will remain. In fact he will make it more and more unbridgeable; the more unbridgeable it is, the more important he is. His importance consists in denying life, destroying life, making you renounce it.

I teach you a tremendous total yes to life. I teach you not renunciation but rejoicing. Rejoice! Rejoice! Again and again, I say rejoice! – because in your rejoicing you will come closest to God.

When the dancer disappears in his dance, he is divine. When the singer disappears in his song, he is divine. Rejoice so deeply, so totally, that you disappear in your rejoicing: there is rejoicing, but there is nobody who is rejoicing. When it comes to such an optimum, there is a transformation, a revolution. You are no more the old dark ugly self. You are showered with blessings. For the first time you come to know your grandeur, the splendor of your being. Say yes to life, say a total yes to life. That's what sannyas is all about. I don't give you concepts, dogmas, creeds. I only give you a certain life-affirmative lifestyle, a philosophy of life reverence.

The Book of Wisdom, Ch 7, Q 2

Three weeks later, he sent another question to his Master:

Beloved Osho,

What is this urge to do something, to create? To free your message, your word, unto the world? I feel like I am in a hurry and that all the people in the commune have the same feeling. It is as if there is no time left, as if any day, this very moment, can be the last moment. Am I dying? I am exploding each and every moment. What is that? What is this urge? Please say something for this thirst.

Sarjano, man is dying, mankind is dying. And in fact there is not much time left. And this is felt not only here around the commune, it is felt everywhere by sensitive, intelligent, creative people. Only the mediocre are unaware of it; only the politicians go on rushing into the danger, the calamity, that awaits, totally unaware where they are going and where they are leading the world.

But people of sensitivity, awareness, meditativeness, people of the heart, are everywhere feeling that the danger is very close, that mankind can commit suicide any moment, that the future was never so uncertain as it is today, that the tomorrow may really never come.

These are moments of great turmoil, but they can become of great creativity too. When one is encountering death, one can bring one's total potential into manifestation. When there is no time left you cannot postpone. Hence the hurry.

When death is very imminent, life flares up to the optimum. And that is what is happening to all creative people around the world, and more so around this commune, because my whole approach is such that only the very creative ones will be attracted to it. I teach sensitivity. Down the ages, religions have been teaching just the opposite – how to become insensitive – because the more insensitive you are the more you can remain aloof, distant, detached. Because it was thought that to attain to God one has to renounce the world, it was a natural consequence, a logical consequence, that one should learn how to be more and more insensitive to beauty, to music, to love, to people, to life itself. In the past, religion has been teaching people how to be unintelligent, because sensitivity and intelligence go together, insensitivity and stupidity go together.

Your so-called saints are not intelligent people at all, but you have worshipped them. And you have worshipped them for the wrong reason – because they were insensitive, because they had dulled their consciousness, because they had grown thick skin around themselves. The spring will come but they will remain unaffected, the clouds will gather and they will remain unaffected. The peacock will dance but they will remain unaffected, the night sky will be full of stars but they will be completely unaware of it. That was the whole discipline in the past: how to become like a rock, so that the world cannot overpower you. It was a kind of paranoia, it was based in fear.

I teach you just the opposite: be sensitive, be alert, be loving, be sensuous – because God is not against the rose flower, God is in it. If you can sensuously feel the velvetiness of the rose you have touched God himself. God is not against the stars and the sun and the moon, he is in them. If you can allow them to enter into your being, if you allow them to stir your heart, if you can allow them to drive you crazy in a dance of joy and celebration, you will be coming closer and closer to home. I teach sensitivity, I teach love.

The people who have gathered around me have a totally different quality to them. This is not an ordinary ashram, it is a commune of creators – artists, painters, singers, musicians. All kinds of talented people have come to me; only they can understand what I am saying. People understand according to their own inner capabilities. I may say one thing, you may understand something else. Communication is not easy, language is not adequate, and you will understand only that for which you have come.

I have gathered around me a special kind of people. Hence this urge will be felt by almost everybody, that something has to be done. First, it will be a very very vague kind of feeling, just a silent voice within your being – heard yet not heard, understood yet not understood…a whisper, not very clear, a little muddy, not very transparent. In the beginning this is bound to be so. You will hear it like a song: it will be more poetry than prose, it will come to you like dreams, visions. Slowly slowly, the unconscious will be able to communicate to the conscious.

And that's what meditation is all about: learning the way to bridge the unconscious with the conscious, so that your own being can give you indications where to move, where to go, so that you don't need a leader, so that you become a guide to yourself, so that you can become a light unto yourself.

Sarjano, you are not dying, but this will be felt like that because you are part of humanity and humanity is dying. All that is human is disappearing, and all that is inhuman is becoming more and more dominating and powerful.

Man is being reduced to a machine, and mechanical values are becoming dominant. The artist is not respected, but the technician is. Poetry is not loved, but plumbing is. The dancer is no more in the center of life, but the businessman, the bureaucrat, the politician are. All that is beautiful is becoming irrelevant to man, because that which is beautiful cannot be used as a means to anything. That which is beautiful is an end unto itself. You cannot use poetry in war; you will need the scientist, not the poet. And you cannot use musicians in the marketplace; there you will need economists.

This whole life is geared around wrong things. Money is more important than meditation. This is a very topsy-turvy situation: man is standing on his head. Man is dying, and the death is very slow. And remember, when death is very fast you can avoid it, because you become intensely aware of it. When it comes very very slow, a slow poisoning....

For example, a person goes on smoking every day. All the experts go on saying that this is dangerous to you, that this will kill you, but he smokes every day and it doesn't kill him! So you may write it on every packet of cigarettes – nobody bothers about your warnings that "This is harmful to health," that "This is harmful to life." Who cares? – because experience says something else! You smoke every day, dozens of cigarettes, and you don't die and you have not died yet.

You believe in your experience. The poison is very very slow: if a person goes on smoking one dozen cigarettes every day, then it will take twenty years to poison the whole system. Now, twenty years is a long time, and man has a very very short vision, he is shortsighted.

The world is being poisoned very slowly. The rivers are being polluted, the oceans are being polluted, the lakes are dying. Nature is being destroyed. We are exploiting the earth so much that sooner or later we will not be able to live on it. We are not behaving well with nature.

Our whole approach is wrong, it is destructive. We only take from the earth, and we never give anything back. We only exploit nature. The ecology is broken, the circulation is broken; we are not living in a perfect circle, and nature is a perfect circle: if you take from one hand and you give from another, you don't destroy it.

But we are doing it: we only go on taking, and all the resources are being spent. But this poisoning is happening slowly, slowly. You don't see it happening because it takes a long time. And then there are politicians who go on gathering more and more atomic weapons – more atom bombs, more hydrogen bombs, super-hydrogen bombs – as if man has decided to commit suicide.

This is what is being felt by you, Sarjano. You have the heart of a poet or the heart of a painter, the heart of a lover. You have immense potential for creativity. You are sensitive, hence you are feeling it. But the feeling is as if "I am dying." No, not you – something far more important is happening, something far more dangerous too.

Individuals have always died, it is not a problem. It is, in fact, part of recycling. Your body goes back to the sources to be renewed, your being moves back into the eternal to be rested, and then you come back again, fresh, young. Life tires, life exhausts, death is a rest. For the individual, death is a blessing – but not for humanity itself; then it is a curse. Individuals go on dying and they go on coming back. But humanity is needed for them to come back. This earth is a beautiful planet and it is in the wrong hands. Hence you are feeling that something is to be done very urgently. Yes, it is urgent, because death is coming closer.

This century's end is going to see either the total destruction of humanity, and with it the total destruction of life on this earth, or a new man being born – a new man who will not hate life, as in the past it has been done; a new man who will love life; a new man who will not be negative in any way, but will be affirmative; a new man who will not desire life after death, but will live moment to moment in sheer joy – who will think of this life as a gift and not as a punishment; who will not be antagonistic to the body, who will respect the body as the temple of the soul; who will love, and who will not be afraid of love; who will move in all kinds of relationships and yet be able to remain himself.

To be in relationship and become dependent is the sign of weakness. And to escape to the Himalayas or to some Catholic monastery because of the fear of becoming dependent is again the sign of weakness; it is cowardly.

To live in relationship and yet remain independent, that is what courage is. The new man will be courageous. In the past, only two kinds of cowards have existed on the earth, the worldly kind and the otherworldly kind – but both are cowards. The really brave man will live in the world and yet not be of it. Either this is going to happen, or a total destruction. Now there is no third alternative. Man cannot survive as he is. Either he has to change himself, transmute himself, or he has to die and vacate the earth.

This is what is felt, this is why you are in such a hurry. That's why I am in such a hurry. My sannyasins can be the new man, my sannyasins can herald the new age. Hence my sannyasins are going to be opposed by all past-oriented people: by Hindus, by Christians, by Mohammedans, by Jainas, by Buddhists – by almost everybody. They are going to be opposed, and that is natural because we are trying to bring a new future in. To bring that new future we will have to destroy the past, because unless the past ceases to exist, the future cannot come into existence.

The past has to die. We have to drop our clinging with the past. What does it mean when you say that "I am a Hindu"? It means you cling to a certain past tradition. What do you mean when you say that "I am a Mohammedan"? You cling to something past.

But when you say, "I am a sannyasin, a neo-sannyasin," you don't cling to any past. Your eyes are focused on the future. Your roots are in the present and your branches are moving towards the future. Then the past is irrelevant. I want you to remember it again and again that the past has to be made irrelevant. You have to cut yourself off from the past.

You say, Sarjano, "What is this urge to do something?"

Yes, something has to be done. You have to give birth to yourself, and you have to prepare the way for the new man.

"What is this urge to do something, to create? To free your message, your word, unto the world?"

Yes, it has to be shouted from the housetops, it has to be hammered – because people are deaf, people are blind, they will not hear what is being said to them.

Just the other day, Neeraj sent me a beautiful parable from Pierre Delattre's Tales of a Dalai Lama. In this beautiful book comes this parable:

All the monks had seen the spirit come out of the wall long enough to utter just one word. But each monk had heard a different word. The event is immortalized in this poem:

The one who wanted to die heard LIVE.
The one who wanted to live heard DIE.
The one who wanted to take heard GIVE.
The one who wanted to give heard KEEP.
The one who was always alert heard SLEEP.
The one who was always asleep heard WAKE.
The one who wanted to leave heard STAY.
The one who wanted to stay, DEPART.
The one who never spoke heard PREACH.
The one who always preached heard PRAY.

Each one learned how he had been in someone else's way.

What I am saying has to be conveyed to as many people as possible, and as fast as possible. Use all modern media to reach as many people as possible. Still, be aware that it is very difficult to communicate. It is almost an impossibility to communicate; still it has to be done. Even if fragments of what I am saying are understood, it will be enough to create the field, the energy field, in which the new man can be conceived.

Even if people misunderstand it…it is better to understand the truth, but even if the truth is misunderstood it is better than a lie. Something of the truth will remain in the misunderstanding too. And truth is a potential power, a great power. Even if a fragment, just a seed of truth, falls into your heart, sooner or later you will become the Garden of Eden. It cannot be avoided. Just a drop, and the whole ocean will find its way towards you.

Sarjano, it has to be done. You have to create my message in as many forms as possible. Compose music, play on the guitar or on the flute, because it is easier to stir the heart of the people, to wake it up through music than through words. Dance, but dance in a new way so your dance becomes a teaching of meditation. Dance in such a way that the one who looks at you starts feeling that it is not only a dance but something more, something plus; so that he starts feeling the vibe of meditation that is happening inside you.

Paint: paint pictures which can become objects of meditation, paint pictures of the inner sky of buddhas. The modern painting is pathological. If you look at Picasso's paintings you cannot look long, you will start feeling uneasy. You cannot have Picasso paintings in your bedroom, because then you will have nightmares. If you meditate on a Picasso painting long enough you will go mad, because those paintings are out of Picasso's madness.

Go to Ajanta, Ellora, Khajuraho, Konarak, and you will see a totally different world of creativity. Looking at the statue of a Buddha, something in you starts falling in tune. Sitting silently with a Buddha statue, you start becoming silent. The very posture, the very shape, the face, the closed eyes, the silence that surrounds a marble statue will help you to get connected with your own inner sources of silence.

Gurdjieff used to say that there are two kinds of art. One he used to call objective art, and the other he used to call subjective art. Subjective art is absolutely private, personal. Picasso's art is subjective art; he is simply painting something without any vision for the person who will see it, without any idea of the person who will look at it. He is simply pouring out his own inner illness; it is helpful for himself, it is therapeutic.

I am not saying that Picasso should stop painting, because if he stops painting he is bound to go mad. It is painting that is keeping him sane; his painting is like vomiting. When you have eaten something wrong, when you have a food poisoning, vomiting is the most healthy way to throw the toxins, the poisons, outside the system; it will help. Picasso's paintings are like vomiting. He is suffering from many illnesses, all the illness that humanity is suffering from. He simply represents humanity, he is very representative.

He represents the whole madness that is happening in millions of people. He is a sensitive soul; he has become so attuned with the pathology of mankind that it has become his own pathology. Hence the appeal of his paintings, otherwise they are ugly. Hence his great name – because he deserves it, he represents the age. This is Picasso's age: what you cannot say about yourself, he has said it. What you cannot pour out of yourself, he has poured it on the canvas. But it is a subjective phenomenon. It is therapeutic to him, but it is dangerous to everybody else.

The ancient art was not only art; it was, deep down, mysticism. Deep down, it was out of meditation. It was objective, in Gurdjieff's terminology. It was made so that if somebody meditates over it, he starts falling into those depths where God lives.

Khajuraho or Konarak – if you meditate there, you will know what the Tantra masters were doing. They were creating in stone something that is felt in the ultimate orgasmic joy. It was the most difficult thing to do, to bring ecstasy into the stone. And if the stone can show the ecstasy, then everybody can move into that ecstasy easily.

But people who go to Khajuraho are foolish people. They look either at Khajuraho sculpture as obscene – then they miss the whole point, then they are seeing something which is within their own unconscious; or they are too moralistic – then they don't meditate on any statues, they are in a hurry to get out of the temple somehow, they just throw glances.

Khajuraho sculpture is not just to see, it is for meditation. Sit silently and meditate for hours. If one goes to Khajuraho, one should live at least for three months there, so he can meditate on each possible inner posture of orgasmic joy. And then, slowly slowly, the at-one-ment, slowly, slowly, the harmony; then suddenly you are transported into another world – the world of those mystics who created this temple. This is objective art.

So too is the Taj Mahal. On a full moon night, if you sit silently by the side of it, not being bothered about the history of the Taj Mahal and who created it and why – those are all nonsense, irrelevant facts, they don't matter : Shah Jahan and his beloved, and his memory of his beloved, he created it.... Don't be bothered by the guides; tip them before they start torturing you, and get rid of them!

Shah Jahan has nothing to do with the Taj Mahal, in fact. Yes, he created it, he created it as a memorial for his wife, but he is not the essential source of it. The essential source is in the Sufi way of life, it is in Sufism. Basically it was created by Sufi masters; Shah Jahan was just instrumental. The Sufi masters have created something of immense value. If you silently sit in the full moon night just looking at the Taj Mahal, sometimes with open eyes and sometimes with closed eyes, slowly slowly, you will feel something that you have never felt before. Sufis called it zikr, remembrance of God.

The beauty of the Taj Mahal will remind you of those realms from where all beauty, all benediction comes. You will become attuned with the Sufi way of remembering God: beauty is God.

Sarjano, don't try to repress this urge. Create in any way that suits you. My message has to be delivered in all possible mediums.

In the new commune we are going to have many guilds. The sculptors will have their own guild and they will sculpt, and the poets will have their own guild, and the painters and the carpenters and the dancers and the musicians and the novelists and the filmmakers. All possible media have to be used to approach as many people as possible, to approach as many different kinds of people as possible – because one who can understand poetry may not understand prose, and one who can understand music may not understand painting, and one who can understand sculpture may not understand poetry.

And the message is so important because the whole future of humanity depends on it. Nowhere else is the experiment being done on such a great scale. There is no other community on the whole earth which is working in such a way as this commune. This is the greatest therapeutic center in the world now.

We need a great therapeutic center so that the modern mind can be helped to vomit, cathart, all that has gone wrong in it. Then we will need creators. And once somebody has catharted and thrown out all that is wrong, a great urge will arise in him to create.

Once pathology disappears, everybody becomes a creator. Let it be understood as deeply as possible: only ill people are destructive. The people who are healthy are creative. Creativity is a kind of fragrance of real health. When a person is really healthy and whole, creativity comes naturally to him, the urge to create arises.

This urge is being felt by many just like you, Sarjano. Do something for it – and whatsoever you do is good. Follow your own urge, don't distort it. In the beginning it will remain vague, but if you follow it, soon it will become clear, more and more clear. And if you start doing something about it, things will become very clear very soon.

There are many things which become clear only when you do something about them. For example, the poet is never really aware of the poetry unless he has written it. It remains a very vague cloudy phenomenon. Once he writes it down it starts taking shape, form; it becomes crystallized into words. No painter is ever able to say anything about what he wants to paint, unless he has painted it.

It is said that the best way to learn is to teach. And I agree with it, because what you want to learn you will not be really clearly aware of unless you start teaching it.

In the future, education will have that dimension. My own vision is that each student should be given an opportunity to teach too. The students who are reading and studying for their master's degree should be allowed to go to lower classes to teach; those who are working for their bachelor's degree, they should be allowed to teach the lower classes.

Every student should be a teacher also, and vice versa. Every teacher once in a while should sit with the students and start learning again. Each teacher once in a while should be a student, and each student once in a while should be a teacher too. This difference between the teacher and the taught has to be dissolved; the teacher and the taught are part of one process.

And the same is true about other phenomena. The therapist and the patient: the therapist should not remain always a therapist; once in a while he should lie down on the couch and let the patient be the therapist and he becomes the patient. And immense will be the benefit out of it. The patient will learn many things that he was not able to learn while he was functioning as a patient: by becoming the therapist, by trying to solve the problem of the therapist – because now the therapist is the patient – he will be able to see many things more clearly. And the therapist as a patient will be able to see more clearly the problem, the anxiety, the anguish of the patient, because he will be standing in the shoes of the patient; now he will know where it pinches.

The therapist and the patient should not be divided; they should become part of one team. It is a therapy team, and sometimes the therapist plays the role of the patient and sometimes the patient plays the role of the therapist – the roles are interchangeable and so on and so forth. A couple making love…the man should not always remain the man, and the woman should not always remain the woman. Sometimes the man should be the wife, passive, and the woman should be the husband, active; they should change roles. The husband and wife should not remain frozen, they should be more melting: once in a while the wife should play the active role, take initiative making love, and the husband should be just passive, receptive. Love will have a greater richness that way than it has today. In fact all frozen roles have to be, by and by, dissolved. Life has to become more liquid.

So do whatsoever you can do, and by doing it, you will know what was the urge. Be articulate, try to convey the message, and don't be afraid.

A great fear arises when you are trying to deliver something immensely valuable; great fear arises, one starts feeling nervous. There is no need to feel nervous, because it is nothing to do with you. The urge is coming from the innermost sources of your being, it is divine. You are in the hands of God; be instrumental, you need not be worried.

You need not be proud if something good happens, you need not be ashamed if something goes wrong. Surrender both right and wrong unto the feet of God, and be free of your self-consciousness – because if you are not free of your self- consciousness you will never really be a creator in my sense of the word.

The real creator has no self. The real creation comes out of no-self, the real creation comes out of inner emptiness. When one is utterly empty, one is full of God. Not to be is the way for God to enter you. If you are too much, he is not there. If you are not, only he is there. And creativity is part of the creator.

No man ever creates; it is always God who creates. Hence the poet while he is creating is divine, and the painter while he is painting is divine. The only thing: if he is self-conscious then God is not there, then whatsoever he will do will be subjective art.

But if he is not there, if he is drowned in painting, completely lost, has forgotten himself and there is no self-consciousness, there is no ego, then God is there. When you find a painter painting , utterly lost, linger around. God is very close by – far more close than you will find him in the temples, in the mosques, in the churches.

When a singer is singing, sit by the side. Feel, God is very close by. When somebody is playing on the flute, hide behind a tree and listen, and you will be able to see something,

something that is not of this world, something that is of the beyond. Creativity is always from the beyond.

The Book of Wisdom, Ch 24, Q 1

Beloved Master,

I don't believe a word about this mystery. Nothing like that exists! My guess is that you are advertising your new commune because the press office is too lazy, and not as clever as you can be.

Sarjano, it is not a question of believing or not believing – it is so. The question of belief arises only because you are not aware of it. Belief is significant, and disbelief too – when you are not aware of the reality. Then either you believe or you disbelieve.

I am not saying believe in the mystery I am talking about. I am not saying disbelieve either – I am saying: Come with me! It is so! Let me wake you up… it is so.

You say, "I don't believe a word about this mystery." *It is very good. Please, don't believe a word, because if you start believing you will not be able to experience. I am not interested in believers, I am interested in inquirers. But please don't start guessing either, because a guess is a guess. A guess is not going to help. It will become a belief – if you go on guessing for a long time, and if you go on repeating the same guess again and again, it becomes a belief. You create your own belief then, and that will become a barrier.*

And beliefs are such subtle barriers, and disbeliefs too. Remember, whenever I say belief I always include disbelief in it – because that is the other side of the coin. Belief and disbelief, both are barriers. Once you have created a belief system around yourself – either borrowed from others or guessed by yourself; either borrowed from the Bible, Mein Kampf, Das Kapital, the Bhagavad Gita, or guessed by yourself, home-made, it does not matter – a belief becomes a barrier, an invisible barrier. And once it settles, it won't allow you to see anything else that goes against it.

Just the other day I was reading about an experiment. Sarjano, meditate over it.

A certain naturalist made the following experiment: a glass jar was divided into two halves by a perfectly transparent glass partition. On one side of the partition he placed a pike, on the other a number of small fishes such as form the prey of the pike. The pike did not notice the partition, and hurled itself on its prey with, of course, the result of only a bruised nose. The same happened many times, and always the same result. At last, seeing all its efforts ended so painfully, the pike abandoned the hunt; so that in a few days, when the partition had been removed, it continued to swim about among the small fry without daring to attack them. Does not the same happen with us?

Now the partition is no longer there – it has been removed – but a belief system has arisen in the pike's mind. Now he believes that there is a transparent partition. Now the belief is enough; he never goes beyond that partition which is no longer there. Now he can go! Now there is nothing to debar him but his belief... he has created a belief. And, of course, out of his experience, Sarjano – not even guesswork – it was his experience, a repeated experience. He tried again and again and again, and each time a bruised nose and pain – of course, a belief has arisen.

You have to forgive him – a poor pike has come to conclude that it is futile: "There is a barrier, transparent, so I cannot go..." and he never tries again. He will never try again his whole life. Now he can go and eat the fishes, they are available, but he will go only up to a certain line, and from that line he will come back.

This is the situation of human beings too. A Hindu has a barrier around himself, a Mohammedan another, a Jaina still another – all people live hidden behind transparent barriers, and because of those barriers they cannot see beyond.

Life is a mystery, Sarjano. And my commune is going to be just an experiment in total living, an experiment in moving into life beyond all barriers – barriers of belief, barriers of ideologies, barriers of Catholicism, and communism...going beyond words. Man is not what he appears to be: he is far more. Neither are flowers only what they appear to be – it depends on you. When a scientist goes to a flower, he only sees a part of it, the scientific part of it; he has a barrier, a transparent barrier. He never goes beyond that. He will see the scientific part, the material part of the flower. The rose is no longer beautiful, because beauty is not his concept. He will weigh, measure; he will look into the constituents of the flower, how much color, how much water, how much earth etcetera...but he will never think of the beauty.

When the poet goes, he never bothers about the weight, measurement, earth, water, and other elements that constitute the rose. For him, the rose is constituted of pure beauty; it is something from the beyond which has descended to the earth. He has a different kind of vision, far bigger than the scientist's, far more significant than the scientist's.

But when a mystic goes to the same flower, he dances – he dances in tremendous joy, because a rose is nothing but God. A rose contains the whole universe for him – all the stars and all the suns and all the moons, all the possible worlds and impossible worlds are contained in the small rose flower. It is equivalent to God – neither less nor more – exactly equivalent to God. He may pray, he may bow down.

The scientist will laugh, the poet will feel a little puzzled. The scientist will laugh at the stupidity of the mystic: "What is he doing? – praying to a rose, praying to a tree or praying to a river or praying to a mountain? All nonsense, superstition!" He rejects it. He simply denies the world of the mystic.

The poet will feel a little puzzled. Enjoying the beauty of the rose he can understand, but praying to the rose, bowing down to the rose, shouting "Alleluia!" to the rose? That he cannot understand. That is beyond his perspective. He will feel puzzled. He will think this mystic a little mad.

The scientist will think him superstitious, ignorant. The poet will think him a little eccentric, a little mad – because he is going beyond his barrier, the mystic is going beyond the barrier of the poet. The mystic is going beyond all barriers – that's why he is called the mystic, because he lives in the mysterious.

Sarjano, what I am saying about the new commune is absolutely true. And I am not saying much about it, because it is dangerous to say much about it. I don't want to attract the wrong kind of people to it. So just a few hints only for those who will be able to understand the hints. I am speaking in a special code which can be understood only by those who are searching for the mysterious and the miraculous. Others will be debarred – not by me, by their own prejudice, by their own transparent barrier.

You can see it happening here! People are coming from all over the world – who is debarring the Poona-ites? They are welcome, but they won't come on their own – their transparent barriers are enough. And it is good that they are not coming, because they will be only a nuisance here. Only a few people from amongst them are coming who are capable of understanding the beyond, the incomprehensible, who are capable of comprehending something of the incomprehensible.

But whether you believe in it or not, listen to this anecdote:

Two homosexuals are talking. First homosexual: "Have you heard of the latest scientific discovery? Normal intercourse causes cancer."

Second homosexual: "Is that so?"

First homosexual: "No, of course not! But spread the rumor."

Sarjano, whether you believe in it or not, please spread the rumor. The rumor has to reach to the farthest corners of the earth. Let it be a rumor! Don't be worried. It is up to me to make it a truth or not. If I find the right people – and I am finding them – it is going to materialize.

This mystery that I am talking about is going to materialize. But it will be materialized only for those who are ready to risk all their prejudices, who are ready to sacrifice all their conclusions. Sarjano is one of those people. I trust in him. He has not asked this question for himself, he has asked it for others – because I know he is perfectly mad. He is not only a poet, but just on the verge of becoming a mystic. He has asked this question for others; it is not his own heart's question. His heart agrees totally with me.

You cannot hide your hearts from me. The moment you come close to me, the only thing that I am interested in is your heart. I talk to your head and I go on looking into your heart. Even in the first encounter with me, I know what is possible with you and what is impossible with you.

I have loved Sarjano from the very first moment. In his head he may have many theories and much knowledge and information – that is not my concern at all. My concern is that he has a beautiful heart – the heart that can be transformed into the heart of a mystic.

The Dhammapada: The Way of the Buddha Vol 2, Ch 4, Q 2

Osho,

Once I thought about energy as if energy was mine and I liked to think that I had a lot of energy. Now I have realized that I am only a passage, a medium, a vehicle for the energy of the divine. So how come that sometimes I am so full of energy and overflowing from each pore, feeling that it is impossible to contain that much and I will explode – and after a few hours I am empty with no energy even to say that I would like to have more energy? Is there no way to keep the flow of energy constant? And again, sometimes I feel such appetite for life that literally I am going around hugging everybody, and I would like to hug trees and stars and flowers, and then after a few hours I feel that life is no longer worth living and it is only out of respect for life that I don't kill myself. But I start asking God, "Please, take back your life – it is too painful and boring." Is there some relation between these phenomena? Would you please talk more about energy?

You are coming closer to the point, to the target of understanding, but you have not come exactly to the point yet; you are missing only by inches.

You say: "Once I thought about energy as if energy was mine and I liked to think that I had a lot of energy. Now I have realized..."

Still that 'I' continues; before it was identified with energy, now it is identified with realization.

"Now I have realized" – *you say,* "that I am only a passage, a medium, a vehicle for the energy of the divine."

To be a passage means you are no more. You cannot realize that "I am only a passage," otherwise you are still there – and if you are there you cannot be a passage. You have to disappear completely. Nobody remains there to realize that "I am a passage": then you are a passage.

That's why this problem is arising. Sometimes you are less and sometimes you are more: when you are less, more energy is flowing; when you are more, the flow stops. When you are a little more there as a realizer, as a spiritual being who has understood the flow of energy, when you are there identified with this new idea of being a passage and a medium, energy disappears because you obstruct it. Sometimes when you are not there – not even as a realizer, not even as a medium, when simply you are not there – the energy starts flowing.

You ask: "So how come that sometimes I am so full of energy...?"

Whenever you are not, you are full of energy; whenever you are, energy disappears. God can exist only in your absence; you cannot coexist with God. But you are still there in a subtle way.

You ask: "...how come that sometimes I am so full of energy...?"

Who is this 'I am'? You are enjoying this: "I am so full of energy." Energy comes when you are not, and immediately you jump in and you say, "I am so full of energy," and energy starts disappearing.

You say: "...overflowing from each pore, feeling that it is impossible to contain that much...?"

Who is there to contain? Who is there to count how much it is? Who is there to weigh? In a subtle way you are hiding by the side or looking from the corner of your eye.

A guest had come to Mulla Nasruddin's house. Mulla Nasruddin was giving him food. The guest was saying, "Now it is enough – I have taken five puris, *now no more."*

Nasruddin said, "Five? You have taken eleven, but who is counting?"

This is also counting! Who is there to contain? You jump in – it always happens. Not only with you, Sarjano; it happens with everybody. Whenever those rare moments come when you are not, energy flows, suddenly the mind recoils, comes back, feels great: "So much energy, impossible to contain!" And immediately you fall to the opposite polarity.

You say: "...and after a few hours I am empty, with no energy even to say that I would like to have more energy? Is there no way to keep the flow of energy constant?

Who wants to keep the flow of energy constant? Just see the point: it is you. The old habit goes on coming back in new ways.

Rosenfeld, a New York men's clothing manufacturer, was returning to America after a business trip to Israel. On the way back he decided to stop off in Rome and take in the sights.

Two weeks later he finally arrived home. "How was the trip?" asked his sales manager.

"Fantastic!" replied Rosenfeld. "In Israel I sold a thousand more suits than any of us expected. Then I stopped off in Rome and saw all the historical sights. I got in with a sightseeing group and we had an audience with the Pope."

"The Pope himself? You don't say!" exclaimed the sales manager. "What does he look like?"

"Oh," said Rosenfeld, "I would say about a forty-four short."

A tailor is a tailor, a businessman is a businessman. Even if he goes to see a Buddha he will come with this information – a forty-four short.

They say that a shoemaker never looks at people's faces, he goes on looking at their shoes. In fact, that is his only way to judge about people. Seeing the shoe he knows whether you have money in your pocket or not. He knows how things are going in your life, whether you are happy or unhappy. In fact, a good shoemaker can predict everything about you just by looking at your shoes; the psychoanalysis of the shoe will show everything about you.

Old habits, Sarjano…and it is so with everybody. The 'I' is the most ancient habit; for millions of lives we have carried it, so 'I' comes again and again. You will have to be a little more watchful, a little more alert. Who wants to keep the flow of energy constant? Exactly the same entity that wants the flow to remain constant is the cause of it not being constant. Be a little more alert.

Mrs Hatton wanted to scare her husband out of his terrible drinking habit. One night she dressed up like the Devil and waited for him in an alley.

Soon the bar closed for the night and Hatton staggered towards home. Mrs. Hatton jumped out at him and yelled, "Yah! I am the Devil!"

Hatton held out his hand and said, "How da ya do? I married your sister!"

This is awareness – even drunk!

Learn a little more awareness, be aware. The 'I' will come in many forms, shapes, disguises. It can become spiritual, it can become holy, it can become saintly, godly. It can try every possible way to save itself.

When you are feeling full of energy you are not, hence great love arises. The ego poisons love; you start hugging people, trees. People have complained to me and trees too, because they may not be in the same energy space as you are, Sarjano. Be a little watchful!

But I know, when the energy flows one is constantly in a sharing state; one would like to share with everybody, even with trees and rocks. But when it disappears you will feel very very empty, so empty that you would like to commit suicide. This happens only when you reach a peak of energy, and then coming back to the valley is very disturbing. People who live in the valley and never go to the peak never think of suicide.

That's why in poor countries suicide is rare, in primitive countries absolutely non-existent. Animals don't commit suicide – they never go to the peak. Because they don't know anything about the peak they never feel the ugliness, the darkness of the valley. Because they have never smelt the fragrance of the divine they can never smell the stinking existence that they are living.

So this is going to happen to every sannyasin: you will reach peaks of joy and then when you fall from the peaks the only desire will be to be finished with it all. But the fall is not happening on its own – you are the cause of it, it can be stopped.

And the only way to stop it is: when you are on the peak, enjoy the peak, enjoy the sunlit peak, the pure air, the whispering of the clouds, the closeness of the stars, enjoy that; and when you fall into the valley, enjoy the darkness of the valley, the dangers of the valley –

and don't bring yourself in – both are good. In fact, the valley will allow you a little rest so that you can again be ready to go to the peak. The valley is a kind of sleep; it is needed after a day's hard work. Tomorrow morning you will be again rejuvenated, you can again track your path towards the peak.

Enjoy both – and you can enjoy both if the 'I' disappears. And if the 'I' disappears – I would like to give you the real mystic statement about it – if the 'I' disappears there is no peak, no valley; everything is the same. Wherever you are, God is flowing through you; wherever you are, you are in a state of blessedness. Wherever you are, not only are YOU blessed, you bless the whole existence too.

Be Still and Know, Ch 7, Q 3

Osho,

You said today that there is nothing like a 'group soul', but I have been strongly feeling something like that in the commune. Not only that, but this feeling of a collective soul is becoming more and more intense and attuned day by day. It is something new for me, and very beautiful, and actually I experience it as the most beautiful thing that is happening for me here. I know that each of us has to awaken alone, but I feel that this 'collective soul' is a tremendous help, at least for us not to create other dreams.... Am I dreaming now of a 'collective soul'?

Sarjano,

No, it is a fact, you just don't know the right word for it. 'Collective soul' is not the right term; it is very misleading. Soul can only be individual. Then what is happening here in this commune? Anybody who enters the ashram for the first time immediately becomes aware of something. He can see it on people's faces, he can see it in their walk, he can see it in the way they are working. He can see that it is no ordinary humanity. Some grace he can feel, some joy permeating the whole place, some playfulness, some sense of humor. And people are working seven days a week. Nobody is looking at the clock...except the Indians!

People are enjoying the work: it is play, it is creativity. They are not tired. In fact, the deeper they go into this creativity, the more nourished they feel, the more energy is released in them.

Anybody can see that something is there like an inner connection that connects all the sannyasins into one whole. It is not a collective soul; it is only falling into the same rhythm. I have a rhythm. The closer you come to me, the more you start falling into the same rhythm. Then my breath and your breath synchronize, then my heart and your heart synchronize.

And all the sannyasins are getting synchronized with me; hence they are also synchronized, as a consequence, with each other. It is a synchronicity. It is an orchestra. We are all playing different instruments, but in harmony, in accord.

That harmony, Sarjano, you are calling the 'collective soul'. It is not a collective soul. An army has a collective mind, no soul at all, because soul can never be collective. Soul is always individual. It is found in your deepest aloneness; there is no other way to find it. But in a commune...this is the chemistry of a commune, that it helps you to become harmonious with others. And the more harmonious you are with others, the closer you come to your own soul, because harmony brings you closer to the soul. When a person is absolutely in harmony with the universe he becomes enlightened.

A paradox to be remembered: the Buddha is one who is absolutely in harmony with the universe, and yet a Buddha is one who is an absolutely unique individual. He plays his flute or his guitar, but he plays his flute or guitar in absolute accord with the whole. He does not go in his own egoistic way – he is not an idiot.

Remember : either you are a Buddha or you are an idiot! The word 'idiot' is beautiful; it simply means doing something privately. Literally it means doing something privately; hence the words like 'idiosyncrasy'. The idiot does not mean a fool; the idiot is far more potent a word than the fool. The idiot simply means one who is trying to live through his ego, who is playing his instrument against the whole and trying to succeed. He is an idiot: he is going to fail, he is doomed to fail. His life will never know any blessing, any benediction.

Sarjano, your feeling is right; you are just using a wrong word. Yes, a harmony is being created. I am in tune with the universe. You don't know what the tune of the universe is; it is invisible. Right now you cannot connect yourself with the universal rhythm directly. But I am in tune with the universe – call it God, nirvana, *enlightenment – I am utterly lost in it. I have no song of my own to sing; I am singing the song of the universe. You can fall in tune with me.*

That is how you become a disciple: when you find somebody with whom falling in love brings joy. Falling in love is falling in tune with somebody.

Your ordinary love affairs are ugly, because you are both in discord. Your love affair is superficial. Because you like the blonde hair of a girl, or the shape of the nose, or the color of the eyes, or the curves of the body...and you fall in love. Now, curves of the body, color of the eyes, the blonde hair, are not going to last long. Sooner or later you will be fed up with them – the same curve, the same eyes, the same nose – sooner or later you will stop seeing them. This is not love! Hence conflict arises immediately. All so-called love affairs are nothing but conflicts disguised – jealousies, possessiveness, domination, ego trips.

But when you fall in love with a Master it is a totally different phenomenon. You feel the rhythm of the Master; and, slowly slowly, your heart feels the call and you enter into an adventure. Slowly slowly, more and more people enter into that adventure...a commune is created.

First the Buddha: Buddham sharanam gachchhami– *I go to the feet of the Buddha. Then the disciples arise, those who have gone to the feet of the Buddha:* sangham sharanam gachchhami. *Then many many disciples gather, and they start feeling attuned not only with the Buddha but a certain attunement with each other also arises naturally: they are all attuned to one center, hence they start feeling an attunement with each other. A brotherhood, a sisterhood, arises; that is the* sangha *– the commune.*

And when you have fallen in love with a Buddha and have fallen in love with a commune, the ultimate surrender arises: dhammam sharanam gachchhami. *Then you know that it is neither the Buddha nor the commune: behind the Buddha is the universal law, the ultimate law –* dhamma. *Buddha only represents the ultimate law in a visible form; his commune represents it in an even grosser way.*

These are the three shelters. First you take shelter in the Buddha, then you take shelter in the commune, and then you take shelter in the ultimate law. This is what is happening here.

Sarjano, you are moving in the right direction; your feeling is perfectly right. Intuitively you are right, just intellectually you are using a wrong word. Drop that word!

Be Still and Know, Ch 9, Q 4

Beloved Master,

Having had the adventure of looking through ancient scriptures of yours, I have noticed that for at least ten years you have kept on repeating this legend: "There are four times more female disciples than male disciples. The same was the case with Buddha, the same with me too."

About Buddha I don't know – I was not there – but about you, after documented and meticulous research, I am happy to inform you that you have fifty-two thousand, three hundred and eighty-seven female disciples and fifty- three thousand, nine hundred and forty-six male disciples.

As the old Bob Dylan used to say: "The times they are a-changing" – fortunately! Would you please say something about this? A disciple does not live on legend only.

Sarjano, you will have to do a little more meticulous research. Just look into those fifty-three thousand, nine hundred and forty-six male disciples: how many of them are really male? And then you will understand that my legend is still exactly true; it can't be otherwise. Buddhas don't lie! If facts don't fit with the legend, the facts have to be changed!

To be male or to be female is more a question of psychology than of physiology. One may be a male physiologically and may not be a male psychologically, and vice versa. There are aggressive women – and unfortunately they are growing in the world – very aggressive women. The whole Women's Liberation movement is rooted in these aggressive women's minds. When a woman is aggressive she is not womanly.

Joan of Arc is not a woman and Jesus Christ is a woman. Joan of Arc psychologically is a man; basically her approach is that of aggression. Jesus Christ is not aggressive at all.

He says: If somebody hits you on one cheek, turn the other. Give him the other cheek, too. That is psychological non-aggressiveness. Jesus says: Resist not evil. Even evil has not to be resisted! Non-resistance is the essence of feminine grace.

Remember that if a man is totally receptive, physically he remains a man but his interiority becomes more a womb. And only such men whose interiority becomes feminine are capable of receiving God. To be receptive, totally receptive, you will need to learn how to be a woman. Each seeker of truth has to learn to be a woman.

Science is male, religion is female. Science is an effort to conquer nature; religion is a let-go, dissolving oneself into nature. The woman knows how to melt, how to become one. And each seeker of truth has to know how to dissolve into nature, how to become one with nature, how to go with the flow, without resisting, without fighting. And then you will see: the proportion will always be the same.

Here also you will see that change happening. Many women have reported to me, complained that "What is happening here to men? They are becoming more and more feminine!" That is true – that is bound to happen. As you become more and more meditative, your energies become non-aggressive. Your violence disappears; love arises. You are no longer interested in dominating; instead, you become more and more intrigued with the art of surrendering. That's what makes a feminine psychology.

To understand feminine psychology is to understand religious psychology. The effort has not yet been made, and whatsoever exists in the name of psychology is male psychology. That's why they go on studying rats, and through rats they go on concluding about man.

If you want to study the feminine psychology, then the best examples will be the mystics – the purest examples will be the mystics. Then you will have to learn about Basho, Rinzai, Buddha, Jesus, Lao Tzu. You will have to learn about these people, because only through their understanding will you be able to understand the peak, the highest crescendo of feminine expression.

Because the woman has been dominated for centuries, religion has disappeared from the earth. If religion comes back, the woman will again gain respect. And because the woman has been dominated, tortured and reduced to a nonentity, she has become ugly. Whenever your nature is not allowed to go according to its inner needs it turns sour, it becomes poisoned; it becomes crippled, paralyzed – it becomes perverted. The woman that you find in the world is not a true woman either, because she has been corrupted for centuries.

And when the woman is corrupted, man cannot remain natural either, because after all, the woman gives birth to the man. If she is not natural, her children will not be natural. If she is not natural, she is going to mother the child, male or female: those children naturally will be affected by the mother.

Woman certainly needs a great liberation, but what is happening in the name of liberation is stupid. It is imitation, it is not liberation.

Here there are many women who have been in the Liberation movement, and when for the first time they come here they are very aggressive. And I can understand their aggression: centuries and centuries of domination have made them violent. It is a simple revenge. They have become insane, and nobody is responsible except man. But, slowly slowly, they soften, they become graceful; their aggressiveness disappears. They become, for the first time, feminine.

Real liberation will make the woman authentically a woman, not an imitation of man. Right now that's what is happening: women are trying to be just like men. If men smoke cigarettes then the woman has to smoke cigarettes. If they wear pants then the woman has to wear pants. If they do a certain thing then the woman has to do that. She is just becoming a second-rate man.

This is not liberation, this is a far deeper slavery – far deeper because the first slavery was imposed by men; this second slavery is deeper because it is created by the women themselves. And when somebody else imposes a slavery on you, you can rebel against it, but if you impose a slavery on yourself in the name of liberation, there is no possibility of rebellion ever.

I would like the woman to become really a woman, because much depends on her. She is far more important than man because she carries in her womb both the woman and the man, and she mothers both, the boy and the girl; she nourishes both. If she is poisoned then her milk is poisoned, then her ways of bringing up children are poisoned.

If the woman is not free to be really a woman, man will never be free to be really a man either. The freedom of woman is a must for the freedom of man; it is more fundamental than man's freedom.

And if the woman is a slave – as she has been for centuries – she will make a slave of man too, in very subtle ways; her ways are subtle. She will not fight with you directly; her fight will be indirect, it will be feminine. She will cry and weep. She will not hit you, she will hit herself, and through hitting herself, through crying and weeping, through using these Gandhian methods, she will dominate you.

Even the strongest man becomes henpecked. A very thin, weak woman can dominate a very strong man simply by using Gandhian methods. Gandhi is not the inventor of those methods; they have been used for centuries by women. He simply rediscovered them and used them politically. The woman has been using them for centuries, but only in a family context.

The woman needs total freedom so that she can give freedom to man too.

This is one of the fundamentals to be remembered: if you make somebody a slave you will be reduced to slavery ultimately, finally; you can't remain free. If you want to remain free, give freedom to others; that's the only way to be free.

The Dhammapada: The Way of the Buddha Vol 7, Ch 10, Q 5

A few weeks later, Satya Bharti wrote a letter to the Master, a simple question that read:

Beloved Master,

Is it possible to love an Italian man without wanting to kill him?

Satya Bharti, it is impossible. But remember, the moment you stop thinking of killing him, love will also disappear. To fall in love with an Italian in the first place is very crazy, and then this desire to kill him is natural. Love is a kind of fight – Italian or not Italian. Love is a kind of fight; it is a struggle. And when you stop fighting, when you stop struggling, love disappears. I am not talking about the love of the buddhas; I am talking about the love Satya is asking about.

And do you know who this Italian is? Sarjano, the most Italian out of all Italians!

After the Ark had pushed off, Noah assembled all the animals in the central cabin and made a short speech. He pointed out that the trip was liable to be a long one, and that quarters were somewhat limited. "Therefore," he said, "I want to emphasize that we can't have any population increases at all until the flood subsides and we can get to land. I am appointing the giraffe, as the tallest of you, to stand guard and make sure my instructions are carried out."

Finally the water subsided, the Ark landed and the doors were opened. Out came the animals, two by two, as they had come in – no more of any species. Then the cats came out – followed by a litter of little kittens. As they passed the giraffe, one of the cats looked up and winked. "I will bet," he said, "you thought we were fighting.

The Dhammapadda: The Way of the Buddha Vol 9, Ch 2, Q 6

Believe it or not, there were people who used to waste the energy of our Master with such risible and petulant questions, to which Osho, in his infinite compassion even answered with ultimate grace.

***

CHAPTER 04

Premal's Story

Premal was a little girl, thirteen years old and the daughter of two German sannyasins who had divorced a few years back, but remained very good friends, and every time they would come together with their little daughter to the Commune they were always coming to the kitchen to ask if they could work with him because they liked to be part of his maddening loud crew.

Their daughter used to come every day to pick them up when they had finished their shift, and then they would go eat together, and every time he would find a way to tease her in one way or another.

Either he would tease her because her tits were growing abundantly, or he would pat her head from the back, without being seen and then turn to the other side, or any other little joke of this kind, because she was really cute and he had a great sympathy for this young (but very promising!) girl.

Then one day the entire family left and they came back only after one year. However, a few months before that, a girl arrived from Munich, the city of Premal, telling him that she had a message for him from this girl.

"Premal has asked me to tell you that you are an 'arschloch' (an asshole)!" She said that very seriously, and in that moment, for no apparent reason, the only feeling he had was that this little girl must have been desperately in love with him, and time would confirm this impression!

A few months later the family arrived in Pune with Premal, and they came back as usual to work with him in the kitchen.

Osho,

There's no question about it, Sarjano is my LSD: a Latin seducing Don Juan. The ashram seems to be the right environment and I know you are guiding me through the trip, but what's the right dose to take him in?

Satya Bharti,

Sarjano IS a ladies' man, so don't waste your time in thinking about the right dose to take him in because tomorrow he may not be available. Eat him totally if you can! There is just one thing you have to be aware of: if you don't like spaghetti, then eating him is going to be a torture – it will be all spaghetti!

What did the cannibal say after he ate the Italian? "The meat's a little on the greasy side."

So eat him while he is available and don't waste time in thinking about right proportions – how much and how much not.

Sarjano is like the wind: today he is here, tomorrow somewhere else. And remember perfectly well: eat him before he eats you, because these Italians are really dangerous people!

Just the other day there was a question: "What is more dangerous than an Italian?" Of course, two Italians!

Walking in Zen, Sitting in Zen, Ch 3, Q 9

Beloved Master,

"Hold your mouth," you said.

Difficult! Almost impossible for an Italian. My approach to the bodhisattvahood in these days is contained in this little story that has been haunting me for months:

There is this little man (anyone) that I meet in a street (anywhere) and he looks very miserable, like all the little men everywhere. And seeing me after a long time, he says, "Hey, you look great!"

"Hmm," I reply, "I would like to say the same thing about you, but you look so sad!"

"Well, you know my life…I feel so miserable. But what about you? How come you look so radiant?"

"Well," I say to him with a smile, "I have found a master." "Ah!" – he looks at me sadly. "And why didn't you tell me?"

So please, you and the other guy, Buddha, don't tell me to hold my mouth. I can't bear this little man knocking even when I am dancing, and asking, "Why didn't you tell me?"

Sarjano, now you have told him, what happened? The little man has not come to me yet. Just your telling him is not going to make any difference; he will simply think that you are crazy.

The miserable people think that if you are looking blissful you are mad. They can't believe that anybody can be blissful; that is beyond their grasp. Their whole life is such a misery, how can they believe there is any possibility of being blissful – unless you are mad? If you tell them that you have found a master they may not say anything to your face, but behind your back they will laugh at you; they will think something has gone wrong. They are not going to believe you. How can one become blissful by finding a master? They can't see any relatedness between their problems and finding a master. If their wives are nagging them to death, how is finding a master going to change it? Now the master will nag you more! If they are suffering from nightmares – and everybody is suffering from nightmares, day in, day out – how is finding a master going to help? They can't make any sense out of the statement.

I can understand your difficulty, Sarjano. It is very difficult to keep silent when you know the answer, but part of being a bodhisattva is to learn the art of being silent. Let them ask again and again. Let them feel that your bliss is not just something crazy, that your bliss is something real, authentic. Let them feel it of their own accord. Let them come and knock at your doors again and again.

Only in a right moment, when you see that they can understand, when you feel that their hearts are open, when you see a real thirst, a longing in them, when a search has arisen in them, only then tell them; otherwise you will simply be wasting your breath. And if you go on telling everybody and nobody listens, sooner or later you will feel very tired of the whole thing.

Buddha is right – that guy is almost always right. Of course, he was not talking to Italians! That was not his problem; that is MY problem! But I know how to manage it.

Truth insists that it should be spoken, although it cannot be spoken – that is the paradox – but it insists that it should be spoken.

When you know and you see that others can be helped, it is impossible to resist the temptation to tell them – but that is part of being a bodhisattva.

Somebody else has asked: "Beloved Master, you say fifty percent of enlightened people become arhatas and fifty percent become bodhisattvas. Still you say again and again that there are many mystics but very few masters – there seems to be a contradiction in it…?"

There is no contradiction in it. Yes, apparently there is, but only apparently. Not all bodhisattvas are masters. The bodhisattva is one who tries to help others; the master is one who succeeds in helping others. Just trying does not mean that you will succeed. Many try, very few succeed. Whosoever attains truth is bound to have the temptation to tell it. If he is not by nature an arhata *then he will try to say it to each and everybody, and he will be thought just crazy. Communication is a difficult art, and communicating the ultimate truth is the most difficult phenomenon in the world. A master is one who waits for the right time.*

Many people have asked me why I kept silent although I became enlightened in 1953. For almost twenty years I never said anything about it to anybody, unless somebody suspected it himself, unless somebody said to me on his own, "We feel that something has happened to you. We don't know what it is, but one thing is certain: that something has happened and you are no more the same as we are – and you are hiding it."

In those twenty years not more than ten people asked me, and even then I avoided them as much as I could unless I felt that their desire was genuine. And I told them only when they had promised to keep it a secret. And they all fulfilled it. Now they are all sannyasins, but they all fulfilled it, they kept it a secret. I said, "You wait. Wait for the right moment. Only then will I declare it."

I have learned much from the past buddhas. If Jesus had kept a little quieter about being the Son of God it would have been far more beneficial to humanity. I had made it a point that until I stopped traveling in the country I was not going to declare it; otherwise I would have been killed – you would not be here.

Once I had finished with traveling, mixing with the masses, moving from one town to another.... For twenty years continuously I was moving, and there was not a single bodyguard. Shiva and his samurai had not yet arrived! And I was in constant danger. Stones were being thrown at me, shoes were being thrown at me.

I would reach a town after traveling for twenty-four hours in a train and the crowd wouldn't allow me to get down at the station; they would force me to go back. A fight would ensue between those who wanted me to get down from the train and those who did not want me to get down, in their town at least.

If I had declared it I would have been killed very easily. There would have been no problem in it; it would have been so simple. But for twenty years I kept absolutely silent about it. I declared it only when I saw that now I had gathered enough people who could understand it. I had gathered enough people who were mine, who belonged to me. I declared it only when I knew that now I could create my own small world and I was no more concerned with the crowds and the masses and the stupid mob.

Sarjano, there IS a difficulty. I can understand your difficulty. But please keep your big mouth shut – Italian or not Italian! Otherwise you will simply be thought crazy. And if you cannot keep your mouth shut, then I will declare, "He is crazy!" Then nobody will listen to you. Then you can go on saying to these little men, "I have found the master," but they will say, "The master says you are crazy!"

The Dhammapada: The Way of the Buddha Vol. 11, Ch 2, Q 7

Beloved Master,
What do you mean by calling Sarjano a big mouth?

Nirmal, exactly that: a big mouth!

I will tell you a fictitious story:

I was going to the Himalayas; Radha was accompanying me. The train was stopped in the middle of the night in the jungle and the whole train was robbed. The robbers came to our compartment also.

I told them, "Don't disturb us. Take whatsoever you want."

So they carried away the two suitcases. I was worried about Radha, that she might get very much frightened, might become very much concerned about her things, but I was surprised. When they left she started laughing, "Ha, ha! Ha, ha!"

I said, "What is the matter, Radha? What's-a matta?"

She said, "I befooled them! I have saved your fifty-thousand-dollar diamond watch, I have saved my Rolex, I have saved my earrings, I have saved my gold and diamond ring , and all the valuables."

I said, "How did you manage?"

She said, "I kept all of them in my mouth."

I said, "That makes me feel very sad."

She said, "Why?"

I said, "If we had brought Sarjano with us, he would have saved the two suitcases! Next time we come to the Himalayas never forget: Sarjano has to accompany us!"

The Dhammapada: The Way of the Buddha, Vol 11, Ch 4, Q 3

Beloved Master,
I am leaving soon on a trip with Radha. Before hearing about your experience of traveling with her I felt confident and safe about our luggage, but now do you think I need Sarjano also to come along with us?

Anand Amito, no, categorically no! Sarjano may help to save your boxes and bags, but what about Radha? Radha will be in danger. It is better to risk the suitcases – you will not be able to save Radha from Sarjano. Avoid Sarjano, even if he wants to come. Certainly he will help you to save the suitcases, but Radha will be gone.

So it is up to you. If you are too much attached to your suitcases, then you can take Sarjano with you; otherwise, that incident is not going to happen every time. And it was a fictitious journey that I talked about – you are going on a real journey. On a real journey things like that don't happen.

The Dhammapada: The Way of the Buddha, Vol 11, Ch 8, Q 5

Osho,
I am leaving for Italy. Would you please tell me a joke to tell to the Italiano?

Sarjano,

Never ask for one joke. You can ask Laxmi: whenever I order one thing she always orders two – she knows me! So whenever you ask for one joke you have to suffer two.

First:

Two Italian nuns were sitting at the table talking about the beauty of the flowers, plants and vegetables in the garden of their nunnery.

One of the nuns says, "Did you see the big, red, juicy tomatoes in the vegetable garden?"

As she is talking the nun joins both hands into a circle, showing the size of the tomatoes.

"Yes," answers the other nun, "and did you see the size of the cucumbers this year?"

While she is describing them, her hands indicate the size of the long cucumbers.

An elderly nun sitting in the corner of the same room, nearly deaf but not blind yet, asks with an eager voice, "Which Father are you talking about?"

And second:

An explosion once happened in an Italian salami factory and one of the salamis is blown into heaven. An angel flying around heaven bumps into the salami and grabs it with her wing. "This is a funny thing," she says. "I wonder what it is?"

She flies to Joseph and asks him, "Have you ever seen such a thing before?" swinging the salami in front of his nose.

Joseph, staring at the salami, says, "No, I've never seen one before!"

The angel flies away and meets Mary. "Mary, do you know what this is?" she says, swinging the salami in front of her.

"Oh!" exclaims Mary, "You know, if there wasn't that funny net around it I would say it is the Holy Ghost!"

Walking in Zen, Sitting in Zen, Ch 9, Q 11

After he returned, he met an American girl called Champa, who was a photographer of great talent, so much so that she was not only doing all the pictures for the 'Osho Times' – the monthly publication of the commune which was translated into five languages and distributed all over the world – but she was also doing all the portraits of the Master that were hanging everywhere.

Privately he had started to shoot some photos himself, since this had been his profession for the past ten years, and he was enjoying making portraits of his closest friends, often also of a therapist who needed a photo to advertise for his group. He had developed a great passion for a technique that can be called 'super impression', that he mastered with perfection using this simple method: he would shoot first a roll of film with subjects like flowers, plants, rosebuds, palm leaves…then he would re-enroll the film and shoot again with the same film, making sure that he was starting exactly from the same point, and then on top of the first images he would photograph some faces, with the result of creating a double image, most often with an extraordinary poetic effect, and certainly very original…

He was hoping that at some point Champa would mention his name to Osho, so that maybe one day he would call him too to make his pictures, but this never happened for over three years!

What happened instead was that he became a good friend of Vivek, Osho's companion, the woman who was taking care of him almost like a real wife, and in fact she was sleeping in his room and taking care of all the necessities of the Master.

One day he made some portraits of her, asking her to sway her arms as if she were dancing and to show to the camera some kind of blissful feeling, if not ecstatic! Naturally he had previously prepared the film in the usual way; that day he had photographed a variety of skies: early morning, later with some clouds, then at sunset, so now his film was full of small swatches of sky, and with this base he shot several portraits of Vivek.

The pictures where in black-and-white, and the result was truly poetical, because it gave the total impression that she was floating and dancing in the sky! After he printed some of the best shots he presented them to Vivek, who liked them very much and was absolutely happy about the unexpected gift.

Some days later, during his morning discourse, Osho answered to a woman who had asked him about levitation, because she had heard that there were still some fakirs in India who were practicing it with great success…

The Master told her,

> *[…] You go to the photographic department here and learn a little bit about trick photography – and there is nothing more in it. Krishna Bharti, Champa, they will be of immense help to you. Or if you want really a crazy man then go to Sarjano; he will teach you trick photography. It is all trick photography, nothing else – no siddhi, no flying, nothing else.*
>
> *But stupid people become very much interested in such sheer nonsense. If transcendental meditators can fly, what is the need for Maharishi Mahesh Yogi to have an airplane? There is no need at all! We have met – I have met Maharishi Mahesh Yogi just by accident. I was having a camp in Pahalgam in Kashmir and he was also having a camp in Pahalgam. His disciples became very much interested and they wanted me to come to them and to talk to them, so I went there. We met. The man is simply ordinary, nothing special. And what he is teaching in the West is a very traditional thing in India; any stupid person knows about it.*
>
> *Just by repeating a mantra you can create a false sense of serenity. It is just autohypnosis and nothing else. You need not go to anybody, you need not learn any Sanskrit mantra, you can just repeat your own name. Your name is Mandira – you can simply go on repeating "Mandira, Mandira, Mandira, Mandira…" Go on repeating. If you repeat it for fifteen minutes you will feel a tranquilizing effect; it is a non-medicinal tranquilizer. It is good as far as tranquilizers go, but it has nothing to do with meditation. Transcendental Meditation is neither meditation nor transcendental. But now it is flopping, and because*

it is flopping, something new has to be invented. Now they have invented siddhis and this is nothing but trick photography.

Tao: The Golden Gate Vol. 2, Ch 8, Q 5, Excerpt

He understood immediately that Vivek must had shown him his pictures, and he was sincerely hoping that this, along with all this appreciation, would have convinced Osho to call him one day to photograph him. However, this was not going to happen for a long, long time, until he finally understood that this was the way in which the Master was working on his ego, and mainly on his photographer ego, which was more or less immeasurable!

Champa was sharing a room on top of a beautiful roof with Aneeta, the leader of Sufi Dance, and she used to invite him to sleep there all the time; so he ended up always being in the ashram, and now he was really feeling at home, until one day he got 'the first Zen stick' from his Master….

Osho,

I never feared anything and never chose to escape in my life. There is only one thing that scared me and gave me an unbearable feeling to escape – boredom. Why am I so afraid of boredom? What am I trying to escape really?

Sarjano,

It is one of the most important questions, because man is the only animal who feels boredom. Buffaloes don't feel it, although they look very much bored. Donkeys don't feel it, although they too look very much bored. Except man, nobody feels boredom; and even as far as man is concerned, all men don't feel boredom. It needs intelligence to feel boredom, so very few, the most intelligent people in the world, feel boredom. Buddha felt it, Mahavira felt it. The rarest people feel boredom because it needs tremendous intelligence to experience it. So in a way it is not a curse, it is a blessing.

It is out of boredom that the inquiry for the meaning of life arises. Those who have felt bored simply show that whatsoever ordinary meanings life has, are no longer fulfilling for them. There are people who are perfectly happy with money, accumulating more and more money, and they seem to be immensely interested in it, perfectly happy with their search for more. These are not really developed human beings: they are the most mediocre human being, the lowest kind. Their intelligence has not yet become a flowering; it is still in the seed, only a potential.

You can see it. The people who are greedy may be clever and cunning – they have to be – but you will never see any intelligence in them. You will not see the sharpness, you will not see any creativity in them. You will not see any fragrance in their lives; they will stink. The greedy person stinks.

And so is the case with the power-hungry, the politician, who is always running after more and more powerful positions, far higher status, who wants to become the president or the prime minister, whose whole life is devoted to the single purpose of dominating people.

These people are dull people. Their life is that of the ugliest form. They don't have any sense of beauty, poetry, music. They don't have any sense for aesthetics. Their whole interest is in bigger chairs, as if by sitting on bigger chairs they will become bigger, as if by becoming a president of a country they will have attained some spiritual integrity, as if by dominating millions of people they will become masters of their own being. They are empty people, hollow; their inner life is utterly dark. But you will never see them bored. They are always on the go, always interested in stupid efforts of gaining power, prestige, money. But they are contented; if they are succeeding you will see them very joyous.

It is the most intelligent people who feel boredom, who cannot see any meaning in money. Of course, there is certain utility in money, but no meaning. Who cannot see any meaning, any significance, in power politics, in ego trips, who can see the utter futility of it all – now for people of such intelligence the greatest problem in life will be boredom.

The first thing, Sarjano, I would like to tell you is: feel blessed. This is a symptom of a higher intelligence. Out of this boredom the person starts moving inwards; finding everything futile on the outside he turns in – because there is nowhere else to go. His intelligence is so clear, so transparent that he can see that he can have all the money of the world, still he will be the same person. He can have all the power of the world, still he would not have become a new being through it, he will not be reborn. He can have all the knowledge that is available, but still he will remain the same stupid person inside; his knowledge will be just parrotlike. He will repeat beautiful clichés without exactly knowing their meaning, because their meaning can be known only through experience of one's own. He can talk like Jesus, he can sermonize on the kingdom of God that is within, but he has no glimpse of it. He has learned only mere words.

The intelligent person becomes aware very soon that "All this is an exercise is sheer futility. Nothing on the outside can ever give me an inner fulfillment, an inner sense of significance." And unless that is experienced, boredom will remain and will become heavier every day.

Now there are two possibilities. One is the western possibility. If you look only through reason then you will never find any meaning in life; then boredom will become more and more acute, chronic. It will pervade your whole existence, it will permeate each moment of your life. It will not allow you to live at all. It will become such a burden that suicide will seem to be the only possible way out.

That's what Fyodor Dostoevsky says: that "If I can meet God, the only thing I am going to say to him is, 'Why you created me? For what? And without even asking me! Is this right?' And the only thing I want to see God for is to give him the ticket back. I don't want to be a part in this futile, meaningless existence."

Marcel says, "The only real metaphysical problem is the problem of suicide. Why man should go on living? For what?" If you look only through the head, only through the reason...that's what the western approach has been up to now. It is head-oriented, it is rational, it is Aristotelian, it is logical. It has given great technology and science, but it cannot provide meaning for your life. Life has become more and more boring; people are utterly bored. They go on living because they are cowards, because they cannot gather courage enough to destroy themselves, so somehow they go on pulling, dragging. West has come to a cul-de-sac; the road ends. Now there is no more possibility for western approach to grow.

But the East has a totally different alternative. When the mind fails, when the reason fails, it does not mean that life has failed. It simply means that whatsoever reason could do it has done; now you have to look for deeper realms of your being – and there are deeper realms. Deeper than your mind is your heart. Deeper than logic is love. Deeper than science is art. Deeper than mathematics is music.

The East drops the mind, not life, and starts moving into the heart, into the world of feelings. And then suddenly great meaning arises, the boredom starts disappearing. And remember, the heart is not your innermost core either; it is only a midway rest. Moving from the mind to the being, the heart is exactly in between. When you have reached to the heart then you will become aware that there is a still deeper layer. But the heart will fill your life with joy, with great thrill, with excitement. The boredom will be gone, and with the boredom gone you will become aware of a deeper realm, the deepest: the dimension of your being, your innermost core. That innermost core fulfills you totally, absolutely. Reaching it is the goal of sannyas. Reaching it is the purpose of meditation.

Sarjano, move from the head to the heart. But the heart has to be used only as a stepping-stone. The head gives you science, the heart gives you art; and the being, which is beyond the both, gives you religion. Religion is bliss, ecstasy, and we are searching for it.

The feeling of boredom simply shows that you are ready to go for the inner journey; if you don't go you will feel stuck. Now the head cannot fulfill your longing. The heart will give you something, a glimpse, a window will open. You will know something of the sky through the window, something of the stars, something of the moon and the sun and the wind and the rain and the flowers, but only through the window. You have to come out of the window too, under the sky, because when you look from the window everything is framed – and the frame is false. If you look from the window towards the starry sky, it feels as if the sky is framed, as if the sky has a limitation, a boundary.

When you reach to your innermost core, all the boundaries disappear...you have entered the unlimited, the unbounded, the infinite. That infinite is called God.

Boredom is a blessing. It is a goading for the search. It is a goading towards God, towards Tao. The western approach has failed; it has come to a point that now there is no more to go. The West is stuck, but the eastern approach has not failed and it is never going to fail. But the West can also move towards the East only when its approach fails. Now the time has come that the West can understand the East and the meeting can happen.

I am not against reason. Whatsoever reason can give it has to be used as a means, but one thing is certain: don't ask for things which it cannot give to you. It cannot give meaning, it cannot give significance, it cannot give dignity, it cannot give you your ultimate flowering. That is possible only through meditation, through discovering your innermost self, your ultimate, eternal being which is never born and never dies.

Use boredom as a jumping-stone towards the ultimate and then you will feel grateful, even grateful to the experience of boredom – which is painful, full of anguish. But the wise man can transform even misery into bliss, and the fool goes on destroying all opportunities for bliss and goes on creating misery out of the energy which could have created a paradise within you. The paradise is already there just you have to take a one hundred-eighty-degree turn.

Zen: The Special Transmission, Ch 8, Q 2

[…] This confusion prevails all over the world. Just a few days ago, Sarjano wrote to me saying, "Osho, it seems I have a strong individuality and I cannot surrender to the commune. I cannot possibly become part of the commune. I want to cook in my own way." *Now he thinks he has a strong individuality; in fact, he has no individuality at all – not yet.*

When you come to me you come only with a personality, a persona. And my work is an absolutely thankless job because I have to destroy your personality; that is the only way to help you to discover your individuality. The individuality is your original face: it is the way God wanted you to be, it is the way you were made by him. Your individuality has the signature of God on it, but your personality is a social phenomenon. Hence there are Christian personalities, Hindu personalities, Mohammedan personalities, and so on and so forth.

Individuality is simply individuality. It is neither Christian nor Hindu nor Mohammedan, it is neither Catholic nor communist, it is neither Eastern nor Western. In fact, individuality is neither male nor female. It is the personality that has all these divisions, categories, aspects.

Sarjano wrote, "I feel I have a strong individuality." *Individuality is never strong; it is very fragile, as fragile as a rose flower. Of course, even in its fragility the rose flower has a certain strength. It can dance in the wind, in the rain, unafraid. It is fearless, but it is not strong in the sense steel is strong.*

Buddha is not as strong as Joseph Stalin is. The very name "Stalin" comes from "steel." It was not his real name; it was given because he was a man of steel. Buddha is not a man of steel; he is made out of very fragile elements: the rainbow, the lotus, the fragrance of flowers. He is very feminine – feminine not in the sense of being female but in the sense of being very vulnerable, receptive, very available to existence.

The strong person is one who is stubborn.

Theologia Mystica, Ch 6 Q, Excerpt

Meanwhile, the little girl had grown up tremendously, and has been transformed into a beautiful woman, with a body that would have certainly attracted Botticelli or any other Renaissance painter. She had developed some harmonious roundness all over, and she had a renaissance face such as the Venetian Fornarina, and all in all she had become a little masterpiece, something that he would have liked to photograph one of these days.

They started seeing each other alone, once in a while, just for a cup of tea or a little chat, until the first kiss happened, then the second, and then one day she told him that she wanted to make love with him!

He wasn't too surprised, because it was very clear that even if he was 38 and she was only fourteen, a difference of 24 years between them, she was clearly in love with him, and he was about to follow her deeply too.

One evening she told him suddenly that tonight she was going to stay with him and sleep together…but first she wanted to go home and inform her mother, because otherwise she would have started worrying not seeing her coming back, so she took a rickshaw and left.

To his surprise, she was back in less than five minutes! He asked her what had happened, and she told him that she had stopped the rickshaw in front of her mother's house, asking the driver to wait. She then had entered and saw her mom in bed half asleep, so she went close to her and whispered into her ear: "Tonight I'm going to sleep with Sarjano…" – to which her mother turned on the other side and simply said, "I knew it!" – and then fell asleep again. Hence Premal came back running, and now she was ready to become a woman in every aspect.

Their first experience was incredibly sweet, but not very hot, because he had the feeling that her sexuality had not yet reached its peak, as she was still a teenager somehow, so much so that next morning, when he got up early as usual to go to his translator's job, she grabbed him like a little girl almost imploring him:" Don't leave me, please, stay here a little longer…I love you so much!"

He felt deeply touched by her ways, and yet he had already decided not to give much rope, nor hope, to this little girl, and most likely he was going to see her only once in a while, if she was lucky.

His life was continuing as usual, but there was now a little change, represented by the circumstance that suddenly there were five books of Osho that needed to be translated before the end of the year. He was therefore asked (on the Master's suggestion) to quit his job in the kitchen, and to put all his energy into translating, at least for the next few months.

He was so much taken by his job, that most often during the night, after the evening darshan, he would go back on the roof where the translators' department was, to work for a few more hours, until some kind soul would come to drag him off to sleep, after the usual sexual performance, of course!

At that point Osho had created such a reputation of a Don Juan, of a great Italian lover about him, that there were always plenty of women who wanted to verify in person if all these stories were true, hence he was having practically different company every night!

Osho,

You have been speaking on several occasions against socialism, and yet I feel that in this commune the first experiment of an alive socialism is happening. Is this another of your contradictions?

Swatantra Sarjano,

The real socialism can only be the fragrance of a commune deep in meditation. It has nothing to do with the social structure or the economy. Real socialism is not a revolution in the society, it is not social: it is the revolution in the individual consciousness.

If many people who are going through an inner revolution live together, then there is bound to be a new quality. You can call it socialism; the better word will be "communism", out of "commune". Only a commune can have communism, but a commune exists only once in a while. When Buddha was alive a commune grew around him; he called it sangha, *another name for commune. The meaning of* sangha *is: where the initiates have dropped their egos and are no more functioning like islands but have become one with each other, where a communion is happening. Communication is between the heads; communion is between the hearts.*

Whenever so many hearts open, become flowers, a great fragrance is released. That fragrance surrounds a Buddha, you can call it a Buddhafield. The energy is totally different: there is no politics involved in it.

Politics belongs to the world of the ego. The game of politics is an ego number : how to be more powerful than the other. It is ambition in its ugliest form. It is sheer cunningness, exploitation. It is an effort to enslave others. It is not possible at all to the meditators, because for meditation the basic requirement is to drop the ego. You cannot play the games of the ego any more. There is no question of being higher, more powerful than the others. In fact, there is no question of "the other".

The moment "I" disappears, instantly the "thou" also disappears. I and thou exist together; they are like two sides of the same coin. Drop your "I" and you will be surprised that for you there is nobody who is other than you; the reality appears as one organic whole. But it is possible only with a center.

When Buddha died his commune existed at least for five hundred years, but slowly died; slowly it withered away. It remained alive till...few people continued to become enlightened and went on replacing the Buddha. When there was nobody enlightened any more, when there was not the center, the whole field disappeared. When there is no sun, how can there be rays? It is an individual phenomenon.

If Buddha is there, the commune is bound to happen; it cannot be prevented. It is inevitable. The real seekers will start moving towards the Buddha from the farthest corners of the world. It is just like when a fragrant flower opens, bees start queuing from faraway places. Suddenly the fragrance becomes a magnetic pull – but only for the bees, not for everybody. The dogs will pass by the flower without ever looking at the flower; it does not exist for them, they are not sensitive towards it.

The Buddha exists only for those who have the sensitivity, the perception, the availability, the openness, the search. Many came across Buddha and missed him. Millions of people encountered him, but could not recognize him. To them he was just another learned man, just another saint. And India has always been full of saints. There was nothing special for them in him. They listened to him, they gathered a little bit of knowledge from him and went on their way.

But those who had the sensibility, who had the heart which can dance with this fragile energy of a Buddha, this delicate perfume, were lost, completely lost and dissolved, merged. Out of these merged individuals the commune arises, the Buddhafield, the sangha.

It happened with Jesus, of course on a smaller scale, because Jews have never been much interested in the interiority of man. They are extrovert people; their whole religion has remained extrovert. Jesus was recognized only by very few people; those few people can be counted on fingers.

It happened again and again around these precious diamonds – Lao Tzu, Chuang Tzu, Lieh Tzu, Lin Chi, Baso, Bahauddin, Jalaluddin, Kabir, Nanak – again and again. But the problem is: when the Master dies, the commune starts withering away. Maybe for a time being a sequence of Masters continues…

For example, after Nanak nine other Masters followed. After Adinatha, the first Jain Master, twenty-four teerthankaras *followed – from Adinatha to Mahavira, a long span of time, almost of three thousand years. But it is very rare. It cannot be enforced by the government, by any outside agency; then it will be plastic.*

Sarjano, you are right – it is one of my contradictions. I am against socialism which is imposed as an economic, political ideology on people, because then it destroys something which is very precious: it destroys the individual. Rather than destroying the ego it destroys the individual; it enhances the ego. The ego is represented by personality.

These two words have to be understood very clearly: the personality is that which is given to you by the society, and the individuality is that which you have brought with you from the beyond; it is a God's gift. The individuality has no ego in it, it is egolessness. The personality is nothing but ego.

The society imposes a certain structure, a certain pattern around every individual. The society is very much afraid of authentic individuals. It creates a false personality, because the false personality can easily be manipulated, enslaved, dominated. The personality is very obedient, the personality is very dependent on the society, because the society has created it.

If you go against your personality that the society has created, you will lose all respect; your ego will start collapsing. And that creates great fear in you, so you go on fulfilling the demands of the parents, of the teachers, of the priests, of the politicians, of all kinds of people who surround you and are trying to exploit you in every possible way. They depend on personality, and they go on enforcing the personality against the individuality. The individuality has to be repressed, completely forgotten, so that you start living in the false and the phony.

Socialism destroys individuality more than any other kind of political ideology, because socialism means society is the goal, not the individual. The individual has to be sacrificed for the society, not vice versa; the society cannot be sacrificed for the individual. And in fact "society" is a beautiful word; behind that beautiful word is hiding the ugly state. It is really the state that dominates in socialism, and the state does not want any kind of individuality in people. It effaces all individuality, it creates robots. It wants everybody to be just an efficient machine, nothing more.

This kind of socialism I am certainly against, but there is certainly a different kind of socialism which I am absolutely for. But the process is totally different, just diametrically opposite: the individuality has to be saved and the personality has to be dissolved.

That is the meaning of surrendering to a Master : you surrender the ego, not the individuality; individuality cannot be surrendered. When you surrender on your own, when you are not forced to surrender, when it is not a question of submission…out of your love and joy, out of your understanding you surrender – it is your choice and your decision. When you surrender, of course you surrender the false; the true cannot be surrendered. You are the truth! You simply put aside all that has been imposed on you, conditioned upon you. In the presence of a Master only the false disappears, and the true comes in its absolute flowering.

In a commune of a Buddha everyone has individuality, nobody has any personality. Nobody is egoistic, but everybody has his uniqueness; he contributes to the commune in his own unique way. And everybody is respected for whatsoever he is doing; there is immense respect for the individual.

You can see it happening here. The well-trained psychoanalyst who could have earned thousands of dollars per month in the West, maybe having a Ph.D. or a D.Litt. and other educational qualifications, is respected in the same way as the toilet cleaner; there is no difference. The toilet cleaner has the same respect, the same individuality; he is contributing in his own way.

And many times it is happening here that a Ph.D. decides to drop all that he has learned and he wants to become a cleaner. There are few Ph.D.s who are toilet cleaners. This may be the only place in the world where Ph.D.s have found the right work! There are M.D.s who are cleaning the toilets. They have been told, "You are M.D.s, why don't you work in the Medical Center?" They say, "Cleaning is so beautiful, so relaxed! We don't want to bother with the Medical Center anymore."

There are poets, painters – famous, well-known – authors who have published much, and they may be making shoes or just working in the carpentry or doing some manual work in the garden, because one thing is absolutely clear : that your job makes no difference, your individuality is intact everywhere. Your job does not give you any higher position, it does not create any hierarchy. Everybody else is doing in his own way, wholeheartedly.

The commune can happen only in the presence of a Master : otherwise, your awareness is such you will start fighting, quarreling, and your ego games will come in. That happens each time a Master dies. If there is a chain of Masters then it is okay, otherwise very difficult.

For example, Jesus could not create a chain; he was not given time enough. He worked only three years, from the age thirty to thirty-three. There was not enough time for him – he was crucified at thirty-three – he had no time to work.

Buddha worked for forty-two years; he created a great line. He triggered many people, from Mahakashyap to Manjushri, Sariputra, Modgalyayan, Purnakashyapa...and many others became enlightened while he was alive and they carried the torch.

If a chain is created then the commune goes on living, but it is a very fragile phenomenon, very unpredictable; it may happen, it may not happen. Even if it happens, then too it cannot be a permanent phenomenon. One cannot conceive that it will go on and on forever; it can stop anywhere. The world is such a desert, and the stream that Buddhas create is such a small stream; it can be lost in the desert anywhere.

But the only true commune exists while the Master is alive. I am all for that kind of commune.

But the communism that exists in Soviet Russia or China is not my cup of tea! It is really exactly the opposite of what I am trying to do here. Communism should arise spontaneously, and differences are many. For example, Karl Marx, Friederich Engels, V.I. Lenin – the communist unholy trinity – these people were talking of the dictatorship of the proletariat; that means dictatorship of the lowest.

In the commune of a Buddha, in the first place there is no dictatorship, although for the outsiders it may seem that there is a dictatorship. For the outsider, if he comes here, he will think this is my dictatorship, although I never order anybody. I never have even visited the office once in these six years! I don't know who is living where, how many people are living in the commune. I have not visited the other houses of the commune. I simply know the way to my room! I cannot find even in my own house where I live, Lao Tzu House, the rooms of other sannyasins who are living with me. Vivek has been telling me that, "One day give us a surprise – come to the kitchen!" I have never been there; I really don't know where it is. So in fact I will not be able to find it unless I am guided by somebody. I have some idea where it should be, but it is very vague.

But anybody from the outside will think that I am the dictator; that is absolutely wrong. People are here working out of their love, nobody is ordered. And if they ask me and I say something, it is always a suggestion, never an order. They are free to accept it or not accept it. They always accept it – the credit goes to them; it has nothing to do with me. If they don't accept it they are perfectly free to do that way.

In a real commune, the commune of my vision, the highest becomes the center. In the communism of Karl Marx, the lowest dominates; it is the dictatorship of the proletariat. Naturally, these are two different things, polar opposites.

When the highest...and by "highest" I simply mean one who is no more, one who has become one with the whole, one who has no more any separate existence. One who is no more pushing the river, one who is flowing with the river, one who is in a deep let-go, one who is just a vehicle, a hollow bamboo on the lips of God. And if God sings, of course the hollow bamboo becomes a flute, but it all depends on God. The song does not belong to the flute, it belongs to the singer.

Through the Buddha, through the enlightened person, God starts flowing. It is the highest, the suprememost that creates a real commune. The communism that exists in Russia and China is dominated by the lowest. Joseph Stalin and Mao Tse-tung belong to the lowest type, the most violent, murderous people that have ever existed on the earth.

The name of Joseph Stalin means a man of steel; that was not his real name. Stalin means a man of steel; it is not his real name, it is because of his hardness.

A Buddha is represented by a lotus flower, not by steel. The lotus flower has been in the East the symbol of all the Buddhas – very fragile, very delicate, with a subtle perfume, not aggressive at all.

If you surrender to a Buddha it is your decision, it is your freedom; you are not made to surrender. And when many people surrender to a Buddha they are really surrendering to their own future, to their own ultimate potential. Buddha simply represents what can happen to them. He is just a reflection of their ultimate flowering.

When you surrender to a Buddha you are really surrendering your lower reality to your own higher reality; the Buddha is just an excuse. Then a real commune comes into existence. It is out of love, out of meditation and prayer. It is not based on violence; it is not rooted in the lower qualities, animal qualities of man.

Sarjano, in that sense you are right, that a real commune is happening here, but it is the not the first experiment, remember it. The experiment has happened many times before. But it always looks like that. When you fall in love you think, "Such kind of love has never happened before; it is something unique." And in a way it is – for you it is a new experience. You have never been in love with a Buddha, so to you it is a new experiment. Otherwise, for thousands of years humanity has existed, and many times small oases in the desert have arisen. But the desert is vast and hard...

And remember one fundamental law: whenever the lower comes in conflict with the higher, the higher is destroyed, not the lower. If you clash a rock with a lotus flower, don't hope that the rock will be destroyed by the lotus flower; the lotus flower will be destroyed. The higher is more fragile.

That's why I say the woman is a higher sex than man: she is more fragile, she is more flowerlike. Man is harder, a little bit of rock is still in him. Man is more closer to the animal than the woman. Man is more aggressive than the woman; the woman is receptive. And because of this higher quality of the woman she has been destroyed by man. The rock is always going to win against the flower.

Such communes have existed again and again. They cannot be totally destroyed because God has a tremendous investment in these communes. They CANNOT be destroyed, they will go on coming again and again, but the vast world is desertlike. The greater humanity has not yet been transformed, although the possibility of such communes is becoming more and more.

Man has evolved, has matured, and particularly today. The time has come when thousands of such communes can erupt, explode all over the world. And that's what I am intending to do by creating so many sannyasins and then sending them back to their countries so that thousands of communes start functioning.

I would like to create a chain of communes all around the world, so this commune does not remain only one oasis in the vast desert but becomes interlinked with many communes. That type of interlinking has never been done before; that will be new. Communes have always existed, but many communes functioning all around the world was not possible before; it is possible only today. Science has made it possible. The world is now so small, it is almost like a village, a global village. Man has come so close that now this possibility exists.

I have got two hundred thousand sannyasins working all around the world, two hundred communes slowly growing. Soon there will be thousands of communes all around the world, and this will be the first chain of communes surrounding the whole globe! And the possibility of their success is becoming more and more than it was ever before, for the simple reason that science has come to such a growth that unless religion also reaches to the same point, humanity is doomed. Everything has become lopsided. It was never so before, in fact just the opposite was the case.

Buddha's commune was far more advanced than the technology and the science of Buddha's day. Mahavira's commune was far more advanced, far ahead than the society, than the inner growth of man; there was a big gap. Now the gap is there, but it is a totally different gap. The society, science, technology, have gone far ahead than man's inner growth. Now the society and the science and the technology have prepared the ground; we can use this opportunity. We can help man come to the same growth, and that will be a balancing thing. All those communes in the past created an imbalance; they were out of tune. They were far ahead of their time, hence they were doomed to fail.

But this time we can hope we may succeed, for the simple reason that we are not going against or too ahead of time. Time is ready and ripe and we are in tune with it. Only we are in tune with it; the whole society is falling behind – the modern technology, the modern science. All your so-called churches, religions are far behind modern science.

What I am doing here is a very balancing phenomenon. Now religion can exist on a far higher level than it has ever existed, because science has provided the right background. And moreover, science has created a tremendous fear in the world that science can destroy the whole humanity. And now the only hope is that religion can save it. And when it is a question of survival, millions of people are bound to become interested in meditation because only meditation can save them; nothing else can save. If man remains the same and science goes on developing, then the very developing science will become a mountainous burden on man.

It is a well-known fact that somewhere in the past, one hundred thousand years back, there were huge animals, far bigger than elephants, ten times bigger than elephants. What happened to those huge animals? They suddenly disappeared from the earth; only their skeletons are discovered. What calamity happened? No calamity from the outside, but they became too huge. The burden of their bodies became so much that they could not carry it; they became incapable from inside. Their inner being remained very small and their outer body became too big; it lost balance.

The same is happening today with man: his inner soul is too small and his outer technology, his science, has become too huge. It can bring a Third World War, a total war, because it is a question of life and death; it has never been such a question before. There is a hope that religion can explode, and millions of authentic seekers are searching for it.

We can create a chain around the world of such communes, and the whole world can be transformed into a Buddhafield. Then only there is a possibility of a communism arising out of love and arising from the highest sources, from the Everests – not a dictatorship of the proletariat, but a trust, a surrender to a Buddha. And out of that trust and surrender a totally new kind of communism can be given birth.

In that sense I am for communism – but communists will be very much against me because if my type of communism succeeds then their type of communism is bound to fail.

I am That, Ch 15, Q 1

During all this, he was seeing Premal more or less every ten days, but he realized that she was quite sad about seeing him so little.

***

CHAPTER 05

Saswad

A few months passed, and the ashram started to be suddenly full of people like never before, to the point that the residents had become so many that there was literally no more space for all of them, and it was becoming a problem where to accommodate all these people!

You need to know that in those times the Commune had acquired a huge castle amid a very large property, located somewhere in the hills about twenty kilometers away from Pune, in a village called Saswad. This property was supposed to become one day – as a future project – the next ashram, much, much larger than the present one. So one day, to somehow deal with the scarcity of space, it was decided to transfer to this castle in Saswad all those departments that weren't functional to the survival of the commune.

Naturally they wouldn't send there the cooks, electricians, plumbers, carpenters, all those people that were necessary for the functioning of the Commune. He was now working full-time in the translation department, and this was one of the departments that had been decided would be moved into the hills. Also his friend the 'engineer' and the entire mala shop (which was the workshop where the malas for new sannyasins were made), and all those people that would make no difference if they stayed in Pune or not were shifted.

All of them were granted the opportunity to come to the ashram every other day to attend the morning discourse, traveling with a private bus that would wait outside until the discourse was over, to take them back to their castle a few hours later.

In that moment he thought that he would never again spend a night in Pune, and most of all he wouldn't be able to see Premal, and he found out that this circumstance pained him more than he could had ever imagined, because he realized in that moment how affectionate he had become about this young woman.

The next time they saw each other he told her the news, with the result that Premal almost started crying, and then asked if she could come to Saswad too.

He told her that this was certainly possible, and all that she had to do was go with her mom to see Sheela, Osho's secretary, and ask her what she thought about it.

Premal decided to go there by herself, with none of her parents, and once in front of Sheela she told her the whole truth – that she was in love with Sarjano and that she didn't like the idea of seeing him leave for Saswad all alone, because she would like to go with him, if possible…

Sheela asked her simply what job she was presently doing in the Commune and Premal told her that she was cleaning the rooms of the residents, including Sarjano's room!

"Then it is perfect!" – answered Sheela – "They are certainly going to need someone to clean the rooms up there at the castle, hence you can go with Sarjano whenever you wish, and take care of him, would you!"

He thought that it was very beautiful, and even a little incredible that they had tackled the entire issue between themselves, like two women; that Premal, even though so young, was considered a grown-up to that effect, and that Sheela hadn't bothered to know if her parents were in agreement, that she had thought Premal was solely responsible to choose her life the way she wanted, and he was very grateful to Sheela for that.

Life in Saswad

For the two of them, life in Saswad was idyllic, even though amongst most people was a feeling of being 'confined' or even 'exiled'!

To tell you the truth, nobody seemed happy to be there in the hills and so far away from the Master, besides of course our two lovers who were totally immersed in this special honeymoon.

They used to go to the little lake nearby to swim naked, they would eat the wild fruit they found on the bushes; once in a while he would prepare some delicacy in the kitchen, which seemed to him more like a hobby, since he was used to cook for thousands of people, and here there were just a little more than one hundred stomachs to fill!

One day there was even a beautiful party, for which all the musicians of the ashram had come to play and to dance the whole night; the beer was running in rivers and everybody was having great fun. The entertainer for that evening was one Pramod, who – besides being in charge of the Translation Department – was also his crazy accomplice, sending to Osho most of the jokes that he recited during his discourses.

A few days before they had both decided to play him a trick, because the Master had become even more irreverent and out front in telling jokes lately, to the point that he was often offering up the most lurid little stories that could be found, and of course with his usual smile! So they teamed up to put together a joke so extremely lurid and revolting, just to see if the Master would dare to tell that too!

The story they managed to pen together, was about a poor guy who – in order to be able to survive – had a very weird job, which consisted in squeezing and even sucking out people's pimples. One day he was called by a fat black woman, weighing in at more than one hundred and eighty kilogram, who wanted some pimples removed from her ass…

The joke continued with some disgusting details I wish to spare you, and it was sent to Osho with the following note: "Let's see if you dare to tell this joke too!"

Naturally the Master never told this joke, because, let's say it clearly, more than provocative, it was explicitly disgusting. However, that night at the party, Pramod announced to the audience that he would now narrate a joke that even Osho didn't have the guts to tell!

He had barely finished speaking when Arup, one of Osho's secretaries, stood up and shouted on top of her voice: "Pramod, you don't dare!"– and thus the joke remained suspended in air and was never told.

Beloved Osho,

God knows I would never wish to contradict my master, but the other day you went too far! You said that all the enlightened ones have been Italians in one life or other. No doubt about you, or Jesus or Buddha, Lao Tzu or even Nanak, and Ramana…but Krishnamurti?

My god! How can you honestly assert that someone so sane and sober as Krisnamurti has ever been an Italian? We hope you apologize.

Swatantra Sarjano, in fact, I myself, Jesus, Buddha, Lao Tzu, Nanak and Ramana may not have been Italians at all; hence still the attraction. I love the Italians – that is proof enough I have never been an Italian before! But Krishnamurti? – it is absolutely certain that he has been an Italian, and not only in one life but many lives; otherwise, how can he be so sane and sober? The Italians have done so much damage to him, he has not been able to recover yet – he is still under the impact. He is so much afraid of laughing in case somebody may discover that he has been an Italian! His seriousness is just the other extreme.

I can understand, Sarjano, your question, because Krishnamurti is deadly serious about things; that is one of his flaws. A really totally enlightened person cannot be so serious.

Seriousness is a disease of the mind. When the mind is no longer there, seriousness has no ground to stand upon. But Indians have respected seriousness very much; it is a long tradition. And Krishnamurti has been brought up by very serious people, the Theosophists.

That whole bunch of Theosophists was very determined to show the world that they are the only spiritual people. Their whole investment was in proving to the world that they had come to redeem the world of all its problems, illnesses, diseases. They were bound to be serious. When you are a savior you cannot joke around; you have to destroy your sense of humor absolutely. You have to be continuously concerned about the misery and the suffering that people are passing through. And when people are passing through so much suffering, how can you laugh? how can you enjoy? how can you even smile? That will be cruel.

The Theosophists had this idea – a very ancient idea that has clouded many people's beings – that they wanted to redeem the whole world. In fact, it is nobody's business to redeem the whole world – and who has the right to redeem anybody else? If the other person is enjoying his dream, you have no right to wake him up. At least his permission is needed, at least you have to ask him. Unless he wishes, you have to keep off. It is interference – maybe for his own good, but who are you to decide? If somebody chooses hell, then it is his freedom to choose it. You can feel compassion for him, you would have liked him not to choose hell, but what can you do? Who are you?

But these saviors of humanity are bound to be serious people; they are bent upon it. Whether you want it or not, they will force you into paradise! They will not leave you alone. And the Theosophists were preparing for a great event: to declare a world teacher. They had chosen Krishnamurti to be the messiah. Of course they conditioned him in every possible way: they regimented him, disciplined him for so long that the traces of it have not left him yet; the wounds are still there. For twenty-five years continuously he was in this wrong company.

Sarjano, look into the training of J. Krishnamurti, and it will help you to understand why he is so serious. He was never allowed to mix with ordinary children – to play with them, to laugh, to giggle, to climb the trees, to swim the rivers, to fight, to be beaten. He was never allowed to do anything that every child has a right to do. His childhood was completely crushed. He was only nine years of age when he was taken away from his parents. His mother had died, and his father was a poor clerk, so poor, and he was not economically in a situation to educate his children. He had two children, two boys, Nityananda and Krishnamurti.

Seeing that the Theosophists were interested in the children he was thrilled – a great opportunity was opening up. They would not only teach him in ordinary schools, they were promising that they would educate him at Oxford, and in some very special schools meant only for royalty. They would take him around the world, they would arrange for private tutors, the best possible. What more could the poor father have desired and dreamt of ? He willingly gave the children to the Theosophists.

And then a long struggle began between Krishnamurti's father and the Theosophists, because when the father became aware of what they were doing to his children, he was aghast. He could not believe it, that they were being forced like slaves.... They had to get up at three o'clock in the morning and read the scriptures – Tibetan, Chinese, Japanese, Sanskrit. And they were almost asleep, repeating them in their sleep. Even in sleep they were not allowed to have a normal sleep; they would be sleeping, and the man who was in charge, Leadbeater, would go on repeating sutras and scriptures softly in their ears.

That was the first experiment in teaching children through hypnosis. Now it is a recognized scientific method, and particularly in Russia where hypno-teaching is becoming very common. Children can be taught with no need even for somebody to sit by their bed. Earphones can be put on, and the tape recorder can go on repeating silently, very whisperlike, so their sleep is not disturbed but still the message can go on penetrating to their unconscious. Even in their sleep they were not allowed the freedom to dream. Even their dreams were controlled.

You will be surprised to know that dreams can be controlled – your dreams can be managed by others. For example, when you are falling asleep, a certain program can be given to you for the whole night so that these will be your dreams. And those dreams can be manipulated from the outside also. For example, when you are falling asleep, there comes a moment, an interval, when you are not awake and you are not yet asleep either – just in between, that boundary line. That boundary line is the most sensitive part of your existence because you are changing the gears from one gear to another gear. Before you change gears you have to pass through the neutral gear, and when you are in a neutral gear anything can be put into your head. That's the whole secret of hypnosis: the neutral gear. That is the time when you are absolutely vulnerable; you cannot defend, you cannot argue.

So Leadbeater, Annie Besant and others would be sitting around when Krishnamurti was falling asleep, waiting for the moment, for indications. And there are very simple methods to know whether the child is in the interval or not. For example, the child can be told, "Go on looking at the roof continuously without blinking your eyes." A moment comes when the eyes become glassy; they are seeing and yet not seeing. That is the time when the neutral gear has come into existence. Wakefulness has gone, sleep has yet to come. It is the evening time; the day is no more, the night is entering. It is the most vulnerable, the most sensitive time. Say anything and it will go directly to the heart of the child. It will condition the child the deepest.

So they were conditioning the child, even managing his dreams, telling him, "You will be dreaming of a great desert. For miles and miles there is nobody – sand and sand and sand, and you go on and on...." And you can help the dream from the outside too. You have put the seed inside; then just a little heat near the feet and the child will start dreaming of the desert, because the heat near the feet will give him the feeling of walking on hot sand. A little heat near the head and he will feel he is under the hot sun, and you have triggered.... You have done both the things: you have put the idea in the unconscious, and you have triggered the process from the body. The child is bound to dream about the desert, and of course he will follow the program that you have given.

This way Krishnamurti was conditioned while awake, while asleep. He was moved from one country to another country. He was never allowed to become friendly with anybody; he had no friends. How can he know what laughter is? He was never allowed to fall in love with a woman, with a girl – how can he know what laughter is?

And the people he was with were really a strange group of people. This Leadbeater was a homosexual; he was not interested in women and hence he was very much against women. And he was found in very suspicious postures with Krishnamurti – a small child.

When the father became aware of what was going on, he went to the courts. The case went on for years in the high court of Madras. The father proved in every way that Leadbeater was a homosexual. He produced witnesses who had seen him doing wrong things with his children. But then Leadbeater escaped from India, and before the court could decide that the children should be returned to the father, Annie Besant escaped with the children out of India, and the father could never get the children back.

Nityananda, the elder brother, died because of all the work that was being imposed upon them. When he was suffering from delirium, they thought that he was being influenced by great spiritual masters – Kuthumi, et cetera – that he was being transformed by the spiritual hierarchy. And that is all bullshit! There is no spiritual hierarchy, nothing.

Even Gunakar has started writing about spiritual hierarchy. He has issued letters and messages to all the U.N. members, and they must think that I am behind it, because my name, my picture is on his letterhead. And Gunakar goes on suggesting to them that there is a spiritual hierarchy working in the world. First he used to call me "Master," now he calls me "Elder Brother." Sooner or later I am waiting for him to write, "Dear Younger Brother." He is rising higher in the hierarchy! Now I am just an elder brother. It will not be a surprise if one day he writes, "My dear son."

Leadbeater was the most cunning of the people who were trying to manipulate these small children in the name of some hierarchy. He was writing books in the name of Krishnamurti. He has written a book, 'The Past Lives of Alkayoni'. Alkayoni is the fictitious name for the many many lives of Krishnamurti. Because in each life there was a different name, Alkayoni is the fictitious name for all these lives, thousands of lives. Leadbeater wrote these books and they were all signed by Krishnamurti. And now Krishnamurti says, "I don't remember at all when I wrote these books, when I even signed. I know nothing about them." They were all written by Leadbeater.

In fact, a child of ten or twelve years cannot have written those books; he cannot have any such stupid ideas – no child can be so stupid. And all this spiritual jargon.... And then, finally, Leadbeater and his colleagues started writing a very famous book which became a world-famous spiritual treatise: 'At the Feet of the Master'. That too was published in the name of Krishnamurti, and Krishnamurti simply says he knows nothing about it.

These twenty-five years of all kinds of unnecessary torture, no ordinary life available.... He was not allowed to walk in the gardens where other people were. He was not allowed to meet and mix with people, because he was "the world teacher" – how could he mix with ordinary human beings? Naturally he has lost all sense of humor. It is sad – and all because of that idea of the world teacher. He renounced the idea finally, and that is the only good thing that he has ever done in his life. He renounced the idea that "I am a world teacher," but that renunciation was only superficial; it never came through his innermost core. Deep down he continues to be the world teacher still. That's why he becomes very angry if you don't listen to him; he even starts hitting his own head. Even talking to people, if they don't understand him and the way he talks – it is so monotonous, it is so boring, that unless somebody is doing some research on boredom, nobody can be interested, people cannot understand – then he starts beating his head, shouting, becomes enraged. But the whole idea deep down is to redeem the world.

If you don't understand me it doesn't matter, it is your freedom. It is my freedom to talk; it is your freedom to understand or not to understand or to misunderstand. How can I decide for you? I cannot be enraged. Even if you all fall asleep I cannot be enraged. I will have a good laugh! Even the idea of giving so many people a good morning sleep is such a consolation that one is doing some service to people!

You say, Sarjano: "...but Krishnamurti? My God! How can you honestly assert that someone so sane and sober as Krishnamurti has ever been an Italian?"

For me to assert anything honestly or dishonestly makes no difference. Whatsoever is right at the moment, honest or dishonest, right or wrong, true or untrue.... I believe in Gautam Buddha's definition of truth: that which works. If honesty works, perfectly okay. I am a nonserious person; these are also serious things. Honest? – why should I be honest? Things should be taken playfully. What is wrong in being dishonest once in a while, just for a change?

And you say, "...so sane and sober...." *If a man is one hundred percent sane, then he is insane. Something of insanity is a basic ingredient of real sanity.*

Zorba the Greek says to his boss, "Boss, everything is right in you, only one thing is missing – a little touch of madness."

A man without a little madness is flat – flat like a flat tire! A little bit of madness brings some spice to your life – some color, some intensity, some passion, some dance, some celebration.

Krishnamurti, even if he enters paradise, will remain sane and serious. I don't think he will be welcome there. He will start talking about the same things he has been talking about on the earth for sixty years, and he will beat his head because even the angels are not going to listen to him! Angels don't listen to spiritual discourses. Their whole work is playing their harps, sitting on the clouds and shouting "Alleluia!" They will fit with me perfectly, but can you imagine angels playing "Alleluia!" on their harps and dancing around Krishnamurti? He will commit suicide: All this "Alleluia!" and the whole world has to be redeemed! Everybody is suffering, and these fools.... But I can enjoy! I may even start learning how to play on the harp. I have tried a little bit, just in order to be ready at least, so I am not an absolute outsider there!

But if he is so sane and sober, it must be the spaghetti that has gone to his head! Too much spaghetti in the head makes people very sane and sober.

And you say to me, "We hope you apologize."

I have never done that, and I am never going to do it – that is not my way. I never repent, I never apologize – for what? I am doing my thing. If somebody feels angry he can do whatsoever he wants to do. He can shout at me, he can condemn me; there is no problem for me at all. In fact, I enjoy all this. Whenever people become interested – this is a kind of interest, if somebody is offended – I rejoice. A connection has been made – not a very good connection, but a connection is a connection anyway! If it is bad today, tomorrow it can be good.

Mrs. Carbotti went to the doctor complaining of fatigue. After the examination, the doctor decided she needed a rest.

"Can you stop having relations with your husband for about three weeks?" he asked.

"Sure," she replied, "I got two boyfriends who can take care of me for that long!"

That's why I like the Italians – they are so human, so truly human!

Giovanni said to his daughter, "I no like-a that Irish boy taking you out-a. He is-a rough and common, and besides-a, he is-a a big-a dumbbell!"

"No, papa," replied the girl, "Tim is the most clever fella I know." "Why-a you say-a that?"

"We have only been dating nine weeks and already he has cured me of that little illness I used to get every month!"

A vet goes to Giuseppe's farm to artificially inseminate his cows. While there, he gets an urgent call to another farm. He decides to give Giuseppe the syringe and explain how to do it, then rushes off.

A little while later the local parish priest doing his rounds knocks on the farmer's door. Pierino opens the door and the priest asks where his father is.

"He is-a down at-a the cowshed," replies the little boy, "but it is-a better not-a to go there. It is-a the third-a time that he tries to inseminate the cow and he is-a swearing like hell-a!"

"What, what…what are you saying?" says the priest. "Ah, my God! And does your mother know what he is doing?"

"Of course-a," replies Pierino. "She is-a the one-a who keeps-a the cow's fanny open and shouts, 'Come on-a, Giuseppe, this is-a time you will-a make it!"

Now these beautiful Italians…who cares about enlightenment?

A teacher was getting acquainted with her fourth-grade pupils by letting them get up and talk about the best thing they did during the summer holidays.

"And you, Johnny?" asked the teacher.

"Well, I played with my train set," reported Johnny.

"What about you, Gloria?"

"Ah, we took a wonderful trip to the mountains for the whole summer," said Gloria.

"And you, Liza?" asked the teacher of Little Black Liza. "I like to fuck!" reported Liza.

"Ah, Liza, what a terrible thing to say! I want you to go home and not return until you have a note from your mother, informing me that she is aware of what you have said!" demanded the teacher.

Two days passed before Liza finally returns to class.

"Do you have that note I asked you to bring, Liza?" asked the teacher.

"No, teacher, I ain't got no note. I told Momma what I said, then I told Momma what you said, and Momma said that if somebody don't like to fuck they must be a cocksucker, and she don't want to correspond with your kind!"

Come, Come, Yet Again Come, Ch 15, Q 2

Osho,
Again you invite us to shout the truth from the housetops.

Yes, since I am here, creativity is becoming more intense and vast, and my song is becoming more and more full of colors and dance and grace.

But on the other side an empty space, a cool silence is calling me more and more gently, more and more seducing, more and more scary, because in this silence all the colors of my creativity fade away. The dance loses its passion. The song breaks. The words fall from my hands and there I am sadly, empty- handed, with no song to sing any more.

What am I going to shout from the housetops?

Sarjano, it is one of the most significant problems, almost perennial. In every time, in every country, in every mystery school, the meditators have faced it. If one becomes ecstatic, blissful, one loses silence, because ecstasy, after all, is a beautiful kind of excitement. It is a disturbance – lovely, but a disturbance all the same.

Blissfulness brings its own chaos, its own turmoil, its laughter, its tears, its creativity, its song. And one is bound to get tired of it – it is exhausting. You cannot be ecstatic all the time. Sooner or later you would like to move to the other polarity: silence.

Ecstasy is the logical end of all that is beautiful, passionate, intense, but because it is such a peak of passion and intensity you cannot remain on that peak for long. You have to go back into the deep, dark valleys of silence to rest, to sleep, to get nourished, to be rejuvenated.

Hence the desire for silence arises, a tremendous desire for silence, and of course it feels as if you are going to lose all your creativity, all your joy. And from the peak of ecstasy, silence naturally looks empty and the very idea of moving into silence seems to be suicidal – alluring, enchanting, seducing, but suicidal too, because you will lose your song, your dance, and a sadness arises. But even if the sadness arises one has to go to silence; one has to move to the dark valleys which look empty, which look like death. Hence the fear, the scary feeling.

Those who have tried to live on the peak of ecstasy have remained only poets; they have not been able to become mystics. A few people have tried, but then they have to find a certain kind of relaxation on the peak. Hence all the poets, all the creators – painters, dancers, singers – sooner or later become attracted towards intoxicating drugs, because the excitement is too much. One has to forget it all. Either you move to the silent valley, or you can remain on the peak but fall into deep oblivion.

It is not just an accident that since the very ancient days of the Rig Veda *the poets have always been interested in some kind of psychedelic drugs. In the* Rig Veda *it was soma, now it is LSD or marijuana; all kinds of drugs have been used by creative people. The logical reason is that nobody can live continuously in excitement – it will kill you. If you don't want to move into silence, then the only way to avoid the constant, passionate, feverish state is through some intoxicant – alcohol, opium, or whatsoever it is.*

The people who have moved to the silent valley, who have lived in silence, become afraid of going to the peak of ecstasy because they start feeling that once they move to the peak of ecstasy they will lose their silence. These are the monks; the monasteries were created for these people. These people moved into hidden caves in the Himalayas and other mountains, not to come back into the world, not to relate, not to love, not to live. They lived only at the minimum so that the silence they have achieved can be preserved, but then they become cold. In the beginning it looks very cool, but soon it starts getting colder and colder. They become almost dead.

The people who live in the monasteries are dead people. If you are not creative you cannot be alive. Life can have only one meaning and that is creativity.

God is ultimate life, hence he is the ultimate creator. If you want to live intensely, totally, fully, wholly, you have to create, you have to relate, you have to love, you have to be multi-dimensional. In a monastery people live a one-dimensional, flat kind of life. Of course there is no excitement, hence they are not tired, but because they are just sitting there without any songs arising in them, without any spring ever visiting them, they become deserts, empty deserts.

This has been one of the most significant problems for all the meditators: either you choose silence, but then you become dead, cold, unloving, hard, frozen, or if you choose creativity, you live an intense life, passionate, but very tiring.

My effort, Sarjano, is to bring these two polarities into your life together. If you ask me to define meditation, I would define it as the art, the alchemy of transforming the polar opposites into complementaries. There is no need to choose.

One should be liquid, fluid, flexible, to move from one pole to the other, knowing that they are supportive to each other, they are not against each other; they are not enemies, they are friends. Just as electricity cannot exist without the positive and the negative poles, just as the day cannot exist without the night, just as life cannot exist without death, creativity cannot exist without silence. And vice versa is also true: silence cannot exist without creativity.

And my own experience and observation is this: that a life which has both is really a whole life, and I don't see any real problem except the old conditioning of centuries. Thousands of years of programming has made the division, otherwise there is no division.

Just as you come out of your house when it starts getting too cold inside, out into the sun, or when it becomes too hot outside you move inside into the cool shade… is there any opposition between the two? Do you need great effort to synthesize this coming out of the room and going back into the room? There is no question at all – you can simply walk in and out. It is your own house, it is your own garden! And the same feet and the same walk takes you out and in, only your direction is different. Sometimes you are facing inwards, sometimes you are facing outwards.

And one thing to be remembered: when you are capable of moving easily from the inner to the outer and from the outer to the inner you transcend duality, you are no more caught in duality.

That's the whole message of the Mandukya Upanishad*: transcendence of duality. And the transcendence cannot happen by choosing one of the two; that is not transcendence, that will be clinging.*

Sarjano, you say: "Again you invite us to shout the truth from the housetops."

Again and again I will do it, because I would like your silence to be a singing silence. Remember, even the silence has a song of its own. It may not be your *song – let me emphasize: it may not be* your *song, in fact it cannot be* your *song – the silence has its own song. You may lose* your *song; it* has *to be lost, only then can the silence sing.*

What you are feeling as creativity, passionate and intense, is still adulterated with your ego. That's why silence looks empty. Because in silence there will be no ego.

You say: "…on the other side an empty space, a cool silence is calling me more and more gently, more and more seducing, more and more scary, because in this silence all the colors of my creativity fade away…"

Creativity will not *fade away –* your *creativity* may *fade away, and they are totally different phenomena. In fact,* your *creativity is not of much value. When you are no more there* and *a creativity arises which you cannot claim as yours, then something real has started happening; then it is the song of the silence.*

You say: "Since I am here, creativity is becoming more intense and vast, and my song is becoming more and more full of colors and dance and grace."

It is still my *song. Let it be just a song! Let it be just creativity, a dance without any dancer, a song without any singer, a creativity but without any creator. Then things are very simple. You can move from the peak of creativity easily, gracefully, into silence, and you will enjoy it and it will not be empty. It will be overflowing, it will be pregnant, not empty, because it will nourish you; it will nourish your sources of creativity.*

Your songs will be born in your silence; they may not be expressed *in your silence, but they will be born in your silence. And when the creative phase comes – which automatically comes, just as the day follows the night and the night is followed by the day… it will come. There is a balance: half the time you will be silent and half the time you will be creative. When the creativity comes you will know these songs were sown in your silence, your silence was pregnant with them.*

For nine months the child is in the mother's womb; the womb is not empty. Of course you can't see the child, but the child is growing. In fact, it is better that nobody can see the child, because seeing the child may hinder its growth; it may be a deep interference.

Hence all things grow in darkness. Roots grow in darkness, seeds grow in darkness, children grow in darkness. In fact, everything grows in darkness, underground, hidden; nobody can see it, it is not visible, nobody even knows what is growing underneath the ground. And then one day suddenly the sprouts are there, but they were prepared by the silence. And the spring comes and there are flowers, but they were prepared by the phase that preceded it. One day the child is born – if the womb is empty, from where can the child come?

So don't call the silence empty. It looks empty to you Sarjano, because of a lingering shadow of the ego. It is dying, but dying very slowly. That too is perfectly okay! – there is no hurry. And if you do it in a hurry it may come back. In a hurry it will be only patchwork. In a hurry you may hide it somewhere but sooner or later it will find its way back again – if not from the front door, then from the back door; in some subtle way it may come in. It is better to let it die slowly, with deep understanding, so nothing is left of it.

It is because of the ego that the silence seems to be empty. It is because of the ego that you feel that all the colors of my creativity fade away. Once the ego is gone, it will be the same scene but your interpretation will be different. Then you will not say all the colors fade away. You will say: all the colors mingle and merge into one color, and that is white. Then you will see the beauty of whiteness.

White is not a color, it is the synthesis of all the colors. It represents purity, innocence, egolessness. You will see it as tremendous whiteness, snow-white, and you will be able to decipher all the colors in it – of course now in a latent form, a silent form, sleeping resting. When all the colors rest in the womb of existence they become white. They don't fade away, they only go to rest. It is seed-time.

Every tree comes out of a seed and one day disappears again into seeds. It will come back – those seeds are carrying the whole program. All the leaves – their structure, their pattern, their gestalt – all the branches, all the flowers, are hidden in the seeds, small seeds. But to see into the seed you need tremendous clarity, and the ego does not allow that clarity. Ego is contaminating, polluting your vision.

You say: "The dance loses its passion."

When the ego is gone you will not see it in that way. You will see the dance loses the dancer, not its passion. And when there is no dancer, the passion is not tiring, the passion is no longer exhausting. It has intensity, but now the fire no longer burns – it only gives light. It is the same fire, but now it gives light.

You say: "The song breaks."

It is not the song that is breaking, it is the ego. But because the ego is identified with the song, when the ego breaks you feel the song is breaking.

I can say to you from my own experience – and I have all the Buddhas of the past supporting me – the song has never broken. Buddha became enlightened and for forty-two years he was singing, for forty-two years his each gesture was a song, his silence was a song, his words were songs. Whether he said something or not, the song continued. The song is not breaking.

You say: "The words fall from my hands, and there I am sadly, empty- handed, with no song to sing anymore."

No, your interpretation is wrong, Sarjano. You feel sad because the ego is disappearing and that has been your joy up to now. The only joy that people know is the joy of ego succeeding. Now the ego is by and by withering away and you feel sad, empty-handed, because your hands were full of the ego.

Once you have understood it you will not see your hands as empty, in fact you will see them having the whole space of the sky available – sky in your hands, not emptiness. You will see it as spaciousness, not emptiness.

I have always lived in empty rooms – no furniture, just the bare necessities, one chair, not even another chair for a visitor because nobody comes to visit. And I have always watched: whenever somebody came to see, either they said the room was empty or they said the room was spacious – but very rarely. Out of a hundred persons only one person would say, "The room is very spacious. I love it!"

The English word 'room' simply means spacious, roomy; it does not mean empty. So I have the biggest room in the world, the most roomy room – just space, nothing to hinder, the whole sky available. Only once in a while has somebody said, "It is spacious," and that man had a certain understanding; otherwise they say 'empty'. And both are right according to their vision.

But you have to understand, Sarjano, it is not empty, and it is not that you have no song to sing any more, it is only that your 'I' is disappearing. You are disappearing, not the song! And believe me, when you are completely gone, then only does the song arrive. Then it is divine.

We have called it in India, Bhagavad Gita – 'the song celestial'. Then God sings through you, you are just a hollow bamboo flute.

Philosphia Ultima, Ch 6, Q 1

As a consolation, he found something new to ask his Master, even being far away on the hills.

It happened during those days that John Lennon had been shot, and he had known him personally ten years ago when John got together with Yoko Ono, who liked to bring him to discover all the underground clubs of London, where naturally they had met. He had participated in a "happening" with Yoko some years back, and since then they had remained good friends and she couldn't wait to introduce him to her new and illustrious boyfriend!

Now he was dead, and in the ashram everybody was talking about him, as if one of them had left his body, and there was a lot of commotion all around, to the point that somebody even started to cry. He then wrote to the Master, just to invite him to speak about John Lennon and to give some words of comfort to all his orphans…

Osho,

We're playing those mind-games together, pushing the barrier, planting seeds. Playing the mind-guerilla, chanting the mantra 'peace on earth'. We've all been playing those mind-games forever… Love is the answer, and you know that's for sure. Love is the flower, you got to let it grow. Yes is the answer, and you know that's for sure. Yes is surrender and you got to let it grow…"

This song was written by John Lennon about ten years ago. Now he is dead. Lennon was very much in love with you, even though he declared that he was not ready to become a disciple. I can feel this connection myself. I really would like you to say something about his death.

Swatantra Sarjano,

Words have their own magic, and the poets, the singers, live in the magical world of words, not of realities. They are skillful, very skillful and efficient, as far as the delicate, subtle waves of words, imagination, dreams is concerned, but all that they go on doing is utterly unconscious.

John Lennon on the one hand sings:

'Love is the answer, and you know that's for sure."

He himself does not know it. He says:

"Love is the flower, you got to let it grow."

But to know it you have to be absolutely awakened, because love is the ultimate peak of consciousness. The poet can imagine about it, the singer can sing about it, the painter can paint about it, but they have seen only reflections of the moon in the lake; they have not seen the moon itself. And, of course, the moon reflected in the lake is just made of the same stuff as dreams are made of. The poets, the singers, are dreamers, they are not seers. So he says:

"Yes is surrender and you got to let it grow…"

His words sound true, but they are only reflections of the moon in the lake. If you dive in the lake you will not find the moon there. In fact, the moment you jump into the water, the reflection will disappear, will be broken into thousands of pieces. It will spread all over the lake; you will not be able to catch hold of it. The reflection IS beautiful, but one has not to forget that it is only a reflection and it cannot transform your being.

So he sings: "Love is the answer… Love is the flower… Yes is the answer… Yes is surrender… And you know that's for sure" – *but he himself is absolutely unaware of it; he has not experienced it. A beautiful man, but still lost in dreams and imagination.*

The poet lives unconsciously, the seer lives consciously. Sometimes their words are exactly the same – don't be deceived by the words. If you really want to know whether those words represent reality or just empty wishes you have to look into the life of the man.

Kahlil Gibran has written tremendously beautiful words. They come so close to Christ, to Zarathustra, to Lao Tzu, to Gautam the Buddha, and there is every possibility many people will think that Kahlil Gibran is enlightened. He may even surpass Lao Tzu and Buddha and Christ as far as expression is concerned; his expression may be far more beautiful because he is a skilled poet, a very skilled painter. He has the sensitiveness to appreciate beauty, but howsoever he is appreciating it is unconscious.

Buddha may not say things so beautifully because he is not a poet in the ordinary sense, but whatsoever he says is the truth. His words may fall short of it… in fact, words always fall short of the truth; they are never adequate enough. So don't decide by words.

Sarjano, you are deciding by words. That's why you say:

"I can feel this connection myself."

Sarjano himself has the quality of a poet, has the sensibility of a creative person. That's why I have given him the name Sarjano; Sarjano means creativity.

But Kahlil Gibran or John Lennon have to be watched to know whether their truths are really truths or only fabrications of dream, fantasy, imagination; whether they have really experienced those things or they are only empty wishes. You have to watch the Buddha….

Buddha is reported to have said: "Don't be too bothered about what I say, rather look at me, rather watch me, rather feel me. Let the words disappear. Don't let the words stand between me and you. Experience my silence, feel the energy that surrounds me, resonate with me – only then will you be able to understand what I am saying."

If you want to understand a Buddha, his words, you have to watch his life.

Buddha has also said, very poignantly: "Don't follow my words, rather, follow what I am doing, follow what I am being."

Sarjano, I can see these words are beautiful:

"We're playing these mind-games together, pushing the barrier, planting seeds."

But there is no need to go on playing them forever. There have been people who stopped all those mind-games, but the only way to stop those mind-games is meditation; there has never been any other way. Meditation means entering into a state of no-mind.

If he was really in love with me, then there was nothing to prevent him from coming here. To be in love with me means to be in love with meditation, but he must have been afraid of meditation. If he said that he was not ready to become a disciple he must have been afraid of meditation, of surrender, of saying yes, of falling in love. Why? – because the poets, the singers, the painters, the sculptors, the musicians, are the most egoistic people in the world. They talk about egolessness, saying yes and surrendering and love, but that is mere talk.

They are very egoistic people, in fact they far surpass even the politicians and the priests, for the simple reason that they are talented people. The politicians are not talented people – they are third-rate, they belong to the world of the mediocre. But poets, singers, musicians, painters, they are talented people. They really have something which they can brag about – they have got something. Their ego has a solid support. The politician is making his house on shifting sands, but the poet – any kind of creative person – is making his ego on solid ground, on rocklike ground. His foundation is concrete; it is not made of just shifting sands. Hence he has every reason to feel egoistic, but then the danger is even far greater : he will be the last person to surrender, and his whole life he will talk about surrender and about egolessness and about love.

Kahlil Gibran talked about love, surrender, saying yes, but his whole life was quarrelsome. The people he loved, he always fought with them. He was talking about compassion, but he was a very angry man. He would go into childish tantrums for small reasons – any excuse would do. He would throw things, he would break things – he would go mad! The people who lived with him were always afraid of him, the women who loved him were continuously in misery.

And this is the man who wrote the great book, The Prophet. *It stands as one of the ten great books of the whole world and it will remain one of the greatest ever; there is no possibility for somebody to surpass it. And this is coming from a man who was very angry, very violent, very jealous, very egoistic.*

Wilhelm Reich *has written about how to get rid of jealousy – because jealousy is the poison for love, it destroys the roots of love. And Wilhelm* Reich *is one of the greatest creative psychoanalysts after Sigmund* Freud. *But his wife writes something else – she writes about him: "I have never seen such a jealous person in my life. He was taking all kinds of freedom, he was moving with many women!" – because he was talking about freedom and that relationship should not be any kind of bondage, but about his wife he was very jealous. Almost twenty-four hours a day he was detecting, spying on where she was, with whom she was, what she was doing, was she looking happy with the man. When he went out of the town he would tell his friends to keep watch....*

Finally his wife had to divorce him – it was too much of a torture. He was taking every kind of freedom – he was moving with many women – and his wife was not even allowed to have friends, not to mention lovers.

You have to look into the life of the person, because only that is decisive.

Now, Lennon was continuously fighting with his own woman – many times they separated and many times they got together again – and he is talking about mind- games, and he was playing those mind-games himself!

Sarjano, the words are beautiful: Love is the answer. *I also say love is the answer, but I mean it! He does not mean it, he is simply saying beautiful words. Beautiful words have their own hypnotic quality. They catch the mind of the singers and the poets and the musicians; they fall in love with beautiful words. He must be in love with the word 'love' – and remember, the word 'love' is not love, the word 'God' is not God, the word 'yes' is not yes.*

Yes is a totally different existential experience. To say yes means to drop your ego entirely. Surrender means disappearing into the whole. He was a nice man, but as unconscious, Sarjano, as you are. That's why you say:

"I can feel this connection myself."

You must be feeling it!

Now the poor man is dead. Somebody played the game – the mind-game – killed him. Many questions have come to me asking that I should say something about his death. To me, birth and death have no significance at all. There are many ways to die, and the best way is to be killed – at least you are not responsible! The worst is to die in your bed and ninety-nine percent of people choose to die in their beds. Beware of the bed, because that is the most dangerous place in the world! All the accidents happen there: birth happens there, love happens there, death happens there. If you can simply renounce the bed you are enlightened!

He died a good death – somebody killed him. One has to die anyway; when one has to die one should choose a good way. I don't think he chose it and I don't think the person who killed him chose it either. People are living – all people are living – in utter unconsciousness.

A patient lying on the operating table started screaming, "I don't want to be cut open! You'll kill me! I don't want to die!"

The surgeon tried to calm the patient.

"Just take it easy, sir," he said. "Look at my long white beard. I've done thousands of operations and nothing has ever gone wrong."

"Oh, doctor, you're right! I know I can trust you!" replied the patient.

When the patient awoke after the operation, he looked around and saw the same white beard and said, "Oh, thank you, doctor! You are a saint!"

"It's okay, son, you don't have to thank me. I am not your doctor – my name is St. Peter!"

So what can I say about his death? It is perfectly okay! Everything is okay. Just…if he had really come here he would have died a totally different kind of death. He would have died celebrating, he would have died rejoicing. He would have died without any regrets, without any complaints. He would have died in love, in surrender, in yes. That he has missed this time – I hope next time he does not miss it."

Philosphia Ultima, Ch 10, Q 1

***

CHAPTER 06

Osho In The USA

Between one party and another, six months passed, and then one day the news came like a bomb that Osho had left the ashram, had left India, and had gone to America, to search together with his secretary Sheela for a vast piece of land to build the biggest ashram in the world!

The project was to create a real city with its mayor, its administration, and its own police force; a place totally autonomous and completely self-sufficient.

The Master had come by then to the conclusion that his people would be able to give birth to the greatest revolution in history, a city-state where blacks and whites, Hebrews and Muslims, Christians and Buddhists, Indians and Pakistanis, even Sicilians and Sardinians, could live peacefully and in great harmony!

The Master would end up paying dearly for his utopian project, because he probably didn't know...but if he had asked him, he would have told him that any other place in the world would have been more suitable than the U.S.A. for his experiment, even Australia or some remote island in Oceania; a North European country such as Sweden or Denmark would have been more appropriate, but certainly not the U.S.A., because it was the most fascist country in the entire world, and if the Master would have had consulted him first, he would have certainly told him to find a different place!

Too bad that Sheela, his Indian Secretary at the time, had grown up in the States; she thought that she knew the country quite well, and she was totally fascinated by it, and being the simpleton that she was, she was still believing in things of the past like "The New Frontier" or even "The American Dream"; so in the end Osho followed her to the States, where he took temporary refuge at a castle in New Jersey, from where the search started to find the place that would host the first "Orange City" in the world.

A New Italy

Three months after Osho had left they went back to Italy together, when there were only ruins left of the commune and everything had been demolished or stored away. It was a sad scene to watch everybody leave, the total dismantling...it seemed like the end of a dream to him.

They landed in Rome, where they were welcomed at the airport by Silvia, who meanwhile had become 'Prem Silvia', by Bill, who had become 'Satyamo', and by Amore, who had become 'Marco'!

What had happened was that after six beautiful and totally unconventional years in Sicily, Amore was sent to school in Rome; there all these straight kids were teasing him constantly because of his name – you can imagine these little Roman delinquents – so after a while of this torture and of all this teasing, he came running home from school one day, declaring that from now on he wanted to be called 'Marco', in homage to his friend in Sicily, and he also said with great authority, that he wanted to be called by his new name even at home!

Premal, however, just to remain on the subject of school, had been warned by her parents that as she hadn't finished all years of the compulsory school, which she had left to be in Pune, she would now have to complete the one missing year, otherwise there would be a lot of problems for them, as the uncaring parents!

Premal had to go back to Munich and suffer an entire year at school, spending months with some creatures that compared to her were just like little kids; but she handled it quite well, because they had learned meanwhile how to administrate her holidays in the best way.

If she had only a Sunday off, he would fly to Munich and spend two nights and one day with her; if she had two days off, they would meet at the train station in Verona, because there were two trains that were leaving almost simultaneously, one from Rome and the other from Munich, both with the destination of the city of Romeo and Juliet! In Verona they would spend a romantic weekend, to return with the last train available to the place they had come from; and finally, if she had one week or more of holidays, she would come to Rome, where they always had a lot of fun!

One year later, the new Commune in Oregon decided to open its doors to the world and to invite all the sannyasins and friends to come for a visit, so he managed to have an endorsement from a magazine called 'La Domenica del Corriere', which included a check for expenses and a paid ticket to fly to Oregon. A week later he arrived.

The editor of this magazine had come to know that in the new Commune there was, amongst others, the former Nicoletta Macchiavelli, who had been a very famous actress during the sixties and seventies. Hence this paper had the brilliant idea of having her narrate the whole story, which was published later in two parts with the title "Come to Oregon – We Are Building a Paradise!" by Nicoletta Machiavelli (text composed by Carlo Silvestro).

At that time, when he was working as a journalist and writing reports about the Commune, or conducting an interview with Osho, he preferred to use his legal name, because this gave more authoritativeness to the story, while if he signed with his sannyas name, the readers would most likely think that he was a little partisan, and of course that he was making up all those beautiful things! On that particular occasion he also had to send to the magazine, besides the story of the actress, some pictures of the Master, possibly one while he was driving his Rolls Royce.

Whilst on this subject, some light needs to be thrown on all these legends and bullshit that have been said and written about 'The Rolls' of the Master'. First of all, Osho didn't own any of these Rolls Royces (that at a certain point reached the number 99!), and he was using them only for his daily tour of the Commune, just to see and be seen by everybody, since he was in silence and wanted to at least show his face.

His drive at that time usually started at two in the afternoon, and it took him more than one hour to drive through the whole Commune at the slow pace he kept in order to give each one of us the chance to wave to him. Sometimes Osho, who was always driving himself, would stop for a minute, slide down the window of the car to give a little present to some child and sometimes even to his lucky parents.

When he decided that it was the right time to make some pictures of Osho driving, and hoping his car would slow down a little, he had placed himself in a crowded corner, and advanced a few meters ahead of everybody else, waiting there crouched like a paparazzo!

As soon as Osho saw him, he stopped his car just in front of him, slid down the window and said with a smile: “So, Sarjano, are you ready for this picture?” And he almost posed for the occasion!

In that moment he was, as usual, completely overwhelmed by that ancient wave of love that simply melted him every time he was near him, and he saw his hands throwing the camera in the air, while his head was reclining almost inside the car’s window.

Osho patted his head, saying softly: “Good, Sarjano, good…but now do you want to take this picture or not?” Then, addressing the people around, he said: “Is there anyone that can collect his camera and place it in his hands, so that he can make this photo?”

Behind him stood Silvia, his old companion and the mother of his only son, who was almost in tears, seeing all the attention that our Master was showering on her former man, so she went to collect his camera from the ground a few meters away and placed in his hands.

He looked again at Osho, who was there, still smiling and waiting for his click, and said just two words: “I can’t!” – and in saying that he threw his expensive camera in the air again, while Osho continued his drive still smiling and chuckling.

He would travel to Oregon at least a couple of times every year, always as a correspondent of some magazine or other, and on top of this was also paid abundantly! He thought that it was immensely fortunate to be paid liberally just to go to have a chat and make a couple of photos of your Master!

He went there also for the 1985 Festival, the last year of the Commune, even though in that moment there was nothing that could have anticipated the end that would follow, and in that year, or perhaps for this occasion, Osho started to speak again in public, after a self-imposed public silence that had lasted about four years.

For this occasion – the return of his discourses – Osho asked the Commune’s press office to invite all journalists possible, all the radio and TV stations reachable, in one word all the media that could be possibly contacted.

More than one hundred and fifty journalists and cameramen from all over the world arrived at the Ranch for the event, including a certain Carlo Silvestro who attended first a general press conference:

Carlo Silvestro
Grazia Magazine, Italy

Yes, another Italian. Bhagwan, I would like you to speak on what kind of love is possible between a man and a woman, and also if there is any hope for a relationship between a man and a woman which is not going to be entangled in the usual pattern of sado-masochism.

It is a very significant question. Ordinarily, religions have made it impossible. Any beautiful relationship between man and woman – they have destroyed it. There was reason to destroy it.

If a man's love life is fulfilled, you will not find so many people in churches praying. They will be making love, early morning love, on Sundays. Who bothers about the idiot who is preaching in the church? If people's love lives are of immense content and beauty they won't bother about whether God exists or not, whether the philosophy preached in the Bible is true or not. They are so contented with themselves.

Once in a while it happens that I pass on the road and two lovers are hugging each other. They don't even look at me. I feel so happy; they must be in an immensely groovy place.

Religions have destroyed your love by creating marriage. Marriage is the end, not the beginning. Love is finished. Now you are a husband, your beloved is a wife. Now you start trying to dominate each other. It is politics, no more love. Now every small thing becomes a point to be argued.

And marriage is against human nature, so sooner or later you are going to be fed up with the woman, and the woman is going to be fed up with you. And it is natural, there is nothing wrong in it. That is why I say marriages should not be there, because marriages make the whole world immoral. A man sleeping with a woman, and they are not loving each other but still are trying to make love because they are married – this is ugly, disgusting. This I call real prostitution.

When a man goes to a prostitute, at least it is straightforward. He purchases a certain commodity. He does not purchase the woman, he purchases a certain commodity. But he has purchased the whole woman in marriage – and for her whole life. All husbands and all wives without exception are caged, trying to get free of it. But even sometimes in countries where divorce is allowed and they manage to change the partner, within a few days they are in for a surprise. The other woman or the other man proves an exact copy of the one they have left behind.

I remember hearing about one man who married eight times – of course, it must have been in California. When he married the eighth time, after two days he recognized that he had married this woman once before too. And then he started thinking, "What have I gained by changing women? It all comes back to the same rut."

Stability in marriage is unnatural. Monogamy is unnatural. Man is by nature a polygamous animal, and anybody who is intelligent will be polygamous. You can't go on and on eating Italian food. Once in a while you want to visit the Chinese restaurant!

I want people to be completely freed from marriage and marriage licenses. The only cause of their being together should be love, not law. Love should be the only law.

Then what you are asking is possible. The moment love disappears, say goodbye to each other. There is nothing to fight for; love was a gift of existence. It came like the wind, it has gone like the wind. You will be grateful to each other. You may part, but you will remember those beautiful moments you had been together.

You may remain friends, if not lovers. Ordinarily lovers when they part become enemies. In fact, they become enemies before they part – that's why they part.

Ultimately, if both persons are meditators, not just lovers, trying to transform the very energy of love into a meditative state....And that is my whole approach towards man and his relationship with woman. It is a tremendous energy. It is life. If, while making love to your woman, you can both move into a silent period, utterly quiet, no thought passing through your minds – as if time has stopped – then you will know for the first time the real taste of love. That kind of relationship can remain for the whole life, because it is no more just biological attraction which fades away sooner or later. Now you have a new dimension opening.

Your woman has become your temple. Your man has become your temple. Your love has become your meditation, and this meditation goes on growing, and when it is growing you start becoming more and more joyful, more and more nourished, more and more strengthened. There is no relationship, there is no bondage to remain with the woman. But who can renounce joy? Who can ask for divorce when there is so much joy? People are asking for divorce because there is no joy, just despair and twenty-four hours a day nightmare....

My people here and around the world are learning that love is only the jumping board. There is much more ahead of it, which is possible only if two persons remain intimate for a longer period of time. With a new person, again you begin from scratch. And there is no need for a new person, because now it is not the biological or the physical aspect of the person, but you have come into communion spiritually.

To transform sex into spirituality is my basic approach. And if both are lovers and meditators, they will not mind, once in a while, if you visit a Chinese restaurant, or she goes to visit some continental restaurant! It is not a problem. You love the woman; if she is feeling happy once in a while with somebody else, what is wrong in it? You should be happy that she is happy, because you love her. Only meditators are capable of dropping jealousies.

Be a lover – that is a good beginning, but not the end. Go on trying to be more meditative. And be quick, because your love may be finished the day the honeymoon is finished.

So meditation and love should go hand in hand. If we can create a world where lovers are meditators too, then there will be no problem of continuous torture, nagging, jealousies, hurting each other in every possible way.

Love without meditation is bound to turn into hatred any moment – beware – but love with meditation will become deeper and deeper, more and more intense. And perhaps two persons will feel together so attuned, a kind of at-one-ment, that they would love to be together forever.

But that is not a condition. Any day, even if one partner decides, "Now I am moving from this crossroad, away from you. Thank you for all you have done. I remember all these beautiful moments, but I cannot continue" – that's enough. No court is needed to decide for you that you are married, to decide for you that you are divorced. What an insane world we are living in! Even our love is not free.

And when I say that love should be our freedom, they condemn me all over the world as the "free-sex guru." Certainly I am all for freedom of love. And in a way they are right: I don't want sex to be a commodity in the market. It has to be freely available, just two persons agreeing, that's enough. And this agreement is only for the moment; no promises for the future, because they become chains around your neck. They will kill you. No promises for the future, just relish this moment. And if next moment you are still together, you will be able to relish it more.

So I don't use the word relationship. I use the word relatedness. You can relate, but don't create relationship. If your relating becomes a lifelong process, good. If it does not, that is even better. Perhaps this was not the right partner, and it is good that you separated. Find another partner. There must be someone somewhere who will be waiting for you. But this society does not allow you to find out who it is who is waiting for you, who is the person who will fit with you.

They will call me immoral....To me, this is morality. What they are trying to practice is immoral.

The Last Testament Vol. 1, Ch 3

He also had come on invitation of the weekly magazine 'Panorama':

I'd like to say a few words about our magazine, which is a weekly magazine in Italy with a reputation of an opinion maker, like 'Newsweek' in America. Since it is the first time any Italian journalist has this opportunity to speak with you, we will have quite a lot of questions and we hope that we have an answer for all of them for our readers.

The first question is: You say that you are not a prophet, you are not a messiah, you are not a god, you are not a saint. So we want to know, who are you?

Is it necessary for anyone to be a messiah, to be a prophet, to be a son of God? Cannot one just be a human being? I am simply a human being as everybody else is, with a very little difference: I am awake and others are asleep.

It may look like a great difference to the person who is asleep, but to the awakened there is no difference at all. Just a little shaking, shocking, and the asleep one will be awake and they both can laugh at the whole stupid game of Master and disciple, of messiah… of the savior and the saved. Except for laughter there will be nothing, because they will know that they are both exactly the same. And because these names – prophet, messiah, incarnation of God – have been used in the past to exploit people, to create bondage for their spirits, for their psyches, these names have divided people into different religions and the result was thousands of wars. Five thousand wars in three thousand years…crusades in the name of God, people killing thousands of other people, burning people alive in the name of God, and with the authority that they are the representatives of the messiah or the prophet or the successor.

I don't want to be in this company of criminals. I want simply to be an ordinary human being – that's what I am.

In any case, do you think that you have a big power?

I don't have any power. I have love, big love, but love knows no power. Power is desired by those who are incapable of love. Only the loveless become politicians, power hungry. They think that if they have power over people perhaps their desire for love will be fulfilled. It is never fulfilled. No politician dies contented. It is impossible – he has gone wrong from the very beginning. The path of power leads farther away from yourself, and from love. The path of love brings you closer home to yourself.

I have immense love to give, inexhaustible love to give, but no power to order or command or tell somebody to be this, be that. I don't give any ten commandments.

Why have you said that you are a guest here? Do you plan to leave, to travel?

No. I have always been a guest wherever I was, because I belong to the whole universe. So anywhere I am, that particular place is only a guest house. I am not planning to leave – I never plan. I can leave any moment, I may not leave ever.

You said, 'I must choose, I prefer to be Zorba rather than Buddha.' What does it mean?

It means that Zorba is the foundation and Buddha is the palace. Buddha is the peak, but the foundation stones are laid by Zorba. It will be foolish to choose to be a Buddha without having the foundation stones.

I am absolutely mathematical about it: Zorba should be there and the stronger a Zorba is there, the better a Buddha is possible. So I can become Buddha any moment; Zorba is absolutely needed as the basic energy out of which the Buddha

is going to be carved. Zorba is the marble rock out of which the Buddha statue has to be carved. I choose the rock…and Buddha is easy.

It is just a question of opening your eyes. I don't bother about Buddha; I am worried about people who are not Zorbas. How will they become Buddhas? They don't have the basic material out of which a Buddha is made.

And this poverty has been given to people by our religious leaders. They have been told not to be materialists. They have been told to be celibate. They have been told to live in poverty. They have been told that life exists out of sin. All these things have destroyed their Zorbas. Otherwise, every man is a born Zorba the Greek.

And if everything goes according to me, every man will die as Zorba the Buddha. Between the Greek and the Buddha there is not much distance, but first you must be the Greek.

What do you mean when you say that you are the guru of the rich people? Are you as rich as many of your sannyasins? Your critics – and I'm trying to understand – say that you collect money just as you collect the Rolls Royces and the watches. Are you against the poor?

First, I collect nothing. There is not a single thing that I possess. For thirty years I have been the poorest man in the world. And on the judgment day, if there is a line, you will find me in the front, ahead of Jesus Christ.

But my people who love me are there. That is my possession; that makes me rich. Their love is more to me than power over the whole world. I would not like to become Alexander the Great. Out of their love, whatsoever they want to do, they do.

If they want me to have Rolls Royces, they are free. If they want me to have diamond watches, they are free. They know my taste, and for that simple reason my people can manage to offer me everything that not even a king or queen is capable of having.

The reason is very simple: whatever I teach can be understood only by the very intelligent and creative people. So only the cream of intelligence comes close to me.

I am against poverty and against the poor. I don't want any poverty, any poor people in the world. I am not in agreement with Jesus that the poor are the blessed; they are the cursed, they shall inherit the kingdom of hell. There is no need for anybody to be poor. We have enough intelligence; we have everything that can make the whole earth a beautiful garden. But politicians will not allow it to happen; priests will not allow it to happen, because if the Garden of Eden can be created here, then what is going to happen to their paradise, their God, their hell and all the business that goes on around those bogus words which mean nothing?

Politicians would not like that there are no poor people in the world. If there are no poor people in the world, communism will lose all hold immediately. If there are no poor people in the world, it will not be easy for the capitalists to exploit anybody. In the capitalist countries, the capitalist wants there to be poor people because they can be purchased easily. In India you can purchase any vote for two rupees; that is the highest price for any vote. Now what kind of democracy can exist where you can purchase a vote for two rupees?

The rich people want the poor to exist, the priest wants the poor to exist, because without the poor, who is going to go to the church? The rich people have their Rotary Clubs, their Lion's Clubs, the Club of Rome – who is going to the church? The priest wants the crippled, retarded, blind, sick, old, starving, all kinds of people who are not wanted at all. The priest needs them; otherwise, who is going to gather around Billy Graham?

If there are not orphans, who is going to give a Nobel Prize to Mother Teresa? These people are exploiting. With all the scientific and technological developments in the twentieth century, I am saying that it is absurd to allow poverty to exist for even a single moment longer.

We've been here a few days now and the commune looks so peaceful and people are really beautiful. Your words are very beautiful, too. What I am asking myself now is, how come the press and the Oregonians are so unusually aggressive against you and your people?

Because I want them to be aggressive. They are simply following my wishes. If they are not aggressive, then there is not much hope. If they are aggressive, we can put them right.

Their being aggressive is their first step towards friendship. They may not understand, but I understand it. For my whole life I have been creating enemies and turning enemies into friends. And in fact it is better this way, rather than vice-versa; you put all your energy into creating a friend and then he becomes your enemy. That is sheer wastage. The better thing is to put your whole energy into creating enemies, and then let them turn into your friends. And they are bound to turn, because whatsoever they are carrying is absurd. The moment they come to know the truth, they will become your friends.

And it is a simple psychology: the deeper their hate, the deeper will be their love, in the same proportion. I do not believe in people like Dale Carnegie. I work just in the opposite way, and you can see my business is succeeding. And where is Dale Carnegie? And how many people has he turned into friends?

I want the whole earth, the whole humanity, to be divided into two camps – no more Russian, no more American – either they hate me or they love me, but both ways they are connected with me, and I love both of them. They are like the two wheels the bullock cart moves upon; they are not aware that they are playing into my hands.

You said, 'I am a simple man.' But why do thousands and thousands of people, simple men, follow a simple man?

Because it is very difficult to find a simple man. Nobody is simple, everybody thinks himself extraordinary. He may not have the guts to say it – that's another matter – but everybody, deep down, thinks himself to be the most superior, the most beautiful, the most intelligent person in the world. And if he is not succeeding, it is because the whole world is hostile to him, everybody is preventing him. Otherwise, he would be on top of Everest.

I am a simple man with no ambition to be anybody other than I am, and these people have been attracted towards me just because of my simplicity, humanity. They have fallen in love with an innocent man who has no secrets and no privacy, who is absolutely open, available.

You cannot find people open, available, innocent, simple. Even the most idiotic people think they are great geniuses. I am not a genius, just an average, ordinary person.

Do you have any kind of personal strategy for the future, any message to leave? Do you have any idea of Rajneeshism and Rajneeshpuram after you? Do you have any successor?

No, because all the religions that have followed those lines have turned poisonous, have turned into curses on humanity. I don't want to be a curse to humanity. I am a blessing and I want to remain a blessing.

So nobody is going to succeed me.

And my message for my people is that the moment I am gone, your religion is gone. Then whatever remains is just a corpse. Don't start worshipping the corpse. I am a free man and I want every sannyasin to be a free man. My love is the only binding force between them; otherwise, there is no theology, no belief system, no agreement on anything.

Only one thing is keeping them together around the world, and that is their love for me. When I am not there, nothing can keep them together. There is no bridge. Each sannyasin is individually connected to me. You don't ask the sun, "If one day you stop rising, what is going to happen to the rays?" You know that the rays will not be there the moment I am dead and gone.

They have lived with me, they have danced with me, they have enjoyed with me – now they know the secret of how to enjoy life, how to live life. And there is no need to go on making a church, popes, successors…because they have done so much harm. I will not allow my people to do that.

When I am gone, then you disperse. What is the point? My love was keeping you together, and I am there no more. It is good that I am no more, because now your last attachment is also dropped. I was the last attachment to be broken, now you are totally free. You were free from your family, from your nation, from your religion, but a small thin thread of love was binding you with me. Now I am no more there; I give you the last, the final taste of freedom.

And then whatever happens, happens. I am not responsible for it. The people who will be coming after me will have the responsibility. And I never think about the future. I am so totally involved with the present...I am talking to you, and at this moment only you exist for me. The whole space has disappeared and the whole time has stopped. Just you and me...only then can there be some communication.

And I don't think about what is going to happen tomorrow. I am not thinking of what you are going to write about me; and I am not going to read it, whatever you write! It doesn't matter at all. What matters is that we enjoyed this moment together, loved this moment, laughed together, felt each other's humanity.

I cannot see anybody as a journalist, as a doctor, as an engineer. Those are not your realities, they are just your jobs. When I look at you, I put aside your journalist; I am talking directly to you. Journalism is just your way of earning bread and butter. What importance does it have? I cannot love bread and butter, but I love you as a person, as an individual, and whatsoever I am saying is totally different from what you would have found in the past with the many other people you have interviewed. Even in the future you may not come across a man like me.

My whole interest in this moment is in how to help you enjoy the time you have been with me. Your magazine, your writing, does not come between me and you, so when you started introducing the magazine, I was going to stop you, but just out of politeness I listened. What concern do I have with magazines, newspapers?

My concern is purely with the individual, and then it is up to him. Whatsoever he wants to make out of it, he will make out of it. I trust in my love, and I trust in the dignity of the individual that is sitting before me, and the trust will take care of everything. I never think of tomorrow.

But you don't think that you are responsible for all the sannyasins living here, for the life and the future of the children I have seen in this city?

I am not responsible for anybody. I am not even a member of this commune. I live outside the City of Rajneeshpuram. And I am not a sannyasin, as you can see. It is the commune's responsibility. I am very irresponsible.

When I was leaving the university, one girl used to love me. But just the way girls are – and particularly in India – she was shy, and I am not the one to chase anybody. I do chasing sitting in my chair...I am just a lazy man. She loved me; and continuously she was sending messages to me. She wanted to get married to me. Then the day of departure came and we were leaving. We had passed our final examinations and then she could not contain it any more.

She pulled me aside and told me, "I have loved you for two years, but I had not the courage to say it. And you are a strange man...I made so many efforts and so many messages, and you just remained as if I am not here."

I said, "You do not know. It is just out of compassion that I have remained that way, because I am a very irresponsible man. I may marry you, and tomorrow morning I may forget all about you. I may give birth to children and then I will not bother at all what happens to you and your children."

Just out of compassion, I kept out of it. It is enough that I am carrying my own responsibility towards myself. That's why I have never accepted any responsibility for anything.

India's first prime minister, Jawaharlal Nehru, wanted me to join politics. I was introduced to him by India's very old senior-most parliamentarian, who had been a member of parliament from 1916 up to 1976. He was known as the father of the Indian parliament. Jawaharlal used to stay at his palace – his father was given the title of Rajah, king, so his house had become the palace, and it was palatial.

And Jawaharlal was a man of tremendous intelligence. He talked just for five to ten minutes with me and he said, "You'd better join politics. You don't waste your time here and there, you have a great future and I am with you and I will support you."

I said, "Thank you for your generosity, but I am not going to be in any position where I am responsible for anybody."

Politics means responsibility, and if you are not responsible you have to become a hypocrite. That's what all the politicians have become. They talk about being responsible and nobody is responsible.

Now, millions of tons of food in Europe have been thrown in the ocean, but they will not send it to Ethiopia. One hundred thousand dollars were needed to take it to the ocean, and they dumped it there – fresh fruit, fresh food. But its presence was going to bring the prices down, and that they would not like. And who cares about Ethiopia? And why should anybody care?

In speeches, everybody will talk about Ethiopia and responsibility, but the real face is totally different. The prime minister of India, Rajiv Gandhi, is one of my friends. He is Jawaharlal's grandson. If I had accepted Jawaharlal's offer, perhaps I would have been in his place. He is selling wheat to other countries while half of India is starving and dying.

And they go on talking about sympathy and compassion for the poor…but he needs nuclear weapons. For that he needs money, and India has only raw materials to sell. It has no technology, no high technology. The poor man works his whole life producing wheat and dies starving while the wheat will be sold to purchase uranium to make nuclear weapons.

I don't take anybody's responsibility. In this way I help whoever comes close to me to be responsible for himself. People who take others' responsibility are responsible for creating retarded, dependent slaves all around the world. If nobody had taken their responsibility, they would have taken the challenge of life and struggled for themselves.

I have heard about a very super-rich woman. She had come to a holiday resort, to the best hotel. Her boy, who looked perfectly young and healthy, was carried from the car on a stretcher. Even the hotel manager and others thought that there must be something wrong. The young man looked perfectly healthy, in the best of health. They said, "What is wrong with this young man? What has happened?" She said, "Nothing has happened, but he can afford to be carried on a stretcher. Why should he walk?"

Now, this woman thinks she is making the life of the boy luxurious, but she is crippling him. He may become crippled, he may not ever be able to walk. Somebody took the whole responsibility.

It is a known fact that in the whole history of humanity, not a single genius has come from superrich families. And the reason is simple. All that he wanted was available, there was no challenge. When there is no challenge intelligence goes out of function, it is not needed.

It is strange. It should have been otherwise. The richer people should have given birth to better geniuses, better Einsteins, better painters, musicians, poets, but they have just given birth to buffalos.

I don't take anybody's responsibility, because I love people and I have compassion enough not to take their responsibility on my shoulders. They have to take their own responsibility.

I want to explain to our readers who the sannyasins are. Is the sannyasin a sort of new man? You say that the sannyasins are innocent children. Your critics say that they are your slaves, slaves of your attitude towards work, life, love, sex. May we have your opinion of the sannyasins?

I don't care at all what the critics say. They all can go to hell – the sooner the better. But I can tell you about my sannyasins.

I don't have any dogma that they can follow. I have no philosophy that they can live. I don't have any catechism that they have to repeat and cram.

Being with me, all that happens is a very delicate deprogramming, and once a person is deprogrammed I don't have any program for him. In fact, my sannyasins are simply losing what they have, and I am not going to replace it with anything. They will lose Christianity, they will lose Hinduism, and I will not replace it with another program. I will leave them to themselves.

They are not my slaves; neither am I their slave. Slavery is a very strange phenomenon, it is a double-edged sword. The master is dependent on the slaves as much as the slaves are dependent on the masters.

I am nobody's slave, nobody is my slave, because I know that if you create a slave, you become a slave immediately. My sannyasins cannot even expect anything from me for the simple reason that I never expect anything from them. When I said that I am not celibate because I am not unnatural, a few sannyasins were shocked. They started writing letters to me, and I informed them that they cannot have any expectations about me. I can do anything I want. We don't have any contract that I will follow your expectations or you will follow mine.

I have no contract of any kind. My sannyasins cannot expect what I am going to do tomorrow. I can do anything, and they also are absolutely free. They can do anything they want: they can be here, they can leave. It is their freedom.

Out of freedom they have become sannyasins, out of freedom they can become non-sannyasins. There is no problem. It is not a church and it is not some contract which has always existed between the leader and the follower, the Master and the disciple. But this delicate thing is rarely understood – that they both become dependent on each other.

I am reminded of a beautiful story about Diogenes. Greece has given a few beautiful people to the world, but none comparable to Diogenes. He is not much mentioned in the history of philosophies or even if he is mentioned, it is only in the footnotes – for the simple reason that the man was so rebellious and such an outsider that the professors of philosophy would find it difficult to explain the man and his behavior.

He lived naked. Now, in India it is a tradition, there are many naked sannyasins. But in Greece, he was the only one in the whole of history who lived naked. Just like Buddha in India, he used to carry a begging bowl to beg food or to drink water.

One day he was thirsty. It was hot and he was rushing towards the river to fill his begging bowl with cool water. Just before he was going to dip his begging bowl, a dog came running in and started drinking. He stopped, for a moment he thought, and he said, "This dog seems to be more independent than me. I have to depend on this begging bowl. If a dog can manage without a begging bowl, then Diogenes is going to manage it, too."

He immediately threw the begging bowl into the river. Even in small things – what to say about human beings – when you make human beings your slave, you are entering into a mutual slavery, a mutual dependence.

I have no contract with my people. I have not promised them that I should be this or that, so they can never question my behavior. I remain individual; and that's what I want them to remain, individual.

Now, the persons who were shocked when I said I am not celibate had carried the idea for centuries that a religious person should be celibate – and particularly nobody has heard that an enlightened man had made love to any woman after his enlightenment. Naturally they were shocked.

It is up to them. They can think that perhaps I am not enlightened. Perhaps it is time for them to leave this place. Perhaps they have come to a wrong person. But as far as I am concerned, I am going to be totally free, absolutely frank, no secrecy, no privacy.

I know for certain that celibacy is unnatural unless you are impotent; and I don't think any impotent person has ever become enlightened. No, there is no mention of it. In fact, just the opposite is the case. The people who became enlightened were really too much sexual, that's why I call them Zorbas; they were really too much sexual – so much that finally they understood that there is nothing much in it. They experienced it through and through and found nothing in it. And that was the point from where they started searching for something else. That led them towards Buddhahood, enlightenment.

But once they had become enlightened – they were fulfilling people's expectations because they wanted to be great enlightened Masters, prophets, messiahs – they could go on fooling with women. Buddha would not even look at a woman. What cowardliness! Buddha would not allow any woman close to him, she had to remain eight feet away.

Is this enlightenment? – so afraid, so shaky that even a woman coming close and you become afraid? This is repression, this is not enlightenment.

I want to declare to the whole world that unenlightened people can have only sexual relationships, which they call love. This is not right. They should stop calling it making love; they are simply making sex. Only an enlightened person can make love, because it is no more his need. He can be without it for years and not even for a single moment will he feel its need. But he can enjoy it as fun.

I can play cards; it is not a need. I can drink once in a while; it does not disturb my enlightenment. I can make love. I don't see…but it can disturb people's idea of enlightenment. That is their business. My enlightenment is not made of such fragile matter. It cannot be disturbed by anything. In fact, they have been asking whether enlightened people transcend sex, and I have sent the answer to them that the enlightened person finally transcends enlightenment, too.

And I have transcended enlightenment, too. Now I am again the same old ordinary man I was before all this round trip jet journey. I am back home.

I have passed through everything, all meditation, all enlightenment, and come back home, with new eyes, new clarity, new vision. It is almost like living continuously on LSD.

Why are so many women sannyasins?

"Because I am a man, and it is natural for women to be attracted to me. You can see my grey beard. This beautiful grey beard is the work of the ladies. The whole credit goes to them; otherwise, I would be having a black beard by this time. But so many ladies…but I don't bother about the color of the beard – the grey is so beautiful!

It seems the whole commune is run by women. Is there a particular purpose or strategy to that?

Certainly there is a particular strategy. Man has dominated women for centuries and forced the idea on them that they are the weaker sex, that they cannot do anything that man can do. They can do small homely things – that is their world. I want to destroy that idea completely. And you can see I have destroyed it.

My communes are run by women, and they have proved far superior to men in every possible way. My sannyasins are doing better business than any man can do, finding better bargains than any man can find. I wanted it to be a solid argument before the whole of humanity that women are not inferior, that if you give them a chance, they can even prove superior in many matters. At least they are going to prove equal.

And this is a strange way: to keep half of humanity in a downtrodden state. How much is the loss? – half of humanity means that women, if they were accepted equally, would have produced a Dostoevsky, a Turgenev, a Chekhov, a Gorky, a van Gogh, a Picasso, a Nijinsky. They may have proved a Buddha, a Jesus....Half of humanity! – it is a vast ocean to whom you have denied all possibilities of creation, expression. And you have behaved with women as if they are cattle, not human beings.

It is not going to be so in my commune.

But I do not agree with the liberation movement of women, because that is going in a reactionary way, creating hate for men – so much so that their basic approach is now that no woman should love any man, that they should all be lesbians.

Here, women are running the whole commune, everything, but no man who is here has ever felt that he is inferior. In fact, for the first time he feels a respect for women. He can see the dignity of women. Every day I receive letters from my male sannyasins asking, "What is happening? The commune sannyasins, the women, are becoming juicier and juicier, more and more graceful, more and more beautiful. And they are working so hard!"

For the first time, they have been given the chance to show their mettle. It is not a loss to men: they have found a companion, equal to themselves, side by side with them.

You were missing half of humanity.... And remember, because you have repressed that half, that half was trying to take revenge in every possible way. Of course, the woman has her own ways of taking revenge, and every man knows how the woman can take revenge. Every woman has been taking it for centuries. She will be nagging the husband, she will be spying on the husband. She will make the husband just a henpecked person.

All husbands are henpecked! I have never come across another category. Outside they may roar like lions, but that is not to be believed. Just look through the keyhole in their houses – the woman is roaring and the husband is hiding like a rat behind this chair, behind that table. It is natural, because if you repress their energy, somehow they are going to revolt against it. Here, men also are feeling tremendously relieved because no woman is nagging them.

Women's liberation is automatically men's liberation. Women's slavery is automatically men's slavery. They go together.

But this is only a transitory period.... Once I have proved my point, all around the world in different countries and different communes – even where I am not present – women will be on the top, once the point is proved and people can see.

Just four years ago, when we came here, we did not have a single dollar. My women sannyasins managed to purchase 126 square miles, an area three times bigger than New York. In four years we have poured almost two hundred million dollars into creating this oasis, and all has been managed by women. They have proved their mettle – and without insulting men, without putting them down, without in any way taking revenge. And they are not lesbians.

So it is, in fact, a tremendous revolution which is needed, which has been needed for centuries. And the sooner the whole world goes the way my communes function, the better, because I don't think women will be ready to use nuclear weapons in the third world war. Women won't want to kill; that is not part of their feminine psychology. They would like people to come closer, to be more loving.

If the world is run by women – and man can take his place more significantly in scientific research, in the service of life and creativity – and the governments and all other functional things are run by women, we will have a tremendous balance.

It will take a little time for women to produce Einstein and Picasso and Michelangelo. It will take a little time to bring a Mozart, a Leonardo da Vinci, because for thousands of years – in fact, for the whole history – they have been repressed, so it will need a little time. And once the repression changes into expression, it will be just like land which has been lying fallow for thousands of years gathering all kinds of fertilizers, rain water, and nobody cultivating it. When you cultivate it, it is going to give you a bumper crop. All other fields will look poor because they have been exploited every year; they have lost their energy to produce more.

The same is the situation of the human mind. The feminine mind has not been used, has not been allowed to function. If it is allowed, it may take a quantum leap. And it will be a blessing for all.

An intelligent woman, respected as equal to men in the society, will not become a lesbian because it is unnatural, absolutely unnatural. She will be heterosexual. And if all women turn to heterosexuality, we will be declaring war on homosexuality, too, because from where are they going to find men? They will chase the homosexuals to their deaths. They are chasing them here. We have got a few homosexuals, and they go on writing letters of complaint to me: "We are homosexuals and women are chasing us. We are not interested, but we do not want even to declare that we are homosexual." I say, "What can I do? Drop your homosexuality."

We can make a better world together. Men and women should be really half-and- half of a whole. There are qualities which men have and women do not have; there are qualities which women have and men do not have. Both together, the human being will be richer in every possible way.

Just think of a woman pilot dropping the atom bomb on Hiroshima and Nagasaki. I cannot conceive of it. If there had been a woman pilot, she would have refused to follow the order. She would have preferred to be shot dead, but she would not go to kill innocent people who have nothing to do with war.

And anyway, the war was ending. Germany was already on its knees, it was only a question of a week or two until Japan would surrender. There was no need of an atom bomb to create a hell for two beautiful cities.

I don't think a woman could have done that. A woman would rather have said, "You can court-martial me. You can shoot me. That seems to be easier than killing 100,000 people in one city, and 120,000 people in another city."

But what did the man pilot do? He dropped atom bombs on both the cities, came back to his base, had a good dinner, smoked the best cigar, joked with his friends, and went to sleep with a woman. In the morning when the journalists reached him, they asked the man if it had been very difficult for him to sleep having caused 220,000 people's deaths.

He said, "No, I slept beautifully. I did my duty, and once the duty was fulfilled – and it was a great duty to be fulfilled – I was feeling so happy that I managed to do it that I went to sleep with a woman and had a beautiful sleep."

Because it had been his orders, President Truman was asked early in the morning the next day, "How was your night?" He said, "I felt immensely relieved. Now there is no question of the war being prolonged any more. Not only that, we have made a point to the whole world: Don't come in conflict with America, otherwise the result will be more Hiroshimas, more Nagasakis" – not a single word of sympathy for those innocent people. They were civilians; they were not in military camps.

I have seen a picture that I cannot forget. One friend from Japan sent me a photograph of a small child, maybe eight or nine years old. His bag hanging on his shoulder, his books in the bag, he was going upstairs into the attic which was allotted to him as his place to study and sleep. And just when he was on the middle of the staircase, the atom bomb fell on Hiroshima. The boy simply got burned and got stuck into the wall – just a burned body with a burned bag, burned books.

When I saw that picture, I could not believe that man can do this to man. If a woman was president of America, I don't think this could have happened. Man has been given enough chance; now let the woman come up, and man can pour his energies more into scientific fields. Meanwhile, women will pick things up.

Yes, there is a certain basic strategy why my communes are run by women. But you can meet my male sannyasins. They are not in any way thought to be inferior. No woman is treating them as inferior in the way they have always treated women as inferior.

Perhaps it is that the male ego functions in that way: unless it makes somebody feel inferior, it is not satisfied. The woman functions in a different way: unless she feels somebody needing her, desiring her, she feels frustrated. A man's need seems to be to dominate, and the woman's need seems to be to be needed. That is a far better need – to be needed.

And I am doing an experiment, I am not a philosopher. I hate philosophy because it is simply a wastage of time. My commune is my experiment, and everything that I have envisioned has come true in it. The same can happen all over the world. This is a prototype.

You have also said, 'We are not missionaries.' Why? Don't you want more sannyasins?

We are not missionaries because we don't want anybody to be converted into sannyasins by us. We are available for anybody who wants to join us. He is welcome. We are receptive to anybody without conditions, but we are not going after people like the Christian missionaries or the Witnesses of Jehovah, forcing their Bible on you, knocking on your doors every morning. We are not going to knock on anybody's door.

Yes, we will spread the message – that's why I am talking with you. We will spread the message and if anybody wants to come with us and join our caravan, we are perfectly happy.

But this is a very different approach from missionaries. It is not aggressive, it is receptive; it is not masculine, it is feminine. That is the difference I make between these two psychologies. The male psychology is to go after the woman – that is the missionary. The woman's psychology is to escape from the missionary, but remain receptive. She never escapes too much. She always remains within the boundary so you can catch hold of her, but she lures by running away. By running away she becomes more beautiful; by running away she becomes a dream girl, a very homely girl can become a dream girl.

I trust in the feminine psychology because these missionary types of people around the world are aggressive. They are in a kind of war; very subtle, but it is a war. They are in politics – very subtle, but it is a politics of numbers. What has the pope got that he should be respected? I have seen his statements, which are not even his statements; his secretary goes on writing them. Even then, all those statements prove only a thick head. Nothing of importance ever comes out of these popes.

And the missionaries I have been in touch with in India were of a very high caliber – men like Stanley Jones – but the whole effort is how to convert people into Christianity. What did Stanley Jones do? He created a Christian ashram. To exploit Hindus, he used the word ashram. He managed his ashram just the way Hindus live in their ashrams: getting up early in the morning, going to the Ganges for the bath, then going to the church to pray. Every ritual of the Hindus was copied.

The only difference was that Krishna was missing, and there was Christ. And that is not much of a difference because there are scholars who say that Christ never existed, it is just another name for Krishna. I was looking at how Krishna can become Christ in Indian languages, and then I came across Bengali: in Bengali, Krishna is called Christo. Now that comes very close to Christ.

you published a mega photo-pictorial about that Commune of sannyasins in Sicily, do you remember it? It had been full of splendid images of beautiful, naked girls, covered only by the mala around their neck, and the photos of the meditations were beautiful too, and now we would like you to do some photos like those ones here!

"If you can manage to stay here a few days more until the place gets rid of all these visitors, after they have gone, we can all go to the naturist's lake, where we can lie totally naked under a tree, and you can make some of your beautiful pictures: what do you say?"

He told her that it was really a great proposal and confirmed he would stay at the Ranch a few days more; meanwhile he would go around looking for some beautiful girls, just to make the pictures a little juicier.

After three days he was taken to the lake in Sheela's car by her driver, along with Premal and a beautiful blonde friend of her, who was the daughter of Osho's lawyer, so at least he had two great models, and for the rest he would see later.

As soon as they arrived at the lake, Sheela immediately removed all her clothes, which seemed very strange to him, given her position of President of the Commune, and besides the fact that she was Osho's secretary, but since she was surrounded by a dozen beautiful girls, he started shooting happily. After half an hour he had made at least ten rolls of film, and the photos would not only be published in a huge reportage in 'Playmen', but were eventually seen all over the world thanks to his idea of sending copies of these pictures to four large photo agencies – one Japanese, one German, one Italian and one American.

Too bad that later (much later) he would come to know that Sheela had done this – amongst others even meaner things – with the only intention to defame the Commune, to show it in a bad light, or at least in a libertine light!

Later he would get to know that Osho hadn't appreciated this kind of publicity at all, but at this point it was already done, and all that he could do was to retrieve all these images from the four agencies and destroy them, which he did in no time.

Beloved Master,

I work in Europe as a journalist, and everybody is asking me about Sheela, "is it true that she betrayed her master?" the only answer I can give is, "I don't know." When they ask me what I feel about the recent events, I say that I feel tremendously grateful to Sheela, whatever she has done.

At this point, everybody thinks I'm crazy. My question is, do you? Please comment.

Certainly you are crazy – for two reasons. First, nobody can betray me. You can betray Jesus Christ because he asks faith from you. You can betray Gautam Buddha because he requires total surrender from you. How can you betray me? Faith can be betrayed; but I ask you to doubt, to be skeptical, to be rational, to be intelligent. How can you betray me?

Sheela has not betrayed me, she has betrayed herself. She has fallen in her own eyes, and she will live with all the crimes heavy on her heart for her whole life. As far as I am concerned there was no expectation. I have never demanded any commitment to me. I have never said that you have to be loyal to me: how can you betray me? This is the first point which proves you are crazy, when you say to people that you do not know. That means you do not know me and you do not know my work.

Secondly, you are telling people that Sheela has done great work and the commune should be grateful to her. She has certainly done great work, and the commune is grateful for all the good that she has done. But side by side she has been committing crimes. The commune cannot be grateful for those crimes – crimes ranging from killing people, attempts on people's lives, to bugging houses – and taping phone calls, which cannot be forgiven, because that is trespassing on individual privacy. And she was planning bigger crimes.

People are accustomed to see things as black or as white. In life it is very rare to find somebody who is absolutely black, or somebody who is absolutely white. People are different in degrees between these two polarities. But one thing has to be remembered, that you may be doing ninety-nine percent good work, but a single crime will destroy your credibility completely. Your good work cannot save you.

You are saying that the commune should feel grateful because Sheela burned the planning office of Wasco County? That she tried to poison one of the judges of Wasco County and one of the attorneys of Jefferson County? That she tried to kill Doctor Devaraj and Vivek, here in the commune? You are going to be grateful to her that she was lying to me continuously?

She bugged my room. She bugged almost the whole commune. Nobody was left their independence, their freedom of privacy. One hundred and forty-five rooms in the hotel were bugged. Nixon looks like a pygmy before her!

I have heard that she placed guards, thirty-two guards at my house, pretending that they had to be protection for me. But she ordered the guards not to speak to anybody who lives with me in the house – my physician, my kitchen people, my cleaners, my seamstresses, people who do everyday work for me.

The guards were ordered not to recognize that the people in my house even existed. They were not to smile at them, they were not to wave at them, they were not to talk with them; they were not to create any kind of contact with them.

One guard must have asked "Why? If we are there to protect the Master, then what is the point of this precaution?"

She said, "The precaution is absolutely necessary. One day you may have to shoot all those people who live there."

Yes, you should be grateful to her. She has made roads, she has made houses – but she has also stolen forty-three million dollars. Even before I came to America she had stolen three hundred thousand dollars, and managed in the court to show that that money had gone to Rajneesh Foundation. Now the court has decided one point four million dollars is to be returned to the person. And the money had never come to the Foundation. All those papers were bogus.

Yes, we have to be grateful to her – she was doing great work. She created this fascist group. She threw out every person who was capable, far more capable than herself, of making the commune better, more comfortable, less tedious. She harassed those people – the vice-chancellor of the university, the chancellor of the university, many psychotherapists, doctors. People who were competent like

Sushila, Makima – they had to leave. Not that they were leaving me, because they are all coming back. They had to leave simply because there is a limit to suffering humiliation, harassment.

And why should a person like Sushila be thrown out?...Because Sushila could have managed this commune far better than Sheela. But you are not aware of it, that when we came here, we had not a single dollar, and Sushila managed to collect thirty-three million dollars to start the commune with. Now, she was a dangerous woman in the eyes of Sheela, because she had done such a great job to get the commune started. This was the reward for her – to be thrown out from here!

In Australia Sushila was managing, with another sannyasin, a company which was capable of producing millions of dollars. And her idea was that that money would come to the commune. I prevented Sheela...I told her, "Don't interfere. They are working well." But seeing millions of dollars and the possibilities, she unnecessarily went there and forced Sushila from there too – in my name. She told her, "The Master says you should leave. I am going to take charge of the company."

That was a pure lie; I had told her just the opposite. When Sushila was in charge there, there was no problem. I have known Sushila for many more years than I have known Sheela. I know her love towards me, and I have great respect for her capacities. But when Sheela used my name, finally Sushila left. And the moment she left, the whole company fell into pieces. Those millions of dollars disappeared; the company is in a mess, under litigation. Yes, you are right, we should be grateful to her.

What has she done? – forced you to work twelve, fourteen hours a day, made you slaves. I told her, "I see people don't have good clothes; in winter they don't have enough clothes. So go and purchase clothes." Because I had said to, she purchased clothes, but they were never given to you; they were locked in a warehouse. Now they have been found.

So what you see is not always the whole truth; there is much more behind it.

She destroyed hundreds of centers around the world which I had created. People were running them with love, joy, and new sannyasins were coming through those centers. She destroyed those centers and concentrated sannyasins into six communes in Germany.

Everybody who has an ambition for power wants centralization. Those centers were independent, they were not under anybody's rule. They were spreading my love, my message to people on their own; there was no need to destroy them. But they were not under her.

In England Poonam had a beautiful commune – four hundred sannyasins were in the commune – and a beautiful place, lush green, with all the facilities. Sheela called Poonam here and took power over the commune, then sent all the sannyasins to European communes. And she was going to sell the commune property. She was destroying all the centers of England – she had almost succeeded. So you know only one side of the story, you don't know the other side.

And I understand your mind....The question is from an Italian sannyasin, Sarjano. Italy has lived under the authoritative rule of the popes, which ended finally in the fascism of Benito Mussolini. Somewhere deep in his mind there is no place for democracy and democratic values.

Yes, she did some good work – as a facade! But behind the facade, she was doing every kind of criminal activity. Two persons she placed in Desiderata declaring that they had positive AIDS tests, for the simple reason that they were not willing to do something that she wanted them to do. This was a punishment – you cannot find a better punishment. Their blood was either mixed with the AIDS virus, or changed, so the test came back from outside as positive. And after she left, their blood was checked again – they have no AIDS.

Do you see the criminality of the mind? Putting two people who don't have AIDS with eight other people who have AIDS is putting them in great danger. And they cannot say anything, because the report is coming from outside. But the blood that was sent must have been taken from the people who have AIDS.

Sheela's intimate, her assistant in crime, was Puja, who was trying to create the AIDS virus. I don't understand what is the need of creating the AIDS virus, of culturing the AIDS virus. Perhaps that would have been their next step: anybody who does not listen to them goes to Desiderata. Without killing him, they have killed him.

If you look at things...for example, Adolf Hitler : you will find many good things that he did. The superhighway that he has created across Germany is the only superhighway in the whole world of its kind. It is straight – few curves, few turnings; hence, you can go at any speed, there is no problem. He changed the old pattern of crossroads; there are no crossroads because that delays the speed. Roads meet, but first they run by the side of the road and slowly slowly merge with the road. So there are no crossroads. You can go very easily one hundred and twenty, one hundred and fifty miles an hour.

You can say he has done a great work – but the same man killed ten million people in the world. A person who wants to see the wholeness of any situation has to look from all sides, from all angles.

Sheela has done a few good things. She has made houses – but anybody could have done that, and in a far better way, not making you slave workers. She has made roads, which cannot be said to be very great, nothing to be compared with Adolf Hitler's superhighway. She was managing sufficient food for you – but she was also poisoning three thousand street people for twenty-one days continuously through their food, to keep them drugged so that they could vote for her. She wanted to take over the county.

I have been insistent that sannyasins should not be in any way involved with politics. I am absolutely against politics. I want the world to be freed from politics – it is a cancer of the society.

So I would like to say to you, first look at the whole picture, all the sides of it, before you say anything.

That's why I say you are certainly crazy.

From Bondage to Freedom Ch 27, Q 1

After he left, the dramatic events unfolded in Oregon that you must know about, and if you don't, you can read the book 'Passage to America' by Max Brecher, and you will know what incredible adventures Osho had to go through, how he was arrested, how he was dragged from one prison to another, how he got poisoned in one of these jails with Thallium, which is a substance that erodes the bones completely from the inside without leaving any trace, and finally narrates about the farce of his court hearings, and how he was expelled from the country forever.

***

CHAPTER 07

Osho Returns To India and Moves On To Nepal

After the events in the USA, Osho decided to finally return to India, and after a short stop in Delhi he chose as his destination Kulu Manali, a small remote town in the Himalayan mountains, where naturally he went immediately to see his master.

As mentioned before, there was this weekly newspaper called 'La Domenica del Corriere' in circulation, which had an editor who was a real gentleman, and who proposed for him to ask Osho only one or two initial questions, and then narrate the whole story, which would carry the signature of Osho, followed by the usual formula, 'Text compiled by Carlo Silvestro.'

Before leaving, he was approached by a journalist who was working in a TV program anchored by Enzo Biagi, perhaps the most famous of all Italian anchormen, who told him that his director would like very much to have an interview with Osho for his program, and since he was going to see him now, he should ask him personally if he was willing to be interviewed by this Biagi or not.

He promised to do so as soon upon arrival and in fact, once he reached Kulu Manali, where Osho had taken shelter in a fantastic resort in the middle of a forest, this was the first thing that he asked, after his emotional namaste.

He further explained to his Master that this Biagi was the most famous anchorman in Italy, that he had interviewed heads of states and most of the personalities on the planet, and that he seemed to him like a good fellow, truly honest, and with courage about his opinions, even if they were often going against the mainstream.

Osho told him instantly to bring him there and to be his interpreter, and meanwhile he got ready for the interview that he was supposed to have with him.

He started by giving him some information about the kind of magazine it was, of the incredible honesty and moral rigor of its editor, and about the fact that it was read by millions of people, until Osho laughingly stopped him and said,

> *I answer to you, Sarjano, then what you are going to do with your interview is none of my business, and you don't have to tell me all this, because I don't give a bit about newspapers, I'm just answering to you!*

He asked Osho then to explain shortly who he was, why he had gone to America, what had really happened there, and what were his plans now, but since Osho didn't know the expression 'in short', it took him two days to answer, in the sense that for two days in a row he was there to narrate his entire life for hours, with the result that in the end he had material not only for an article, but almost for an entire book!

When he transcribed his long interview it turned out to be more than fifty pages long. As he didn't know what to do with all this material he called the editor of the magazine, asking him if he was ready to publish Osho's story in two separate chapters.

The editor told him that this was not possible, that it didn't match the policy of their paper, hence he had the hard task to chop that massive interview until it would be reduced to a story no longer than ten, twelve pages!

He thought that this was really a cruel job for him, almost painful – to cut the words of his Master in such a way, but in the end he almost managed it and was capable to condense everything on twenty pages. More than that he couldn't do, not even with all his effort and good will, and the editor told him that he could understand and he could just send those twenty pages, and he would have taken care of it personally.

He sent this manuscript then, telling the editor to be gentle in completing the cutting work, because he himself couldn't do more than this, for he had already chopped too many words from the mouth of Osho, and the rest would be his job!

Somehow the editor managed to cut this article in an intelligible and sensitive manner, and published it with the title "Who is Afraid of Me?" – written by Osho – and followed by the usual formula – 'text compiled by Carlo Silvestro'.

The article resulted in being so beautiful and so intense that the Milanese sannyasins made a huge poster out of it, posted it everywhere on the walls of the city.

Once he came back to Italy, he got another visit from the emissary of Enzo Biagi, to whom he reported that the Master had given his consent to the idea of being interviewed by him, so he was invited immediately to meet the anchorman, in order to define with him the time and logistics of their departure.

The next day, Biagi and his troupe went to the Indian Embassy to ask for the necessary visas, specifying in their request that they were going to India to interview the famous Guru Osho; after one week they found out that the visas had been denied everybody, Biagi included!

He went out of his mind from this surprise, and anger, because he understood that the American Government was still doing everything in their power to isolate Osho from the rest of the world, even putting undue pressure on every Indian Embassy in the world, so that not only his visa would be denied, but denied even to all of those who want to meet him!

He immediately proposed to Biagi to make a big scandal about this ugly story, to write about it in every newspaper, to talk about it on television, and to expose all this medieval fascist story…but Biagi asked him to cool down and not to create any trouble, because he knew Andreotti, the Foreign Minister at the time, and that he would have a talk with him in order to solve the whole question one way or another.

While Biagi was involved in his mediation, he had informed Osho about what was happening with the Indian Embassy, with the result that the Master, who had already had enough of India and its attitude, proposed to everybody to quit and move to Kathmandu.

It happened in fact that in those days the entry visas of all those disciples who were taking care of him, such as his doctor, caretaker, driver, etcetera, were expiring, and when they went to the local authorities to ask for a simple three month extension, the visas were denied to everybody; hence all these people were supposed to leave the country within 48 hours!

The story of Biagi, plus this latest injustice, convinced Osho to leave his own country, and after two days he was in Kathmandu with all of his court.

Meanwhile Biagi, when he got to know that the Master had moved to Nepal, asked for a visa to Nepal for all his crew, which naturally was accorded to them immediately, and the next week they were all flying to Delhi.

In order to have some rest along their trip, they decided to spend the night in Delhi, from where they would leave the next morning for Kathmandu. They took a taxi to The Intercontinental, one of the most hip hotels in town, where they met half an hour later at the restaurant to have a late dinner, and possibly to make a plan for the next day.

While everybody was in their rooms to refresh themselves before dinner, he thought that it would be a good idea to call an old girlfriend living in Delhi, because she had always asked him to give her a call were he ever in town. He invited her for dinner at the restaurant of the hotel, or after for some coffee or a glass of wine. The woman arrived in a car with her husband, who after having dropped her off left quietly without a word and left her there to chat with her Italian friend.

When Biagi saw the woman coming out of his room the next morning and realized that she had spent the night with him, the first time they were alone he said: "I really like this sannyasin philosophy! Her husband has brought her here to you, then he went home to sleep, knowing that his wife would have been staying with you all night…but you know, you orange people are really peculiar!"

The next morning they took the first flight to Kathmandu, and after a couple of hours they were already in front of the hotel reception of the immense Crowne Plaza Kathmandu-Soaltee where Osho was staying with all his people. The hotel was truly mega-galactic, and the rooms were probably costing a fortune, but it was RAI TV who would pay the bills, so he chose for himself a spacious room on the third floor, just opposite the one of the Master. By doing that, he sometimes managed to meet Osho in the elevator, when he was descending for a walk in the immense garden to greet all the people that were rushing to Kathmandu to see him.

Biagi meanwhile was acclimatizing himself with the place and was getting ready for his interview, and he was doing it with great interest and participation, because it was clear that he didn't have any preconceived ideas in mind, neither any theories to prove, but he was approaching the meeting with the Master in total innocence and humbleness, 'in wonder', as we say among us!

The first question is, what is your teaching?

I do not have any teaching at all. I am not a teacher, in the sense that I don't give any philosophy of life, any discipline to live, and programs to follow. I have a certain approach to life which I share with my friends; my approach begins with de-programming. That is a key word as far as I am concerned.

Initiation into my friendship means initiation into de-programming. Everybody is programmed by birth – either as Christian or Hindu or Jew or Mohammedan.

The child is born innocent, but he is burdened very soon with hundreds of concepts, and he lives with those concepts his whole life. This is living a borrowed life; it is not authentic, it is not sincere, because it is not yours.

You have not discovered any of those things that you are trying to live. So my first thing is to help you get rid of all your conditionings. Those who come to me, if they are Christians, will no more be Christians; if they are Hindus will no more be Hindus; if they are Mohammedans will no more be Mohammedans. I simply give them back their innocence, their humanity, their purity, their individuality.

So my basic work is destroying their conditionings. And it is a very simple work, because none of their conditioning is based on logic, intelligence. It is all superstitious. They have been provided with certain logical structures, but those logical structures are all phony. They are not authentic. For example, all the religions are based on the greatest lie in the world – God. No religion has been able to prove logically, scientifically, has not been able to give any evidence, and yet they go on burdening every child that comes on the earth with the idea of God. It is very simple to take away the idea; I just have to show to the person that your idea is enforced upon you. It is not your intelligence that has accepted it; it is your innocence which has been corrupted by your parents, by your teachers, by your priests, and all logic that they have given to you is phony.

For example, all the religions say that the God is needed, otherwise who will create existence? Existence is there, and there must be a creator. Without a creator, how can there be creation? But they stop there. An intelligent person will go a little further, he will ask, "If this is the case, then who created God?"

God is there, and he has no creator. Then where has your logic gone? Existence needed a creator, and the creator himself needs no creator. This is not logic, this is just fallacious exploitation of human innocence. A child cannot argue. He simply accepts it.

I am reminded of a beautiful anecdote. A professor of philosophy in the University of Paris was a little eccentric, which is not rare. Professors of philosophy are rarely not eccentric. And he was the head of the department and used to make statements which were absurd, and one day he went a little too far. He began his lecture with the statement "I am the greatest man in the whole world."

This was too much. One student stood up; he said, "You are a great philosopher, a great logician, hence we ask you to prove this statement. Give us the logical background." The professor was absolutely ready, willingly, happily. He spread the map of the world on the board, and he asked the students, "What country do you think is the greatest in the world?"

Obviously they all said, "France." And the professor laughed. The students could not understand why he was laughing.

And then he asked, "What do you think is the greatest, most sacred place and city, in France?"

And they all said, "Paris, the most beautiful." And he laughed again. The students were feeling a little uncomfortable. Perhaps he is leading into some unknown logical conclusion. But still they were not aware where he is leading. And then he asked, "What is the greatest thing, the greatest place in the greatest city of the greatest land in the world?"

And they all said, "Of course, the University. The temple of wisdom."

The students said, "Of course the greatest place in Paris is the University."

And the professor laughed again, and asked, "Which department is the greatest in the university?"

Now the students were caught. They knew that he has managed a phony argument. Looks like logic. But it is not logic. They had to say, "Of course it is the philosophy department."

And the professor had a hearty laugh and he said, "Now do you understand why I said 'I am the greatest man in the world'? I am the head of the department of philosophy."

All arguments about God, about heaven, about hell, are just like that. My work is to destroy the phony structure of logic and your rocks simply start disappearing, your mythologies start disappearing, leaving you a pure space. And from that pure space arises your individuality. You are no more part of the crowd.

That's my basic work – to make you an individual, not just a cog in the wheel, not just a part of the crowd. To give you an integrity and to give you a freedom of the soul, that you are no more bound into any slavery called Christianity or Hinduism or Judaism; for the first time you are just yourself. And now it is your search for truth, your inquiry into truth. And remember, all the answers that have been given by others to you, can never be a salvation to you. Only your own answer found by your own hands, by your own search, can deliver you from ignorance, from misery, from anguish.

I don't have a teaching. I have only a device.

I am not a teacher, I am a master.

Teachers have teachings, the masters have a certain device and methodology to transform people.

Why have you been in jail in America, and forced to leave?

Why was Socrates poisoned? Why was Jesus crucified? Why were many attempts made on the life of Buddha? They have not done much to me. They have simply arrested me without any arrest warrant, without showing any cause why they are arresting me, without allowing me my birthright to call my attorneys.

They did not answer me; their only answer was twelve loaded guns around me.

But I enjoyed the whole experience. They were far more kind to me than people were to Socrates; they did not poison me. They were far more kind to me than people were to Jesus; they did not crucify me. They simply harassed me for twelve days, from one jail to another jail. And it does not matter at all to me. In fact, it was a great experience. I always wanted to visit hell, though hell does not exist. Yet America provided me the opportunity to visit it. And after twelve days… because there was no case against me. I had not done any harm to anybody, I had not committed any crime against anybody; my only crime was that I had created a commune of five thousand people who were so happy and so rejoicing that their joy and their blissfulness caused jealousy among the neighbors, the politicians, and particularly the Christians.

Christians have been coming to the East converting millions of people to Christianity. This was the first time there was somebody who had taken thousands of Christians out of their fold, and they were absolutely helpless. And the people that they have converted in the East are not educated, are not cultured, are not of the higher strata of society. The people that Christians have converted in the East are beggars, aboriginals, primitives, orphans, people dying on the streets. They have not been able to convert a single intellectual, a single intelligent person in the whole East.

Naturally they were very much offended, because I was not converting beggars, I was not converting orphans, I had converted their best minds; I had converted only the intelligentsia. And I was not converting the intelligentsia into another religion either, which is easier – to take one toy from you and give you a new toy.

Everybody is happy with something new. The old was rotten, getting dirty, was almost dilapidated, has been used for many centuries by many people, and it is beautiful to get a fresh, new toy. But I was not converting those people into another religion. I was simply deprogramming them and they had no answers.

So it was Christianity behind the politicians which pressed them that I should be thrown out of America. It was simply a question of the poverty of Christian theologians. Otherwise they should have come up front. I was ready to argue about everything.

Stop. We are changing the reel.

Are you a Christian?

My being sent out of America is simply an indication of the poverty of Christian theologians. If they had guts they would have invited me to have an open encounter. But they knew that they don't have any logic to support them. So they tried a criminal way to throw me out of the country. But that is not going to stop me. Wherever I am, I will be doing the same. They cannot throw me out of this planet.

So it is simply the defeat of Christianity , defeat of the great powers and the great nation, United States of America, that they could not manage a single individual who was standing against them – not by any armed force, but by simply proposing a new way of looking at things. They wanted to remain blind. And this is my whole life's experience, that I am selling candles in the city of the blind.

It is not their fault that they get angry with me, it is my own fault. But I am helpless; I have to commit it, and I am going to commit it again and again, until my last breath.

How have you and your community managed to become so rich?

It did not manage to become rich. Only the rich are attracted to me, because only the intelligent are attracted to me. You have to understand a certain hierarchy of values. You never ask, "Why is a poor man not attracted to the paintings of Picasso?" You never ask, "Why is a poor hungry beggar not interested in the music of Mozart?" But you continuously ask why only rich people, cultured people, intelligent people, educated people are attracted towards me.

Religion is the ultimate luxury. And of course those who can afford it will be attracted towards it. It is not for the poor. The poor do not need religion. In the name of religion the poor have been given only opium, consolation. In the name of religion, something pseudo, something false, has been provided to the poor.

True religion is not possible for the hungry man, for the man who is dying from sickness, disease, old age. He cannot be interested in the flights of consciousness. He wants something to eat, he wants some shelter to live in, he wants some clothes. It is too cold and he is naked and you are talking about meditation, you are talking about consciousness? You are talking about how to attain the ultimate peaks of your being? It is simply absurd.

So it is not that my people have managed to be rich. In fact whoever comes to me is already rich. That's why he comes to me. Religion starts only when you are bored with your richness, when you have everything that money can provide and still you find you are empty. You have everything that you can possess. And still you find that something is missing which money cannot give to you, and you have to find some other way.

When money comes to the end of its capacities, it has given you everything, you soon start getting fed up and bored. That is the point where either you commit suicide, or you start a search that can bring you to a man like me. So I simply attract the rich. And I don't provide any opium; so my way of life is not for the poor.

How do you explain your charismatic effect on people?

It's very simple; because I am not a politician. The politician says whatever the people want to hear.

I speak about whatever is my experience. I don't care whether you like it or you don't like it. When I am speaking, I am speaking with my whole heart – irrespective of your reaction – my simplicity, my honesty. I am not in any way trying to influence you.

There is no desire to convert you. All that I am doing is enjoying sharing my experience. You will find people in the world who are all interested to convert you. You will not find people who are not interested in converting you, who are simply interested in sharing their heart and their soul with you.

So I don't know what charisma is, because I have never come across any charismatic personality in the whole world.

I am not interested in influencing anybody. I am tremendously happy to simply share my vision with you. Perhaps my sincerity, my truth, my authority behind it, becomes a charismatic influence on you. And when I say my authority, I do not mean that I am an authoritative man. There is a vast difference which has to be remembered.

An authoritative man always has a borrowed authority. When people say, "Listen to me, because my word is God's word," this is the voice of the authoritative man. He is using God's name to enforce his authority. When the Pope speaks, he is speaking in the name of Jesus Christ. He is authoritative.

I am not authoritative, because I am not speaking in anybody's name. No God to support me, no Holy Bible to support me. It is simply my own experience. That gives me tremendous authority. Perhaps all these qualities together – the authority behind my word, my own experience, no desire to influence you, my sincerity to expose the truth, and my obligation to you – make you listen to me. You are not obligated to me. I am obligated to you, that you gave me a chance to unburden my heart. It is something like a raincloud when it is full of rainwater. It wants to shower somewhere.

It is just like when a rose opens its petals it wants the breeze to come and take its flavor, its fragrance, to faraway places. I am obligated to you.

Perhaps that's what impresses you as charismatic. Otherwise I am a very simple man. I don't do miracles; I don't make wine out of water, because I am not a criminal. That is a crime, to create drugs out of water. I don't pretend to be the only begotten son of God. I don't say that you have to believe in me. On the contrary I say that I will provoke you to think, to doubt, to be skeptical. Because I know that if you doubt, if you inquire, you are bound to find the truth that I have found.

It is only people who are afraid of their truth who force you to believe, who say "Have faith." Because they are afraid if you inquire you may not find anything of what they are saying. Their insistence on faith simply proves that they themselves don't know. Otherwise, why be afraid of doubt and inquiry?

My invitation is to inquire. Because I know whatever I am saying is there within you, just as it is within me.

It has been said that in your communes there is limitless sexual activity. Is that true? And what is sex, and what is love?

In the first place, there can never be limitless sexual activity. Biology prevents it. It is not within your hands. How many times can you make love in one night? You will know that it cannot be limitless. There is a limit, and it comes very soon.

It is absolutely absurd to say that in my community there is limitless sexual activity. In fact, there are so many activities going on that nobody has time for sexual activity. And I am not for repression; that does not mean that I am telling you to be licentious. When I say, "Don't repress" I simply mean, "Listen to the body. It has a wisdom of its own." When you are eating, can you eat limitlessly? You know perfectly well that your body gives you clear cut indications when to stop.

And if you listen to the body, you will be healthier.

There are two kinds of extremists: one who will fast, will not listen to the body saying "I am hungry", and the other who will go on eating when the body is crying "I am overloaded. Stop!" In America I came to know that there are thirty million people who are dying because they have no food, no clothes, no shelter. And another thirty million – the exact number, thirty million – people who are dying because they are eating too much. Now we must be living in an insane world. Just one simple thing has to be decided. Sixty million people are dying from a simple misunderstanding.

Thirty million starving and thirty million overeating: sixty million people can be saved within a minute.

Just what do you do with your food? What do you do with your thirst? You don't go on drinking. You know when your thirst is gone: you stop. Then why has sex become a problem? In my commune, sex is as natural a thing as everything else. Neither too much nor the other extreme. Just the middle way, the golden medium.

And you are asking me "What is sex, and what is love?"

Sex is something biological. All animals are sexual beings. Only man has the privilege to have something higher than sex. Not just the meeting of the bodies but the meeting of two souls. That's what love is.

Love can contain sex. Sex cannot contain love.

Sex is a small thing. Love is vast and tremendous. It can be without sex too; it is not necessary that a love relationship should have sex. In fact, my experience is that the more you go higher than sex and you start enjoying a spiritual communion with a friend, with a woman, with a man – from that state of communion sex seems to be so far away, so much in the hands of blind biology. Love seems such a freedom, and such a growth, that it goes on growing, so that you may not even like to get down to the dark valleys of sexuality.

But I am not preventing it. I am simply saying that as love grows deeper, sex becomes shallower. When love reaches its optimum, sex disappears.

It seems so childish. Just think of yourself, just put yourself a little far away, and look at yourself making love. And you will be surprised – is it you doing all these gymnastics? Stupid, idiotic.

The real transformation of sexual energy is love. But it happens only if you allow sex a natural acceptance. It does not happen to the monks of all the religions.

They are the loveless people. They cannot love, because they have not even gone into sex. They have avoided the basic energy which can be transformed into love. So they may talk about love but their talk is just bullshit. They don't understand anything about love – and they cannot understand. You have to go step by step; and your body is your first step.

You cannot ignore it; it is so basic, so very rooted in existence. Ignoring it is simply committing suicide. Ignoring it means perversion. So all the monks of all the religions, all the nuns of all the religions are perverted as far as sex is concerned. They will have to find some way. They will become homosexuals, they will become lesbians. And that is an ugly state.

And religions have forced people to become homosexuals, lesbians, make love to animals – and we still go on respecting celibacy. It should be declared a crime.

Nobody can be celibate, because that is against nature.

You have to learn acceptance of nature, and through that acceptance is transcendence. By being in a sexual relationship, perhaps the relationship and the intimacy will create something new, which is love. And as love grows, sex starts sinking, because it is the same energy that is changing; it is moving into a higher form. When love comes to its maturity, sex disappears. That is true celibacy. But you have not done anything for it to happen; it has come to you as a gift from nature.

When celibacy comes as a gift from existence, it is tremendously beautiful; but when you impose it upon yourself you create homosexuality, and then one day you will create AIDS. Just the other day, somebody was telling me that Mother Theresa is opening a hospice in New York for AIDS patients. And the person told me, "She is doing a great service to humanity."

I said, "This is nonsense. These are the people who created AIDS. So if they

are opening hospitals, nursing homes, it is simply repentance. It is not service. The whole Vatican should be converted into a hospice for all the AIDS patients, because these are the people who created it. And it is not service; it is simply repentance."

I simply teach acceptance of your nature; and through acceptance, immense transformations happen. But they come on their own accord. You don't have to force them.

Love has a beauty. Sex is ugly. Sex is something like the roots of a rose bush.

Those roots are going to be ugly. Love is like the roses; although those roots are continuously sending energy to the roses, it is the roots and their energy that are becoming roses. So I will not say to you, "Cut your roots because they are ugly."

Do not cut the roots; help them to be strong, nourish them, and you will have thousands of roses blossoming.

And that will be what I call love.

What is your recipe for happiness?

Every child is born happy. Every child is born innocent and beautiful. And then something happens; all those beautiful children get lost. All their innocence is destroyed. All their joy is turned into misery.

Just look at a child, collecting seashells on the beach. And he is happier than the richest man in the world. What is his secret?

That is my secret too.

The child is in the moment, enjoying the sunshine, the salty air of the beach, the beautiful expanse of the sands. He is here now. He is not thinking of the past; he is not thinking of the future. And whatever he is doing, he is doing totally, intensely; he is so absorbed within it he has forgotten everything.

And that is the simple secret of happiness. Whatever you are doing, don't let the past move your mind; don't let the future disturb you. Because the past is no more, and the future is not yet.

To live in memories, to live in the imagination, is to live in the non- existential. And when you are living in the non-existential, you are missing that which is existential. Naturally you will be miserable, because you will miss your whole life.

All the time you are simply missing. And you are never given two moments together by existence; it gives you only one moment at a time. And that one moment either can be lived, or can be missed. There are two ways to miss it: let the past burden you, let the future attract you, and it is gone. You are losing the real for the unreal. And this is the whole misery of humanity.

All that I try to help my friends understand is to live in the present. Just now, there is no misery, no suffering, no anguish. Just move away from the present, and you have gone into something unreal. And the unreal is bound to be miserable.

Reality is ecstatic; and to join with reality the only way is not to miss the present moment. And if you know just the taste, once, how it feels to be in the present – looking at the sunrise or the sunset… Just be there, so that you can have a little taste of the present, and you will be surprised that you have the key all the time with you. The master key that can open all the doors of the mysteries of life; its ecstasies, its beauties.

You don't need a Jesus Christ to lead you into paradise; you are capable of being in paradise right now. Because paradise is not somewhere up above. It is somewhere here.

I am reminded; there was a great atheist and he had written in his sitting room the motto of his whole philosophy: God Is Nowhere. So anybody coming to visit him was bound to see it in gold letters on the wall; it was impossible to miss it. And then, naturally, the discussion would start. And then a child was born to the atheist, and the child was growing up. He was learning the alphabet and he was learning slowly to make words. And one day he was sitting on the lap of his father, the great atheist, and he started reading the sentence on the wall.

He could read 'God is' but 'nowhere' was too big a word; he could not make it. So he cut it into two pieces. He read "God is now here." The father was shocked. He had never thought about it, that 'nowhere' can be also read as 'now here.' And it is said that this disturbed his whole atheist philosophy. He started thinking of 'now here' and the implications of it. Not that you will find God if you are now here....

Not that you will find God now, here; but you will find something more than God. You will find godliness. That is my word for the ultimate experience of bliss.

Remember these two words 'now here' and you know the secret of ultimate happiness. There has never been any other secret, and there will never be another secret. This is it.

And it is so simple, and so easily possible for every human being. You need not be part of any church, any organization. You need not carry a Holy Bible , or the Vedas or the Gita or Koran. All that you have to do is just have a little understanding of your own mind, its function, how it functions.

Your mind is never in the present, and time is always in the present; so time and mind never meet. This is the misery – that you are missing the train every moment; and you will go on missing, your whole life.

One great mystic was dying. And his disciples were surrounding him, and they asked him, "What is your last message, Master?"

The dying master opened his eyes, and indicated towards the roof of his small hut. A squirrel was running on the roof making noise. All the disciples looked at the roof. For a moment, there was utter silence.

The master said, "This is my whole life's message: Be in the moment." How beautiful it is just to listen to the squirrel on the roof and not to bother about anything else. And he said, "Can I die now?" And he died, with a smile on his lips, with bliss on his face; but even in that last moment his message was just to be here now.

That is my message.

The Last Testament, Vol. 5, Ch 19

The meeting was in fact extraordinary, and they appeared like two good old friends who hadn't seen each other since a long time; it was truly touching.

Osho had been informed about Biagi's by-pass operation, and took care immediately to ask him how his heart was, to which Biagi replied laughingly, "The heart is always young!" Then the interview commenced, which by now is history, and in the end they all retired to their rooms to watch the footage that had been shot and to decide if it would be necessary to shoot some more.

According to Biagi, it was the case, because the whole interview had happened between two people sitting in a room – since he himself was just sitting in a corner, out of the camera's way, to translate the questions of the Italian journalist, and all in all the whole shoot looked a bit static. It was decided to have another shoot of Osho in the garden while walking with Biagi, just to give a little more movement and respite to the interview.

He very much liked the idea that Biagi wanted to have a walk with the Master, even though nobody knew yet that Osho not only accepted the idea, but that when he was in the garden he took immediately the journalist by his hand!

It was exactly at this moment that something happened to Biagi.

Since he was a very sensible person, he had immediately realized that he was talking with someone very different compared to all the personalities that he had interviewed in the past, but couldn't figure out what this difference was… Biagi told him later that he had felt the diversity of this man, his immense charisma, but he was incapable of placing it anywhere! He said further that when the Master had touched his hand, he had felt a great shock inside, and

something of him, his most secretive part, had answered to the invitation…

"But it must have been a dream, an open-eyed vision, an instant of vertigo" – and by saying so, Biagi was confessing that he was denying the whole experience that had befallen him, with all the rationalizations possible and with a massive dose of what we call in psychoanalysis 'remotion'. When he finally returned to Italy after a few weeks, the program had just been aired and he called Biagi to compliment him for a beautiful job done, but the journalist diminished himself by simply saying, "I just did my job!"

He asked Biagi if he could at least do something in order to get a visa for Osho, since he had mentioned knowing the Foreign Minister well, but Biagi answered that he was about to leave for another mission, and that he had no time.

"But as you have met him and know him now, you can at least say to everybody that Osho is not a dangerous individual," he told him impetuously.

"I've only seen him for a couple of days; you can't say that I know him! – replied Biagi almost annoyed.

And so this feeling of an absurd 'remotion' surfaced again, and he felt even a little pain for this man who had just met a living Buddha, and something inside of him had absolutely recognized him, but he had to deny his experience at any cost.

Too many things to reexamine, too many certainties to put under judgment… better to forget all about it, better….

Once he finished the work for which he had come, Biagi went back to Italy. But he decided to stay there with Osho at least a couple more weeks, irrespective of the cost of the hotel, now he had some money in his pocket and he could easily afford it. Italian RAI had given him 15 million of the old lire, for his job of taking Biagi to interview his Master, hence he could have squandered all the money he had just earned, in spite of the fact that this type of old farmer from central Italy had warned him, with his patriarchal wisdom, of not spending all the money that he had earned by remaining any longer in this super-expensive hotel!

This famous anchorman was really a great guy, and when Osho died a few years later he wrote a loving epitaph called "A Little Flower on His Grave", which was published in an alternative magazine. In this piece he narrated his trip with Biagi to Kathmandu, of Biagi's unexpected love for Osho, of his rationalizations and of his escape...

In reality he would have liked to call his piece "You'll be back!", but he was afraid that hardly anybody would understand it!

He then asked for an interview for Corriere della Sera:

Osho, you never stop surprising us. How come you decided to go on a world tour?

It is very simple. People don't live in the moment. They plan for the future. Hence they are surprised.

I live in the moment; I don't know about the next moment. So it is not only that I surprise others; I surprise myself too. I keep the coming moment open, unplanned. I don't know what is going to happen. This way, life is juicier, more adventurous, more spontaneous. This way one is always young, never gets old. This way even death is a surprise, not a shock.

One enters into death too with great joy, to discover something. And if the whole life has been a moment to moment journey, discovery, then death cannot be otherwise. Because death is not the end of life; it is the very culmination, the very peak, the height.

When can we expect you in Italy?

Any time. Perhaps I may start my world tour from Italy.

Do you expect to be welcomed in Italy by the Pope and the Vatican?

Certainly. In fact because of them, I am going to be welcomed in Italy. The Pope and his company have exploited Italy for centuries and I don't think Italians are dumb or retarded. They can see the parasite in the Pope.

I am going to be welcomed by the intelligentsia of Italy, by the youth of Italy, and by all those who are bored and fed up with the rotten Christianity that the Pope represents. I have always felt Italy to be my country, more than any other country. It does not belong to the Pope. It belongs to me. In fact, Jesus Christ was crucified by the Italians. They should do the same with the Pope.

It is not a coincidence that Italy became the citadel and the center of Christianity, because Jesus Christ was crucified by the Italian governor general, Pontius Pilate in Judea. It created guilt in Italy. And out of that guilt, Christians have exploited Italy. They destroyed the Roman Empire, they destroyed the whole glory of the country. They destroyed its fundamentals of philosophy. The Roman philosophy of life is very close to me, because it was the philosophy of a pagan. It was not devoted to a god, a fiction. It was not devoted to the other world – another fiction. It was basically devoted to man, his life, his joys. It was a very earthly and pragmatic world view. That's why I say Italy belongs to me, not to the Pope.

The German government has already stated that they don't want you in their country. Why do you think they are so afraid of a man they have never seen before?

Every government is afraid. And every organized religion is afraid, for the simple reason that I am against all kinds of establishments. I am against the whole past of humanity. I want to begin its history anew, fresh. The past has been ugly, and the responsibility goes to the politicians and the priests. And I don't want it to be repeated again in the future.

Naturally, I am the greatest enemy of establishment today in the world. They are afraid because they don't have any argument against me. Whatever I am saying is so true that they cannot deny it. They are aware that their intelligentsia, their young people, are going to understand.

Germany particularly is afraid. The reason is Adolf Hitler, and what he has done to the world. He is the politician par excellence. With Adolf Hitler, Germany was completely disappointed in politicians, and the politicians know perfectly well that the German youth is seeking and searching for some substitute for them. They also know that even in faraway countries, wherever I have been, German youth has been reaching me.

Their concern is that if I come to their country, I can change the whole mind of their youth – which is the future. I can manage very easily to turn their youth against them. They can see that even without going to Germany, I have the largest number of my sannyasins in Germany – and I have not been there. Once I am there, it will be difficult to find a young man who is not a sannyasin. So those cowardly politicians are trying to prevent me from entering Germany. They don't understand me. This helps my work. This makes their weakness clear, and brings it into the open – and loudly.

Once I have reached Europe, my sannyasins in Germany are going to sue the government in the court because it is absolutely illegal to prevent me. I have never been in the country. Naturally I have not committed any crime in the country. They don't have anything against me. And to prevent a person who has not done anything in your country, has not even entered your country, is simply absurd.

The reason they have given as to why they don't want me to enter the country is so lousy that it makes one laugh. They have said that they don't want me to enter Germany because I am not going to be a help to their country. Then they should make a general law that only people who are certain to be a help to their country can enter Germany. And before I have even entered, how have they managed to find out that I cannot be a help to their country? I have thousands of sannyasins there; I am a help to them. They are a part of their country; they want me to be in the country. They cannot be deprived.

They have been asking me if they should go to court against the government. I have been telling them, "Just wait. First let me be in Europe, then sue the government. With me in Europe it will be a totally different scene. Then all the sannyasins of Europe will be of tremendous help to you; and you will feel stronger, and the government will feel weaker. We are going to defeat them, and I am going to enter Germany. Whether they change their law or not, it does not matter."

Several of your sannyasin friends have suggested that you come to the border of Germany and Austria, and they will come in their thousands and thousands to visit you and dance on the border, so that the German government will be exposed all over the world. Would you like this to happen?

I am going to do many things: that is one of them. I am going to call them to the border to be with me, and declare to the world news media that if our master cannot come to Germany, Germany can come to our master. And I have seen the American jails. I would love to see the German jails too. If they don't change the law, I am still going to enter Germany and show the world how your so-called democratic governments are behaving with absolutely innocent people.

You have attacked all the religions of the world, politicians, philosophers, scientists, gurus, intellectuals, the Pope, Mother Teresa, even Gandhi, the media, the educational system, and the whole world as such.

Is everything wrong in this world? Is there anything we can save?

It looks a little bit strange when I say everything in one stroke. It looks strange because you don't understand that all things in the world are part of an organic unity. They are not separate things, so it may be possible that if you take a fragment, it will look good and worth saving. But it is dangerous. It has been part of a poisonous unity. To save it can pollute your future.

For example, if the politicians have been corrupt, if the priests have been corrupt, if the educationists have been corrupt, who creates your intellectuals? The education system, the theologians, the philosophers, the political ideologies, they are all part of your intellectuals – their minds are conditioned by them. You cannot save the intellectuals. Saving them you will be saving much of the priests, the politicians, the educationists.

Even your paintings, howsoever beautiful, are influenced. Your sculpture is influenced. You can see in the Middle Ages, even your greatest artists, people like Michelangelo, have worked for their whole life in the churches and cathedrals, just painting the stories about Jesus which are all fictitious. Your sculptors have been in the hands of the priests, making statues of Jesus, Buddha, Mahavira, to be worshipped. Your musicians have also been part of this course of history.

Your philosophers have been part of theology, part of the courts; none of your philosophers have the guts to expose the religions and their patent lies. Even men like Kant, Hegel, giants in the world of philosophy, are completely silent about Christianity. Whom are they cheating? They are showing their cowardliness, and they are trying to propound a philosophy that somehow supports religion, the vested interests, the establishment. They are not revolutionaries.

Everything is entangled with everything else. Society is an organic unity. And when you want to make clean the whole human race, the whole human consciousness, it is better to drop it all and begin absolutely fresh, rather than choosing pieces – which may look good as pieces, but they have been part of a poisonous system for centuries, and they carry that poison. They may destroy your whole plan for the future. And what is the need?

We can create a new man, we can create a new art, and we can create new architecture. If we can create a new religiousness, a new philosophical understanding of life, then we can create new art, new poetry, new paintings. Why not get rid of the old, so that you are not chained to the dead?

It is something like when your father dies, your mother dies. Your father had beautiful eyes. They were real, alive, in the organic unity of your father's body. But if you dig out those eyes and save them…

It is not that they were rebels, revolutionaries, that they were against the past. No. They were trying to take help from the past so that they could have the authority of that past. They wanted to be authoritative. The desire to belong to the past is the desire to be authoritative.

I don't want to be authoritative. And there is a difference to be remembered between these two words, authoritative and authority. The authoritative person is always deriving his authority from ancient scriptures, traditions, prophets, and all that. He is not certain enough about his own experience to be an authority. He needs props and supports.

My experience is enough unto itself. It is an authority in itself, without anybody's support. In fact, their desire to belong to a tradition, their effort, the way Jesus is trying continuously to persuade them that "I am your Messiah", the way Buddha is trying to persuade the Jainas that "I am your twenty-fourth Tirthankara" is pitiable. That simply shows these people don't rely on their own experience; their experience is not authoritative. They need some extra authority, some certificates from tradition, some sanctions from holy scriptures.

It happened, one of the very impressive men in this century in India was Ramateertha. He impressed America immensely, Europe and other countries.

Naturally he thought that when he comes back to India he is bound to influence millions of people. When he could influence people of other traditions, other religions, it is a natural corollary that he is going to influence the Hindus to whom he belongs.

So he returned first to Varanasi, which is the center of Hindu wisdom, and thought to be the oldest city in the world. Perhaps it is. There is not a single scripture in India which does not mention Varanasi; the oldest of the scriptures still mentions Varanasi. Many cities have arisen and disappeared; Varanasi has a certain permanency. And it is the most sacred city in India, the citadel of Hindus – Hindu scholars, pundits, priests. So Ramateertha came to Varanasi, because if Varanasi recognizes him as a saint, then the whole of India is bound to recognize him.

But to me, this is the poverty of the man, to seek recognition from others. You don't have your own experience, certainly; otherwise that experience authenticates you. There is nothing else you need. It is enough, more than enough. It is only one who is empty within who wants some sanction from outside.

He called a meeting of the Wise of Varanasi. He stood up to speak. He had not spoken for more than a few minutes when a Hindu scholar, a Brahmin pundit, stood up. And he said, "Stop all this nonsense. First answer me one question: Do you know Sanskrit? Because listening to you for these few minutes, it seems you don't know it. You are quoting from Persian, from Urdu, but you are not quoting from Sanskrit. And your pronunciation is not that of a Sanskrit scholar."

And it was true; he was born in Punjab, near Lahore, which is now in Pakistan. His mother tongue was Urdu, not Hindi. He was educated through the medium of Urdu, and he was a scholar of Persian and Arabic. That was the atmosphere around Rapala; it was a Mohammedan area. He had even read the Vedas and the Upanishads through the Persian translations. He had no idea of Sanskrit or Hindi. He had to accept it. And the Brahmin pundit said, "Then first go and learn Sanskrit; and don't destroy our time and don't waste our energy. Without knowing Sanskrit, you cannot be accepted by the Council of the Wise as a saint."

This was a very shattering experience, very shocking – but it can be shattering and shocking only to a person who has no inner light of his own. And, you will be surprised, he started learning Sanskrit. What poverty! It is shameful. And he was so shattered that the Council of the Wise, which is the topmost council of the Hindus, has rejected him that he dropped his orange clothes, feeling he had no right.

He started wearing white clothes while he became a scholar of Sanskrit – as if to become wise, to become enlightened, Sanskrit is a necessity. That is absolutely stupid. Buddha never knew any Sanskrit. He never spoke Sanskrit. Mahavira never knew Sanskrit, he never spoke Sanskrit. But he went to the Himalayas, learning Sanskrit.

And one day he saw his wife coming up the hill. He had been married before he renounced the world and became a sannyasin. The poor woman had accepted this, as has been the case for millions of women in India, with grace and gratitude, with joy, although it was going to be a very difficult life for her because he had not left her anything. He was not a rich man; he was just a lecturer in a college, he came from a poor family. He was a very intelligent boy, so he was getting scholarships, and that's how he finally managed to top the university in mathematics and became a mathematics lecturer. But he had not much to leave behind. The poor woman was happy that her husband has become a holy man – in pain, in anguish, but still she was not angry.

Hearing that he has come back after years of traveling, she sold the few ornaments she had for a ticket from Punjab to the Himalayas, just to see him. There was no other expectation. One of his disciples, Sadha Bonsingh, was sitting with Ramateertha as he saw the wife coming. Ramateertha told Bonsingh, "Close the doors, and don't allow that woman in."

Bonsingh was a very intelligent man, and he had written a few very beautiful articles, poetry. He said, "This is strange, because I have seen you meeting hundreds of women in the West. I have seen you shaking hands with people, which is against Hindu spirituality. This act seems to be ugly. You left this poor woman. Somehow she is managing by cleaning people's houses, their toilets. And she has come to see you and you are closing the doors. What is the fear? Do you still believe that she is your wife? Then you have not renounced.

What is the distinction between another woman and this woman? So either you allow her, and let her see you; or I am going to leave you. It has been difficult for me to accept that you are learning Sanskrit just to get a sanction from those idiots, none of whom is enlightened. Yet I have been keeping silent. But this is too much."

[…] It is like being named as a holy man by the Pope. Now, the Pope himself has no enlightenment; he is not an awakened being. What meaning does his sanction carry? And the person who starts believing himself a saint because a sanction has been given by the Pope is also not self-realized. Otherwise he will not wait for the sanction.

I don't have any sanction; I am nobody's saint. No tradition supports me. No orthodoxy stands behind me, no holy scripture can certify me. But I don't need any. Even if they want to, I will reject it – because my own experience is more than enough, and it gives me tremendous freedom.

So certainly I am a strange friend and master. And with me begins a new era of religiousness. I want to destroy everything that is old, past, dead. I don't believe in renovating old houses. I want to make a new house, fresh, for the new man to live in.

Describe how is in your vision, your man – East and West, Zorba the Buddha, and a scientist with wings, religion and science. So if you can briefly explain what is your vision of this synchronicity, this unity that we are trying to create in the world and what we call human.

The old man was schizophrenic. He was split between the body and the soul, between matter and spirit, between this world and that world. And he was told by the old religions, the old prophets, the messiahs, the saviours, to choose.

If he chooses the body, he chooses matter, he chooses this world, he is a materialist, he is a Zorba. And Zorba was condemned by all the religions around the world, without exception. If he chooses the spirit, he chooses the other world, he chooses God. Then he is a spiritual being. Then he is a saint. But in either case, he will be in anguish, he will be in suffering, because both are intrinsic parts of his being, and he is being cut into two.

So whatever he chooses, Zorba or Buddha, he will remain half. And the half can never be totally fulfilled. The half will remain always a wound because the other half is missing. So the Zorba is missing; he becomes almost an animal, loses all dignity. And that hurts. The Buddha is missing; he becomes almost a god, but he loses contact with reality. He starts living in a dream, in fantasies. He has lost his roots. Now his flowers cannot be real ones;

they can only be plastic. So all Buddhas have plastic flowers, and certainly plastic flowers can't have fragrance and can't have life.

The Zorba remains only in the roots; and the roots are ugly, and the roots live underground in the darkness of the soil. They can't even see the light of the sun, the stars of the night. They live like thieves in darkness, hiding themselves, hiding their ugliness. This has been the history of the past man. I can say with absolute certainty that the past history of man is schizophrenic; it is sick.

The new man accepts the whole man. It does not divide. It teaches an organic unity. Its fundamental philosophy is that you are one whole – not body and soul, not this world and that world. Your body is only the visible part of your soul.

Your soul is only the invisible part of your body. This world contains that world within it. Just you have to go deeply into it. In each experience, if you are intense and total, you will find within this world that world too. This contains that. They are not separate. There is no guilt, there is no sin.

Yes, you can commit mistakes, which is absolutely human. And you commit mistakes because you are not aware. I say to you, you are allowed to commit mistakes, but don't repeat the same mistake again and again. That means unawareness. When you commit a mistake for the first time, it is perfectly okay, because you have never committed it before, so how can you be aware of it? So it is good learning. Learn something out of the mistake. And be aware that it is not repeated. So commit as many mistakes as you can. But they have to be always new, so you go on learning and you go on growing in awareness.

So all the rituals of religions, and all their prayers, and all their mantras and chanting, are reduced to a simple method: awareness. All their sins are reduced to only mistakes. The original meaning of the word sin is good. It means forgetfulness. So don't commit the same mistake again, otherwise it becomes a sin; it becomes a forgetfulness. But I would not like to use the word sin because it has become so much associated with guilt, and guilt is the heaviest load on humanity. Take it away, and we can make people so light that they can almost fly.

The new man will not have any guilt. The new man will not have any split. The new man will have only one religion, and that is awareness. The new man will have only one world, this world – because that world is hidden behind it. This world is like a circumference, and that world is the center. And I call the whole man the holy man: then he becomes Zorba the Buddha.

Then the whole life – with its whole spectrum, all the colors of the rainbow.... You can live without any fear, without any guilt. You can dance like a Zorba, you can meditate like a Buddha, and I don't see there is any contradiction. In fact, if you have danced totally, deeply – so deeply that the dancer disappears in the dance – that is the time to start meditation.

And when you have meditated, and you are full of silence and peace and blissfulness, so much so that not only are you blissful but you can bless the whole world, that is the moment to dance. Your dance then will be a showering of blessings to the whole world.

I don't see any contradiction. That's why I say, drop the old completely. It was sick, it was schizophrenic. And let us have a new man: organic, healthy, whole.

And with the new man a new world comes into existence, which will not be divided by politics into nations, which will not be divided by religions into different sections, fighting, murdering, killing, burning living people.

We can make this earth a paradise, if we are together – if there are no nations and no churches, no religions, nothing dividing man from man. Then we will have so much energy available, which is now involved in wars, in fighting, in organizing, that this whole earth can blossom into new flowers of consciousness.

Okay, Sarjano.

The Last Testament Vol. 5, Ch 27

A few days later he proceeded with an interview for Il Manifesto:

Your commune in America, Oregon, has been described as both – an experiment of an alternative society and an experiment of a real communist. Would you agree?

Yes, I agree. I agree totally.

It was an experiment for both: as an alternative society and as a higher quality of communism.

The old society has some basic things on which it depends. There have been many critics of the old society but none of them has succeeded to hit the very roots. They have been just pruning the leaves.

So the critics have been criticizing and the old society goes on and on. Their criticism has not made any difference to it.

The roots of the old society are hidden like all roots of all trees. They are not available unless you dig deep.

For example, the family is the basic unit of the old society. Marriage is the basic unit of the old society.

Money as the means of exchange is very fundamental to the old society.

Religious orientation: whatever the religion may be, the old society needs a certain religion. It is the opium that keeps the people asleep and drugged.

In my commune we were destroying the very roots. We were destroying the family; we were dissolving the family into the commune.

The children were not going to belong to their parents: they could love them, they could meet with them, they could invite them, but they could not possess them. They have only been vehicles to bring those children into the world; the children are not their property. The commune will take care of the children.

Hence, marriage loses its relevance.

You can be together with a woman or a man as long as you love them. Except for love, there is no other reason to be together. There should not be any other reason to be together, because any other reason is going to be a wrong reason: no law, no logic, no convenience, no respectability…

The moment you see love has disappeared it is time to depart in deep gratitude, friendship, remembering all the beautiful moments that you have given to each other. Not spoiling it by fighting, quarreling, going to a court for a divorce – it is absolutely ugly.

When there is no marriage there is no question of divorce.

When there is no marriage prostitution disappears automatically.

Prostitution is the shadow of marriage. It is marriage in which love has died that creates the prostitute – the ugliest institution in existence.

The old society forces the woman to sell her body for money. This is a crime which cannot be forgiven. And strange is the fact that all the old societies are against prostitution and they are the cause of creating it. And they can't see the simple logic that when a man cannot feel love for his wife and cannot enjoy her, she is no longer an ecstasy to him, he tries to find… perhaps he can buy ecstasy, he can buy love, he can buy happiness: a desperate effort of a miserable man.

In the ancient times it was not possible for women to have male prostitutes for the simple reason that they were reduced to such slavery that they had no right, no say as to how the society should be run. They had no money. But in this century, as women have slowly become financially independent, simultaneously a new institution has come into being: male prostitution.

Now the woman is doing the same as the man has been doing. She is also hoping that through money those beautiful moments of hers which she has lost can be recaptured…

But there are a few things money cannot buy. It cannot buy love. It cannot buy peace. It cannot buy ecstasy.

The old society is miserable, but is itself responsible for all its miseries.

Then there is money as a means of exchange. And it is money that has created classes. The so-called communism created by Karl Marx and Friedrich Engels does not take note of this basic fact. They miss the most fundamental thing; they want to distribute money equally, but they don't see the point that it is money which has created classes.

You can distribute money, but then you will have to maintain a continuous dictatorial state to keep that money distributed equally; otherwise there will soon be people who will be having more money and there will be people who will be having less money – because to earn money is an art. To accumulate money is an art, to create wealth is an art, and everybody is not so talented. Soon there will be poor and rich.

But they did not see. They both were blind about the most important thing – that the easiest way for this to disappear is to take money out of society; then it is no longer the means of exchange. Then there is nobody poor and nobody rich. There is no need to create a classless society: just remove money and the classless society comes into being.

The commune should take the responsibility of providing the basic needs of its members. Everybody should get whatever is his need. And we had managed, in our small commune of five thousand people, for four years, to create the highest quality of communism that has ever existed on earth. It was an alternative society – because it dissolved the family, it dissolved marriage, it dissolved divorce, it dissolved the whole possessiveness of parents over children. It dissolved money. It made a classless society. It dissolved any need for a ruling class and the ruled. It created a functional structure.

So the president was not more prestigious than the plumber. He was doing his work; the plumber was doing his work. It was possible that the plumber was doing better work as a plumber than the president was doing in his work. Then the plumber has to be honored and respected.

Yes, our commune was an alternative society and a higher form of communism. And we have proved that it is possible. We were not only theoreticians; we have proved it, practically – against all odds, against the greatest, mightiest government. We managed to create an oasis in a world of misery. People rejoicing and dancing. People feeling completely unburdened of the entire past and unconcerned about the future.

In those four years we managed to give reality to a dream which man has been dreaming about for millennia.

Has the fact you left America to be considered a failure of your experiment?

It was not a failure. It was an absolute success. We succeeded in doing everything that we wanted.

We managed to prove that whatever is our theoretical idea is also practical. It is pragmatic, it is down-to-earth. That is our success. I call it absolute success – not in terms of time, that it existed for only four years, but in terms that it existed at all!

It was going to be destroyed: that is not something unexpected. It was going to be crushed. In fact, it threatened the greatest world power – that is its success. It challenged the greatest power – that is its success. That the greatest world power had to use illegal means, undemocratic means to destroy it, is its success.

America has failed – not the commune. Otherwise, a small commune of five thousand people, what harm could it have done to America? It had no nuclear weapons, it was not a danger to anybody, it could not have conquered America.

What was the fear? The fear was not of nuclear weapons; the fear was not that this commune was going to conquer them. The fear was that this commune is transforming from a dream that is hidden in every man's unconscious. This commune is making real something that man has always wanted to experiment with but thought was a dream – good to dream about , but you cannot materialize it.

We proved it. Anybody who thinks it was a failure is absolutely wrong. We succeeded in every way. We threatened the greatest power – what more success do you want?

Such great powers are not threatened by small things. They don't take any notice. They could have ignored it. But they could not really ignore it; they had to take note of it and they had to understand clearly that if this commune goes on growing, sooner or later it is going to threaten their very existence –without any nuclear weapons.

It is going to take away the youth. It is going to take over their people. It is going to take away their most potential power – human power. Then they can go on keeping their nuclear weapons but they will be of no use.

The fear, the paranoia, in the American government's mind, against a single man and his small commune is a proof of absolute success.

Osho, that means that there is no hope for wherever people like you will try an experiment like this – it will, is bound to be, destroyed?

No, there is always hope. They can destroy it one time, they can destroy it a hundred times, but they cannot always destroy it.

Each time they destroy it we will be creating more sympathy, more lovers, more people on our side.

Each time a man like me is jailed, you will find more and more people coming closer to our philosophy, our way of life.

This is how history functions. They will destroy it a few times but each time they will be weakening themselves and they will be strengthening us. We invite them to go on destroying till we are more powerful than them and they cannot destroy any more and they will have to commit suicide because there is nothing else left for them to do.

We also think that there has been some misunderstanding when you talk against poverty. In fact, it has been reported today that you are against the poor. Will you please make it clear: are you against poverty or against the poor?

There is no misunderstanding. I am against poverty. And without poverty how can there be poor people?

If I destroy poverty, I am at the same time destroying poor people too.

Poor people exist through poverty. The misunderstanding is created by those people who would like to say, "Destroy poverty but love the poor." What they are saying is that the poor man can be still a poor man without poverty! They are trying to save Jesus, they are trying to save all the old religions – because Jesus is not saying that he is for poverty; he is saying, "Blessed are the poor."

But how can these people be poor without poverty? And if he wants these people to be poor, he is for poverty, without any confusion.

I am against poverty; hence I am against the poor man because the poor man is nothing but a byproduct of poverty. Once poverty is withdrawn the poor man disappears. So there is no confusion.

It is better I should say that to me, they are both the same thing.

But the distinction has been made down the ages, so I can understand what the question is. They have always said, "Condemn evil, but don't condemn the evil man."

But without evil how can the man be evil? That is beyond my comprehension. They say, "Destroy sickness, but love sick people." But if you destroy sickness, where are you going to find sick people? To me, it is sickness that makes them sick, and if you are really destroying sickness there is not going to be anybody who is sick and nobody who needs your sympathy.

So I am against poverty and I am against the poor man.

I would like every man to be rich in all the dimensions of life.

I am all for riches – and to me riches does not mean only money. A man who cannot understand the greatest literature of the world is a poor man and I hate him! He is living unnecessarily; he is simply a burden on the earth. Either he has to improve, to sharpen his intelligence, or he has no future.

In all the dimensions poverty has to disappear. And with poverty the poor man disappears automatically.

The man remains; just that ugliness of poverty disappears. I cannot say "blessed are the poor", "blessed are the sheep", "blessed are the ugly", I just cannot say this. And I cannot tolerate anybody else saying it; I will condemn him, criticize him to my best. Because I want this earth to be full of beautiful people – multidimensionally rich; contributing more beauty, more joy, more blissfulness.

What is your advice for destroying poverty in the world?

My advice is very simple. First, absolute birth control for twenty to thirty years. On the other hand, after living seventy-five years, the freedom for everybody to choose if he wants to die. Then he can simply go to a hospital and register himself, that he has lived enough and now there is no point in living and he wants to be relieved.

So on the one hand we prevent new people coming and on the other hand we make old people move faster in the queue, so the world's population is reduced to almost a fourth of what it is., Then the earth is plenty – rich, nourishing.

Secondly, nations should disappear from the world. They are one of the causes of poverty, sickness, war, destruction and misuse of the technology, science and energy that man produces.

We need one world. If we want to be rich, we need only one world. No political lines on the earth. Then it will be very easy to see.

There was a time in Soviet Russia when they were using wheat instead of coal on their railway lines, in their engines, because they had a bumper crop of wheat and wheat was cheaper than coal and they didn't have many coal mines.

The whole of the East was dying hungry. They cannot eat coal. They have coal mines – but they cannot eat coal. Yet wheat is being used elsewhere as coal. If it was one world, things would have been simple. Shift the coal from where it is too much and useless and send the wheat where it is needed – don't burn it! It is not something to be burned when people are hungry.

Just a few months ago in Europe, they drowned millions of tons of food in the ocean. And just close by in Nigeria, in Ethiopia, people were dying. In Ethiopia people were dying in thousands because they had no water, no food. And in Europe you are drowning food, fresh food, in the ocean.

In fact, one hundred thousand dollars were wasted just in drowning it, because you need labor to drown food.

If the world was one, Ethiopia would not have died the way it has died. And it has been happening always. America goes on destroying its crops, drowning its food in the ocean, but will not give it to those who are dying. For the simple reason that if you start giving food then your own economy suffers. Then prices come down. And no country wants this; particularly the people holding the markets don't want prices to come down.

And why should they bother about Ethiopia? Ethiopia or no Ethiopia – it makes no difference to Europe. It is good if it is finished: one problem is solved.

We need one world.

Just the idea of one world means that the tremendous energy involved in preparation for war – nuclear weapons, atomic energy – and millions of the best minds humanity has ever produced – all the scientists, and technologists – are freed to do some creative work.

If they can manage the atomic energy to destroy Hiroshima and Nagasaki, if they can manage nuclear weapons to destroy the whole world, why can they not manage, with the same energy, to produce more food? To produce better clothes? To produce better houses? To produce a totally new kind of world which has never been dreamt of, yet is now possible. Unpolluted, ecologically sane.

There is enough food in the oceans; our scientists just have to work on it. Very nourishing food can be found in the oceans.

And ultimately, as science goes deeper into it, there is bound to come a time when science can create synthetic food – just like synthetic clothes and everything else man has made – which will be better, far improved on nature.

Man can live at least three hundred years, very easily. If he just gets the right kind of food and the whole scientific world changes its direction from death to life, it is possible.

Things are very simple. We have just not explored them. If you look back in time, you can understand it.

There was a time when man lived only on hunting. He had no idea that fruits could be eaten, that crops could be grown. If anybody had said that, he would have been thought crazy. Because people had never done that. They had all lived on hunting, and to live on hunting was a very difficult process because some days you may get food, and some days you may not. It was all accidental.

But as the population grew they had to listen to the dreamers who said these fruits can be eaten, crops can be grown. And that was a tremendous revolution – from hunting to cultivation.

And yet we are still hanging there. Standing at my window I see every day, and I feel so sad… One couple has been working since I have come here – they may have been working long before – using their hands, preparing the ground to sow seeds. They have not even come to use bullocks or horses; they are living almost fifty thousand years back in time.

In the middle of Kathmandu, where you have all contemporary technologies available, the whole day from morning to evening they are preparing the ground just by hand. It will take months to prepare, that which could have been done with bullocks or horses within a week – that which could have been done by a tractor in just a few hours.

But perhaps they have no idea. We have to bring science, technology, to every field of life, in every possible way.

Man's mind clings to the past. Everything new seems to be unnatural. It is not true.

I use one hundred percent polyester, and my father was very much against this. He would say, "This is unnatural; you should use cotton." But I told him, "Do you know, there were times people never used cotton. They were naked; and when for the first time cotton was used there were people like you who said it was unnatural, because our fathers, forefathers, had never used it. And I feel perfectly comfortable in it. I have never felt so comfortable in any other kind of clothing. So have I to understand my own experience or just follow the old trodden path?"

Poverty is not a great problem. The problem is divisions of nations, divisions of religions. You can see it in India. A man is poor if he is Hindu; if he becomes converted to Catholicism he becomes rich. Hindu, he will remain poor; Christian, he need not be poor.

But is it right to exploit the man? Is it right to purchase the man's ideology by giving him food, shelter, clothing, education? Why can't you give to him without any conditions – just as a human being? It means,"There is enough, but first you have to be a Christian. Poverty is not necessary: your Hinduism, your Buddhism, is a barrier. Be Christian and poverty disappears."

I want all these religions to disappear, so all their riches can be used for the benefit of all.

Reduce the population, destroy nations, destroy religions, and the world would be so rich, you cannot dream.

It is a very simple phenomenon.

Osho, we agree with you in total and for whatever help we can be, we would like to know in which circumstance would you be willing to create another experiment of an alternative society to offer as a model to the world?

This time I am not going to create a society or a commune, as a model. I have done that.

But my people will be creating communes around the world – on the same model – so that I don't become tethered to one small space; one single spot, with only a few thousand people.

I would like to remain available to all of my sannyasins around the world. Now I am going to be a constant wanderer, a traveler, seeing what my people are doing around the world, helping them to do it better.

So I am not going to put my energies into a small model – that I have done. And this is not my habit, to do anything again. Once is enough.

I have moved on to another experiment. Now I will be moving around the world continuously, travelling, reaching every sannyasin, every lover, every friend, every sympathizer, and creating a worldwide movement And now it is up to my sannyasins to create communes.

This way I will be able to work on a bigger scale, larger scale. And it will become more impossible for any stupid government to destroy my work because it will be spread all over the world.

You talk about meditation. Can you explain the difference between meditation techniques and meditation itself? And how there can be meditation when you drive a bulldozer, or work twelve hours a day?

Meditation techniques are not really meditation.

Meditation techniques only prepare the ground.

They are needed because people's minds are so full of rubbish that before meditation can be started, that rubbish has to be removed.

Meditation techniques are just to remove the rubbish. If that is removed, the meditation starts.

If somebody comes with a clean mind, he does not need any technique. He can directly enter into the space I call meditation.

And the space called meditation has nothing to do with where you are, what you are doing, or not doing. It is simply a constant awareness, an undercurrent of alertness. So you can work twelve hours on a bulldozer or you can just sit silently doing nothing. Deep underneath your work or no work there is a thread of alertness.

I have loved always a story… There was once a master thief; he was never caught and it was thought to be an honor if he stole from your house. People talked about it, saying, "The master thief has visited us." Because it was not an ordinary thing. He never went to ordinary people; he went only to the super rich, to the kings, to the emperors. So people used to brag about being visited by the master thief. It was more valuable than what he has stolen, his visit was more valuable.

He was getting old. His son asked him, "Now you are old and you have not taught me your art."

The master said, "It is never too late. You can come with me tonight – and I am going into a very beautiful palace."

The son followed. He was very much afraid, although he was young and strong. And the old man has passed eighty, but he was unafraid. He made a hole in the wall. The son was perspiring; it was a cold night and a cold wind was blowing and he was so nervous he could not believe that the old man's hands were not even shaking. And he was doing it as if it is his own house. He made the hole; he entered the hole, he called the son. He was very much afraid to enter it, but as he himself has asked, what will the father think of him? So he entered. The father said, "Don't be afraid – can't you see me? And you are with me, so just watch me – and behave! This is not the way to become a master thief: follow me!"

He followed – but his legs were trembling, his breathing was no longer normal, his heart was thumping; he could not believe that the heart can make so much noise. The night was silent, but the old man was as if absent. He opened door upon door – he had a master key. He entered into the innermost chamber. He opened the door of a closet: beautiful, very costly dresses. He told the son to go in and find the best dress he liked. And as he went in the old man closed the lock, locked the door, shouted loudly, "Thief, thief!" and ran back out, through the same hole by which they had entered.

Everybody was awake: the whole household. The servants and the master and the children and the wife and the guests were all there and they were looking around: where is the thief ? And there has certainly been a thief; the hole in the wall was a proof.

And the young man could not believe that his father would do such a nasty thing to him; he has always been nice.

Closing the doors, putting on the lock, and then shouting, "Thief, thief!" and running away. Now how is he going to get out? His mind could not function. Your mind would not have functioned either.

It was such a situation where the mind has to stop, because the mind can work only with known situations. As the unknown comes in, the mind stops, simply stops.

Then a maidservant came in, looking all around. She thought perhaps it is a good idea to look in the closet. She opened the lock, opened the door, she had a candle in her hand, looked inside, and the young man had no idea what he is doing, why he is doing it: he simply blew out the candle, pushed the servant, the maidservant, aside and ran out through the same hole.

But now everybody has seen him. They all followed. And he was running for his life, so he was running at his best. He could not do better; he had been a good runner, participated in university, been a good competitor, been a champion runner, but he could not believe that he is now doing double. If he had done this much before he would have been the national champion.

The people were still following and more people had joined them, neighbours and others, and they were all shouting and had torches. And he comes by the side of a well, and still not knowing what is happening, because he is not in a situation to figure out, to think... there is no time; mind needs time to think.

Those who know, say "mind is time". They are not two entities. If there is no time, there is no mind. If there is no mind, there is no time. He had no time to think, but things were happening on their own accord. This is what I call spontaneity.

He just took up a big rock – and he could not believe he could take that big load in his hands, the rock was too big – and he threw the rock into the well, not knowing what he is doing or why, and ran away. All the people who were following gathered around the well thinking that he has jumped into it, listening to the rock sound falling into the well.

He reached home. The old man was fast asleep! He was snoring!

The young man could not believe that this is his father. He pulled back his blanket and said, "Is this a way to behave with your own son?"

The father opened his eyes half and said, "So, you are back? The remaining story you can tell me in the morning. If you are back, it seems everything went right. But don't disturb my sleep. Just go and have a good rest."

The son could not believe that he is not even curious about what happened to him: his life was at risk at every moment, he could have been caught, he could have been given to the police, the people could have shot him, anything was possible. And he is saying, "You are back, that's enough; the remaining story you can tell me in the morning, that is not very important. What is important is that you are back and I am happy."

In the morning the father said, "There is no need to tell the story. This is the whole art. If you want to become a master thief you have not to function out of the mind, you have to function out of your totality, spontaneity. Now you can choose. This is my business, my whole life's work. I have given you a taste. If you love it, the adventure of it, the ecstasy of it, then you are welcome, my son.

From today you can go on your own because there is only one lesson in this path."

Meditation is a single lesson of awareness, of no-thought, of spontaneity, of being total in your action, alert, aware. It is not a technique, it is a knack. Either you get it or you don't.

Do you think that your sannyasins and friends have now learned the lesson about the danger of an organized religion?

They certainly have. I have been telling them my whole life about the dangers of organized religion. But just telling is not enough. They need something practical. I gave them a practical situation. They have learnt it. They have burnt their fingers in learning it. They will never forget it, they will never repeat the same mistake again.

I am happy. Once in a while people need something actual, not theoretical.

If you have the chance to speak both to Reagan and Gorbachev what would you say to them?

I would say to them that if they have any humanity left in them then the first thing is to help create one world.

They are the greatest powers in the world: if they want to, it becomes a very easy thing. They are in a situation to destroy the whole world. I can show them an alternative that they are also in a state of creating one world. Perhaps it has not dawned on their consciousness, that the power they have is not only capable of destroying the world, it is also capable of creating one world. Because never before in history have two countries had so much power that the whole world will have to listen to them. All that is needed is that they should agree on the point that they want to create one world. Then all these small nations, poor nations, can be given the alternative to choose: either a third world war or one world. And in the third world war only America and Russia are going to lose – nobody else. Because nobody else has anything to lose.

Even if the third world war does not happen, most countries will die from starvation and over-population. Can you understand? I used to think that by the end of this century India would have a population of one billion. Right now it is nine hundred million. For the first time in thousands of years, it will be ahead of China. Up to now China has been the leading country with the greatest population. But just the other day, I came to know that by two thousand – by the end of this century – India will not have only one billion population, it will have doubled its population as it is now. It is now nine hundred million; it will have doubled. That means eighteen hundred million. One billion and eighteen hundred million: these people are going to die by themselves – without any war. In fact, war will be a great release of their tension, of their worry, of death constantly ahead.

These countries alone, one third of the world – the third world – will die of poverty, starvation, sickness.

The remaining world – which is not poor, but which does not have real power compared to Russia or America – will die of AIDS, which is even uglier than dying of starvation. So this world is finished.

Only in the third world war are America and Russia going to lose. They are going to destroy themselves. The remaining world is going to commit suicide on its own – they don't need your help.

So I will suggest to these people to just be clear about the situation. You are all going to lose. If there is a war, only one will be the losers, yet you both will be destroyed by it.

You can propose to the world, "We have decided to be together. Rather than die together, we have decided to live together, and create one world."

And nobody can prevent the Soviet Union, Russia, from creating one world. They can remove all the lines from the map very easily – there is no problem at all.

And once they decide that they are not going to fight, then the tremendous energy which is involved in war efforts will be available for them, and the whole world, to make paradise out of it.

Okay, Sarjano.

The Last Testament Vol. 5, Ch 29

The interview continued on the next day:

Osho, you say that marriage has done its work and is now out of date. We agree. Do you suggest the commune as a new basic unity of lifestyle? And say that the children will grow up freer in this context? It looks beautiful but it's very difficult for a mother, especially an Italian mother, to think that her child doesn't belong to her. Please explain.

Every transformation, every revolution, is difficult in the beginning because you are accustomed to the old and to adapt to the new creates difficulty. The very idea of possession is anti-love. You possess things, you don't possess living beings.

But unfortunately we have reduced living beings to things. It will hurt to drop the possessiveness but it will immensely help the mother in understanding, in spiritual growth, and the hurt will be healed very soon.

It is just an old habit transferred from one generation to another generation that 'you possess me, I possess you'. Dropping possessiveness means 'I am myself, you are yourself': we meet out of independence. We love out of freedom, not any contract.

And once a person has tasted love, non-possessive love, he will be surprised that what he had been thinking of as love was not love but fear.

It is fear which wants to possess, so that you cannot escape, and you remain always part of the house furniture, so that you remain obedient; you are not an independent being but just a projection of the idea of your mother, your father, your wife, or your husband.

The difference is very much as if a bird comes out of the egg: he must be afraid, he is entering into an unknown world. Inside the egg he was safe, secure, no problems. Getting out of the egg is a trauma. But once he looks at the stars and the whole sky is his, once he opens his wings and rises high into the heavens, he knows that the egg was not his home; it was a prison. Now he has found himself.

In finding freedom, one finds himself. And only a free man is capable of loving.

You cannot expect love from slaves. You cannot expect love from prostitutes.

They can pretend – you pay for it. You cannot expect love from a child who feels in bondage; he will pretend, and he will pretend for his whole life because you are training him for pretension, not love. He will pretend with his wife, he will pretend with his children, and this way the disease goes on and on.

Intelligent people are needed to come out of this vicious circle. And I am not saying you are not allowed to love; I am saying you are not allowed to possess.

You can love your children, you can love other people's children – what is special in your children? They are as much strangers to you as other children. Your love should have some unconditional quality about it.

In a commune a boy, a girl, will be getting love from thousands of people. And it is one of the most significant things to remember that when a girl is brought up by the mother she hates that mother her whole life. She cannot forgive her, she cannot forget her – on the one hand. And on the other hand, she is just a replica of her mother. It is the same with the boy.

And it is a known fact that the girl wants to love the father, the boy wants to love the mother, but this is thought to be a criminal act. As the boys and girls grow up the father and mother will create distance between their children and themselves, but the harm has already been done.

Scientists say that the first days of life are the most important because you gain certain impressions which you will carry your whole life.

The boy will carry the impression of his mother his whole life. He could not have the mother, but he will search for the mother in other women – and no other woman can fit with his idea. The same is true with the girl.

People fall in love and you ask them why they fell in love with a certain woman or a certain man. And they are at a loss to answer, because it is something unconscious of which they are not aware.

The reality is you fall in love with a woman who has some similarity to your mother. Maybe the similarity will be very superficial – the hairdo, the sound of her voice, the way she talks, the features of her face, the eyes, anything – just a small thing, and you fall in love. You fall in love with a fragment; but soon after marriage you will discover the woman is not a fragment, she is a whole continent. And so is the man. Both are going to be frustrated, because what will the hairdo do? Even if the nose of your wife is exactly the same as your mother's, it is not going to make your life a joyous pilgrimage.

What does it matter if your father resembles the husband you have chosen? Because he was a professor, very scholarly, always talking of great things, and this man is also a professor talking of great things – but these things don't constitute life. So when you are together twenty-four hours you start discovering so many things which do not resemble your father or your mother.

Finally, when you discover the whole phenomenon of your woman, that small fragment is so small, it makes no difference at all. Then there is frustration, then there is constant quarreling.

This is one of the basic facts as to why no couple is happy – and I say it without any exception. No couple is happy around the world, and every couple is pretending to the outside that they are living in paradise. They are living in hell – twenty-four hours! They pretend to be loving only when guests come, visitors come; otherwise the house is hell.

I have heard: Two men used to visit a restaurant and they both remained there till the manager forced them to leave. This was a great similarity. One day when these two men were just leaving the restaurant, one man asked the other, "Why do you stay so long?"

He said, "I am married, and as long I can remain away from the home it is peaceful."

Then he asked, "What is the cause of your staying – because you are too!" He said, "It is better that you should not know."

But the man insisted on knowing.

So he said, "I am a bachelor. As long as I can remain away from my empty house it feels I am alive. When I enter my house it seems I am entering a grave."

When you are alone you cannot live. When you are together with a partner you cannot live. Certainly the whole human psychology is berserk.

In the commune children will be part of it. They will have many uncles, many aunts, many sisters, many brothers. They will not get a certain fixed idea in their mind as to how a woman should be or a man should be.

Almost ninety percent of psychological problems will dissolve, and for the remaining ten I also have some ideas. As the children grow to sexual maturity they should be allowed absolute freedom, with all precautions so that they don't get pregnant.

Now the Pill is available. First it was available only for the woman, now it is available for the man too. All kinds of birth control methods are available.

After the thirteenth or fourteenth year, the girl or boy is going to be sexually mature. It has to be understood that nature has brought them to maturity. As far as nature is concerned they are capable of producing children. But the society, the family, the old rotten structure will prevent them up to twenty-five years of age. That means a difference of ten or eleven years before they get married; for these ten years every society insists that you should remain celibate. You are asking the impossible.

Nature has matured their sexuality; it is none of their fault. It is as simple as you taking a vow that "I will not allow my hair to grow" – but are you capable of doing that? Your hair will continue to grow. You can go on reading the Bhagavad Gita or the Holy Bible, and you can go on, on your knees, praying to God saying, "I have taken the vow that I will not grow my hair" – but they will go on growing.

Your biological structure is not under the control of your mind. And sex is the most important part of your biology because the whole of nature depends on sex for reproduction.

These ten years are going to be of perverted sex. They could have been a great experiment, a great experience.

In a commune the children will be allowed to have all knowledge, all medical support, so they don't get pregnant. And they should move with different boys, with different girls… there is no hurry to decide. And there should not be any hurry to decide.

First let the boy experience a few dozen girls, let the girl know a few dozen boys: only then can you expect her to decide who seems to be more close to her being, who will be a partner with whom she would like to travel a long way.

And the boy will also be able to see which is the girl, which are the qualities that impress him. And they should go on changing around in the commune, because it is not settled; they are just playing around with their love energy, to have experience before they decide. And my understanding is that if, in a seventy year life, ten years of experience cannot make you come to a conclusion, what more can you want? These ten years will be settling.

Nobody is made for you; neither are you made for anybody else.

It is a search, a groping in the dark, for the most suitable companion who is non-possessive, who loves freedom, who loves to give freedom, who is not only non-possessive but is against being possessed, who is absolutely open to share love, without any conditions.

These ten years will be the most significant of your life. Right now they are a nightmare.

And then you can decide whenever you want – or you can decide that married life is not for you. Perhaps you would like to continue in the same way as you have been doing for those ten years – nothing is wrong in it. It is absolutely up to you! No parent decides it. It is your decision to choose a partner, or not to choose a partner.

One more thing to be remembered: at the age of near about eighteen you have the greatest sexual power that you will ever have in your life. After eighteen your sexual power starts declining. And it is sheer stupidity to decide for marriage at twenty-five, when sexual power has already declined tremendously: you will not be able to satisfy a woman.

The most satisfying sexual orgasm is between eighteen and nineteen; you are at the prime of your energies. But education continues up to twenty-five, twenty-six; and if you are going to do a Ph.D. it may go up to thirty, or if you are really a bookworm it may go up to thirty-five to get a D.Litt.

I came across a man in Varanasi who had seventeen M.A. degrees in seventeen subjects. And that was his only achievement – useless – but he was praised. I was perhaps the only man in the whole world who condemned him to his face. All that he had been doing in his life was moving from one subject to another, and attaining another M.A., to prove that he is the only man in the world who has seventeen M.A. degrees. And the people who brought him to me had brought him with great praise. They told me, "He is a rare individual."

And I looked at him and told him, "You are an absolute idiot. What are you going to do with your seventeen degrees? You have wasted your whole life. Now collect all your papers and keep them in your chest and move to your grave. Perhaps God may be very impressed seeing seventeen Masters' degrees."

At first the man was shocked. And then tears came to his eyes and he said, "Perhaps you are the first man who has told me the truth. I have wasted my life. I have never loved – I had no time. I never got married – I had no time. I was running from one department to another department. My whole idea was to have all the Masters' degrees available in the University of Varanasi. Your attitude shocks me, hurts me, but still I understand: I have wasted my life."

By the age of thirty-five sexual energy is fast declining. That is the reason that most people in the world don't have orgasmic experience – because that orgasmic experience was possible between eighteen, nineteen, somewhere there, when you were so full of energy and the woman was so receptive that making love was a divine dance.

When men's energies have declined, women's energies have not declined. So she feels continuously frustrated. And the man feels deep down that he is the unfortunate one who has never known what orgasm is, but he cannot accept it.

Ninety-eight percent of women in India have had no sexual orgasm. And that is one of the basic experiences that nature gives you, as a gift. With that experience you for the first time become aware that life is not just mundane, it has something divine in it.

My own understanding is that it was orgasmic experience which created the mystics in the world. Because if meeting with a woman, totally, can give you such an experience, meeting with the whole universe, merging with the whole universe, totally – you can imagine how much, how vast, how infinite it is going to be. It is going to be absolute orgasm. But if you have missed the first, you have no possibility of attaining the second. The first was an indication of a new dimension. You will collect money and power and prestige and you will die just as everybody has died.

=In the commune the children will have all orgasmic experiences. And before they decide they will know what kind of a woman or what kind of man brings them to that holy experience. That is going to be decisive – not astrology, not palmistry, not parents; nobody can decide it. That merging and meeting and that great experience overwhelming both the lovers, is enough: it has decided.

Most of us in relationships between men and women look like sadists or masochists. And there are now more and more people who choose not to be and call themselves 'singles'. This is a new phenomenon in the West, increasing every day. What do you think about that? And do you think there is any hope for a relationship between a man and a woman which doesn't enslave them both?

The phenomenon of people living alone is disgusting because it is out of frustration. They wanted to be with someone; they have tried, and they have failed again and again. Now it is out of failure that they have reached a conclusion that it is better to be alone. But their aloneness will be sad, empty, ugly – because it has not come out of any abundance of love, it has come out of the psychopathy of love. And it is true, the best couple in the world is one in which one partner is a masochist and the other is a sadist. They fit very well.

The sadist wants to torture, the masochist wants to be tortured. You cannot find a better combination. Both are happy – there is no complaint. But the situation is ugly. To settle in such a state where one is a sadist and the other is a masochist… Two sick people cannot create a healthy relationship. In fact, their relationship is based on sickness. Most of the couples who seem to cling together are of this type because they are fulfilling each other's need. And it is a natural byproduct – if you cannot find somebody who fits with your psycho-pathology, it is better to be single. But that is not going to make you psychologically healthy. Your singleness may create thousands of perversions.

I have heard a story that two men were going to Alaska. At the last village they stopped to purchase a few necessary things – toothpaste, et cetera – and the shopkeeper said, "I have something more: perhaps you are not aware, you will not get a woman there."

They had not thought about it but that is true. In Alaska, where are you going to get a woman? So the man said, "I have some arrangements: I have a rubber woman. You just pump it up and it is more beautiful than any woman. And it is very easy; it never quarrels, never nags you and is easy to carry. Just take the air out, fold it back up and keep it in your pocket – nobody will know."

They both looked at each other and said, "It is a good idea."

But one said, "I don't have money."

The other said, "I have money." So they purchased the woman – a really beautiful woman which filled with air had all the right proportions of the body.

After two years, one man came back.

The shopkeeper said, "As far as I remember, two men had gone: where is the other?"

He said, "Don't mention him – I shot him."

He said, "Why did you shoot him – he was your friend!"

"Don't call him my friend!" he said. "When I was out, he was making love to my woman. He was cheating on me continuously. I asked him again and again, 'Are you making love to my woman?' – because I had paid for it. And he said, 'No, I am not interested in women.' But one day I came in the middle of the day and saw him making love to my woman. I shot them both."

These singles will find rubber women. These singles will have to come to some understanding about their sexuality. And their singlehood will create the same situation as celibacy has created for thousands of years.

But it is a sign that the old marriage has failed –that people are so tired of it that they choose to be single rather than getting married and entering into a continuous nightmare.

I have lived with hundreds of families: I have not come across a single couple who is happy. But what else to do? Society has managed everything in such a way that they have to pretend to be happy – that is their respectability, prestige in the society. But deep down they are dying of cancer – a cancer which is invisible and cannot be operated upon.

The world can be so joyous; a few stupid ideas just have to be removed. Give children chances to experiment with sex so that before they decide, they decide with full awareness that the person they are choosing fits with them – not on a fragmentary basis but whole to whole. And then too it is not a marriage according to law, it is not a marriage according to social customs; it is a marriage between those two people. Any moment they feel that all joy is disappearing then why continue? Say goodbye, find new partners. The world is so full of men and women; perhaps you may find somebody else, your woman may find somebody else. And don't think of permanency; in existence everything is momentary. What is beautiful today may turn ugly tomorrow; what is so great this moment that you are ready to accept it for your whole life, may turn so sour tomorrow that you may like to kill yourself or the other person.

But there is no need of all these things. It should be a free-floating, free-moving society. In each constitution of the world this should be a birthright of man to choose a partner, to change a partner, without any hindrance from the government or society because it is an individual affair.

And when the children are being taken care of by this society there will be no problem. And children will not be losing you – the mother can visit them, the father can visit them; they will be still calling you 'father', calling the woman 'mother'. To them nothing has changed. To them it is perfectly good. In fact they will be very understanding that if love has disappeared it is good that you have separated, rather than torturing each other your whole life.

Life is so simple. Man has made it so complex unnecessarily.

It seems that the religions of the world, the politicians and other powerful people of the world don't want human beings to be happy. They don't want them to be in a state of euphoria, they want them to be miserable.

There is some vested interest in their misery. If they are miserable, continuously burdened by the wife, the husband, by children, parents, by jobs or by unemployment, they cannot be rebels. They are dying under the burden of their own life. Who has time for rebellion?

But if my idea starts to spread, and people are happy and independent – joyous – then the vested interest will be in tremendous trouble, because when these rebellious people are not burdened with anything their whole energy is available to revolt against anything that hinders human happiness.

Just the other day there was a question about drugs. Alcohol is almost universally legal. Marijuana is not, LSD is not, Ecstasy is not. And the strange thing is that alcohol is the most dangerous drug out of these four I named.

'Ecstasy' has no bad effects, is non-addictive, simply gives you a pleasant feeling, well-being: it is prohibited. I can't understand. Why do you prevent people from feeling well-being? And it hurts nobody. The whole medical research is in favor of it; it is an absolutely harmless drug. It will bring you out of your sadness, make you smile and laugh and dance and sing, but it is illegal. You may have to suffer in jail if you are caught with Ecstasy.

Marijuana grows wild in the Himalayas and has been used by the people for thousands of years, with no bad effect. It certainly gives you hallucinatory feelings, but rather being in real hell it is better to be in a hallucinatory paradise – what is wrong in it? If you cannot give a real paradise, at least let people have some glimpse in their dreams, in their hallucinations.

LSD can be further perfected. It can be perfected to the point where anybody can take it without any prescription and feel immensely good, healthy, full of energy, and see life in its utter beauty: the same rose flower yet you see it for the first time radiating , surrounded by an aura of light. LSD intensifies your sensitivity. Not all people are born with sensitivity, and yet nobody is training them to create more sensitivity for beauty, for joy, for compassion. LSD can do that – but LSD is illegal.

Alcohol , which has no plus points, is legal. Alcohol simply destroys people, helps them to forget – but the next day they fall in a deeper ditch, the hangover.

Neelam reported to me that she has a friend in Kulu who has two friends: one who is an alcoholic and another who lives on marijuana. The alcoholic has destroyed his whole life; his business is ruined, his family is ruined, he is ruined. And the man who has been taking marijuana is fully healthy; his business is good, his family is together. But marijuana is illegal, and alcohol is legal. Why is alcohol legal? One wonders.... It is in favor by the vested interests. Drugs like Ecstasy are not in favor; they are in favor by humanity but they are not in favor by the vested interests.

And the same situation exists on many fronts.

Osho, you have been very hard on the homosexuals, especially lesbian ladies. These people have been so much condemned and discriminated against in our society that we really didn't expect you to add your criticism against them. Can you please say a few words about this?

I cannot support anything unnatural.

It is homosexuality which has brought AIDS to humanity. And AIDS may destroy two-thirds of humanity, without nuclear weapons.

I am certainly against homosexuality. I am so much against it that even people of very great genius, talents, creativity... I have appreciated them on all other accounts but as far as homosexuality is concerned I cannot support even Socrates. He was a homosexual. His homosexuality destroys much of his credibility, that he did not understand Tao – the way of nature.

And homosexuality, moreover, is a religious disease. And in condemning all the religions, for all the harm they have done to humanity, one of the greatest harms is homosexuality. Because it is these religions that started preaching celibacy and started separating male monks from female nuns.

If you go back in history three thousand years, you will be surprised:, nuns were having intercourse with the devil. And a special investigator was appointed by the pope in the middle ages to find the nuns who had had any sexual contact with the devil. And they tortured the nuns, interrogated the nuns, day and night, and finally they managed to make them confess – the way they manage in Communist Russia. They can manage to get people to confess anything – just go on torturing; there is a limit to human capacity. Don't let them sleep, don't give them food. Finally the woman thinks it is better to accept rather than deny, and the acceptance has to be according to the investigator. And thousands of nuns in the middle ages were burned alive because they had confessed. First you force them to confess that they are having intercourse with the devil, and then because they have confessed, you burned them alive: who was responsible?

And the monks created homosexuality. Monks are the cause, if some day humanity is going to die through an ugly disease, AIDS. The whole blame goes to the religions.

I am not condemning, I am simply clarifying the situation that homosexuals should understand that they are victims of a religious tradition and they should come out of it.

And it is not difficult; we just have to create places where homosexuals can be hypnotized and convinced about heterosexuality.

Lesbians, religions created. But more than that, now women's liberation has been created against men. How can a woman love a man? A woman can only love a woman. No-one knows if just as homosexuality has brought AIDS, what dangerous disease lesbianism may bring in the future. It is better to stop it now.

And I am not angry. It is my compassion. I would like religious people to make arrangements for homosexuals to be changed into heterosexuals – men or women. It is their duty, otherwise they should be punished – not homosexuals or lesbians. But I am against anything that is not in harmony with nature. It is bound to create trouble because nature makes your body in a certain way, your biology in a certain way – it is made for heterosexuality; it is not made for homosexuality.

There is no condemnation in me, and there is no criticism either. I am simply putting out the facts. All the homosexuals in the world and all the lesbians in the world should protest against the religions, the churches, the pope: "You are responsible for distracting us from our natural being and you have to pay for it. Now open hospitals, clinics, where we can be put back in harmony with nature – otherwise we are going to destroy your churches, your temples, your mosques. Because we are burning – and we cannot allow you to go unscathed, with nobody pointing the finger towards you."

You seem the most elegant spiritual figure in the world. The look, which seems a very important matter today, is important for you too?

To me what is important is my truth, is my experience. And certainly the truth changes the look, experience changes everything.

It is such a great inner revolution that the whole body is bound to follow it. Truth brings beauty, compassion, charisma.

But the look alone does not matter to me; what matters is truth.

If you had the chance to speak to both Reagan and Gorbachev's wives, what would you say to them?

Wives are powerful people as far as their husbands are concerned. Their husbands may be presidents and prime ministers of countries, but before the wife they are nobody.

So I will tell both ladies that the whole existence of humanity is in your hands. Dictate to your husbands that it is time for the Soviet Union and America to be friends and share scientific wisdom for the benefit of all humanity. Otherwise, nag them, throw clothes at them, wake them in the middle of the night, sit on their chest, beat their chest, until they say "Okay".

Wives can do miracles.

I am reminded of a story: A king was asking his close circle of wise people, "Can you find a husband in my kingdom who is not henpecked?"

They all said, "Of course, thousands of people are not henpecked."

But one man, Birbal, who was one of the wisest of all, remained silent.

The king asked him, "Birbal, why are you silent?"

He said, "I am silent because the greatest king of the country is asking the question and I suspect you are a henpecked husband yourself, and I don't see any possibility of finding another person more powerful than you."

The king said, "You are right – but still try. I would like to see a man who is not henpecked."

So two horses were given to Birbal,one white and one black, great stallions. And he was told, "Take these two horses and if you come across a man who is not henpecked let him choose one of the two. These are the best in our kingdom."

He went to many many people. He knew it was an exercise in futility but finally he reached a small cottage. A wrestler, a very big man, maybe seven feet high, very strong and muscular, was massaging himself in the early morning sun. His body was worth seeing – almost like steel.

Birbal thought perhaps this is the man; such a strong man cannot be henpecked.

He asked the man, "Are you henpecked?"

He said, "If you say the word again I will kill you here and now. Take your words back. Me – and henpecked?"

Then Birbal said, "Where is your wife?"

He said, "She is inside, you can see, preparing my breakfast."

A very small lady, thin....

Seeing both, Birbal was convinced that he is not a henpecked person. This woman he could throw a thousand feet high! What could she do to him?

So he said, "I am satisfied. The order of the king says that he who is not a henpecked husband can choose one stallion. They are the two greatest horses in the kingdom – one is white, one is black; which one would you like?"

He said, "Wait a minute" And then he called his wife: "Darling, should I choose the white or the black?"

The woman said, "Choose the white! And if you choose the black then remember, nobody is going to be as bad as me. I will bring you to your senses."

So the man said to Birbal, "The white."

Birbal said, "Now, no more – because you are a henpecked husband. With all these muscles and this height, you may be a champion wrestler but before your wife you are nothing. And she is just a tiny woman but she challenged you, saying "If you choose the black one then I will show you who I am. Choose the white, otherwise I will make your life a hell!" And you have simply chosen the white. Now I cannot give you either the white or the black and I have to report to the king, 'Drop this search, there is nobody who is not henpecked.'"

So I would like to say to these ladies of the presidents of America and Russia, that you have immense power in your hands. You can change the whole course of history: just scream loudly, break plates, throw things all around, and your husband is going to say, "Forgive me, I will do whatever you say."

What all the pacifists of the world have been unable to do, women can do…

Okay?

The Last Testament Vol. 5, Ch 30

It was beautiful to live in a room close to the Master, a room that had the prerogative, asked for specifically by Osho, to be the darkest room of the whole hotel, something that he realized the day on which Osho agreed to be photographed in his room in his ordinariness.

When he entered Osho's room, he understood instantly that it was too dark to make any pictures, and asked him if he wouldn't mind to come with him to his room just in front, since there it was full of light.

Osho followed him along with Vivek, but once they entered he noticed in horror that there were some noticeable sperm stains on top of his bed!

He thought that there was certainly no point his night's activity being known everywhere and he managed with supreme nonchalance to throw a huge pillow on it. He then asked Osho who meanwhile had accommodated himself on a big chair to do just something normal, something usual to him, so that he could make some pictures of the quotidian life of the Master during a common day, but at this point Osho closed his eyes and seemed to be dissolving into samadhi, and he almost started crying: "No, not like this! Please do something, anything, but do something … have a cup of tea, eat a sandwich, have a little beer, but do something, pleeeease!"

Osho looked at him laughing, and then asked to Vivek to bring him a cup for tea, empty, from where he pretended to sip his drink like the consummate actor that he was. After he had shot a few pictures of Osho while drinking his tea, he asked him if Vivek could comb his beard while he would photograph the entire scene. The Master approved, creating thus a memorable sequence in which the only effort from Osho's side was to not burst out with laughter for how much this scene was amusing him!

He was going to have even more fun when our photographer invited him to come out on the huge balcony to sit at the vast table there, proposing to him to have a real cup of tea this time, along with Vivek, Shunyo, and Anando, his faithful lawyer. According to him it wouldn't only be a nice photo, but most importantly an image that nobody had never seen before, a photo of the Master sitting with his girlfriends sipping tea, just like an absolutely commonplace person, such as an old uncle surrounded by his grand-daughters.

Nonetheless, the three girls absolutely didn't want to sit there to have tea with Osho, because they found it very disrespectful; hence he had to intervene and ask the Master to invite them himself, so perhaps they would stop making all this fuss!

Osho looked at the girls incredulously, because obviously he couldn't understand their pseudo-problem, and invited them all to sit with him and drink tea, making sure that they smile for the camera!

He spent two marvelous weeks there, photographing Osho every day for half an hour, until the day before his departure he asked him through Vivek if he could photograph him sitting in the garden, amongst the beautiful flowers that were blossoming all around.

Vivek came the same day to tell him that it was okay with Osho, and that the next morning he could have his photo session with him, in any spot of the garden that he liked. Then, being the perfect caretaker that she was, she suggested to him to buy a couple of small, nice carpets, "because it wouldn't be nice to have him sit on the grass like a vagabond!"

He went straight to town to buy these little carpets, and he bought even some small colored pillows, but only after he had told her that it was a bit of a weird idea, because it would be much more natural if he could photograph Osho just sitting simply on the grass. However, she insisted on those carpets, and she got them.

The next morning when he went to his appointment in the garden carrying all the pillows in his hands and the carpets draped over his shoulder, Osho asked him why he had brought all this stuff, and he told him that this had been Vivek's request, so that he could have something to sit on and didn't have to sit on top of the grass. To his surprise Osho replied: "It is much better if I sit simply on the grass, it will be much more natural."

At these words he looked at Vivek with that Neapolitan expression that can be translated into words as 'tie'! – and he could finally have his session with the result that (hopefully) everybody has seen those great photographs.

***

CHAPTER 08

Intermezzo In Mumbai

After leaving Kathmandu for a world tour, Osho arrived in Greece from where he was deported after a few weeks staying on the island of Crete. From there his odyssey included many stopovers in Europe, and countries such as France, Switzerland, Germany, Holland, England, Ireland, and Antigua all refused to let him stay for a visit. Even Canada refused permission for his plane to land for refueling on the way to Antigua! However, Osho finally received an entry visa for Uruguay, where he stayed in Punta del Este until the Uruguayan government – under heavy pressure from the US government – had to ask Osho to leave. Osho was flown to Jamaica but within hours the US government's arm had reached there too and he was then flown to Portugal where he stayed for a month but also here difficulties arose. At the end of July Osho returned to Bombay where he soon began to give discourses.

Beloved Osho, yes!

Sarjano, there was no need to say yes because I have seen it in your eyes. I have heard it when you were sitting near me, although you have not uttered it.

Since you have come to me there has never been a no in you. And it is strange, because your type is no-type! You have said no to everything, and perhaps that is the reason that your no is finished. You don't have any no anymore, and you have come to the person with whom you can connect only through yes.

To be with a master is to be in a yes attitude.

That's what I mean by receptivity, openness, vulnerability.

But I know that one wants to say it, thinking perhaps I may not be aware. I am absolutely aware of those people whose heartbeat is saying yes. There are people who are still in two minds – sometimes yes, sometimes no. There are also people who are too much attached to their no – but I don't count them, they are not my people. Only those whose yes is unconditional, absolute, categorical, are my people.

And Sarjano, you are fortunate. You belong to my people.

Yes, Sarjano.

The Osho Upanishad, Ch3, Q 4

Beloved Osho,

Last time I saw you in Poona, you smiled at me and you sent me one of your unforgettable glances. Somehow, deep down I knew that this was the last time I would see you.

I was ready to live without your physical presence, I was ready to live without your morning discourses, but that smile… Oh Osho! In that moment my heart was crucified by the most unbearable pain ever felt in my life, and I thought: "Oh my god, I can live without his presence, but how, how in heaven can I live without this smile? I can't, I certainly can't. I will die without it!"

And suddenly, at the bottom of the agony I heard a voice inside my heart. It sounded like your voice saying, "Just see! If you can just see, you will realize that all of the existence is smiling at you twenty-four hours a day, in the same way, exactly the same way!"

For all these years I've been whispering this secret to myself, every morning, every evening, but now I want to say it loudly.

Would you kindly allow me to reveal the secret, the gift for which I will be eternally grateful to my Master.

Sarjano, there is no need to ask me.

It is nice of you that you asked, but when the urge has come to say the secret loudly then don't wait for anything, not even for my approval. Just say it – because it is neither mine nor yours; it belongs to the whole.

The Osho Upanishad, Ch 11, Q 4

Beloved Osho,

Sitting at your feet, drinking from your wine, the ecstasy of your presence, and your smile showering such a grace on us….

And do you really think someone here would want to disappear? No way! Certainly not 'me'!

It is true, Sarjano; but you have disappeared, I don't see you anywhere.

This is a cunning question.

Everybody is present; only Sarjano has disappeared! But I do understand what he means.

The master is the last barrier on the path. The love for the master is difficult to drop. One can drop everything – one can renounce the whole world, one can renounce himself – but unless the last thing also is dropped, that small clinging with the master remains the base for your ego.

Gautam Buddha has said, "If you meet me on the way, immediately cut my head." He is talking metaphorically. Because when you are meditating everything will disappear, but finally, you will see the master is there. When the whole world has disappeared the master is there. That is your last love, and it is so satisfying, so gratifying, that one wants to be in that state forever.

Only the master can say, "This is not the goal. One step more. remove this attachment with the master too, so you are absolutely unattached."

In absolute unattachment the ego disappears.

And the disappearance of the ego is not the disappearance of you. The disappearance of the ego is really the appearance of you for the first time; the false disappears and the true comes to revelation.

Sarjano, you are right; it is difficult, but it has to be made possible. It is not impossible because many have done it. And you are not doing it against the master; you are fulfilling the last message of the master.

Let the ego disappear.

But it will disappear only when there is no attachment.

And the moment there is no ego at all, for the first time you are.

Then you will feel grateful towards the master forever because if he had not been insistent, you would have remained in that beautiful state. But there is something beyond, more; and the master would not like you to be stuck on the path.

The master wants you to be totally liberated, liberated from everything; he is included in that 'everything'.

But Sarjano is clever : he has put the question here and he has escaped to Italy!

That won't help – I will haunt him wherever he is. He will have to disappear!

The Osho Upanishad, Ch 13, Q 5

Beloved Osho,

'Sitting silently, doing nothing, the grass grows by itself.'… And I fall asleep. Somehow I always feel envy for those people who can sit silently for hours, but I really can't manage it, and I have been trying hard. I'm only good at fighting, at creating troubles, at dancing with creativity, at shouting from the rooftops, at singing loudly. So does that mean that there is no hope for me?

Sarjano, the haiku you are quoting is from a great master, Basho.

I know him. I can tell him to change it a little just to save a poor Italian. And the change that I can suggest to Basho will not be such that he will feel any difficulty.

The haiku is, 'Sitting silently, doing nothing, the spring comes and the grass grows by itself.'

I can tell him to make just a little change: Sitting silently, doing nothing, the sleep comes and the grass grows by itself. I don't think there is any problem. You have every hope.

But don't try your other things; they will not fit. Sleep is a perfect spiritual activity – but shouting from the rooftops, creating trouble, and doing all the things you are saying in your question, they don't fit.

And as far as the grass is concerned, while you are asleep it has more chances to grow silently; otherwise you are going to create trouble.

Basho's haiku is tremendously important. He is simply saying that if you can relax, God grows by itself. It is not the grass. He cannot use the word 'God', but that's what he means: God grows by itself.

So sleeping silently is a perfectly right atmosphere for God to grow. You have every hope.

As far as Basho is concerned, I will persuade him to change the haiku.

The Osho Upanishad, Ch 19, Q 5

Beloved Osho,

In the West, the portrayal of woman's body is used in films, books and magazines. This art form is known as 'eroticism'.

Through the sculptures of Khajuraho and Ajanta I have seen that a similar art form was there in the East.

Can you talk about the difference between these two cultures in regard to the female body?

Sarjano, superficially there is no difference.

Khajuraho, Konarak, Puri, Ajanta, Ellora, Elephanta – they are full of erotic art, just like the contemporary erotic culture where the repressed sexuality of thousands of years has become such a burden that it has to be dropped. And suddenly a great erotic revolution is taking place.

Pornography is nothing but erotic and obscene – in paintings, in films, in dances. They don't create in you a longing for the beyond; they simply create in you more sensuality, more sexuality. But on the surface they look alike.

And in India and in the outside world, they are being misunderstood.

After the country became independent, Mahatma Gandhi proposed that all these sculptures, all these temples should be sunk into mud. They would not be destroyed, so if Ronald Reagan comes to see, then you can clean it and show him – just for special people....

But for ordinary people they would be closed. Because Mahatma Gandhi thought, in the same way as it is thought all over the world, that they are erotic, they are obscene.

But I want to declare emphatically that there is a vast difference between the Eastern art in Ajanta, Ellora, Puri, Konarak, Khajuraho, and the modern Western erotic, pornographic photography, painting , music. The difference is that all these temples….

For example, there are thirty temples in Khajuraho. There were one hundred temples originally – Mohammedans have destroyed seventy temples, which are now ruins. The city was a city only of temples; people just used to come to see the art. One hundred temples must have been built in thousands of years by thousands of artists continuously working on stone – generation after generation may have died working on it.

And they have created the most beautiful bodies in stone. In Khajuraho stone speaks, sings, dances; it is not dead. You can see that the artist has succeeded in transforming the dead stone into a living form. It looks so alive that any moment the statue may walk towards you and say, "Hello." And hundreds of statues….

These statues were not to satisfy your repressed sexuality. On the contrary, they were used as a tantrica method to release the repressed sexuality just by meditating on these naked statues. The method was simply to sit there in silence – only a dim light reaches there, and hundreds of statues surround you.

Just watching them, you will be surprised to find that many of those dreams have occurred to you, many are such that they have been condemned in every society – sexual orgies, but they have happened in your dreams; they are part of your unconscious. And these places like Khajuraho were kinds of universities where people were coming to release, to cathart repressed sexuality.

And all these statues are outside the temple. Inside the temple there is no erotic sculpture. In fact, inside most of the temples there is nothing – just silence, a cool peaceful milieu, with the vibes of thousands of years of people meditating there.

The rule was when you feel, or your master feels, that now the erotic sculpture outside the temple no longer affects you, it does not create any sexuality in you, any sensuality in you, that it has cleaned your whole repressed sex….

It is the greatest psychological method invented by the East. Nobody is told what is happening, and for years there is no need. Once the master sees, and once you see that you are sitting there and nothing happens, it is as if the walls are empty – when you are absolutely certain that they don't affect you – that is a signal: "Now it is time, you can go inside. Now the door for the inner, for the interior is open." All that was rubbish has been dropped – a cleanliness, a weightlessness, and a silence which is full of beauty and song….

Khajuraho or Konarak… these are not pornographic. They are devices for meditation.

What is happening in the West is simply pornography, obscene. It does not help man to get rid of it but simply gives him a temporary relief. The pornographic literature, photography, are all helping you to stay normal; otherwise you will go mad.

So I don't think there is any harm when somebody reads Playboy hiding it inside The Bible. What he is seeing in a pornographic magazine brings up his own unconscious.

This was used as a meditation technique in Khajuraho. In the West it is used to create more thirst for the same sexuality which has been aroused by the pornographic magazine, by blue films, by naked dances and striptease.

The same method was used to transform your energy into spirituality.

In the West it is used to provoke more sexuality, more sensuality.

And then there is a kind of insatiation – almost all painting has gone pornographic, all the movies repeating almost the same stories, the same plot, the same triangle: two women, one man; or two men, one woman, a simple structure – the same story. What attracts people to it? It is not great appreciation for literature!

What attracts is that in the story – needed for the story or not needed – they go on putting your suppressed needs, desires. It is a kind of relief. But tomorrow you will be repressing again, and again you will need the same kind of photography, the same dance.

This way you will never be able to enter into the temple. In fact, pornography in the West has no idea that it is the outer wall of the temple.

The East has used every fragment of human nature for a greater change, a mutation, to bring something higher in you of which you are capable but unconscious.

Sermons in Stones, Ch 5, Q 3

Beloved Osho,
What is your definition of perversion in regard to sex?

Sarjano, perversion means your energy is not going in the natural way; the natural way has been blocked, suppressed, condemned. But the energy is there and collecting, it is bound to find some outlet. That outlet will not be natural. That outlet will be perversion.

And the whole past of man is nothing else – from different directions, for different excuses you have been told to cut off your natural paths for energy and expression.

Man is an intelligent being. Even unintelligent animals are bound to find some way. In the wild, no animals turn homosexual; there is no need because there is no priest. But man is so much conditioned against a few things – sex being the main one – that if he lives sex naturally, he feels guilty that he is going against God, against religion. If he prevents his natural expressions, then soon his energies start moving into perverted forms.

Just the other day, I received the information that by the end of this century, there will be one billion people suffering from AIDS. And this is the lowest estimate. I don't feel the number will be so low. The number, according to me, may be double.

AIDS is the ultimate expression of perverted sexual energy. And the wonder is that you are surrounded with such dangerous things.... AIDS can destroy the whole planet, because we don't have any medicine and the doctors and the scientists are openly saying that there seems to be no possibility, at least in the near future, to find a medicine. So once you have AIDS, your death is certain within six months to two years, and you cannot do anything except wait.

A disease like AIDS has come through homosexuality. It is the ultimate.... And the perversion is not condemned; on the contrary, in different ways it is supported because every religion believes in brahmacharya, in celibacy. Now those who believe in celibacy are standing in the queue – first they will be homosexuals, lesbians and sooner or later, they will receive the ultimate reward, the Nobel Prize – AIDS.

Now religions are responsible for it. But this is what I say, human insanity....

In Texas, they have made a law against homosexuality. Now it is a crime in Texas; you can get five to ten years in jail. Texas is a backward state in America. Even I was surprised that one million homosexuals demonstrated against the legislature and these may not be all the homosexuals in the state of Texas. But one million homosexuals! And they made it clear to the government that by making homosexuality illegal, you cannot prevent it. You have made many things illegal in the past, and what have you prevented? Has theft disappeared? Has murder disappeared? Is rape something of the past?

You cannot stop it with your laws because you have never stopped anything with your laws. You are just befooling the masses, making a law so people feel the government is doing something. But they don't see that what they are doing, they have been doing for ten thousand years, and things have gone from bad to worse.

When I read about it, I had two ideas: one, that to make homosexuality a crime and not to make celibacy a crime.... Because these homosexuals are products of your religion. Your religion condemns sex so much... your monks, your nuns, you have put them almost in prisons. Now these one million homosexuals in Texas will go underground. Just now, they had their clubs, their discos, their restaurants; they were openly homosexual. Now you have made it a crime. They will go underground. When they were open and known, there was a possibility to check them medically, to help them in some way. If somebody had AIDS already, he could be isolated. Places could be made where only AIDS people would be living, working.

Now, nobody is going to accept that he has AIDS – why should he go for an examination? This is the danger. A single person can spread the disease like wildfire because it not only transferred by sexual contact – that is something more than ordinary sexual diseases – it can be transferred by other means.

Blood transfusion... now you don't know whose blood is being transfused into you. And if the man whose blood is being transfused into you has AIDS, you will have it. It can be transferred even just by kissing because saliva carries the virus. Now for the first time, the Siberians have been proved right because they have never kissed in their whole history, and they always laughed when they came in contact with Christian missionaries, watching them kissing each other. They could not believe it. These people have come to teach religion to you and they don't even know hygiene. Mixing each other's saliva, playing with each other's tongues – and these idiots have come to preach religion!

In Siberia, they have never kissed. It is a dirty habit... you just think about it. Siberians rub noses with each other – that is pure hygiene. And as far as love is concerned, it can be expressed in many ways.... But repression is going to grow.

In one monastery in Europe, half of the monastery has just declared that they are homosexuals, so the monastery is now divided in two parts. They are fighting amongst themselves – the homosexuals and the non-homosexuals. I am saying non-homosexuals because I cannot say they are celibate. It is almost impossible to be celibate unless something is wrong with your body.

I have heard that Stanley was a very healthy sperm and the whole day he used to do push-ups while all the other sperm were just relaxing. And they were puzzled:

"What is wrong with this Stanley? The whole day, exercises, exercises."

Finally, one of these lazy people asked Stanley, "Please tell us what the secret is? Why are you exercising so much? The whole day, from the time you wake up till you go to sleep, you are exercising, doing this, doing that. What is the purpose?"

He said, "You don't know? You guys are fools. Only one sperm is going to reach the woman's egg. And next time when the release comes, I am Stanley, the one who is going to get to the egg. That is the purpose."

And one day suddenly they started feeling very hot and they all thought the time had come. Before they could have discussed among themselves what to do, they were released so suddenly... but they all saw Stanley far ahead. He was swimming so fast, they could not believe that one could swim so fast and then suddenly, Stanley turned back, screamed loudly, and said, "Go back, go back! It's a blow job!"

Even poor sperm are laughing at humanity.

If man is allowed to be simply natural, his life can give him immense joy, peace, silence, and finally the truth – but if his energies are perverted, then he goes round and round wasting himself.

I have heard about an army officer who had been around the world, posted at different places – and naturally, the monks and the soldiers are in the same boat because you don't allow soldiers their wives, their girlfriends.

This officer, Major Benson, was in Hong Kong and got into real trouble. He was going to prostitutes all over the world, but he was not aware of Chinese prostitutes. They are the most dangerous. He fell into the trap of a Chinese prostitute and seeing the situation, looking at the naked body of the prostitute, he felt that it was better to have a medical check-up: "This woman seems to be sick and one does not know what kind of sickness she is carrying."

So he went to the American section of the city and found a doctor. The doctor examined him and said, "Nothing can be done. You need an immediate operation; your cock has to be removed."

The man was shocked. He said, "My God!"

The doctor said, "You have so many diseases that in this one life, they cannot be cured."

He came out dazed. He thought it would be better to have another opinion, so he went to another American doctor.

He checked him thoroughly and said, "I'm sorry, the first doctor was right. It is too late. Nothing can be done and if you don't have the operation soon, even an operation may not help; the diseases may have spread all over your body. So don't waste time. I can do the operation tomorrow."

He said, "I will be coming tomorrow," but he was not satisfied with the idea that he would have to live his whole life without a cock.

Suddenly, he saw a Chinese doctor's signboard. He thought, "Perhaps a Chinese doctor might be helpful."

He went in. The doctor looked. The other doctors had spent hours in checking his whole body, this and that. The Chinese doctor just looked with a magnifying glass and said, "There is no need for any operation."

Benson was very happy. He said, "Really? Is there any hope?"

He said, "Every hope. First, you went to a Chinese woman – because these diseases you can get only from a Chinese prostitute. The second wrong thing you did, was you went to American doctors who are just after money, money, money – and money means you have to do something. Even if your cock disappears, they are not worried; they need money. An operation means money. You don't be worried, there is no need of any operation."

Benson was very happy. He said, "Thank you!" He gave much money to him and the old man said, "Whenever there is any trouble, come to me, don't go to American doctors. They are simply cheating people."

Just to have a final word from the doctor, he said, "So now I can go? There is no need?"

He said, "There is no need, I have told you. Just wait two or three weeks and the pecker will fall off by itself."

Sermons in Stones, Ch 16, Q 5

***

CHAPTER 09

Back to Milan and Osho Returns to Poona

At the end of 1986, he moved to Milan to live there for a short while, and enjoyed working for Wild Boys, a multicolored magazine for kids, that had asked him if he was ready to make a series of pictures about street fashion, and since he was living in Ticinese, just opposite of the 'San Lorenzo Columns', he accepted with pleasure.

These colonne are one of the most famous gathering places in the whole city, where all the various youth bands used to converge, from the mythical Teddy Boys to the New Dandys, to the Rockabilly, and then Punks, Hippies, Paninari – the lot!

Every evening, just before sunset, all these gangs gathered around the columns to watch and to be watched, so all he had to do was to go in front of his house and start photographing this colored humanity in the beautiful light of the sunset, a job, that given the conditions of the light, would last at most for an half hour, and it was very well paid!

In those days he was living together with Premal who had completed her education long ago and had moved to Milan with him. After a couple of months of this Milan life, he came to know that Osho, tired of traveling endlessly from here to there and being thrown out wherever he would go, had decided to return to the old ashram in Pune that had been his home for years, and from where nobody could expel him.

He also found out that all the sannyasins from Pune were getting ready for his comeback with a lot of fanfare, and with the idea of creating a parade to start from the airport and to reach the ashram, with flowers, music, dances and songs all along the way. Of course he found immediately an endorsement from a big magazine interested in this story, which included airline tickets and a check for his expenses; he got ready to leave.

A few days before his departure, he was reached by the news that all these plans had changed dramatically, and that Osho would for sure be returning to Pune in a few days, but it would have to be done very quietly, without anybody receiving him at the airport, neither festive parades along the way, and this was due to the fact that, although it might sound incredible, the city authorities were not happy about Osho's return, and there was a possibility they could have turned him back where he was coming from!

Osho returned to Pune quietly a few days later, but at least now he was in his ancient home, and his troubles and peregrinations seemed finished forever.

Once they came to know about his imminent arrival, the local sannyasins had cleaned up the place at its best, had restored Buddha Hall, and had made everything neat and shining. Hence Osho started to give his discourses the very next day after his arrival, but since there weren't many people yet, he decided to give his discourses in Chuang Tzu Auditorium, which was simply a small roofed marble courtyard outside his room.

Two days later he was in Pune, while Premal, who lately had been disconnecting more and more from him, decided to stay in Milan for another couple of months, because she had suddenly discovered she was a teenager who had spent all her life with 'an old man'; now she wanted to hang around with people her age and have fun in some discothèques, so she promised that she would join him in a few months and waved him goodbye.

After a few days in Pune he was so happy to be again close to his Master that he decided to send him a little poem which he had written in a moment of divine anger! It was only a few verses long, and he had previously sent them to his friends in the sannyasin world to let them know his thoughts about what had been done to Osho, and these verses had been published by every Osho Times in the world, even in its Japanese version, and at this point he thought that Osho too should have a chance to read them, hence he sent them to him with a private letter.

The next day when he went to listen to the daily discourse in Chuang Tzu Auditorium, Maneesha, the woman who was reading aloud the questions or the sutras to which the Master would comment, took him by the hand and brought him to sit in the first row, close to her, less than two meters away from the chair where Osho was going to sit, telling him that this was the Master's wish...

He had never sat so close to his Master in his entire life, and he was all excited, and even a little scared! When Osho arrived and sat down, he saw him immediately, and he felt like he was smiling at him. Then Maneesha started to read the first question:

Beloved Osho,
Would you say this is not love?
For behind the tears of absence
is a serene memory
as a constant presence in my center
always, always in the center
of my heart, of my feet,
all the directions of the earth,
the words and the silences,
the embraces and the songs,
but most of all
in the center of my sorrowing smile
sometimes pained with rage.
So would you say this is not love?
Because I shout: "You bastards!"

for I cannot accept in silence or with joy
that they gag your mouth
and they fetter your feet.

Would you say this is not love?
The divine rage that screams within me
singing its furious song
for the thousands and thousands of hearts
who would have loved to meet you
but are hindered by boundaries of fear,
by bureaucracy, passports and masked manners.
Would you say if I could ask you
my eternal question
that I do not love you?
Because I feel to scream to them
that I love you, I love you,
and because I want them all to love you,
to be free
to love you and to meet you
under every tree,
in every country,
on every street around the earth,
and because I wish for every wretch
you could reach out your hand
or your infinite silence.
I would be dead by now
forgotten of myself
if I had not met you.
And so I weep for all of those
who died in forgetfulness
of their own soul
without having met you.
And again and again I scream:
"You bastards!"
into the faces of those
who try to chain you close
in order to keep you
from the thirsty and the lost.

So would you say this is not love?
For the scream is louder still
than the silence.
For the heart is turmoil and the rage

whets the intelligence
like a sword to cut the chains,
to cut the heads of the parasites,
and to open a door
for intuition to enter.
I cannot take this anymore,
the fear and the meanness of those who decide
what is right and what is wrong.
Nor the fear of those who are afraid
of the songs,
of the dance,
of the music that springs up
when a living being
meets you.
So, oh, my love, would you say
this is not love?

Sarjano, I am reminded of a beautiful statue of Gautam Buddha, which was sent to me from Japan by a friend. It was no ordinary statue; it was the samurai conception of Gautam Buddha. In one of his hands was a burning torch and in the other hand was a naked sword. And the beauty and the strangeness of the statue was this: that half of his face was lighted by the torch – serene, silent, peaceful; and the other side of his face had the same sharpness as the sword he was holding in his hand.

Silence can also be a song.

Love can also be a sword.

These great experiences of life – silence or love or blissfulness – are not limited to only one meaning. They include the whole spectrum of the rainbow: all the colors between black and white also belong to them. Love can be as soft as a rose flower, and love can be as hard as a bullet – these are all aspects. One has to remember only one thing: that they are coming out of a loving space. Your revolution has to come from a loving space; your rebellion has to have the flavor of love. Then it is a totally different phenomenon: it is no longer political, it starts taking on a spiritual dimension.

I can understand, Sarjano, you love me too much. You cannot bear to see what the religions, the organized churches of the world are doing to me. You cannot tolerate it; it is impossible for your love to tolerate what the politicians and the bureaucrats have been doing to me.

I have been teaching only silence and love to people, and I have been treated as if I am a murderer!

The Attorney General of America said at a press conference, "We could not put Osho into jail because we don't have any evidence that he has committed any crime." And the same man, in the federal court, produced a long list of crimes, and blackmailed my attorneys, threatened them. They came to see me in the jail, they had tears in their eyes – and they were professional attorneys, they were not concerned about me the way you are concerned about me.

But those twelve days in American jails.... They arrested me without any arrest warrant. And the way the judges behaved... they would not allow me even to inform my attorneys that I had been arrested; they would not indicate even verbally the reason why I had been arrested. The magistrate before whom I first had to appear was a woman magistrate. For three days continuously the U.S. Attorney argued and could not prove anything against me. He had to accept, himself – in his closing statement on the third day – that "I have failed to prove any crime against Osho, and I don't have anything else to say." Still the magistrate did not allow me to be released on bail.

Even the jailer could not believe what was happening. He had brought my things with him, thinking that I would be released. They did not have any arrest warrant, they did not have any cause to show; for three days he had been listening and there was not a single point that proved me guilty or criminal.

When bail was refused, he said, "I have never in my life seen such injustice. The reason why your bail has not been given is something nobody will ever know." The reason was that the government had threatened the magistrate, "If you give Osho bail, you will always remain a state magistrate; you will never move into the position of federal judge. And if you don't give bail, you will soon be promoted to federal judge." And within three weeks she was promoted.

My attorneys were watching all this happening, and the final thing that they could not believe was that the U.S. Attorney did not want the trial. He said to them, "We know and you know that there is no case at all – you are going to win. But it is in our hands not to give him bail, and to go on prolonging the case for ten years, twelve years... so you have to choose. If you insist on a trial, then don't blame us. You will win, but Osho could be in jail for twenty years. If you want him to be released without trial then you have to accept at least two crimes. The choice is clear for you."

For twelve days my attorneys had been running from one jail to another – because they were taking me from one jail to another every day, changing the jails, trying to find some indirect way to kill me.

They put me in a cell with a man who was going to die of AIDS. The cell was meant for two, but for six months nobody had shared it because the doctor had ordered that he should remain alone. They put me in that cell. And while the doctor was present, the jailer was present, the U.S. Marshal was present, as they moved me, the man – who was almost counting his last breaths – told me, "Osho, you don't know me, but I have been watching you on television, and I have fallen in love with you.

"Don't come into the cell; just stand near the door, because I am suffering from AIDS and I am dying. And they have put you knowingly here – because for six months they have not put anybody else in here. Everything in the cell is contaminated. You just

remain by the door, and knock on the door, because it will take hours of knocking for anybody to turn up."

It took almost one hour before the jailer came. I asked him, "For six months this cell has not been given to another person. You know perfectly well this man is dying... why have you put me here?"

Immediately I was changed. They had no answer. I asked the doctor, "You must have taken the Hippocratic Oath to save people's lives. If you have any shame, any dignity.... You were present – you have been preventing even murderers from being put in this cell – and you did not say anything."

He said to me, "We cannot do anything. Orders came from the top that every indirect method should be used – so if the person dies, we are not responsible."

As I entered in another jail, in the middle of the night, the U.S. Marshal wanted me to sign my name as 'David Washington.' I said, "But that is not my name."

He said, "That we don't know. This is the order we have received from the top: you cannot write your own name on the form. In the jail, you will be known as David Washington."

I said, "I see written on your coat in beautiful letters 'U.S. Department of Justice'. At least take this coat off. What kind of justice is this? – and do you think I am an idiot that I can't see your game? – if I sign under the name 'David Washington' you can kill me, and nobody will be able even to find a trace of where I disappeared because I never entered your jail."

I said, "I am not going to write anybody else's name. But if you are feeling tired – I can see it is the middle of the night, the whole day working... you must be feeling tired – you can leave me here on this bench in the office. I will wait. Or you can do one thing: you can fill in the form and I will sign it."

He could not understand a simple strategy. He filled in the form with David Washington and everything as he wanted. It was all fiction: my father's name was fiction, my place of residence was fiction – but I signed my signature. He looked at my signature and said, "What does it mean?"

I said, "It must mean 'David Washington'. And tomorrow you will see in the newspapers and on television... my signature is known all over the world."

My attorneys were watching continuously, running from one city to another city, from one jail to another jail. They were worried that if they did not accept two crimes, the trial would mean my torture and perhaps my death. And if I have to live for twenty years in jail, what is the point of winning? They came with tears in their eyes, and they said, "We are asking you something which we should not ask. We are here to defend you, and to defend your innocence, but the government is blackmailing us." And they told me that this was their strategy.

And he has made it clear, the same Attorney General, "If you want Osho alive, you must immediately accept two crimes… and within fifteen minutes Osho has to leave America."

Seeing their tears, and thinking of the millions of my people around the world, who were telephoning and sending so many letters and telegrams and flowers that every jail was full of flowers…. The jailers were asking me, "What to do with these flowers? Where to keep them? – because we don't have space."

I said to them, "There is no need to worry; I am a non-serious person. I can accept any crime they want. Outside the court the whole world media is waiting, and outside the court I will say, "Under the oath of truth, I have lied. The government forced me to lie." On one hand they force you to take the oath that you will not lie, and on the other hand they blackmail you into lying.

So I said, "Don't be worried." – I accepted, without even bothering what those crimes were. They had not said that if I accept the crimes, there is going to be a huge fine – four hundred thousand dollars, which is nearabout sixty lakh rupees – and that for five years I cannot enter America. And fifteen years of suspended sentence – so that even if after five years I enter the country and the government thinks that I am committing any crime, I will have to go to jail for ten years, and there will be no trial for it and no question about it.

These are their protections, so I cannot go to a higher court and appeal: that this is blackmail. So in fact they have prevented me from entering America for fifteen years.

And my attorneys were perfectly right: as I left the jail, a bomb was found under my seat. The bomb was a time bomb. Now, nobody else can put a bomb inside the jail except the jail authorities, except the government.

The case finished within five minutes, because I accepted – there was no question of argument, and I said, "Any crime they say, I have committed. No need to waste the time of the court. You simply give your judgment." My people immediately produced four hundred thousand dollars, and within ten minutes I was out of the jail. My plane had been kept ready, so that within fifteen minutes I could leave America.

I was wondering why they were in such a hurry, why fifteen minutes? My attorneys said, "They are worried that if you are allowed to stay here for two days or five days, you may go to a higher court and appeal that you have been blackmailed – so you have to leave America immediately."

These are the democratic governments. These are the people who go on saying that their ideals are democracy, liberty, freedom of expression, freedom for the individual to be himself. So I can understand if you call these politicians, these popes, these shankaracharyas, 'the bastards'. It is simply that your love is too much for me and your love for freedom, individuality, and respect for life is too much.

My whole teaching can be reduced to a simple concept: reverence for life and freedom.

So Sarjano, you need not be worried. You must be feeling that I may say this is not love. This too is love – love on fire, love aflame. And love has to learn not to be just a rose flower. It has to know that if the time comes, it can become a sword.

You are asking me, "Would you say this is not love?" *No, I would not say that.*

"For behind the tears of absence
is a serene memory
as a constant presence in my center
of my heart, of my feet,
all the directions of the earth,
the words and the silences,
the embraces and the songs,
but most of all
in the center of my sorrowing smile
sometimes pained with rage."

Love knows to roar like a lion too. Love is not just sweet poetry.

If love were just sweet poetry, it could not exist in this insane world. It has to be strong enough – stronger than hate, stronger than anger. It has to be a lion's roar.

"So would you say this is not love?" *No, Sarjano, this is love in its purity, in its utter genuineness, in its absolute authenticity.*

"Because I shout: 'You bastards!'
For I cannot accept in silence or with joy
that they gag your mouth
and they fetter your feet.
Would you say this is not love?"

I have knocked on the doors of twenty-one countries, but no country was courageous enough to allow me even a tourist visa for three or four weeks.

In Greece they allowed me a four-week visa, but the archbishop of Greece started making a great noise, sending telegrams to the president and to the prime minister, and writing threatening letters to the owner of the house in which I was staying, saying that if he wants to save his house, I should be thrown out. Because if I am not thrown out within thirty-six hours, he is going to burn down the whole house with all the people in it; burn them alive. And this is the archbishop of the most ancient Christian church. He represents Jesus Christ!

The government became afraid. They had no reason – because I had not even left the house in two weeks. I was asleep in the afternoon when the police came. My legal secretary, Anando, was telling the officers, "Sit down, have some tea, and I will wake Him up."

But they threw her from a four-foot porch down onto the gravel, and dragged her over the gravel to the jeep, and took her away to the police station: she was trying to prevent government action.

And as I was awakened by John, I heard noises as if dynamite was being exploded. The police started throwing rocks at the house from all sides, destroying the beautiful ancient windows and doors, and they also had dynamite. They said, "You have to wake him up this very moment, otherwise we will dynamite the house."

No arrest warrant, no reason to be so furious – just because the archbishop had told the government that if I was allowed to stay in Greece, the morality, the religion, the culture, everything would be in danger. In just two weeks I would corrupt the minds of the young people. I had not even left my house, and I had not met anybody. The people who had come to see me had all come from outside Greece.

But I wondered: they have built up this morality and this religion and this culture over two thousand years: what kind of culture and what kind of morality is it which can be destroyed in two weeks by an individual man? It does not deserve to exist if it is so weak, so impotent.

The American government has been telling all the governments of the world that I should not be allowed, even as a tourist, in their countries. One small country, Uruguay, in South America, was very happy that I had come there, because the president had been reading my books, and he had not dreamt that I would ever come to Uruguay. So he said, "We will make every effort to give you land, so that you can create a community. Because not only will we be enriched by your presence and your disciples, but thousands of pilgrims will start coming; and we are a poor country – it will be a financial gain too." And he immediately managed a one-year residence visa for me.

But when the American President, Ronald Reagan, became aware of it – the American Ambassador in Uruguay informed him – he threatened the President of Uruguay: "Within thirty-six hours Osho should leave the country. Otherwise you will have to return all the loans that we have given you in the past, and all the loans – billions of dollars – which we were going to give you in the coming two years will not be given. So you can choose."

Now, Uruguay cannot manage to return the money and cannot afford not to take billions of dollars in the coming two years, because her whole planning is based on those billions of dollars. The whole economy of the country would collapse. The president had tears in his eyes when he told me, "Your coming to our country has at least made me aware of one thing: that we are not independent. We have been living under a delusion.

"You will have to leave. It is illegal – because you have a valid residence visa for one year; and you have not committed any heinous crime – that is the only reason that a residence visa can be canceled." And I had only been there one month. And he said, "It is unfortunate that I have to do it. I am doing it against my own conscience."

Even this much the American president was not willing to concede: that I should simply leave the country. My plane was standing at the airport. I said, "There is no problem; I can leave the country. I will not put your country into such jeopardy."

He said, "The American President insists that you should be deported; you should not leave the country without being deported. I am forced to commit crimes: first, to tell you for no reason to leave the country, you have done nothing. Second, to deport you. But I am absolutely helpless. Still, I want one thing: that on your passport there should be no stamp of deportation from Uruguay. We have a small airport – so move your airplane to that airport, and in the evening leave without informing us; so we can say, 'He left without informing us. There was no time to deport him.'"

But he was wrong. As my jet moved to the small airport – the American embassy must have been watching – the American Ambassador was there with all the stamps and the official whose business it is to deport people. I was delayed there, because they had to fill in all the forms, and as I left the country, I said, "It doesn't matter." In fact, my passport has become a historical document: I have been deported from so many countries without any reason.

When I left Uruguay the President was invited to America immediately, and Ronald Reagan gave him thirty-six million dollars as a 'gesture of friendship'. That was a reward because I was thrown out within thirty-six hours: exactly thirty-six million dollars, one million dollars per hour! In fact, I should start asking these governments for my percentage: You are getting billions of dollars because of me – I should get at least two percent.

America has been informing all the governments; I have seen the documents that they are sending to every government. All that those documents say is: "This man is dangerous. He can corrupt the morality of the country, the culture of the country; he can corrupt the youth of the country. He can destroy the religion of the country."

It is such a strange world. One day the German parliament decided that I should not be allowed into Germany – not only that I should not be allowed into Germany, but my airplane should not be allowed to land at any airport, even for refueling. I cannot understand how I can corrupt their morality, sitting in my airplane for just fifteen minutes.

In England I was not allowed to stay in the airport lounge for just six hours during the night – which was my right. It is an international airport, and my pilots had finished their flying hours and they could not fly any more – it would have been against the law. And just in case they refused, saying that the first-class lounge is not for private air jet travelers, but only for commercial flights, we purchased two tickets also. Just to show them, "If that is the problem, we also have tickets for a commercial flight tomorrow morning."

But the airport official had a file, and every other moment he was phoning the Prime Minister, "What shall I say now? What shall I do now?" – because it was something he had never done before. To tell somebody, "Your staying in the lounge will corrupt the country's morality," does not look reasonable. And finally he came to me and he said, "There is no point in arguing. They have decided that you can stay only if you want to stay in jail for six hours. We will not allow you to stay anywhere else." So for no crime, I had to stay six hours in jail in England.

The U.S. Attorney General has been saying again and again in press conferences, "I don't want to hear Osho's name again, and I don't want any news media to report his ideas. I want him to be completely silenced."

This is their strategy to silence me: that I should not be allowed in any country; and no sannyasins should be allowed into India. That's why I have withdrawn your orange clothes and your malas; otherwise you would not have been able to enter India. Now they cannot figure out who is a sannyasin and who is not a sannyasin. Now the whole world is my sannyasin.

"The divine rage that screams within me
singing its furious song
for the thousands and thousands of hearts
who would have loved to meet You
but are hindered by boundaries of fear,
by bureaucracy, passports and masked manners."

Sarjano understands it perfectly well – he is from Italy. He and other Italian sannyasins have been trying continually for one year just to get a three-week tourist visa for me, and the Italian government goes on saying next week... and one year has passed. Because the Pope has put an embargo on the government: in no case should Osho be allowed into Italy. These cowards are your religious leaders. And just now, Sarjano went there again to enquire, how many more weeks? They said, "Because one year has passed, that application is invalid; put in a new application." So he has put in a new application, and I think that again it will take one year – before it becomes invalid again.

When the Pope was in India, he was opposed by everybody: Hindus, Mohammedans, Jainas, Buddhists – wherever he went he was opposed. I was the only man in the whole country who opposed the people who were opposing the Pope, and said to them, "This is ugly and this simply shows weakness. Welcome him: invite him for a public, open discussion. In every city he enters, he should

have to face a public discussion on the fundamentals of religion; that will be something valuable. Let us see how much he understands about the fundamentals of religion."

For ten thousand years this country has been pouring its whole genius into religious experiments. There is no other place in the world where religion has been so intensely and insistently explored. Christianity looks so childish compared to Buddhism that there is no need to oppose the Pope. It is a good opportunity that he himself has come here; and if he had faced intellectual discussions all over the country, I think that he would never have come back again.

I can understand your rage against bureaucracy, passports, and masked manners.

"Would you say if I could ask you

my eternal question
that I do not love you?"

Sarjano, my eternal answer is that you love me too much.

"Because I feel to scream to them
that I love you, I love you,
and because I want them all to love you,
to be free
to love you and to meet you
under every tree,
in every country,
on every street around the earth,
and because I wish for every wretch
you could reach out your hand
or your infinite silence.

I would be dead by now,
forgotten of myself
if I had not met you.
And so I weep for all of those
who died in forgetfulness
of their own soul
without having met you.
And again and again I scream:
'You bastards!'
into the faces of those
who try to chain you close
in order to keep you
from the thirsty and the lost.
So would you say this is not love?
For the scream is louder still
than the silence."

Sarjano, there I don't agree with you. Silence is always louder than any scream. A scream has a beginning and an end; silence is eternal.

Silence is the scream of the whole existence.

But I would not prevent you from screaming, because the people you are screaming at are so deaf that it is compassionate towards them to scream as loudly as possible; and they are so insane that they cannot understand silence.

Silence can be understood only by those who know what silence is, who have experienced silence. Perhaps your scream may reach the insane minds of the politicians and the bureaucrats and the theologians and the religious leaders – because they are full of mad noises themselves. They don't know what silence is. If they had known silence, I would have been welcomed by them.

The first man from outside America to protest against my arrest was a Zen master from Japan. He immediately phoned Ronald Reagan and phoned to me, informing me, "I have phoned Ronald Reagan, and I have told him that he is committing a great sin, he will suffer for it." He has never met me, but in his monastery my books are read as scriptures – his disciples know about Zen from my books. Zen was born in Japan, but he has found a better expression, a more profound meaning in my words; so rather than teaching them through Japanese scriptures, he is teaching them from my books.

I told him on the phone, "I am grateful that you protested, but there was no need to tell him that he should repent, that he has committed a sin."

He said, "I am enraged. I am a man of silence. My whole life I have been simply meditating and doing nothing. But seeing you on television, in chains, handcuffed, being treated as if you are a murderer, I could not remain silent." And that old Zen monk's prediction is coming true. Ronald Reagan and the Attorney General of America, Mr. Meese, are both going down the drain. Irangate is going to finish them completely.

And just today Neelam has brought to me the news that in the White House, Ronald Reagan's daughter and his son-in-law have seen a ghost – they think it is the ghost of Lincoln. But why should Lincoln be wearing red clothes? Now even Ronald Reagan is afraid to be in the White House – because many other people have seen it; even his dog starts barking when others see the ghost. It seems some old sannyasin is just playing a joke! Soon the White House will be a ghost house; nobody will be ready to live in it. Only dead sannyasins will enjoy living in the White House.

But Ronald Reagan and this Mr. Meese are absolutely finished; they don't have any future. So don't be angry. Even if you scream, your scream should come out of your love, out of your compassion – so that the deaf can hear and the blind can see.

"For the heart is turmoil and the rage
whets the intelligence
like a sword to cut the chains,
to cut the heads of the parasites,
and to open a door
for intuition to enter.
I cannot take this anymore,
the fear and the meanness of those who decide
what is right and what is wrong.
Nor the fear of those who are afraid
of the songs,
of the dance,
of the music that springs up

when a living being
meets you.
So, oh, my love, would you say
this is not love?"

Again, Sarjano, I say: This is too much love.

Just don't forget in your anger and rage that it is love that is roaring like a lion. Basically it is love. Whatever they have done, and whatever they are doing, is just out of unconsciousness. You cannot be too angry about them: they need more pity and more compassion.

Now, here it is going to happen, everywhere it is going to happen. We have had this property since 1974 – we purchased it. But the government has not transferred it to our name. So we have paid the money, but the property belongs still to the original owners. The municipal corporation goes on asking for taxes from us, and we are paying those taxes.

Because I had gone to America for five years, one structure was demolished by our people – because it was of no use anymore. One hall was enough. When I was

here before, then ten thousand people used to be here. Soon they will be coming again, so we have started to raise the structure again. It is an old structure – we are simply putting it back together – but the municipal commissioner is so enraged about it that he has threatened that he will come on the twenty-eighth of February with bulldozers and demolish the structure. And it is our temple.

So the twenty-eighth is going to be a really festive day! You have to lie down across the whole width of the road, with all the musicians playing and dancers dancing, and tell them, "First you will have to bulldoze our people, and then you can bulldoze the whole property – because we will not be here, it will not be of any use. But unless you bulldoze all the people who are here, you cannot move one inch into the ashram land." Now we will see how much guts that municipal commissioner has got.

We are not going to be violent; we will be singing songs of love, we will be playing music, we will be dancing with joy. Let the whole world know that to be joyful, to be peaceful, to be loving, to be nonviolent, to be festive, is criminal. Perhaps it may raise the whole consciousness of humanity.

So you have to be ready for your great celebration. And, Sarjano, it will be a good opportunity, so that I can teach you that you can die for truth – even dancing and singing; with joy, with no anger, just love and compassion.

The Rebellious Spirit, Ch 25

***

CHAPTER 10

Preparing To Die

That last discourse had touched his heart like a smiling death sentence, because he had taken the words of his Master very seriously, or better sincerely, and now he wanted to get ready to die. He made a quick inventory of his life, with the conclusion that he had had a truly marvelous life, that he had been the most fortunate of men, and that somebody up there must have always protected him.

He saw again his fatherless childhood, with his incredible luck in not having had any father figure to replace it, neither any teacher nor schools to impart in him the 'good manners'. At that point he felt totally spontaneous to forgive his father, hence he thought about him intensely and forgave him for having abandoned his only son just after his birth, then he forgave his mother and asked her forgiveness for not having been capable of leading a life the way she would have dreamed of.

One by one he forgave all the people that he had met in his life, and to each one of them he asked for forgiveness; then he saw all his past lovers, a long queue of faces, of eyes full of love, of forgotten gestures. He saw Silvia, the mother of his son and his companion of so many adventures, and he thanked her without words; then it was Terry's face to overwhelm him, poor Terry who had lost her blue prince and not for a more beautiful girl as she had always feared, but for an old man with a beard!

He saw his son Amore and remembered the walks they had together when he was a child, and his marvel at discovering everything, a marvel so innocent to become contagious, to the point that he began to marvel at everything himself, in magic synchronicity with his child. Finally he saw Premal and her Botticellian body, recalling her face looking so similar to a Renaissance Madonna, while listening again to her invocation when he would get up from their bed: "Don't go away please…I love you so much!"

How much love there had been in his life, how many women had loved him, and how many he had loved.

He kept on remembering and forgiving for the whole day and also for part of the night, because although he was in bed since one hour he couldn't sleep, with all these people to say farewell to.

At a certain point he even asked himself if he had deserved all this love, and his conclusion was immediately that it must have been so, because God knew well what he was doing, and who to shower with his gifts!

He finally fell asleep in the early morning hours, but it was a strange sleep, light and heavy at the same time, filled with visions of his beautiful past that continued to appear and then vanish into nothingness, to make space for other images. He also saw that he had been always a troublemaker in his life, and he was very happy and satisfied by that!

He had passed through the most extraordinary adventures, he had met all the people in the world that he wanted to know, from Jean Paul Sartre to Jack Kerouac, from Jimmy Hendrix to Mick Jagger, from Andy Warhol to Alejandro Jodorowsky, and with everyone he had hugs and established an intense friendship.

To end his beautiful life, he had even met Osho, had fallen in love with him, and after living for more than a decade at his feet, he was now ready to die at his feet too, which seemed to him an exemplary end, the end deserved by a hero of his time.

He even wrote a few letters – one to his son, one to Terry, to tell them that he was going, but that they should celebrate his departure with joy, remembering him always with the meaning of his name, which was 'freedom and creativity'.

After having slept just for a couple of hours, he got up and went for a walk; the roads were deserted and utterly silent in those misty hours of dawn, and one could hear only the frogs awakening with their "cra – cra", and the early crickets with their "cri-cri"...when suddenly he felt overwhelmed by an incredible wave of heat around his chest, and in that moment something happened to him that he was never capable to describe!

There were still five days before his appointment with destiny, or with the bulldozers that were supposed to pull down Buddha Hall (whatever comes first!), hence he decided to kill the time writing another letter to Osho. If you think that the massive dose of love received from the Master as an answer to his previous letter ought to be enough to last for the next six months you are totally wrong, because the same day, even immersed in the thought of death coming in a few days, he decided to write him once more:

Beloved Osho,

Last year in Bombay, you said that since I've met you there has never been a no in me. Yes, Osho, that is true. And yet, the other night, I saw my head shaking in a deep no to your words. When you said I love you too much, I felt for the first time a no in me, so total, so deep. For a moment I heard my heart singing, no, no, no – it is not too much, there is space in my being to love you much more. So I guess you were joking, or using poetic license, or a metaphor.

I don't like to say no to you, but if you dare to repeat that I love you too much I will start to laugh and say, "No, Osho, no," again and again, "No, Osho."

Sarjano, words like yes and no are very flexible. They are not opposites; they are two extremes of one single energy. Hence sometimes a very strange phenomenon happens. It is said about women that when they say no they mean yes – the flexibility is so great – and when you were saying no, you were meaning yes.

I can understand why the no arose in you, because love knows no limits. For those who love, even too much love is too little. You wanted to say no, because you are capable of loving more. But that capacity is infinite: At no point does love feel that it has come to a full stop – there are always possibilities, potentialities, and space available to grow more. Your no is not no, it is really a preparation for a greater yes.

So I want to say to you: Sarjano, you love me too much. And even if you say no, it does not matter. It simply means even too much is too little – and you can see that you can love more. Too much is not the end, so your no is, in a disguised form, nothing but yes. You cannot deceive me by words.

You are saying, "Last year in Bombay you said that since I have met you there has never been a no in me." *I still say so. But you are puzzled, because you feel,* "Yes, Osho, that is true. And yet, the other night I saw my head shaking in a deep no to your words." *It is because your love is greater than any words can contain. But your no is not negative; it is another form of saying yes.*

"When you said I love you too much, I felt for the first time a no in me, so total, so deep. For a moment I heard my heart singing, no, no, no – it is not too much...." *You were not saying no to me, you were simply saying no to my statement that you love me too much.*

Suddenly you became aware that you are capable of loving more – this is not too much.

I agree with you: you are capable of loving more. Still, it is too much. It will become even vaster, deeper, greater; but that is not going to change my statement. And you have understood yourself, without being clearly aware of it, when you said, "It is not too much. There is space in my being to love you much more. So I guess you were joking, or using poetic license, or a metaphor."

No, I was neither joking, nor using metaphors, nor poetic license. I was simply describing the simple fact that your love is too much for me. But for you, it may appear too little. That is the perennial experience of all lovers. The loved one feels it is too much, but the lover feels it is nothing: "I have not put my whole being into it yet."

"I don't like to say no to you...." *You have never said no to me. Even when yesterday the no was arising in you, it was nothing but preparing ground for a bigger yes.*

You are challenging me, that "If you dare to repeat that I love you too much, I will start to laugh and say, 'No, Osho, no!' Again and again, 'No, Osho!'"

You can laugh, and you can still say, "No, Osho, no." *But it will mean only "Yes, Osho, yes." And I repeat again and again that you love me too much, Sarjano.*

Language is a very slippery matter.

I am reminded of a small incident. In a monastery, only one hour was given to the monks who lived in the monastery, to go out in the garden. But it was called one hour for praying in the open, under the sky. Two friends were very much troubled by one thing – both were smokers, and since they had entered the monastery they had not smoked: it was prohibited.

One of them said to the other, "Perhaps it is prohibited inside the monastery, but in the garden...? I think we should ask the abbot, the chief monk." Both agreed, and the next day one came out angry, enraged, humiliated, insulted, because the abbot had refused absolutely. He had used the words, 'Absolutely no.' As he came out, he became even more furious, because he saw the other sitting under a tree smoking so joyfully. He could not believe it.

He said, "Have you asked, or are you smoking without asking?" He said, "I asked – but why are you looking so red with anger?" He said, "This is strange: has he agreed?" The monk who was smoking said, "Yes – he said, 'Yes, absolutely yes!'" The other man said, "This abbot seems to be crazy. To me he said, 'No, absolutely no!'"

Still the other man went on laughing and he said, "Just cool down, sit down, and tell me what you have asked." He said, "I have asked simply, 'While outside in the garden, can I smoke?' And he said, 'No, absolutely no!'" The one who was smoking said, "Now things are clear. You asked a wrong question. I asked 'Can I pray while smoking?' He said, 'Yes, absolutely yes!'"

Your no, Sarjano, is nothing but yes. You are not satisfied with too much, you want more. And now you cannot laugh, and you cannot say, "No, Osho no." *– you will have to say, "Yes, Osho yes".*

Even when you were saying no, you were saying yes – you were just not alert why that no was arising in you.

The Rebellious Spirit, Ch 27, Q 1

Then two incredible events happened almost simultaneously: the first was that the Civic Commission of Pune retracted its order to demolish Buddha Hall, hence its glorious end was postponed indefinitely, and the other was that the sensation he had felt a few days before in the morning had come back even more aggressively during the night, and this time it had drowned him in an abyss of ecstasy. He couldn't figure out if it was more similar to death or to enlightenment, which perhaps are the same things, in the sense that their manifestation could even be the same for both phenomena.

What had happened to him was absolutely inexplicable and certainly he wouldn't have dared to tell anybody; hence he decided to write another letter to Osho (the third one within one week!) because he really needed to tell it at least to somebody, and who was better than his Master?

He pondered a little about what to write, because even if the letter was addressed to Osho, it was very difficult for him to explain in an articulate manner what had happened to him; in the end he decided to remain a little vague, because he knew that his Master would understand anyhow, and this is how he expressed himself:

Beloved Osho,

A few days ago it happened, and you must know it; the one who can find words for everything now has no words to describe this experience. I only say what it was not: there were no angels playing their trumpets, there was no celestial music, nor smell of incense, nor flowers, nor colors of thousands of rainbows.

The experience came from the back, with velvet feet like a thief, so unknown and so familiar.

My arms grasped the sky searching for your hand while my feet walked on their own towards Lao Tzu Gate, and my being was only a river-like whisper, murmuring, "Osho, Osho, Osho." But your hand was not there, or didn't I see it, didn't I feel it?

Oh Osho, my beloved ocean, haven't you promised me that you would take hold of my hand?

Sarjano, I have promised you, and I have been fulfilling my promise. But I will not hold your hand from outside, I will hold your hand from your inside – your hand will be my hand. That is true holding; from the outside it is very superficial, but from the inside, it is as deep as it can be. And who do you think was following you with velvet feet? Feet are never made of velvet but my shoes are. But in the night a small misunderstanding is possible.

You are saying, "A few days ago it happened, and you must know it." *Yes, I know it.* "The one who can find words for everything now has no words to describe his experience. I only say what it was not." *But this is the only way to describe a few experiences. All the great experiences have to be described negatively – what it is not. With a negative description there is a beauty.... The positive description confines a thing, the negative description only indicates – it does not confine. So it is absolutely right to describe it by what it is not.*

"There were no angels playing their trumpets." *There are no angels anywhere; and anyway, trumpets are so costly nowadays.... Forget those old days of the Old Testament, when every angel was given trumpets and harps – even people who had reached heaven by mistake.*

I have heard about one person certainly, a man from Munich, Germany. He was a porter at the station, and by some mistake, angels carried him to heaven. He tried many times, "You must be mistaken, I am just a porter, I am not a saint; why are you dragging me towards heaven? This is my time to go to the pub, and I tell you frankly, I am a sinner, just don't harass me." But they went on with their trumpets and their harps, and nobody listened to the poor porter. He said, "This is strange." And then he was presented to the chief of the angels, and he was given a harp, and he said, "What? What I am supposed to do?"

He said, "There is nothing to be done, you just sit on any cloud, and play the harp."

He said, "I am a porter, I have never played on any instrument."

They said, "Don't be worried, in the beginning every saint says so."

He said, "But I am not a saint! And I am concerned that pub may be closed! In all this nonsense, do you think me an idiot, sitting on a cloud, playing on the harp, when it is time to go to the pub?"

But they told him, "You will have to behave, because soon God will be coming here.

He always comes when new arrivals enter into paradise.

He said, "My God, so it means tonight I cannot go to the pub?"

They said, "You stop talking about the pub."

So he had to sit on a cloud. He felt very embarrassed, that this was not a place to sit; but he saw angels and saints were sitting on all the clouds and playing on their harps, "Hallelujah, hallelujah." He has never done any such thing. But then he heard God is coming, so he started doing anything that he managed to do and shouting loudly, "Hallelujah, hallelujah." But again and again he remembered the pub.

God was sitting on his golden throne, on a big white cloud. Just silently the porter was saying in between, "You son of a bitch, hallelujah, hallelujah."

He thought that God would not hear what he was saying very silently, but God heard it. He asked the other angels, "Why are you torturing that porter? It is an accident, he is not supposed to be here, and he is very unhappy, just look at his face. He is saying, 'Hallelujah, hallelujah,' but inside he is saying something else that only I can hear! Just send him back, let him go to his pub."

So he was thrown back to the earth. Although he fell with a thump on the ground he said, "At least there is still time! All those idiots sitting on the clouds look like clowns, and for eternity you have just to play on your harp, and go on singing, 'Hallelujah, hallelujah.'"

He got up and went into the pub and the people said, "You are very late."

He said, "I got into such trouble. By accident people took me to heaven. It was just my old habit of telling people 'You son of a bitch' that helped me. When God heard it, he thought it was better to send this man away; otherwise he will corrupt the other saints."

In the old days it was okay, Sarjano. Nowadays there are "no angels, no trumpets, no celestial music nor smell of incense, nor flowers, nor colors of thousands of rainbows...." *The mystics have been talking about these things, because they could not find words to relate the experience, just as you cannot.*

There are just ways of describing something; thousands of lotus flowers, thousands of rainbows, thousands of suns rising all around – these are all simply indications that language has failed. And what they want to say they cannot say, but there is a tremendous urge to say it. So they are caught in a dilemma. They cannot say it and they cannot resist not saying it. So something has to be said.

One great German thinker – perhaps one of the greatest thinkers of this century – Ludwig Wittgenstein, in one of his most rare books, Logico Tractus Philosophicus, has one statement. He does not write in the ordinary way people write, he writes only maxims. But each of his maxims he numbers one, two, three. Each of his maxims has tremendous value and is pregnant with meaning; he has condensed paragraphs, pages or perhaps books into one sentence.

One of the sentences in this Tractatus is: "That which cannot be said, should not be said." I wrote him a letter, "You have not followed your own dictum. You have said something about it. 'That which cannot be said should not be said.' You have said something about it."

I received a letter from one of his friends; Wittgenstein had died. I was not aware that he is dead – I was only a student in the university. The friend wrote, "Wittgenstein is dead. I am sorry that he could not see your letter because he was such a sincere and honest man, he may have removed his statement from the book – because what you are saying is absolutely right. If nothing should be said about that which cannot be said, even this sentence should not be there – just an empty place."

"The experience came from the back." *It almost always comes from the back. Because anything coming from the front can make you tense, can make you closed, can make you defensive. All great experiences come from the back, because from the back… until they have overwhelmed you, you are not aware and you cannot be defensive. And by the time you become aware, it is too late – you cannot do anything. You are possessed.*

"… with velvet feet, like a thief." *In Hindi, one of the names of God is "Hari" and "Hari" means a thief. India has a longer experience of the mysterious than any other country in the world. It has even chosen names with a very deep awareness that they should not be just names, but they should also contain the experience.*

"The experience came from the back like a thief, so unknown and so familiar." *Whenever any one of you will come to know something of the unknown, you will always find it both; unknown on the one hand, and so familiar – as if you have always known it. And it is both, because it is not something that is coming from the outside. It is something that is really growing within you. It is something that in your unconscious you have always felt, but your consciousness has not been aware of it, and now the consciousness becomes aware. So you have both contradictory statements together, "unknown" and "so familiar."*

"My arms grasp the sky searching for your hand." *Sarjano, that's where you were not clear. You were searching my hand as though it were something outside. But slowly, slowly, as more and more experiences of this type become available to you, you will see that you are seeing through my eyes; and you are trying to search – and it is not your hand but my hand. There is a state of immense attunement, when the master is not outside, but inside you.*

You are not so small as you appear. You are not confined to the body. You are vast enough, you can contain all. Your capacity for containing is oceanic.

"While my feet walked on their own towards Lao Tzu Gate and my being was only a river-like whisper, murmuring: 'Osho, Osho, Osho….' But your hand was not there." *It was there. And next time something like this happens, just look at your hand and you will not find your own hand – but you will find my hand.*

"Or didn't I see it; did not I feel it?" *No, it was just your first experience. And you were looking, very naturally, on the outside. You must have seen one of the great paintings of Michelangelo in which God is creating the world and his hand is touching the hand of Adam. He's hanging in the sky, downwards, and Adam is on the earth. It is one of the most beautiful paintings.*

But Michelangelo has no experience – that God's hand cannot come from outside, and anything that comes from outside is not God's. God can only blossom from your innermost being. He can see through your eyes and he can spread his hand in your hand. He can walk with your feet and he can breathe with your lungs, and he can beat from your heart.

Never think of God as something outside. It is always your interior, your subjective experience.

"Oh Osho! My Beloved Osho! Haven't you promised me that you would take hold of my hand?"

I had promised you, Sarjano; and I was holding it.

The Rebellious Spirit, Ch 29, Q 4

Beloved Osho,

I really dig the idea of being a mirror, but I am Italian. Do you know the Italian mirror? Once I was staying with two friends and a woman, living in the same house. One day the woman left. She had written a message on her lover Hugo's mirror with her lipstick: "Hugo ti amo" – "I love you, Hugo." When the other guy went to the bathroom and saw the message, he became envious. So he put his finger in a pot of spaghetti and wrote on the mirror with the tomato sauce: "I love you, Sugo" – "sugo" means spaghetti sauce.

This is to give you an idea of an Italian mirror. Now do you still want me to be a mirror?

Sarjano, I still want you to be a mirror, but not an Italian mirror. There are more varieties of mirrors. Not only are Italian mirrors full of spaghetti sauce, even Italian heads are full of spaghetti. In this whole world I hate only one thing and that is spaghetti.

But you can be a German mirror, a Belgian mirror – the best of all mirrors is the Belgian mirror; and if you are going to be a mirror, why not be the best? But a mirror you have to be. And avoid spaghetti as far as possible, because that makes the Italians greasy. From every pore of their body you can see spaghetti coming out.

I love the Italians minus spaghetti.

The Razor's Edge, Ch 2, Q 2

***

CHAPTER 11

Questions And Answers

Beloved Osho,
Again, you invite us to kill the Buddha when we meet him on the path. You said that the master is the last attachment and you want me to drop this too, in order to be totally free. Oh my beloved, the problem is not that I love you too much: I can kill you out of love, with no pain at all. But the real problem is that I like you too much! I like your eyes, I like your hands, I like your beard, I like your face, your profile. And I like the way you walk, the way you talk, the way you laugh. I like everything about you, Osho – except for your watches, of course. For all my life I've been in search of beauty: I have photographed the most beautiful women and the most beautiful men in the world, but never, never have I come across a being who contains both: the fragile beauty of a woman and the austere grace of a man. How could I possibly kill you, if I like you more than any sunset, any temple, any painting, any poem, any woman, any river, any sculpture; more than anything I have ever seen? And you must know my hidden secret too: for I keep coming back in the body to please my eyes only. How in heaven could I deprive my eyes of the vision of you, of the ultimate grace of form, in this unaesthetic world?

Sarjano, your question is not a question. It is a statement. The only thing questionable in it is about my watches. So I can say to you, if I meet you on the way, take away my watch.

That will be enough. Moreover, they are not mine, they belong to sannyasins who want me to use them while they are here. And then they can take them back, and they become something precious to them. I don't own anything – even my dresses are not my own. They are also made by sannyasins.

And I agree with you, I don't like these cheap watches myself. But where to find richer people than sannyasins? If you have some idea, either you can inform me or if you can manage, you can bring the right watch, one that you like.

You are an Italian, Sarjano, so especially for you I have a joke here.

An Italian ship has been out at sea for months and all the crew is missing the delight of female company. Everyone is becoming more and more irritable. Everyone, except the captain.

The crew begin to notice that the captain does not seem to suffer from the same frustrations that they do. So they decide to spy on him and find out his secret. That night, they creep down to his cabin and look through the keyhole. They see him enjoying himself with a beautiful and very lifelike inflatable doll.

So when the captain is not in his cabin, they all take turns to go down and enjoy the favors of this magnificent piece of modern engineering.

When the ship docks in Amsterdam, the captain goes back to the shop in the red-light district where he bought the doll. "Good morning, captain," says the attendant. "Are you satisfied with our product?"

"Ah, yes," replies the captain, "She is magnificent! And she is so lifelike that I even got gonorrhea from her."

The Hidden Splendor, Ch 1, Q 2

Beloved Osho,

The other morning before lecture, I suddenly felt an overwhelming urge to touch, with great gratitude, the floor where you walk. In that moment, I heard again that voice – it still sounds like your voice: "If you can kiss in gratitude the place on earth where I have stepped…" I want to tell you, that I've stepped everywhere on this earth. This is really too much, for I see myself in tears, kissing every spot on the earth. And again that voice comes in me, or from me, whispering, "If you can kiss in gratitude all the earth, and all that abides on the earth, you don't need me anymore." Please, Osho, tell me that I was just imagining, that it was just a dream. You haven't said that to me, have you?

Sarjano, the idea is Catholic. You come from the country of the Pope, and that fellow goes on kissing the earth wherever he goes – even in India, where kissing the earth means kissing cow dung. When he kissed it here, that very day I said, "He has tasted something of Hindu religion."

It is just your imagination, Sarjano. There is no need for your gratitude to be expressed in stupid gestures. Just being grateful, your eyes full of tears, your heart just melting and merging with existence, is enough. Kissing the earth is just an idiotic symbol; I could never have said anything like this to you. But you love me, and you are so full of me that even if you speak in your imagination, you may hear my voice.

But remember one thing: except for silence, everything else is your imagination – howsoever beautiful. Only your silence I can say has my support, because only in your silence are you close to the very center of existence. In absolute silence, you become the very center yourself. But remember to avoid any kind of imagination, all imagination, even beautiful imagination, apparently looking like the divine.

It happened once: I had a few Mohammedan friends and they were followers of a Sufi mystic. The mystic used to come to the city once a year to see his disciples, and they were continuously telling me, "This time when he comes, some way has to be found so that you both can meet."

I said, "There is no problem with it. I can be his host; he can be my guest. That will be the best thing because he is going to be here three days, so for three days we can be together."

They liked the idea. The most impressive thing to them in the Sufi mystic was that he saw God everywhere: he would see a tree and he would go and hug the tree and start talking to the tree. Almost in a trance, he would kiss the earth; he would hold your hand and kiss it and he would start talking in a trance and address you as "God! My Lord!" People were very impressed.

He came to stay with me. Before he could kiss my hand, I said, "Wait! Do you really see God in me or have you been imagining for years?" – because that is one of the traditions in the Sufis: you start imagining and, slowly slowly, the imagination becomes a reality.

He was shocked. There was a moment of silence – painful silence, because his disciples were there. But he was an honest man; he said, "Ah, at least thirty years ago I started on the path, and this was the path shown by my teacher : 'Look into everything for God.'

"In the beginning, it was difficult to see God in a camel, in a donkey, in a buffalo. But my master insisted: 'All these forms are gods; you don't have to judge them – your path is just to see God in everything, so that one day you can see God everywhere.' And I succeeded in three years, and I started seeing God everywhere. Now I see God everywhere."

I said, "Just listen to me. For the three days you will be here, stop imagining. Just see things as they are: a table is a table, not God; a camel is a camel, not God; and a buffalo is a buffalo, not God – just for three days."

He was very reluctant and afraid and nervous, but he was staying with me, so I said, "I will remind you about this kissing and hugging – don't forget! After three days you can hug with a vengeance, because no tree can prevent how much you hug it. For three days... you can fill the quota afterwards, but for three days I will be constantly after you. You have to see things as they are."

There was no need for three days. Within just one day, in twenty-four hours, the god that had been there for thirty years disappeared. In the morning, he was very angry at me. He said, "What have you done? I really see a table is a table! Just now I saw a man going by on a bicycle, and I saw neither the god in the man, nor in the bicycle. You destroyed my thirty years of practice."

I said, "Just think a little. If something that you have spent thirty years discovering was really true, then in one day it could not disappear. For thirty years you have lived in a hallucination – you created the hallucination, and the hallucination can be so strong that all doubts disappear. And thirty years is a long time."

I told him a story of Ramakrishna which is very rare in the history of mystics. After attaining enlightenment, nobody ever tries to look into other paths to see whether they also reach to enlightenment or not – there is no point. You wanted to reach here, you have reached – now what is the point of finding out whether other roads also reach here or not? But Ramakrishna had something tremendously significant on his mind, so he gave six months to each religion that was available in his vicinity; for six months he would practice the religion and forget everything else. Of course he was already enlightened so the path was not a problem; in six months he would reach back to the point of consciousness.

In Bengal, there is a small local group of a very strange religion: they believe that Krishna is the only man, and those who follow him are all women. They may be men, but that is only an illusion; in reality, except for Krishna, there is no other man – all are women. He is the lover and you are the beloved. In the night, the followers of that sect, men and women both, dress alike – like women. And even men sleep with a statue of Krishna in their beds – he is their husband.

Ramakrishna followed that path also for six months. For others it was just a ritual; they were born into that religion, just as you are born into Christianity, or Hinduism, or Jainism. You don't really care; it is just accidental that you are born into a certain religion and you follow it, but it is a formality – at the most.

But Ramakrishna was not going into those processes in a formal way: when he was following something, he was following it with totality and intensity. And almost a miracle was seen! Even in the day, he used the same clothes as women use in Bengal. Even the people of that sect told him, "In the day you can use men's clothes; otherwise it looks very awkward."

But he said, "When I follow something, I follow it totally. I cannot divide my day from my night. And I don't care about the world."

His breasts started growing; his disciples became very much afraid. So much intensity of projecting that even the doctors who came to know about it when they visited Ramakrishna and saw his breasts, could not believe it – because this was a physiological miracle. But his disciples whispered in the ears of the doctor, "This is nothing – he is having monthly periods!"

For six months continuously… his voice changed, it became more like a woman's. He started walking like a woman – which is very difficult; difficult because only a woman can walk that way. She has a womb inside her body and that womb gives a different kind of movement to the legs. Man has no womb inside; his legs have a different movement.

He started walking like a woman, speaking like a woman, his voice changed. And when the menstrual period started, then the disciples became really afraid. They said, "We have lost him. How can we get him back?" They tried to persuade him, but until six months was up, he was not going to change his path. They said, "This path is dangerous. We don't think that these breasts and this period are going to disappear even after six months. Your whole life you will be a laughingstock – and we are going to be laughingstocks because we are your disciples."

It took almost six months after he stopped for the change to take place again. Slowly, slowly, he became a man again – before that he had become a woman. Such a deep psychological projection.... It is through such projections that people are experiencing Krishna, Jesus, Buddha – and when they experience it, they see it.

And if you say to them that it is only an illusion, how can they believe you? Their illusion looks more real than you are. Mind has a capacity to project anything and make it appear almost real; or sometimes, if the mind is very powerful, even more than real.

But my path is not the path of imagination: It is the path that does not use the mind at all.

Imagination and projection and hallucination and illusion – they are all parts of the mind. My simple approach is transcendence of mind; so only when you start seeing absolute nothingness, utter silence, can you see that I am very close by.

In that silence, you have heard me; in that nothingness, you have seen me. But if you see something, if you hear something, then it is your imagination – you have fallen from the beyond, back into the mind.

Only one thing has to be remembered: the mind is the world – and going beyond the mind is the beginning of God.

The Hidden Splendor, Ch 9, Q 2

Beloved Osho,
Let's reverse the question for once: what have you learned being with us?

Sarjano, it is the last supper. Jesus has gathered all his disciples together and there is a great feeling of gloom in the air. A single candle lights the room. Everybody can sense that something momentous is going to happen and that this may be their last meal together.

Jesus pours out the wine and passes the glasses around and then divides up the food and personally serves his disciples. The candle burns low and at last, all the food is gone except for one hard-boiled egg.

Jesus says to Peter, sitting on his right, "Peter, my blessed disciple, would you like to eat this last egg?"

"Ah, no Master," says Peter. You must have it."

Jesus then turns to his left and says, "John, my blessed disciple, would you like to eat this last egg?"

"Ah, no Master," says John. "You must have it." Jesus asked all his twelve disciples in turn, and they all refused the last egg, saying that he, their master, must have it. Just then a gust of wind comes through the window and blows out the candle. The room is plunged into darkness and it is filled with an awesome silence.

Suddenly, there is a hideous scream. Someone lights a new candle, and everyone gasps as they see Jesus with his hand stretched out for the remaining egg – and embedded in the back of his hand, are twelve forks! But it was too late to learn....

I have learned much. One of the most significant things that I have learned is not to feel sad when you betray, not to feel sorry when you go astray – in fact, not even to expect that you have to trust.

The relationship between me and you has to be one-sided, only from your side, not from my side at all. You are here of your own free choice; you can move away just as freely as you had come. You love me – that is your decision. You can start hating me – that will also be your decision. I am absolutely unconcerned; only then is it possible not to feel hurt, not to feel wounded.

Jesus was betrayed only once, by one disciple. I have been betrayed continually for almost as much time as Jesus lived on the earth – thirty-three years. So many people I have trusted so totally have betrayed me so easily. There was a moment they were ready to die for me and just some small thing... if I was not fulfilling their expectation, which I have never agreed to fulfill, their love changes into great hate. The same person who was ready to die for me is ready to kill me.

So I have learned it the hard way that if you love, it is your decision. If you hate, it is your decision. I am almost non-existent as far as my side is concerned: neither am I a partner in your love, nor am I going to be a partner in your hate. This is a sad lesson but it is good that I have learned it long before.

If somebody assassinates me, at least I will not have any complaint, any grudge – because to love was his freedom, to hate is also his freedom. I am absolutely out of the relationship.

I will go on doing whatever I feel is needed for the growth of your consciousness. But people have been going on changing – such stupid expectations and if they are not fulfilled... it seems as if they have come to me to change me, to transform me. They want me to be according to their idea of how a master should be.

I give you total freedom to be yourself. I never expect anything, any ideal to be imposed on you. I don't give you any commandments. And yet you go on carrying within your mind certain expectations that I have to fulfill, and if they are not fulfilled... and they cannot be fulfilled. Thousands of people are related to me. They have different ideals, different moral concepts. It is almost impossible – and even if it were possible, I am not a man to fit with those who are unconscious, who are themselves living in darkness.

You are here to go through a transformation. It is none of your business how I live, what I say, what I do – the moment you start thinking to change something in me, the bridge between me and you is broken.

And it is a one-sided bridge; I am not a partner in it. I know it is hard for you but your very question implies, Sarjano – perhaps you have not read it very consciously while you were writing it... You say, "Let us reverse the question for once." You cannot reverse it even for once. You are asking now, "What have you learned being with us?"

I have nothing to learn.

You are here only because of the fact that you have found a person who has nothing to learn – and particularly from you, who are groping in darkness, in unconsciousness, who are almost on the boundary line of insanity – any moment, just one step more and you are in a madhouse.

Neither from you, nor from anyone else.

And my whole approach is – and I have been insisting millions of times – that as far as truth or the ultimate reality is concerned, you cannot learn it from anybody else. And once you have known it, there is nothing that remains to be learned.

So I say to you: not even once can the question be reversed. I have not learned anything from you. You need not feel responsible for anything. Just being with you for all these three decades, it has not been a learning but simply a discovery: that there is nobody in the world who is so awakened that you can even call him a friend, so awakened that you can even call him a beloved. This has not been a learning – this is simply a discovery, slowly slowly, as I have come to know human beings.

And as I went around the world, my discovery has become absolutely clear : this humanity has come to a dead end. To hope for anything from this humanity is sheer nonsense. Perhaps a few people may be saved – and for them I go on creating the Noah's Ark, knowing perfectly well that perhaps when the Noah's Ark is ready, there may not be anybody left to be saved. They may have all gone their own ways.

It rarely happens: never have so many people come in contact with anybody – either Jesus or Mahavira or Buddha – and never have so many people left Buddha, Mahavira or Jesus. It is significant to have some insight into it. Even Gautam Buddha, a man of immense insight, was ready to compromise on minor points with his disciples. And the disciple feels immensely happy if the master agrees with him – although the master agreeing with the disciple is like light agreeing with darkness, truth agreeing with that which is not true, life agreeing with death. But because Buddha, Mahavira, Jesus and other teachers of the past have compromised on minor points, very few people have left them.

I am an absolutely non-compromising person. Either you have to be with me absolutely... without expecting anything from my side, because I cannot agree on any smallest, most minute point if it is not true.

And truth is indivisible. You cannot say, "I may not have the whole truth – but a little bit, a piece of it, a fragment of truth." Truth is not divisible. Truth is almost like a circle. Have you ever seen a half circle? Perhaps you may have misunderstood: if you have seen a half circle, it is no longer a circle at all; the circle can only be full. The half is only an arc, it is not a circle. Just as the circle is indivisible, so is truth, so is life, so is existence, so is love, so is ecstasy.

Either you have it or you don't have it.

If you have it, there is no question of your being here. If you don't have it, then be absolutely clear that you don't have it, because living in the illusion that perhaps you have a little bit of it, is dangerous.

What can I learn from you? – being unconscious? Being greedy? Being jealous? Being violent? What can I learn from you?

As I have gone on discovering more and more people, my hope for humanity has disappeared. If you want to call it a learning, you can.

I don't see any future possible. And the time is so short before the curtain falls that you should not waste it in unnecessary things. Your life has now to be absolutely devoted to the most essential thing, the most fundamental thing: to be enlightened has to be your single-pointed concentration.

Everything else has to be sacrificed for it, because you cannot even postpone it for tomorrow. Tomorrow may never come.

The Hidden Splendor, Ch 13, Q 1

Beloved Osho,

What is this undercurrent of giggling in my heart every time I feel that you are using the whole world as a device for our growth, and that you are using us as a device for the whole world? Would you please comment?

Sarjano, you will have to stop your giggling in the heart. This is not a device. There is no time left for any device at all. Your giggling is simply a rationalization: you don't want to believe that the world is going to end because you don't want to change. You want me to say to you that this is only a device, so that you can relax – relax in your fixed pattern of life. But I cannot lie to you.

When I use something as a device, I tell you it is a device. But this is not a device, either to transform the world through you or to change you through the world. I am simply stating a very sad fact. Your giggling is nothing but an effort to erase the impact which I am trying to create.

Giggle about everything else, but not about your transformation. That giggling is your unconscious trying to deceive you, telling you something or other will happen, so you need not worry.

The unconscious does not want to disappear. Your unconscious is nine times more than your conscious; it is nine times more powerful too. And you have to be very alert not to be caught in the powerful unconscious; otherwise it will close all the doors, all the possibilities, all the potentialities of transformation.

I am in absolute support of your giggling about everything in the world except the transformation that is needed within you. And the problem is that you are very serious about everything in the world, and only non-serious about your own interiority.

During his world tour, the Polack Pope arrives in America. When he comes out of the plane, there is a big crowd standing on the runway waving flags, shouting, "Elvis, Elvis!"

The pope looks at them, full of holiness, kisses the ground and says mildly, "My children, look: I am not Elvis, I am the Pope."

He enters the airport hall and notices a mass of people standing there, dancing, waving flags and shouting at him: "Elvis, Elvis!"

A little bit indignant, he blesses the people, and very softly he says, "Oh no, my dear sheep, I am not Elvis, I am the Pope."

Later on, when he finally reaches his hotel, he can't believe his eyes: in the lobby, hundreds of people are crowded, waving flags, yelling, "Elvis, Elvis!"

A little bit puzzled now, he puts his hands together, makes a cross, smiles as divinely as possible and announces, "No, my beloved little lambs. No, I am not Elvis, I am the Pope."

Centered again, he goes upstairs to his suite, opens the door and suddenly sees two beautiful naked women are lying in his bed, waving little flags, shouting ecstatically at him, "Elvis, Elvis!"

Immediately, jumping out of his clothes, he starts singing, "You ain't nothing but a hound-dog…"

Your unconscious is always there, so powerful that if it gets any chance – pope or no pope – the unconscious will be the winner. You have to make your consciousness so strong that the unconscious, slowly slowly, becomes weaker and finally dies. That's the meaning of the enlightened man: one whose unconsciousness has disappeared, whose whole being is full of consciousness.

Whatever I am saying, it is my absolutely clear vision that the world is very close to its end. Don't giggle it away. Don't find rationalizations; they won't help.

There is no time to waste in any unconscious consolations. An immediate transformation is absolutely needed; it is an urgency which man has never faced before. In a way, you are unfortunate that soon there will be no future. In another way, you are very fortunate because this crisis is so big – perhaps it may help you to wake up.

The Hidden Splendor, Ch 14, Q 2

Beloved Osho,

Is it possible that I always transform my feelings and experiences into words and images only to get rid of them? Is it possible that I come to your feet with tremendous thirst, and when I am filled with energy I am overwhelmed with this absolute need of sharing – only to get rid of it? Is it possible that this urge for sharing is only my illusion, or just my way to escape? Somebody told me that I should be more generous with myself. What can I do if I know not any other way to be generous with myself than sharing? Is it time for me to learn another way? Please help me with your guidance.

Sarjano, what you are experiencing and what you are doing is perfectly right. Sharing your experiences, your energy, your love, your blissfulness, is not an escape from them, neither is it a way to get rid of them. On the contrary, the more you share, the more you will have.

It is not the ordinary economics. In the ordinary economics you share and you lose; in the spiritual economics you share and you get more. In ordinary economics you have to be a miser, then only can you become rich: accumulate, never share. In the spiritual economics, if you are a miser whatever you have will be lost. It can live only if you share; it is a living experience. By sharing, it continues a dynamic movement.

I have heard about a young man who had just received a great lottery prize, and he was immensely pleased. He stopped his car because a beggar was standing there. He used to stand there every day, but he had never stopped his car. But today was different. He gave him a note of one hundred rupees. The beggar laughed.

The man said, "I don't understand. Why are you laughing?"

He said, "It reminds me… once I used to have my own car and I used to be just as generous as you are. I am laughing because soon you will be standing by my side. Don't be so generous! Learn something from my experience."

In the ordinary economics, the moment you give something, that much is less. But have you felt that by giving love you have less love? Or by sharing your joy, have you felt that your joy is a little bit less?

If you have watched, you will be surprised: by sharing, your joy is a little bit more; by loving, your sources of love are flowing more – you are juicier. By dancing , just to share yourself with your friends, you will not find yourself losing something but gaining something.

Sarjano, don't listen to other people. They know only about the ordinary economics. They don't know anything about a higher economics, where giving is sharing and where not giving is very destructive.

The more you give, the more you will have; the less you give, the less you will have. And if you don't give at all, you will not have anything at all.

But the people who are suggesting to you that this is not right are creating a problem in your mind about whether you are doing right or wrong. You are doing absolutely right. Do it with more totality, without any hesitation, and without holding anything back. Don't listen to others. Listen to your own experience; watch your own experience – when you give, do you lose something or do you gain something? That should be the decisive thing, not people's advice. The advice of others is dangerous….

When the Eisenbergs moved to Rome, little Hymie came home from his school in tears. He explained to his mother that the nuns were always asking these Catholic questions and how was he, a nice Jewish boy, supposed to know the answers?

Mrs. Eisenberg's heart swelled with maternal sympathy. "Hymie," she said, "I'm going to embroider the answers on the inside of your shirt, and you just look down and read them the next time those nuns pick on you."

"Thanks Mum," said Hymie, and he didn't bat an eye when Sister Michele asked him who was the world's most famous virgin. "Mary," he answered.

"Very good," said the nun. "And who was her husband?"

"Joseph," answered the boy.

"I see you have been studying. Now, can you tell me the name of their son?"

"Sure," said Hymie, "Calvin Klein."

The Golden Future, Ch 2, Q 2

Beloved Osho,

Once, in Kathmandu, I asked you about the need of the disciple for a master. Then I asked you if the master needs the disciple, and you showered on me some words that I received in tears, like petals of an unknowable flower. Would you please be so kind and speak to us about the need of the master for the disciples. Aren't you the formless form, with whom existence is fulfilling our longing? Aren't we, in some way, your food, your nourishment?

Sarjano, I do not remember what I said in response to your question in Kathmandu. I never remember anything I have said. That keeps me responsible. I cannot repeat, because I do not remember. I can only respond to the question and to the questioner in this very moment.

Between Kathmandu and this moment, neither have you remained you, nor have I remained I. And so much water has gone down the Ganges that any repetition is always out of date. Any repetition is dead, is not alive.

That's how the whole of humanity is only pretending to live, but deep down is dead, because it has forgotten the language of response. It knows only the language of reaction. It reacts according to the memory. It does not respond according to the awareness of the moment, of the need here and now. It is full of the past.

There is no present in millions of people around the world. Millions of people live without knowing the taste of the present. And when you are full of the past you are a graveyard. Howsoever beautiful the past may be, it is still dead. And beauty is meaningless if it cannot dance, if it cannot sing , if it cannot even breathe.

I am here, you are here, why bring Kathmandu in? I don't know what Kathmandu means in Nepalese, but in Hindustani we have a phrase which immediately reminds one of Kathmandu. The phrase is 'kath ke ullu'. *It means, 'You are an owl'. And that too not real, but made of wood. I don't know what Kathmandu means;* Kath *certainly means wood.*

Why bring Kathmandu in? You really want to listen to the same answer again, but it is impossible Sarjano. You will have to forgive me, because I don't remember a single word. Kathmandu is almost as far away as the farthest star, as if it happened in some other life.

While we are alive, why waste your time? You can ask a new question and you can receive a new response. The new will be fresher, and the new will be better. The new will be more mature.

But people have lived to live in the past. It has become almost a second nature to them. It is very difficult to drag them out of their graves and tell them, "You are not dead yet. Start breathing, you are still alive."

An elderly Jewish man walks into a jewelry store to buy his wife a present. "How much is this?" he asks the assistant, pointing to a silver crucifix.

"That is six hundred dollars, sir," replies the assistant.

"Nice," says the man, "and how much without the acrobat on it?"

People cannot forgive the past, people cannot forget the past. Two thousand years have passed, but Jesus is not yet acceptable to the Jewish mind. Not a single Jew in two thousand years has repented that crucifying Jesus was a criminal act, and that he finds himself also part of the conspiracy. You will be surprised to know that not a single Jewish scripture even mentions the name of Jesus. It is so unworthy. Such is our approach to life....

I will take your question as fresh, because we are not in Kathmandu. And I will answer you in this moment, responding to your question and to you. I am not in the habit of quoting myself.

You are asking what is the need of the disciple for a master and, vice versa, what is the need of a master for a disciple? Condensed to its essentialness, the question is,

"Does love exist in the lover or in the beloved? Or does love exist in the harmony of both?"

Only in those rare moments, when there is no "I" and no "thou", love blossoms. It does not exist in the lover, it does not exist in the beloved; it exists in the disappearance of their separation.

That's why all lovers are disappointed, because they cannot remain organically one for more than a few seconds. Just a small thing and the separation returns; it was just waiting. If in twenty-four hours you can find twenty-four seconds of organic unity and harmony, you should think yourself immensely blessed, tremendously rich.

The same is the situation between the disciple and the master. Something higher than love, something deeper than love and togetherness exists in those moments of silence, those moments of communion, when the disciple forgets that he is separate from the master, when the disciple melts and merges into the master.

The master is already merged into existence. Merging into the master you are really merging with existence itself. The master functions only as a door, and a door is an emptiness; you pass through it.

The master is the door to the beyond.

And the beyond exists in the organic unity, in the communion, in the merger, in the melting of the master and the disciple. It is the highest form of love. It is the greatest prayer, the deepest gratitude, and the most ecstatic experience available to human consciousness.

The master is missing something when he is alone; he is like an ocean into which no rivers melt. A disciple is certainly just a nobody without a master. With a master, he becomes the whole existence. Both are fulfilled in a togetherness. And because this togetherness is not of the body, not of the mind, but of that which is beyond the mind in you, it is possible to attain and never lose it.

Love is always up and down, one moment joyful, another moment sad. But the love that we are talking about – love between two spirits, between two beings – only begins, it never ends.

The masters ordinarily will not accept what I am saying, but if they don't accept it they are insincere. And if they are insincere, what kind of masters are they?

The masters have been pretending that they don't need anything – they don't need you, they don't need your eyes, they don't need your heartbeat, they don't need your love, they don't need your merger and meeting. That is an egoistic attitude. And anybody who pretends that he needs nothing is only a teacher, not a master. He himself needs to be a disciple. He has heard many beautiful truths, but he has not known anything on his own.

A true master, out of his sincerity, out of his humbleness, will accept the simple fact that he is not beyond any need. Of course, his needs are of a very spiritual kind.

He cannot live unless he can share. Even to exist is impossible for him – he loses all meaning unless he can wake up people who are fast asleep, unless he can make people who are miserable become transformed into dancing roses. In their fulfillment he becomes again and again enlightened.

His enlightenment is not an incident: the authentic master is becoming continuously enlightened each moment. His enlightenment is a progress, an eternal progress; otherwise, the world would have been far more poor. It is already poor.

If Gautam Buddha needed nothing, then for forty-two years walking the whole land, talking to people, knowing perfectly well that they cannot understand, is an arduous task. Why is he doing it? He is helpless; he has to do it. It comes as an intrinsic part of his own enlightenment.

Before, it was a longing to become enlightened. Now, it is a longing to make the whole world enlightened.

The Golden Future, Ch 14, Q 1

Beloved Osho,

The other day when your body fell a little, some of your sannyasins rushed towards you in a split second to help. There was no hustle and no confusion amongst them, and their movements were in perfect harmony. After the necessary assistance was finished, they sat back in their seats as if nothing had happened. This all happened within a couple of seconds. Osho, is this the reflection of the awareness that you are constantly talking about?

Satyam Niranjan, yes. It is something of alertness, something of silence and peace – a discipline that arises out of awareness, not a discipline that is being forced through training. Only Sarjano missed out because he did not have the camera ready.

After you had gone back to your seats and I moved, I remembered Sarjano, and I remembered a small story….

An American couple are touring darkest Africa on safari. They are walking cautiously through the jungle when suddenly a huge lion springs out in front of them. It seizes the wife with its giant jaws and proceeds to drag her into the bush.

"Shoot!" she screams. "Shoot for Christ's sake!"

"I can't," answers the husband. "I have run out of film."

Everything was right, only Sarjano was not ready with his camera. I have heard he is angry with his camera, wants to sell it. Don't do any such stupid thing! Even if you have run out of film we can get more!

The Golden Future Ch 33, Q 2

Beloved Osho,

The other morning you said that we are all going to be enlightened, and all masters, and I felt simultaneously a great laughter and a tremendous responsibility awakening in me. Is that what you want? Am I listening correctly? Again I feel that I am not receptive enough. Please help me.

Sarjano, I said certainly that you are all going to become enlightened, and masters, and you heard me right. Just one thing more I have to add to it. I could say it because enlightenment is your very nature. It is because of language that many problems arise; otherwise I would have said you are enlightened and you are masters – you are just unaware of it.

It is as if you have a treasure in your house, but you don't know where it is. The house is big – many mansions, many rooms; you know certainly the treasure is there, but you are poor, you are a beggar, and who is going to believe you? Even you yourself suspect a thousand and one times that perhaps it is all a myth, a dream, there is no treasure. But you have not looked into the house, you have not searched in all nooks and corners; you have not made enough efforts to find it.

I have found my treasure! That's why I am absolutely certain that if my consciousness can give me so much peace and so much silence, so much joy, so much blissfulness, there is no reason why your consciousness cannot do the same. Perhaps you have not looked into the possibility, you have not searched in your own being, you have never gone in; otherwise you are enlightened this very moment.

And I could say that not only will you all be enlightened; you all will be masters. All enlightened people have not been masters, but I can say with tremendous guarantee that my people, once they become enlightened, are going to be masters, for the simple reason that I have been preparing you to convey the message. I am giving you all the devices: how to create bridges between you and those who are blind, how to find words which can contain at least a hint of your experience. Talking to you twice every day for almost thirty-five years….

The danger is that many of you may become masters before they become enlightened, because they have listened to so much; just a little articulateness and they can pretend to be great masters. A few are doing that already around the world; they have become mini-gurus.

But what you heard, you heard rightly. It seems difficult, it seems almost impossible; hence you laughed. The very idea of Sarjano as enlightened will create laughter in everybody. Sarjano, the enlightened master – the piesta seller, the pornography photographer. It certainly…. I can understand why you laughed. You know yourself!

But simultaneously you also felt a tremendous responsibility awakening in you, because it does not matter; neither piesta, nor anything else can prevent your enlightenment. In fact, my people are going to be not just like the stone statues of Gautam Buddha, sitting in a lotus posture doing nothing. How many Buddhas like that can we afford in the world? We will need a shoemaker who is enlightened, a piesta maker enlightened – all kinds of people. Your actions don't define you; your being remains undefined by your actions. Certainly your being defines your actions. When you are enlightened your piesta will have a different taste.

In desperation the young bride finally took pen in hand and wrote to the problem page of a newspaper : "I am married to a sex maniac. My husband never leaves me alone. He makes love to me all night long, while I am in the shower, while cooking breakfast, even while I'm trying to clean the house. Can you tell me what to do? signed, Worn Out.

P.S. Please excuse the jerky handwriting."

But even these people have to become enlightened!

My deepest longing is to make all kinds of people enlightened and to make enlightenment a very ordinary, simple and innocent experience – nothing special, nothing holier-than-thou-humble; non-pretending, not claiming spirituality, just being joyous and full of light, radiant with joy, overflowing with love, ready to share their experience in whatever way they can.

Sarjano, there is no need to laugh. You are as capable as any Gautam Buddha. And there is no need to be worried about responsibility, because when you become enlightened you also become capable of fulfilling tremendous responsibilities of which you could have never dreamt before.

[Suddenly the sound of fire crackers is heard in the distance.]

Is this Sarjano making all these firecrackers from his piesta shop? – because I think he is there!

The Golden Future Ch 34, Q 3

Beloved Osho,
I am with Sarjano for a while. Can I survive that?

Prem Sandha, it is a difficult job you have taken in your hands. It is almost impossible to survive with Sarjano. But it is not a curse, it is a blessing.

You should not make any effort to survive either – merge with him. He is mad, but with a method; he is full of energy and love. Just don't fight with him – become one with him. The way to survive with Sarjano is to become one with him. But that is the way for everyone who wants to love. Love is basically committing suicide.

Two egos have to commit suicide to place them in a position for merging and melting, to create the space in which love can grow.

Sarjano is full of energy – sometimes too much! But an understanding woman can help him to be more centered if she can love unconditionally and without asking anything. If she can enjoy his abundance of energy, then there is no problem. But if you want to dominate him, you cannot survive; if you want in some way to be bitchy, you cannot survive.

He is not a man who will accept any handcuffs, any curtailment of his freedom. Neither do you have to curtail your freedom; enjoy your freedom and let him enjoy his freedom. Two freedoms can exist together beautifully, but two slave-makers cannot exist together; they are after each other's necks. Unfortunately, that is the situation in the whole world: people are killing each other in the name of love, destroying each other in the name of love.

Love is a creative act. It enhances both. It gives freedom, it gives joy, it gives courage, and nourishment; but that seems to be only theoretical. In actuality, millions of people are suffering because of love. It is very rare to find someone who is growing because of love, who is becoming spiritually strong and integrated because of love.

But at least my people should understand it, because I don't want you to be just like the unconscious crowds that fill the whole earth. I want you to experiment with new ways of living, new styles of living. And one of the most important things for new styles of living is that love should never be used as politics, as an effort to dominate the other.

Love should make you humble and simple, innocent, available and open – childlike, with no expectations. Then you can survive even Sarjano, or even nuclear weapons. He is a nuclear person!

I love people like Sarjano; they are so full of energy, they don't know what to do with it. They are running hither and thither for no purpose, just to exhaust their abundance of energy. A right woman can help him to be centered, can help him to transform his abundance of energy into something creative.

A man walks into a bar looking for his friend. After finding him, he proceeds to tell the friend how much he hates his own wife.

"Why don't you have her murdered?" asked the friend. "I know a guy called Artie who will do it for you really cheap." This sounds great to the man. So he goes off to meet Artie who agrees to do the job for a dollar.

He asks the man where his wife goes shopping – he plans to do the murder there. So Artie waits outside the supermarket until he sees the woman go in. Then he creeps up behind her and, in a deserted corner, strangles her.

When he has finished, he notices two old ladies staring at him, so he has to strangle them too. On his way out of the market, he is caught by the store detective and handed over to the police.

The headlines in the newspapers read, "Artie Chokes Three for a Dollar in Supermarket."

But it is not a rare case that husbands hate their wives and wives hate their husbands, although they go on saying, "Darling, I love you." The more they hate, the more they repeat, "I love you." They have to repeat it to create a facade to hide their hate.

I have heard about a very great surgeon. His friends had arranged a beautiful party and celebration as a golden jubilee of the surgeon's married life. They all were drinking and dancing and enjoying. Suddenly, somebody looked around; the surgeon was not there, so his most intimate friend and advocate went out in the garden to see where he could have gone. He was sitting under a tree very sad.

The advocate said, "What is the matter? Everybody is enjoying, and it is a moment of celebration, and you are sitting here sad." The surgeon said, "Don't come near me! I may strangle you. You are the person who destroyed my whole life."

The advocate could not believe this outburst. He said, "What do you mean?" The surgeon said, "You may have forgotten, but remember : twenty-five years ago, I had come to you to ask that if I murder my wife, what will happen? And you said, 'Never do it, because you will get at least twenty-five years in jail.' I am feeling sad that if I had not listened to your advice, today I would have been a free man."

In the name of love, people have been torturing each other for centuries – men in their own way, women in their own way.

Love has not yet entered into the world. It is still in the poems of the poet, in the songs of the musicians, but it has not become part of humanity. I hope that when we get rid of the old man and his whole so-called barbarous attitudes and approaches to life, love will become the very foundation of a new humanity. This love will not be a bondage, an imprisonment, but a tremendous freedom.

Unless love becomes freedom, you don't know what it is. Freedom without love is dry, is a desert. Love without freedom is fake, just a hypocrisy; it does not exist.

Love and freedom are two sides of the same coin.

It is one flower, and it can blossom only when both are allowed dignity and respect.

You can survive Sarjano. He is not a dangerous man. He has a very loving heart.

If you can love him, you will find hidden in him one of the most beautiful hearts. There is no question of "surviving" him. You can dancingly live together, helping each other in creativity, in meditation, transforming each other into higher peaks of consciousness – which are our birthright.

Osho, The Golden Future Ch 35, Q 2

Beloved Osho,

When I visited Sarjano's pizza parlor yesterday, I found him sobbing by a huge vat of spaghetti. He said that, in spite of your assurances, he feels it is all hopeless. He said, "I can-a never get-a enlightened-a. I'm-a too much-a attached-a to my past-a." I tried to cheer him up by saying that you were helping us to return to the source, and where there is sauce there must be spaghetti. But he was inconsolable. Beloved Master, please, can you help?

Maneesha, Sarjano need not become enlightened – he is already. Those who have been to his place have tasted enlightenment in his spaghetti.

It is true, he is too much attached to the past-a. I would like to suggest to him that in our place he should change these names a little bit – because I am against the past, I cannot allow any past-a here. So I have to rename his pasta; it will be called from tomorrow: futura. And his pizza should be called presenta. The language should be meaningful. Pizza reminds one of pee – that's why I have never been calling it pizza. I have been always calling it "piesta" just to avoid that pee.

And Sarjano need not worry about enlightenment; those who are with me are already enlightened. They may recognize it, they may not recognize it – just out of humbleness....

A very large elephant was moving sedately through the African jungle when he caught sight of a mouse. He stopped in astonishment; he had never seen a mouse before. "My God," he said, "you are small!" "Yes," said the mouse, "I have been ill lately."

Following an ancient custom, the rabbi of the local synagogue prostrated himself before the Ark of the Lord, "Oh Lord, forgive me, for I am as nothing." Then the cantor followed, "Oh Lord, forgive me, for I am as nothing." A little old man praying nearby in his tobacco-stained shirt and old shoes called out, "Oh Lord, forgive me, for I am as nothing." The disgusted rabbi said to the cantor, "Look who thinks he is nothing!"

In the society where everything turns into ego, even humbleness – which should be egolessness – becomes a subtle ego in itself. But my people are not egoists; hence

they need not be humble either – because humbleness and ego are two extremes of the same energy. My people are simple; they are just exactly in the middle, they follow the golden mean.

Nirvana, enlightenment, kaivalyam, moksha, *all great experiences, are not to be proclaimed. People will recognize them just by your joy, by your playfulness, by your presence. And Sarjano is playful, joyous – sometimes a little too much. Once in a while he goes to the extreme, but most of the time remains normally mad. I am going to visit his place one day. I have heard too much about it. He and Kuteer are both doing great things there.*

Sarjano has made a great futura for me, a huge wristwatch with numbers and hands. He must have devoted so much time and so much love... and it came with the message: "Bhagwan, I can only offer you this kind of watch." You can see his humbleness, his love. He is one of my most beloved disciples.

You all have to remember that I have changed the names. We are thinking about the new man and we are thinking about the future of humanity – and this is the last talk of this series. It is perfectly the right and ripe time to give Sarjano's creativity new names: futura and presenta.

The Golden Future Ch 40, Q 1

***

CHAPTER 12

Towards The Big Stick

Beloved Master,
Can we help each other? Can I be helpful to someone, can someone help me? Is becoming aflame the only way to be really helpful? Please, throw some light.

Sarjano, the blind cannot help the blind. Those who are groping in darkness cannot lead others to light. Those who don't know immortality cannot help others to drop the fear of death. Those who are not living totally and intensely, whose song is not yet of the heart, whose smile is only a painted smile on the lips, cannot help others to be authentic and sincere. Those who are hypocrites, pretenders, cannot help others to be honest.

Those who are not yet themselves, know nothing about themselves, have no idea of their individuality, who are still lost in their personality which is fake and created by the society, cannot help anybody else to attain individuality. Even with all good intentions, it is simply not possible.

If your flame of life is not burning, how can you make the unlit lamps of others aflame? You have to be aflame, Sarjano; only then can you put others on fire.

This is what I mean by being a rebel: you have to be rebellious, then you can spread rebellion all around you. If you are on fire, aflame, you can create a wildfire which goes faraway beyond your vision. But first you have to be aflame.

The blind man leading another blind man… Kabir says both fall into the well. His original words are: andha andham thelia dono koop padant. *'The blind led the blind and both have fallen into the well.'*

You have to have eyes to lead the blind to a physician – there is no other way. You can only share with others that which you have got: if you are miserable, you will share your misery. When two miserable persons are together the misery is not only doubled, it is multiplied. The same is true about your blissfulness, the same is true about your rebelliousness, the same is true about all experiences.

Whatever you want the world to be, you will have to be a model first. You have to pass through a fire test to prove your philosophy of life by your example. You cannot just go on arguing about it. Reasoning and argument will not help; only your experience can give to others the taste of love, of meditation, of silence, of rebelliousness, of religion.

Before you have experienced, never try to help anybody – because you will simply mess up the other person more. They are messed up already. Centuries of heritage have been messing up everybody. It will be very kind of you not to help, because it is going to be dangerous; your help will be very risky for the other person.

First travel the path, know perfectly well where it leads – only then can you hold the hands of others and take them on the path.

An American Jewish visitor in Russia says to his guide, "In America I can say that Ronald Reagan is an idiot and nothing would happen to me."

The guide says, "You can say that in Russia and they will give you a medal."

It is very difficult in this world to communicate. You have to learn how to communicate your experiences so that what reaches others is exactly what you want to say; otherwise you may be thinking of sharing nectar and it may turn into poison in their lives. They are poisoned enough already!

It is better to first cleanse yourself, make your eyes more transparent so that you can see better. Perhaps – then too, perhaps – you may be able to help others. The desire is good, but good does not happen just from good desires.

The ancient saying is that the way to hell is paved with good intentions. There are millions of people who are helping with good intentions, advising others – not even bothering about the simple fact that they don't follow their own advice. But just the joy of advising is so much… who cares whether I follow my own advice or not?

The joy of advising others is a very subtle, egoistic joy. The person you are advising becomes ignorant; you become knowledgeable. Advice is the only thing in the world which everybody gives and nobody takes; and it is good that nobody takes it because it is given by people who know nothing – although there is no bad intention behind it.

You are asking a very compassionate question – but in the very nature of things, if you want to change the world, you have to change yourself first. The revolution must come to you first. Only then can you radiate it into others' hearts. First the dance must happen to you, and then you will see a miracle, that others have started dancing too.

The dance is catching; so is love, so is gratitude, so is religiousness, so is rebellion – they are all contagious. But first you must have the flame that you want to see in others' eyes.

The Rebel, Ch 5, Q 2

Beloved Osho,
Sometimes I am blessed by this overwhelming feeling that this commune is becoming gently one body, one organism, one heartbeat. Am I dreaming? Am I once more the usual utopian? Oh, amore, please tell me it is not a dream.

Sarjano, it is a dream that is coming true, but it is a dream – not your dream, but the dream of everybody who is here.

It is impossible to find a man who is not carrying a dream of utopia, of a world which is better, more human, more beautiful, more loving; a world without conflicts, wars, discriminations, a world sensitive, compassionate, understanding. Every human being carries in some corner of his consciousness the dream, and it is not a new phenomenon.

From the very beginning the dream has been present in humanity, and efforts have been made to make a reality of it. Almost all efforts have failed, not because of any intrinsic difficulty, but because of a vast world that surrounds you. Your dreams are not in tune with the vested interests of the world, and they are more powerful – immensely powerful. The dreamer is very delicate, very fragile, just like his dream.

It is a communion of dreamers.

We created a dream in America, but the American establishment could not tolerate it, because the dream of human beings living in peace and love as an organic unity is against all politics, against all those who are in power. It is against all the so-called religions, because if you succeed in creating a dream here and making it a reality, who is going to bother about their heaven and hell and God?

Bertrand Russell is right when he says that if people were really happy, religions would disappear. Religions have a vested interest in the misery of people. The people have to be kept miserable; otherwise, what will happen to Christianity, to Hinduism, to Judaism, and millions of priests who are living as parasites because you are miserable? In your misery you need some kind of consolation!

In the first place they make you guilty, and in the second place they ask you to go to the church to confess to the priest. The priest will fine you and will pray for you to God that you should be forgiven – it is such a game! And it has been going on for centuries and still man is so asleep that he does not see in what ways he is being manipulated.

No child comes with any feeling of guilt and if you don't teach him guilt he will never know about it. He will live a natural, uninhibited, beautiful life, but that will destroy the whole profession of the priests. And now the psychoanalysts have also joined in that profession; they are the latest version of the priest.

Just the other day, I was reading that a patient said to the psychoanalyst, "Last night I did not dream." The psychoanalyst was saying, "Tell me about your dreams. Unless I have your dreams I cannot analyze them and I cannot help you."

The psychoanalyst became very angry. He said, "You are very uncooperative. Why did you not dream? Without dreams what can I do? My whole profession, my whole expertise depends on your dreaming. Continue to dream, and unless you cooperate, I am at a loss; I cannot help you."

The psychoanalyst wants you to continue dreaming. That has become his vested interest. The priest wants you to go on committing sins. The priest will be at a loss if nobody commits any sin.

In a small school, the teacher was telling the children how to go to heaven. And after one hour's continuous effort to make those small boys and girls understand, finally she asked, "Can anyone tell me, what are the requirements to go to heaven?"

One small boy said, "You have to commit sin."

She said, "What? How have you managed to get this idea in your mind?"

He said, "Without committing sin, how is God going to forgive you? And without forgiveness, nobody can enter into paradise."

The child was saying something immensely significant. The priests, the saints, go on teaching: Don't sin. But they don't mean that; remember, they go on saying it because they know the human nature, that you will sin. If they were for a moment made aware that people had decided not to sin, they would be in difficulty. You would have taken their whole profession.

The Pope this year declared that anybody who confesses to God directly is committing a grave sin, you have to go through the right channel. Naturally, because if people start confessing to God directly, raising their hands to the sky and saying, "God, I have committed this sin, please forgive me," what will happen to the church? What will happen to the money that goes on flowing into the church because you commit sin?

I have heard...

A bishop was very friendly with a rabbi. They became friends because both were interested in golf. And they had decided that on Sunday after the bishop was finished with the confessionals they would go to the golf course. The rabbi waited, but it was becoming late. So finally, he came to the church to see what was the matter. He went inside.

In the Catholic church the priest sits behind a small window with a curtain. On the other side stands the man who confesses his sin, and the priest gives him the punishment: "Donate ten dollars to the church and never do such a thing again," although deep down he wants him to do it every day. It is natural, because from where is the money going to come?

The rabbi said, "It is becoming late."

The bishop said, "What to do? There is still a long line waiting, but you can be of help. You just sit here, so I can wash, change my clothes, and get ready. Meanwhile, you do the confessional."

The rabbi said, "But I don't know what confessional is."

The bishop said, "It is very simple. You have just seen that man who raped a woman; I have fined him ten dollars. So just five dollars, ten dollars... fine them and tell them that they will be forgiven, and not to do it again."

The rabbi said, "Okay, I will try."

Of course, on the other side the people were not aware that there had been a change: the bishop was no longer there and the rabbi was sitting there. And one man said, "Father, you have to forgive me, I committed rape twice this week.

The rabbi said, "Son, don't be worried. Just put thirty dollars in the donation box."

The man said, "But last time when I committed rape, you asked only for ten dollars. Is the rate going higher?"

The rabbi said, "Don't be worried my son, ten dollars are in advance. You can commit another rape."

Utopia is what every human heart carries within him, particularly the younger generation, because as you become older you become less and less optimistic. Seeing the reality and its ugliness, seeing that all the powers are against any utopia, any freedom for human heart, any love, they don't want the world to become a paradise, because then they will be out of employment, and nobody is ready to lose his bread and butter.

So as you grow old, you slowly slowly start thinking that utopias are utopias, and you start compromising with the society. But there are a few crazy people like me who go on dreaming in spite of the society, in spite of the whole world. And howsoever difficult the dream seems to be to materialize, still my heart says there is no harm in making another effort. Perhaps one day, if not in my life, then in the life of future human beings, utopia will become a reality.

When the commune in America was crushed, almost bulldozed criminally, anyone in my place would have dropped the idea – but I am stubborn! I will go on till my last breath… or even after that.

Sarjano, what is happening here again is that the dream is becoming true. And we have learned much in the destruction of the commune in America – it has not been a bad experience. Learning is always good, and learning always comes through failures. The commune had succeeded, almost succeeded.

Here, we will avoid those possibilities of destruction. It is better to continue to dream for a better humanity than to settle into sadness and pessimism. Things are still coming together again. People are returning and they are more experienced now. They know not to have a structure that is capable of being destroyed. Something totally new, a more organic body; not a dictatorial regime, no enforcement of ten to twelve hours' work but more joyous, life-affirmative, each according to his need, each according to his choice. We are making every effort not to disturb anybody's individuality, not to sacrifice any individual for the commune. On the contrary, make every individual as strong as possible, because that will be the total strength of the commune – and the seeds have started sprouting.

You are right, Sarjano, when you say, "Sometimes I am blessed by this overwhelming feeling that this commune is becoming gently one body, one organism, one heartbeat. Am I dreaming?" *No, it is a reality that is happening.*

"Am I once more the usual utopian?" *We are making every effort to change the meaning of the word 'utopia'. The meaning of the word 'utopia' is 'that which never happens' – and we are determined to change the meaning. We are committed to the idea that utopia is that which can happen. Its old definition has to be changed totally. Utopia is the very heart of human beings. A man without dreams for a better humanity is not a man, he is a desert.*

"Oh, amore, please tell me it is not a dream." *Sarjano, it is both: it is not a dream because the dream is turning into reality, but it is still a dream because much more has to be done. You should not be satisfied.*

This is a dream which goes on growing with new possibilities, with new dimensions. But we are determined to create it, to make it a reality. This is our religion. We are not interested in going to paradise; we are interested in making the paradise come here. It all depends on our love, on our silence, on our peace, on our meditation, and being aware and alert not to fall again into any trap of the vested interests.

Once the tree has become strong, has gained roots in the earth, it will be difficult for anybody to destroy it.

I believe in the earth.

I repeat Zarathustra who said to his disciples, "Never betray the earth." All the religions have betrayed the earth.

The earth is the only reality.

Everything else talked about by religions is only fiction to distract you. We don't want religions which are interested in a future heaven after death. Our interest is here, now – before death. What is the point of thinking about after death? This has been the routine because people could not succeed to create something beautiful in life. They started postponing it beyond death because nobody knows what happens beyond death; so it was a very good postponement.

I am not for postponing it, not even for tomorrow. Whatever can be done should be done right now.

Don't betray the earth; don't betray the present.

Don't betray your dream; your dream is your very soul.

At a party an elderly bishop tired of social engagements sank wearily into a chair. His hostess rushed up suggesting that he have a cup of tea.

"No tea," grunted the bishop.

"Coffee?"

"No coffee," was the solemn reply.

"Scotch and water?"

"No water."

Sarjano, just avoid Scotch. Just avoid unconsciousness. Water is perfectly good. Be clear in your vision, be conscious in your efforts. The dream is gaining roots and I hope soon we will see the flowers. They are not far away.

The Invitation, Ch 1, Q 3

Beloved Osho,

You don't exist as a person and yet you are the being that I love most. You know nothing and yet I put all my questions at your feet. You are just silence and yet I can only sing your song. You have no name and yet I'm helpless in crying your name. You tell us every day the inexpressible cannot be said, and yet I can't help but try again and again.

You know my gratitude and yet I cannot resist to touch your feet and whisper Thank you, Osho. Even more today, because you free me from saying no to you.

But now I have a question:

Seeing how painful it is to say no to you, how can I ever dare to ask you anything?

Sarjano, you are asking: "Now I have a question: Seeing how painful it is to say no to you, how can I ever dare to ask you anything?"

It is very natural to say yes when you love, just as it is natural to say no when you don't love. But there is still a deeper layer where you love so much that you can even say no. Your love gives you that power. Your love does not make you a slave, particularly as far as I am concerned.

You can say yes out of fear. Then your yes has no value. Your yes is valuable only when it comes out of your love. The value is not in your yes; the value is in your love. If you can understand this then you can understand another thing also: if your no comes out of your love, it has the same value as your yes, because the value is neither of yes nor of no; the value is of your love. Love is absolutely capable of saying yes or no, because love knows no fear.

Love trusts so much that it can say no without any difficulty. Saying yes is very natural, but there may be times when you have to say no. But the no is coming from a loving heart without any disrespect; on the contrary, with great respect. You respect so much that you know that your no will not be taken as a disrespectful or negative attitude.

Love gives freedom.

Love is freedom.

So you need not be worried that you cannot ask for anything. Always remember that you are free to say yes or no to me; I am not your enslaver, I am not your jailer. Not in any sense is there a bondage between me and you. All that exists is freedom and the love that freedom brings.

In this freedom and loving atmosphere everything is acceptable: your yes is acceptable; your no is acceptable. And unless this is possible, your love is not deep enough.

What you have said in your whole question is more a statement and very truthful, honest and sincere. There was only one question in the end that I have answered, but I would like to discuss your statement. I am not answering it because there is no question in it. I am discussing it so that it can become clear to all those who are present here. Because one day everybody has to come to this state from where Sarjano is speaking.

He is saying, "You don't exist as a person, and yet you are the being that I love most."

It is not only true about me. Anybody who does not exist as a person, but only as a presence, will be loved more than anyone else. Simply because he does not exist as a person, he attracts, provokes, invites your love. His absence is a tremendously

powerful magnet. His absence is not emptiness; his absence is overflowingly positive. The person is not there, but the presence is intensely there. And what is the difference between the person and the presence? – the same difference as there is between the flower and its fragrance. The flower is a person; the fragrance is only a presence. You cannot catch hold of it, yet you can be overwhelmed by it.

A person has boundaries, limits. And one who has limits cannot give you unlimited freedom. He himself is not unlimited. Only a person who has died as an ego and has resurrected only as a pure being, a presence, has no boundaries. Obviously he is capable of giving you freedom; in fact, he cannot give you anything else. He has no boundaries. He can also give you a world without boundaries. And naturally, you will love such a presence more than you can love any person.

A person is a very small thing.

A presence is a vast sky full of stars.

"You know nothing and yet I put all my questions at your feet." *I know nothing , it is true.*

And only a man who knows nothing is innocent. Knowledge corrupts because it gives you prejudices, it makes you mechanical. If you ask a question to a knowledgeable man he will not answer your question directly, he will simply repeat some dead, ready-made formula. He knows; his answer will come from his knowledge.

My answer will come from my innocence; hence, my answer will be a direct response to your question. A learned man cannot respond to you – he appears to answer you, but the answer is ready made; it is not a fresh, spontaneous response. It is a prerecorded answer; it does not pay any attention to you. The answer would have been the same even if it was asked by somebody other than Sarjano.

But my answer will be different to each person, even though the question is the same, because I am responding each time not only to the question, but more basically to the questioner. The questioner is the context. The question is symbolic only. I have to answer the questioner more. The question is only an excuse, so my answers will be different although your question may be the same. It creates great difficulty to so-called scholars.

One professor of Bhagalpur University has been doing research for his doctorate on my thoughts almost for seven years, and he becomes more and more confused. He has inquired several times, "Which answer is right? Because for the same question you have given so many answers. You have created such trouble for the scholars who will be working on your work when you are gone."

That's the way scholars work. They never work on living people, they work on dead people. They will work on Kabir, they will work on Gautam Buddha; they will work on Raidas, Meera, whom they condemned when they were alive. Raidas was a shoemaker and in India a shoemaker is not supposed to be a saint. But what to do if a shoemaker becomes a saint? He was ignored, condemned. No Brahmin could go to him to ask a question.

Kabir used to live in Varanasi, which is the Jerusalem of Hindus or the Mecca of Hindus. It is their ancientmost city, and perhaps it is the most ancientmost city in the world. All Hindu learned scholars belong to Varanasi. And Kabir lived in Varanasi but he was not a Brahmin. In fact, by his profession he was a weaver. And weavers belong to the fourth class of the Sudras, untouchables. But only by profession was he a weaver; by his birth nobody knows whether he was Hindu or Mohammedan, because their parents… certainly he was illegitimate, as people call children if they are not out of marriage.

According to me, there are no illegitimate children; there are only illegitimate parents. And when I say illegitimate parents I don't mean those who are not married, but those who give birth to children without any love. Marriage is a formal thing. Love is the reality, the substantial reality. Any child which is born out of a formal marriage without any love, I call those parents illegitimate.

Perhaps Kabir was born out of a pair who were not married. Out of fear of the society they left the child on the banks of the Ganges. A Hindu monk, certainly a great sage,

Ramananda, had gone to the Ganges early in the morning in darkness. And the little baby who was to become Kabir was lying down on the steps of the Ganges. And as Ramananda passed by, the little baby just took his feet in his hand. Now Ramananda could not leave the child touching the feet of the master, although it was going to be a condemnation for Ramananda, as to where he got the child – most probably it is his own child and illegitimate!

Persons like Ramananda don't care at all about the crowd and their opinions. The child has caught his feet and he could not leave the child there, knowing perfectly well that some parents have left him. He brought the child to his monastery. He was a famous Hindu monk and had thousands of disciples and they were all against him: "What are you doing unnecessarily taking a condemnation? Give the child to us; we will leave it there or we will leave it in some orphanage."

Ramananda said, "It is not that there is any question. The child has touched my feet, and I cannot refuse anybody who is ready to surrender himself."

They said, "You are getting into unnecessary trouble. The child knows nothing; it is just accidental. You must have been passing by and he caught hold of anything. It was not addressed specially to you, 'I am your disciple.'"

But Ramananda said, "You don't understand. I know this child, not to whom he belongs in this life, but on his hand is written 'Kabir'.

Kabir is a Mohammedan name which means God; it is one of the names of God. In Mohammedanism there are one hundred names of God. One of those one hundred names is Kabir. So certainly the child seems to be born either out of a father who is Mohammedan or a mother who is Mohammedan, or perhaps both are Mohammedan, but it does not matter.

Ramananda said, "I can look into the past life of the child. He has been my child, my disciple before too. It was not accidental that he caught my feet. He simply reminded me, 'Your poor disciple…'"

People said, "You are getting into unnecessary trouble. Nobody is going to believe these stories. And you will be unnecessarily thought immoral, characterless." Ramananda said, "That doesn't matter."

He raised the child and his prediction became true. Because he said, "One day this child will be a greater man than me. I will be remembered only because of Kabir."

And it is true. Ramananda would have been forgotten. There have been many Ramanandas, many Hindu saints whose names have been forgotten. But Kabir proved to be such a great man that obviously while Kabir is remembered you cannot forget Ramananda.

But because Kabir was not a Brahmin, and certainly he was illegitimate in the eyes of the society, Brahmins, the higher cast people, were not even ready to go to listen to him. They heard him secondhand. They wanted to know everything about him because the people who were going to him were changing so miraculously. He was one of the highest categories of consciousnesses. The same category as Gautam Buddha or Lao Tzu or Mahavira.

You reminded me of him by saying, "You know nothing and yet I put all my questions at your feet." *Knowing that I know nothing, if you still put your questions at my feet, you are sure to find the answer. It won't come from me; it will arise within your own being, out of your humbleness. Just because you have put your questions at my feet shows immense trust, an innocence. And your trust will not go unfulfilled.*

"You are just silence and yet I can only sing your song." *It is true. I am just silence; but I am not a dead silence, I am not the silence of a cemetery. I am the silence of the mountains, the silence of the deep forests. My silence and my song are not different. My silence is a song; it has a music of its own. It has a dance too of its own. So you are right, Sarjano.*

"You have no name and yet I'm helpless in crying your name." *Knowing that I have no name, if you cry my name in your helplessness you will be helped, because you are not calling me in ignorance, just believing in my name. You know perfectly well that I don't have any name. But one has to address some name – it is arbitrary. Namelessness is the reality – but you cannot point a finger towards nothingness, towards silence; you cannot pinpoint. Still it is our human weakness, we have to use names.*

Silence has no name but we have called it silence. Existence has no name but we have called it existence. Enlightenment has no name but we have given it a name. It is our human weakness and frailty. But if we are aware of the fact that we are calling the nameless then there is no problem, any name will do.

I told you Mohammedans have one hundred names for God. I must remind you that in fact they have only ninety-nine names. One name they have left as nameless. That is the real name. Unfortunately the language is incapable, but they have done well. They say, "God has one hundred names," and then they give the list. The list has only ninety-nine. I have asked many Mohammedan scholars, "How do you explain this? Is there some mistake, some error? Either the man counted wrongly or he has forgotten one name." And not a single Mohammedan scholar could give me the right explanation because learning is very poor.

And when I said to them, "I have my own experience. I am not a Mohammedan, but I can give you the answer. The reality is the man has done it deliberately. Whoever has written these ninety-nine names knows perfectly well that one name is missing. But that is the true name which cannot be pronounced; hence he has left it. The number one hundred is given, but the name is not written. So the man was neither counting wrongly nor has he forgotten it."

When Jews write God they never use the O in the spelling. They use G-D, because the real essence, the very center is not capable to be pronounced. They have found a beautiful way; they leave out the O. And in a sense the English O is also exactly the same as the English zero. You can take it in both the senses, that God's real name can only be zero, nothingness, what Gautam Buddha called shunyam, *zero; he has exactly called it zero.*

It is perfectly right if you know that I don't have any name and still you call my name in your helplessness; you are not committing any wrong.

"And yet I'm helpless in crying your name. You tell us every day the inexpressible cannot be said, and yet I can't help…"

Nobody can help. The inexpressible cannot be said, but yet every effort has to be made to say it, knowing perfectly well every effort is going to fail, but just making the effort is significant. Whether it succeeds or fails, that is secondary. You make the effort knowing that it is inexpressible, yet you tried. You tried and you gave ninety-nine names, but finally you accepted your defeat that no name can be given.

But a number can be given at least: the number one hundred. It is beautiful that the man gave the number at least. Just as the English O in God can also be interpreted, in fact should be interpreted, as zero which is God's name. And that has been dropped because it is not possible for human lips to utter it. The number one hundred has also tremendous meaning. One meaning is that the inexpressible is perfect; one hundred is a perfect number. There have been different mystical ways but all have failed. But that failure is not something to be taken in sadness. That failure also shows that although we have not been able to express his name, we have caught hold of the nameless. We will not be able to count him but we have counted everything and only he remains uncounted; that is a way of counting.

"And yet I can't help but try again and again. You know my gratitude and yet I cannot resist to touch your feet and whisper Thank you, Osho."

It is true for every seeker past, present, future, that nobody can show gratitude to existence but still one has to say something. Not that that saying expresses the real experience of gratitude, but at least symbolically it gives you a certain satisfaction. You cannot express it in its totality, but you can give it a symbolic name.

In fact what do we know, even about small things? You call a rose flower red, but what do you know about red? If it was called yellow what difference would it make?

One of the great philosophers of the contemporary world, G.E. Moore, has asked the question, "What do you mean by yellow?" And all that you can do is take him to yellow flowers, marigolds, and show him that this is yellow. And he said, "That's what I am trying to tell you. Even a small and mundane ordinary thing like yellow is inexpressible; it can only be shown. And you ask, 'What is good? What is beauty? What is God? What is consciousness?'"

You don't understand that these things also can only be indicated. They can be shown.

I can take your hand in my hand and show you the path. I can give you the direction where you will find consciousness. But I cannot express it; I cannot give you any explanation right now without your own experience. And if you have experience you don't need any explanation.

Sarjano, lastly you are saying, "Even more today, because you free me from saying no to you. But now I have a question: Seeing how painful it is to say no to you, how can I ever dare to ask you anything?"

There is no question, no problem at all. You can say yes to me, and you can say no to me with the same love, with the same trust, and I will understand your love. I don't care about your words. I will know your heart and I will know the depths of your being.

Yes and no are just trivia.

Sarjano, you have made people serious, and I hate seriousness; hence this joke… The psychiatrist had been working with the patient, a sex maniac, for many months. Finally, things had reached a point where the doctor thought that only hypnosis may help the unfortunate patient. The doctor swung a pendulum in front of the man's face and said, as the hypnotists do, "I want you to imagine that this is a big old clock pendulum, ticking away, and soon you will be asleep. Ding-dong sleep. Ding-dong sleep."

The patient lay still for a moment and then jumped up, shouting excitedly, "Doctor, it works! It works! My ding-dong is asleep!"

The Invitation, Ch 17, Q 3

Beloved Osho,

Every time I come to you, I feel like one of those ancient warriors who came to pay his respects to the emperor. He would enter into his presence, take off his helmet and put it at the feet of the emperor.

The only difference is that I am putting my head at your feet. More so when I ask you a question, and even trembling inside, I put my head as close as possible, for you to cut it with your sword.

But every time, to my infinite surprise, you shower the nectar of your grace on my poor head, the fragrance of your compassion, and an ocean of love in which I find myself drowning deeper and deeper each time.

Beloved master, what has happened to your sword?

How many times will I have to provoke you to cut my head?

Sarjano, it surprises me to know that you have a head. Some idiot guy must have given you the idea.

I have not lost my sword; you have forgotten your head somewhere – maybe drowned in spaghetti! Or do you prefer pizza?

But as far as I know you don't have any head. I have tried to cut it, but what to cut? Certainly you are brave enough to go on trying again and again and again. This does not suit the Italian; this is the American stupidity! Try again and again and again... For what? For the sake of trying. Everybody in America is so busy trying, and nobody knows for what. Trying itself has become the goal; speed itself has become the destination.

But Italians are far more loving beings, far more centered in the heart. Perhaps that's why you go on living without a head – the heart is enough. And no master in the whole of history has cut anybody's heart with the sword. But I am not a reliable man, so you be alert!

A story for you...

The English pirate ship was alone on the high seas. Suddenly the lookout came running. "Captain! Captain!" he cried, "There are five Spanish galleons on the horizon!"

"Quick!" said the captain. "Bring me my red coat."

So he did, and the captain put it on, and the pirate ship defeated the Spanish galleons.

The next day the lookout came running again. "Captain! Captain! There are ten Spanish galleons on the horizon!"

"Okay," said the captain. "Bring me my red coat."

He put it on and they defeated the ten galleons.

"Captain," asked the lookout. "Would you tell me why you always ask for your red coat before we go into battle?"

"Oh, that's because if I'm wounded, the blood will not show; then the men will not be frightened and we will fight to victory!" the captain replied.

The next day the lookout came running. "Captain! Captain!" he cried, "There are a hundred Spanish galleons on the horizon!"

At these words the captain's face turned white, and he called to his lookout, "Quick, bring me my brown pants!"

Just be alert!

I love you, so I'm going to kill you – that's certain. Love is a sure killer. But I kill gradually, because in my experience if you kill suddenly, people start escaping. Gradually, they don't know what is happening; they come to know only when they are gone.

And this place is for only those who are ready to be gone. You become your ultimate flowering only when you are not. It is a strange fundamental law of existence, and there is no way to change it.

The more you are, the less you are.

The less you are, the more you are.

If you are all, then you don't exist. If you are a nothingness, you have tasted existence for the first time.

So, Sarjano, while I go on taking small pieces from your ego, from your so-called personality, you keep yourself engaged in spaghetti and pizza. It is a perfect art!

The authentic master kills the disciple, so that he also can become a pure nothingness, and can become one with the universe. The ancient sages of this country have said that the master is a death. Unless you find a master who can be a death to you, don't waste time. Go on searching, somewhere you will find a master who is going to erase you completely. He will give you your real and authentic being.

Your question is right: I have not lost my sword. It is just because you don't have your head, so you can't see it. But you can feel, and that is far better – to function through the heart.

The Great Pilgrimage: From Here to Here, Ch 6, Q 2

Perhaps he never mentioned that Osho used to arrive in Buddha Hall in a Rolls Royce always with the same driver, a distance of only 200 meters from Lao Tzu House where he lived. He would descend in front of the Hall, where Avirbhava would open the doors of the car, and would then walk towards the podium from where he was giving his discourses.

Once in a while he made a habit of scaring this innocent woman, pretending to hit her below her chest, or shouting something in her ears, managing always to catch Avirbhava by surprise, with the result that she would literally jump into the air with a terrific cry of surprise that resounded in the entire hall!

This sort of little ritual had become so recurrent that he wrote him a little note of complaint about his 'crudity', with the result that although he never got an answer, after one week Osho mentioned it during a discourse, hitting him at the same time with the most tremendous and unexpected Zen stick that he had ever received in his life as a disciple! The opportunity was given to him by someone who had asked something about sex and meditation and the apparent contradiction between those two, to which Osho started answering but then changed subject abruptly and went on his case out of the blue, as he was to do every time he wanted to hit him.

His words were…

[…] Meditation is a way to open your wings and fly into the sky. It does not believe in gravitation. You cannot have both.

So always remember, if I am saying something, do it. You are not here as my examiners so that you have to find out what contradictions I have been telling you. But people take such self-appointed positions….

Now Sarjano has written a letter to me. He goes on writing stupid letters almost every day. Just because last night, when I went out, Avirbhava was on the outside door to open the car. And I have my own way of relating to people; I scare her, and she is so innocent, she gets scared – at least she pretends. She never disappoints me. Now, who is Sarjano to write to me, "I cannot forgive you that you scare simple Avirbhava."

Now, who is he?

I used to think that Swabhav is in charge of the ashram – has there been some change?

Sarjano is neither in charge of the ashram, nor is Sarjano a guardian to Avirbhava, nor is Sarjano my boss. So who gives him all these appointments? He cannot forgive me! And who has asked him that he should forgive me? I will not ask even God himself to forgive me. Even if I can manage to forgive God, that will be enough. For this whole stupid idea that is going on all around, God is responsible – if he is still alive. And the day I am going to encounter him is going to be really the last judgment day!

But who are you to judge me, in my own place, amongst my own people? First he was a disciple; it seems now he has become my master.

But I will not tolerate anybody here in the commune behaving as if he owns the space. If ever again I get any letter like this, you will be turned out of the door. Whoever he is – because he seems to be very tricky: one letter he writes which is absolutely ugly, then another letter he writes praising me, and great poetry and great gratefulness. This Italian spaghetti cunningness will not do here!

As far as I am concerned I have never contradicted myself. Certainly when I speak on Tantra, I speak not as a scholar on Tantra or about Tantra; I speak as an insider who knows what Tantra is. When I speak on meditation, I don't speak about meditation; I speak about my experience of meditation.

Whatever I speak, I never speak without the support of my own experience, and in my experience there is no problem. The Tantra vision, meditation, sex, enlightenment – all come into one single organic unity.

But that does not mean… According to you, do you want me to say everything every day the same? Then what is the need for me to be here? Just a tape recorder will do.

I am not a tape recorder. I am a living human being, growing continuously, and according to my growth my answers will grow, will become different, have different colors, will have more depth, will have new angles, new dimensions. I am not a system maker; I am simply an explorer of the whole field of consciousness.

So I will make all kinds of statements. Whichever suits you, do it. Don't be worried about my being contradictory, because that is my problem. If I am contradictory you are not going to be responsible for it. I will arrange on the last judgment day with God, who is contradictory: am I contradictory or is he contradictory? But that is my problem. God will not ask you about my contradictions, he will ask about your life, how you have lived it – have you lived it at all?

Always remember it as a criterion: if there is a God and on the final judgment day he asks you, What is in your hands? – they will be just empty. You will not have even a few flowers to offer him, because your concerns are all absolutely unnecessary, irrelevant. Your concerns should be absolutely just you, and nobody else.

First solve your own Gordian knot, first cut yourself asunder, first explode your own potentiality; and then you have the right to advise, you have the right to say something about these great things – meditation or Tantra or enlightenment. Right now you don't have in any way, any right at all, to say anything.

Do something! Be something! Then your very being will resolve many problems that right now you feel are great problems. You think this is a great problem, and you say, "I am puzzled." *Why should you be puzzled? I should be puzzled; it is my contradiction, not yours. But I am not puzzled; nothing puzzles me.*

If you can enjoy me, that is enough. If you can celebrate me, that is enough.

I call this kind of Bible really holy: this is the service of the poor, of the lonely, of the lost.

Here, you are to rejoice. This is not an academical institute; it is just a divinely mad communion of people who know how to love, how to laugh, how to sing, how to dance. And you bring academic questions that I said something and now I am saying something else….

If you go on looking that way you will simply waste your life, because I will go on saying anything every day. But whatever I say is relevant to somebody. If you watch carefully, you should choose whatever is relevant to you, and not only keep it in your memory, but materialize into a realization.

Just a joke to make this silence deeper…. First experience this silence, so that after the laughter you can experience the deepness of it… how laughter can make silence deeper, how laughter can make love deeper, how laughter can make meditation deeper. But first, feel it….

A traveling salesman was passing through a small town in Virginia when he saw a little old man sitting in a rocking chair on the porch of his house. The little man looked so contented that the salesman could not resist going over and talking to him.

"You look as if you don't have a care in the world," the salesman said, "what is your formula for a long and happy life?"

"Well," replied the little old man, "I smoke six packs of cigars a day, I drink, I enjoy a large bottle of whiskey every four hours, and six cases of beer a week. I play the guitar and I go out chasing women every night."

"My goodness," exclaimed the salesman. "That's just great! And how old are you?"

The little man took the cigarette out of his mouth and said, "Twenty-five."

The Great Pilgrimage: From Here to Here, Ch 9, Q 2, Excerpt

Beloved Osho,
Am I really getting old, because everyone is gossiping about it?

Devageet again! Just two days ago you had become old, and I had to take so much trouble to bring you back. And you slip again! One time is okay, but twice is too much – it is becoming really a serious problem.

And don't listen to gossip; you are here to listen to the gospel!

But I have also heard the gossip that is making you worried. So first the gossip:

One day at the Poona drugstore, Milarepa, Sarjano and Devageet come in to buy some condoms. Milarepa goes first and says he would like a week's supply, which is six. "Why only six?" asks the druggist.

"Well," says Milarepa, "these days I like to have Sunday off."

Next, Sarjano walks up and asks for eight condoms. "Eight?" says the druggist. "Why eight?"

"Mama mia!" says Sarjano. "I-a always like-a to do it twice-a on Sundays."

And last, Devageet walks up and asks for twelve. The druggist, looking at his size and age, is astonished. "Twelve?" he says. "That is pretty impressive for a man of your age. But tell me, why twelve?"

Devageet replies, "January, February, March…"

That is the gossip that is going all around. And I have to suffer from all these gossips; now I have to bring Devageet back to his senses.

The Great Pilgrimage: From Here to Here, Ch 13, Q 1

After this terrific hit, he couldn't even wait for one day and after twenty-four hours, where he was feeling like a piece of shit, overwhelmed by anguish and by the remorse to have been (even if unconsciously) disrespectful towards his

Master, he wrote him a timid letter hoping as usual for his infinite compassion, which regularly arrived like a deluge! It took a few days to be answered…

Beloved Osho,

What do you see in my eyes now, after you hit my head so hard? Oh beloved Master, the blessing of your sword has left only one wound that even the silence blossomed out of this meditation hasn't healed: have I really been disrespectful in my unawareness? For I will rather cut my tongue before saying anything against you, and I will kill myself with joy rather than be unloving to you.

Surjano, I know your heart. I know your love. I know your deep gratitude and respect – but it is human, once in a while to slip from the path. And it happens from a necessary psychological principle: you start taking me for granted. This is one of the ancient-most diseases of the mind. Once you start taking me for granted, then you are bound to behave unconsciously.

Never take me for granted.

I am simply alive just for you.

My work is finished, and my boat has been waiting for long to take me to the other shore, but your love and the fear that without me you may be lost... and you are coming so close that if I can manage to wait a little longer on this shore, I can give all of my people what I have received from existence. But the moment you take me for granted, immediately you forget, become unconscious, create distance.

I don't want to hit anybody, but except hitting you I cannot wake you up when you have fallen asleep. Consciously, whatever you say is absolutely right, that you would rather cut your tongue than say a word against me, that you would rather die than offend me. These are not just poetic assertions. I understand you perfectly, but you still have the unconscious mind and that unconscious mind manages to sabotage whatever you are gaining in your consciousness.

In mythological terms, it is a conflict between good and evil. In a more contemporary psychological way, it is the conflict between the conscious and the unconscious. The unconscious is afraid – and its fear is real. If your whole being becomes conscious, it will be the death of the unconsciousness in you, and the death of mortality in you, and the opening of eternal life.

Your unconscious mind does not want to commit suicide. It will give you every resistance; hence once in a while it will catch you unawares, and something will come out of you that you had never meant. But if I let it go without hitting you, then your unconscious will be gaining more and more power over your conscious. Hitting you is simply a loving way to put the unconscious back and to help your consciousness to be stronger, more powerful, more capable to understand what comes from your unconscious and what comes from your conscious.

The unconscious is not your friend.

The unconscious is all the past centuries; it is carrying the whole evolution of man. It is barbarous, it is animal. Only a small part of your being has become conscious, but that small being can manage to dispel the whole unconsciousness if you don't become a victim of it again and again.

Now Veena is sitting in her perfect beauty, relaxed, but she does not know: the whole night I have had to sharpen my sword for her! The closer you come to me, the more you love me, the more you should remember that at any time I can hit you.

I have told you the most beautiful story in Zen, about a master thief. He was no ordinary thief, because in his whole life nobody had been able to catch him red- handed. Even the emperor was amazed at his craftsmanship, his art in stealing. The man was so perfect – but he was getting old. The situation had come to the point in Tokyo that whosoever's house was visited by the master thief, bragged about it. It was a great honor, because it was not that he would go just to anybody, but only to the super-rich. It was a certificate that the master thief had stolen things from some family, that they bragged about it.

But as he was getting old, his son said, "I don't know anything of your art, your fame – and you have the strangest fame. Before you leave the world, please let me understand the secret of your greatness. Your stealing is not just for money; your stealing is simply to keep your mastery sharpened so you don't forget the art."

It is almost like a musician. Once Yehudi Menuhin was asked, "If you don't practice one day, what happens?"

He said, "Only I understand that the thing is not as perfect as it would have been; nobody else will find any difference. If I don't practice for two days, then the critics will become aware that something is missing. If I don't practice for three days then everybody will be able to hear that something is wrong, the master is not at his height."

Every musician practices for hours, sometimes eight hours per day. Even the most famous musician practices for hours, because the art is so subtle and so delicate that it can slip out of your hands if you miss just a few days' practice.

So the boy said, "Before you leave the world, help me to know the secret so that I can practice in front of you, and you can correct where I am going wrong."

The father said, "Tonight you come with me."

They went to a very rich house, and the young man was trembling with fear and the old man was going as if he were going for a morning walk – so at ease, with such tremendous confidence. The old man made a hole in a wall to enter into the house... the young man was perspiring, and it was a cold night. But the old man was doing his job so silently that although he was making a hole in the wall, there was no noise. When the hole was ready, the old man slipped in, and signaled the boy to come in.

His heart was throbbing, naturally, but he was wondering... his old father is going as if it is their own house! He had the master key that can open all the doors.

He opened door upon door, and the boy became more and more afraid, he started cursing himself: Why have I asked him to teach me? This is not for me. If I can manage to survive tonight, finished – I don't want to learn this art. It is beyond my capacity.

The man was doing things, so at home, and he took the boy into the innermost part of the house, opened a big cupboard and there were very costly things inside, valuable diamonds, very costly, and rare clothes. Everything was dazzling. The boy could not believe his eyes, that people have so much money.

The old man said, "Get in!" He got in and the old man went out and – it was such a great surprise – closed the door, locked it with the boy inside, and shouted "Thief! Thief!" and ran out!

The boy said, "Is this my father, or my murderer? And what kind of teaching is this? I was wondering if I could survive – now there is no possibility." The whole house was awake. The servants were awake. People were searching every nook and corner, and a maidservant came into the room where he was inside the cupboard. He knew nothing of what to do, but spontaneously he started scratching on the cupboard – as if there are rats inside.

This was not a calculated act, it was absolutely spontaneous. Even he could not believe what he was doing. And the maidservant, just to look for the rats, because there were valuable clothes, opened the door. She had a candle in her hand, and the boy blew out the candle, and rushed out. But he was seen, so the whole family and the whole neighborhood followed him. He had never run so fast in his whole life – he could have become an Olympic champion the way he was going, just like the wind!

It was a question of life and death, and he was praying to God, "This is the first and last time, just save me!"

Then suddenly he came across a well. He took up a big rock and threw it in the well – the whole crowd that was following him stopped. They thought he had jumped in the well: they had heard the sound, so they stopped there, and they said,

"Now there is no worry. Either he will be dead, or in the morning we will pull him out and shoot him."

And the young man reached his house, and again a great surprise: the old man is fast asleep, snoring! He could not believe that this man was his father! He shook him, and the father said, "Don't disturb me. You have come back, that's enough. I know the conclusion; the rest of the story you can tell me in the morning. There is nothing else to learn, I have given you my whole art.

I am not acting out of mind. I am acting out of no-mind, in utter silence. It is my meditation. Just go to sleep."

The boy was amazed that he did not even want to know through what difficulties he had passed. He had been almost on the verge of being caught! He could not sleep the whole night: his heart was throbbing, and again and again as he would close his eyes, he would see the nightmare that those people had caught him, and he would wake up again. In the morning the father did not say anything, he was just sitting, with his tea. The boy said, "But at least ask me what happened!"

He said, "You have come home; everything has gone right. You could not have come back if you had acted out of your mind, so you don't need to learn anything more. All that you need to learn is how to act out of no-mind."

"Still," the boy said, "please listen to my story."

He said, "Okay, if you want you can tell it. But I am not interested. All my interest was in whether you came back or not."

He told his whole story, and the old man asked, "Scratching like the rats were destroying the clothes – was it your thought?"

He said, "I had never thought about scratching the cupboard like rats destroying the clothes… I don't know how it came to me."

His father said, "That's the way – you don't come in. Let your no-mind take possession of the whole situation. How did you figure out that to throw the rock in the well would stop them?"

He said, "I don't know… just the rock was there, the well was there, and the people were just on my heels. Suddenly a flash… and I took the rock and threw it in the well. It was not my act."

The old man said, "This is what the ancient masters have said – action without action. I am not a thief; I have just chosen stealing as a way of enlightenment."

You cannot believe it; anything can become a way to enlightenment, even stealing. But it has to be not your action; it has to come from your no-mind.

So now there are three things, Sarjano: the conscious mind, which you know and out of which whatever you have written to me has come. Behind and below is the unconscious mind, from where all kinds of sabotage will come, disruptions, to destroy the whole possibility of consciousness.

Without your knowing, you have been disrespectful. I know that with your knowing, you will be the last person to be disrespectful, and it does not matter to me whether you are disrespectful to me or not. The point is, I don't want your unconscious mind to sabotage the beauty that has arisen in your consciousness.

Below is unconscious, above is no-mind, or super-conscious. I will hit you if I see that the unconscious is pulling you down, and I will hit you if I see that you are not moving fast enough from the conscious to the super-conscious. Those are the two times when I will hit you.

It does not matter… I have not hit you because you were disrespectful. Remember it – because I have been condemned my whole life: from my very childhood I don't know a day when I was not condemned for doing things not in the way people wanted. I have become so accustomed and at ease with condemnation, disrespect, notoriousness – everything – so that is not the question. Just Sarjano's disrespect will not add anything; it will be just a dewdrop in an ocean, so that is not the problem. The problem is that it will disrupt your consciousness, your love, your peace that is growing, your meditativeness that is growing, and I cannot see that happening.

And this is to be understood by all, because today it is Sarjano's case; tomorrow it can be your case. These hits are out of sheer love. If I don't care about you, why should I bother? The whole night I could not sleep… because I have not used the sword for many years, but just to prepare it for Veena – and she is sitting just here, laughing. If she had laughed before, I could have slept at ease.

I don't want to cut your heads, but if you insist I will have to do it – reluctantly, but there is no other way. If you only understand the language of the sword, then I will have to speak that language. I am not using it; I am using only words.

So be careful. Whenever you start getting angry at me, remember : it is your unconscious that is disrupting your love; it has nothing to do with me. When you start thinking something against me, remember it is your unconscious that is feeding the idea to you.

Otherwise, whatever you said is so beautiful, Sarjano, I would like to read it again so that everybody understands clearly. It is not only a question, it is a statement from the very deepest core of his heart.

"Beloved Osho, What do you see in my eyes now, after you hit my head so hard?"

I see your eyes. I see you – the same as you were before the hit, after the hit. But if you were not hit you would not have been so full of love, with tears of joy in your eyes.

"What do you see in my eyes now, after you hit my head so hard? Oh beloved Master, the blessing of your sword has left only one wound, that even the silence blossomed out of this meditation has not healed: have I really been disrespectful…?"

No, you have not been disrespectful. But you don't know: there are so many dark sides of you which you don't identify with – they were disrespectful.

"… in my unawareness? For I will rather cut my tongue before saying anything against you."

No, that won't help. You can cut my tongue, your tongue; we both can sit in silence because we cannot speak – but I will go on doing what I am doing without the tongue, and you will go on once in a while being disrespectful, without the tongue. The tongue is not needed, just your face can show it, your eyes can show it. Just the smallest gesture can show it.

Don't think in terms of cutting your tongue. Think in terms of from where within you any ugly thing crept into your conscious – and destroy that unconscious. The tongue has nothing to do with it; it is only a means, which the conscious mind can use, the unconscious mind can use, the super-conscious mind can use. I am using it; it is a perfect mechanism to convey things which cannot be conveyed.

And finally, you say, "And I will kill myself with joy, rather than be unloving to you."

That is easier, to die for someone.

The real difficulty is to live for someone.

Many have died in the name of love, because death is a single-blow thing; but living for someone because of your love is a long- time process. I don't want you to make this commune a Jim Jonestown – that is the Christian stupidity. I want this place to be the place of life and love and rejoicing.

If you love me, rejoice. If you love me, sing. If you love me, dance. I don't ask you for death. Death will not prove anything; it will simply prove your incapacity to live for my love. But that has been taught for as long as we can go backwards, that dying for love is a great martyrdom. It is sheer stupidity.

I am not here to teach you all these stupid things that have happened in the past. People have died for Christ, people have died for Mohammed, people have died for Buddha. But that does not show their love, it simply shows their unconsciousness.

The unconsciousness was destroying their love, now it has destroyed even themselves.

Here you have to learn a totally new alphabet, the alphabet of rejoicing. If you love me, rejoice. In spite of everything, rejoice. The more blissful you are, the more you are laughing, the more you are dancing, the more I know you have given me, offered me your flowers of love.

This is a temple of love and laughter. Never forget it for a single moment.

As the boat was sinking, the skipper called out, "Does anyone know how to pray?"

"I do," replied Pope the Polack, who was on board the ship.

"Okay, go ahead and pray," said the captain. "The rest of us will put on life jackets; we're one short."

An old English gentleman was on trial before the high court of Australia, for the crime of making sexual advances to an ostrich.

"Before passing sentence," announced the judge, "do you have anything to say?"

"Your honor," said the Englishman, "if I had known you were going to make such a fuss about it, I would have married the bloody bird!"

Here we are not masochists or sadists. This is not a sick psychological place as all the churches are – belonging to any religion. This is a pagan, natural, simple, playful place. If you can laugh heartily, this is your prayer. If you can dance with abandon, if you can sway with the music, that is the only yoga I teach.

I don't believe in distorting your bodies.

I believe in transforming your souls.

The Great Pilgrimage: From Here to Here, Ch 18, Q 1

Two months passed…

Beloved Osho,
Sometimes I have the feeling that sex has dropped me, but it seems I have not got it yet. Or I just don't want to accept the fact of it. Can you help me to understand what is going on?

Sarjano, the Western mind has completely forgotten that sex is not life; hence everyone born in the West carries in his unconscious the idea that the moment sex is finished, all is finished. This is not true. On the contrary, the moment sex falls away from you, real life begins. On the graveyard of sex grows the mystic rose. It is not only happening to you, it is going to happen to every sannyasin who is honestly and sincerely seeking the truth.

Sex is so childish, so stupid that if you take a photograph of yourself making love, you will be surprised to note a few things: the woman you are making love to has closed her eyes because she cannot bear to see you in such a stupid activity. The only way is to keep the eyes closed and let this ugly moment pass. And that's why people have chosen the nighttime to make love – except a few idiots. You will see yourself doing such gymnastics, huffing and puffing and perspiring over the poor woman – and you are not even ashamed that the fragile woman is under you and you are on top!

But you are so much engaged in this futile activity that you are not aware of it. In fact, in a few cities in Europe and America there are restaurants, hotels which have a very special attraction.

I have heard about one man who asked, "What is this special attraction?"

The manager said, "The fee is high, but if you are interested and you have the money, you will get one of the most gorgeous women to make love to."

He could not resist the temptation, so he paid the money and he was led into a room. Certainly the woman was gorgeous, and as he started making love, he started hearing a few giggles from this side, a few giggles from that side. He could not understand what was happening. He has made love many times, but giggles? – and from all sides?

When the lights came on, he could see that those people had made a great arrangement. There were peepholes around the room – it was a round room – and people were watching him through magnifying lenses; that's why those giggles were coming. He said, "My God, these restaurant people are cheating!"

He went back out and he said, "What is all this? You never told me."

The manager said, "The fee for watching the show is much more. There is no harm; tomorrow you can watch the show. And what is a show if there is no watcher?"

He paid the money – because he felt that the people who were giggling were enjoying more than he was enjoying – and the next day he sat by a magnifying hole and he enjoyed it so much that he started giggling himself. The person who was watching the show by his side said, "What you are giggling at? This is nothing; you should have come yesterday! The man was absolutely mad!"

Sex has been kept hidden for centuries, in the darkness of the night, with the eyes of the woman closed. When it begins, at nearabout thirteen or fourteen years of age, it is a biological device for reproduction. It has nothing to do with you; you are just being used by the blind forces of biology. And if you are understanding enough, my own calculation is that by the time you are forty-two you will start feeling that sex is dropping. Not that you have to drop it – let me insist again and again, you should never drop it because that is the only way to keep it alive to the very last breath of your life.

What you will do by dropping it is what has been done by monks – Hindu, Christian, Buddhist – all over the world. They call it celibacy – a beautiful name for an ugly fact. In the name of celibacy they are repressing their sex.

Sex is a vital energy because it reproduces life. You cannot repress it; it will find perverted ways to come out – in homosexuality, in sodomy. And the ultimate perversion of all the religious teaching is the disease AIDS. It is the outcome of your so-called celibacy.

But nobody is condemning the Vatican, nobody is condemning shankaracharyas *that they are responsible that at least ten million people in the world today are sufferers from AIDS. These are the data only from the Western world, because the East has not yet the facilities, the processes, the experts to find the AIDS virus. So these ten million people belong to the Western part of the world.*

Hundreds of people are dying every day because AIDS has no cure; it is slow death. Between six months and two years, you will be dying slowly. Dying quickly has a beauty about it; you don't suffer. But hanging in the limbo, knowing perfectly that there is no cure, two years of your life becomes a horrible nightmare. You don't think about anything except death.

If you repress sex, you are not going to transform the immense energy contained in it. But if it drops by itself through your meditations and through your understanding, with no effort on your part, it will release such a tremendous beauty and openness to your being that all you have been always dreaming and thinking will become a reality.

And just as I said, Sarjano, it is going to happen to every sannyasin. I call it celibacy only when sex drops, not before it. If you force it before it drops by itself, you are simply becoming perverted. This is a fundamental law of life.

You can change the natural flow of life energy, but once it gets perverted, then it becomes very complicated. First you have to bring it back to the natural state and then only transformation is possible. Perversion cannot be transformed.

It is not only you; your ancient girlfriend has also written to me. Her name is Prem Premal. She says,

Beloved Osho, Is it possible that sex has dropped me and I did not realize it?

It seems it is very hard for the Western conditioning to realize the disappearance of sex with joy and as a blessing from the beyond. Because they believe only in the material body, sex becomes the only possibility of having any moments of orgasmic joy – if you are fortunate enough, which millions are not.

Only once in a while somebody will get a little glimpse of orgasmic joy. Your conditioning prohibits it. In the East, if sex drops by itself it is a celebration. We have taken life in a totally different way; we have not made it synonymous with sex. On the contrary, while sex continues you are not mature.

When sex drops a great maturity and centering comes to you, and a true celibacy, an authentic brahmacharya. *And now, because you are free from the chains of biology which are the only chains that are making you a prisoner of blind forces, you open your eyes and you can see the beauty of the whole existence. You will laugh in your days of celibacy about your own stupidity, that you once thought that is all that life has to offer.*

I have heard about an old drunkard who was sitting early in the morning on the sea beach, and he saw a young man doing pushups. The drunkard could not believe it. He went around the young man; he looked from this side, he looked from that side. Finally he could not contain his curiosity, and he said, "My poor boy. Why are you unnecessarily perspiring and doing these pushups? Your girlfriend is not here." – because he knew only the pushups which people go on doing in the name of love.

Sarjano and Premal, it is perfectly okay – and not just okay – that sex is disappearing. As sex disappears you will find authentic love growing in you. Sex is not love; it is just a fallacy, a blindness. You are tricked by biology into believing that this is love.

But once sex has disappeared your whole life energy is redeemed from its animal past. And just as sex was reproducing more and more children, sex-freed energy starts giving you every moment a new birth. Your whole life becomes fresh, growing in a new direction. Sex is horizontal; love is vertical, it takes you upwards to higher realms of being. And the higher you are in your love, the closer you are to the ultimate truth. The day your love has reached to its climax, you will experience what I have been defining as satyam, shivam, sundram – *the truth, the godliness and the beauty.*

Then these experiences are not momentary glimpses any more. They become part of you, you become part of them. They become just like the heartbeat – they are with you for eternity.

But I can understand your problem: up to now you have known only one joy and that was sex. You are absolutely unaware that there are skies beyond skies and you are just creeping on the earth. You are not aware that you have wings and you can fly just like an eagle across the sun into the faraway sky. The whole sky becomes your kingdom.

Because of this fact, a misunderstanding arose. Down the ages mystics have experienced it, and because they experienced that sex is functioning as a blinding force, as imprisoning you, they started condemning sex. The misunderstanding was that people started thinking that if sex can be repressed, they will also become part of the mystical world and its experiences.

Nobody has had the courage to say that this is not a true understanding of the fact. Celibacy is not something to be practiced, it is not something to be rehearsed, it is not something to be imposed on you by any method, any effort, any doing. Celibacy comes when sex disappears on its own accord. Certainly the word 'celibacy' has tremendous meaning in my sense.

But the misunderstanding was that seeing the mystical people rejoicing and dancing and singing and their eyes and their faces and their charismatic pull, people started repressing sex, thinking it is sex that is preventing them from knowing higher realms of being. There lies the great misunderstanding.

My effort – which has brought me condemnation from all over the world from all religions, because they are all living in this misunderstanding – has been to destroy this misunderstanding. I am not for sex, but I am not against sex either. It has a time, its season, its climate, and that time should be given to it. It is absolutely a natural phenomenon, but it should not spread beyond its limits. Just as at the age of fourteen it appears, if you live it totally, intensely, without any guilt created by religions, you will be out of the imprisonment by the age of nearabout forty-two. This is an average; those who are more intelligent may get out of it sooner. Those who are a little dull witted will take a little more time.

But misunderstandings are everywhere.

Just before the operation, the high-powered surgeon was explaining all the new recovery techniques to his patient. "Now, you should begin walking as soon as possible," explained the doctor. "On the first day, you must walk around for five minutes; on the second day ten minutes, and on the third day you walk for at least an hour. Do you understand?"

"Yes, doctor," answered the apprehensive patient, "but is it all right if I lie down during the operation?"

Things were not going so well for Gilroy and Loretta when they went to bed together for the first time. Gilroy was working away hard, but Loretta was not responding at all. Finally in exasperation he asked her, "What is the matter?"

"It's your organ," Loretta replied, "I don't think it is big enough."

"Well," Gilroy replied indignantly, "I did not think I would be playing in a cathedral."

There is so much misunderstanding in the world. It creates confusion, it creates chaos, and when everybody has misunderstood something and you stand alone to make them understand, they feel offended.

Not a single religious leader has refuted logically whatever I am saying, because they don't have any logic. But they have been condemning me without refutation, and because they are all together in the same boat, naturally it seems that I am alone against the whole world.

But what I am saying is a simple truth to understand. You cannot bring sex in forcibly – can you make a seven-year-old child potent enough to reproduce children? The very idea looks absurd. Sex comes on its own accord; it is a certain maturity of your body, of your chemistry, of your physiology that brings it at the age of twelve.

If the coming is not in your hands, the going is also not going to be in your hands; it will go at the age of forty-two without any problem. Just one thing has to be remembered: don't be corrupted by your religions, don't be corrupted by your scriptures, don't be corrupted by your so-called saints. They are the most poisonous people on the earth. They have destroyed man in so many ways that their crimes are uncountable.

The greatest crime is to create a guilt against sex, because it keeps sex alive beyond its natural boundary. So even a person of seventy is still thinking of sex. In fact there is nothing else for him to think about – retired, what else can you do? You have to simply think about it and talk about it. Sex, which used to be a part of the physical body, has moved and become just cerebral, just in the mind.

Even at the time of death, most people die with some sexual image floating in their minds. This is ugly, and the responsibility is on your so-called saints. Neither do they understand the psychology and the science of the transformation, nor do they care that what they are teaching is going to destroy people's lives.

I teach you that when the sex energy is starting to function, allow it full support. At the age of nearabout eighteen or nineteen man has his greatest sexual energy; that is the peak point. But your society prevents you: you have to go to the college, you have to go to the university, you have to come back after university – maybe twenty-five years old – and then you will have to be married.

But at twenty-five years old, you are already six years downhill. This is absolutely unscientific. Boys and girls in the colleges and in the universities should live together, not in separate hostels, and they should be given all that the scientific approach has found out about sex. In the past, of course, it was a little difficult, because of the problem of the girl becoming pregnant. But now there is no problem at all. The pill has been the greatest revolution in the world – even greater than the Russian Revolution!

And now two more pills have come into existence which have made sex simply a fun, nothing to be worried about. The first pill was to be taken by the woman for a certain period of time; only then was it possible to prevent pregnancy, and that too was not a hundred percent sure. It used to happen that you were not expecting your lover and he suddenly comes and you have not taken your pill.... And the human mind is so stupid that it goes on thinking that nobody gets pregnant every time; it is very rare, so there is nothing to worry about. You can take the chance. But that chance has always proved very dangerous.

I have heard about a man traveling with a busload of children. Somewhere he stopped for the children to take some drinks, tea or something. The manager of the small hotel asked him, "My God, are all these children yours?"

He said, "They are not my own. I am a salesman for birth control methods; these are my failures. I am going to take them to the factory to show the owner that something is wrong with his birth control methods. Just count these children.... And all the parents are now waiting with loaded guns to kill me, because I have given them a one hundred percent guarantee."

The first pill was not a hundred percent guaranteed. The second pill is tremendously important. The second pill is to be taken after you have made love, so there is no problem, there is no risk. And the third pill is even more important because it brings about the equality of men and women. Why should only the woman take the pill? The third pill can be taken by the man.

If one looks in a scientific way without any prejudice, then every young man or young woman who is at the peak of sexual potency should be allowed to make love without any guilt. But we force them to remain repressed about sex, and by the time they are declining in their energies we allow them to get married.

Two problems arise out of it. First, for twenty-five years you have been telling them that sex is wrong, to prevent them from getting into any sexual relationship. Twenty-five years is one third of your life; it is a long time to create a great prejudice against sex.

And then suddenly in one day everything changes; you allow them to get married. This is idiotic – because what will happen to twenty-five years' propaganda against sex? And those who are getting married are also idiots; they don't ask the priest and their parents, "What will happen to that twenty-five years' conditioning?

Now you are giving us license to make love, but what about those twenty-five years that you prevented us?"

So the first problem is that man is the only animal in the whole world… Man is the most intelligent animal, but absolutely unintelligent as far as sex is concerned. There are no sex classes for deer and lions and horses and donkeys. They don't need to be taught about sex at all; it comes naturally.

But because of twenty-five years' constant insistence from the religion, from the society, from the university, from the parents, man gets confused. On the honeymoon he does not know what to do.

I have heard about a young man who got married and went to the honeymoon hotel in a holiday resort. It was a full moon night. The woman immediately undressed and lay down on the bed, but the young man was sitting at the window looking at the full moon. Minutes passed, hours were passing, and the woman said, "What is the matter with you? What are you doing there? It is our honeymoon."

The man said, "Shut up. When I was coming here, I asked my mother, 'Any advice?' She said, 'This is the greatest night of your life. Don't miss a single moment.' So I am waiting and watching the night, the greatest night. Don't distract me."

But this is bound to happen. And then the second thing happens: a deep guilt feeling about sex, that it is sin. If you are carrying the idea that something is sin you cannot really enjoy it. Your sin will be holding you back. Your guilt will be making you feel ashamed of yourself: What are you doing? So no man, no woman is prepared to make love in deep joy, in freedom. On the contrary, everybody is prepared against love.

This is the reason why people don't get rid of their sexuality at the age of forty- two; they will continue even if they live eighty years. Society spoils people in such a way – and perhaps they are also doing it absolutely unconsciously. They are taking away your home – the experience that was possible for you, but which happens only when sex drops on its own accord.

Then the freedom has a totally different meaning. You have not achieved it; it has been bestowed upon you from the beyond. Existence has accepted that now you are ready for greater mysteries. You are no more to cling to your teddy bears; you can move on into ecstatic lands, into experiences of bliss that know only a beginning but no end. You can move towards finding the truth of your being and the truth of existence.

It seems very strange that I am condemned for teaching sex to people. In fact I am teaching them the natural celibacy; but to bring the natural celibacy the sex also has to be natural. Sex is not the goal, but only a staircase.

If it can be natural, without any guilt, without any poison, you will reach beyond it and you will be immensely surprised that only now you have become mature. Now the bodily pleasures don't have any meaning, because in comparison to your spiritual blessings, blissfulness, they all fade away.

Sarjano, what is happening is perfectly good – but particularly for an Italian it is a little difficult to accept. But the moment you became my sannyasin, you dropped all boundaries and discriminations that make men different from each other. My sannyasins are simply the first world citizens. They don't belong to any nation and they don't belong to any church.

The other day I received a letter from Australia. Just like other lands and other continents, Australia also has a Rajneesh Foundation, and we have thousands of sannyasins in Australia. The Theosophical Society of Australia was selling my books up to now, and those books were their best sellers. This time, when the representative of the Australian Rajneesh Foundation went to the Theosophical Society, they said, "We have been ordered by our world headquarters that your books should not be sold."

The sannyasin saw that books that were written against me were being sold, and he asked about it and the man said, "I love Osho myself, and his books were our best sellers. I even wrote a letter that this is not right, but they overruled my letter and they said, 'You have to do what you have been told. Books against Osho can be sold, but literature of Osho or any literature written in his favor is banned.'"

It was not a surprise to me – but it is very inconsistent with the Theosophical Society's own philosophy. They pretend that they are synthesizing all religions, all philosophies, all approaches – just excluding my standpoint! They are exposing themselves, because this letter banning my books must have gone not only to Australia; it must have gone to Japan, it must have gone to America, it must have gone to other countries in Europe.

What is their fear? Their fear is that they cannot make my approach fit with all other religions' approaches. It stands aloof and apart and alone in its own majesty.

They cannot answer, and they are not ready to confront me publicly. So from the back door they try to destroy whatever I'm trying, which is to help humanity come out of the garbage that has been accumulating in you for centuries behind very good names.

Sarjano, it is a festive moment if sex has dropped from you – and it must have dropped, because the certificate is there from Prem Premal. Now you can move from ordinary animal life into authentic transformation. It is the same energy that is involved in sex.

If sex drops you have so much energy for meditation, you have so much energy for friendliness, you have so much energy to be creative – and you are a creative person.

Now with all this energy released you can manage so much creativity in your work that you may not have even dreamed about. This creativity will bring to you your self-realization.

Satyam Shivam Sundram, Ch 19, Q 1

This is the poignant story of a very crucial day in his life. He has no explanations. No regrets. Or does he?

He would visit the ashram every day. The beautiful, silent early morning darshan was the best part of his day. He lived a few blocks away from the auditorium and would walk down the quiet road in the misty mornings. Alone and blissful.

A woman used to walk just ahead of him. If she wasn't ahead of him, he would slow down to let her pass. He loved watching her graceful stroll. Her beauty would make the sun shine for him. Blonde and tall, she was everything he ever dreamt of in a woman. Enchanted, he would follow her, praying that she turned towards the ashram so that he could continue to follow her. Invariably she did. Still, every day he would hold his breath until he saw her turning. Had she gone the other way, he may have followed her and missed the satsang with the master.

It was not about a woman. It was not about love. It was not about sex. She symbolised sheer beauty, and in those moments he realised that if he had to choose between God and beauty, youth and beauty, silence and beauty… he would have chosen beauty!

He followed the same enthralling routine morning after morning, month after month, year after year. He never spoke to her and would later lose track of her in the crowd of pilgrims.

One day, as he was returning home, lo and behold, she was walking ahead of him. In the glowing light of day, she was even more beautiful. The rays of the sun gave her movement, her dancing, a rare dimension.

He found himself walking faster and faster, till he was abreast of her and invited her for a real Italian coffee. His face must have been familiar to her, as she accepted gracefully.

While sipping coffee together, she revealed to him that this was her last day in Pune and she was to fly back to Europe that night.

He told her that he was a photographer, an artist and a worshipper of beauty. He told her everything – the morning walks, his sheer joy in her dance towards the auditorium, his fears and his prayers. They had a great laugh. She asked him why he had never stopped her before, and he told her that he was waiting for it to happen some day.

"It had to be today, the day you are leaving."

This had to be the only day, the only opportunity, the only moment. Tomorrow would have been too late. It was here and now!

They dissolved into each other without even sharing their names.

What they shared was love, song and dance.

They shared eternity.

She had all the colours of his love. Overwhelmed by her beauty he cried. Occasionally he would open his eyes and look at her in wonderment.

In one of those moments, his eyes fell on the bedside clock!

A clear reminder of time. It was a quarter to one and his friends would soon descend on him for lunch.

In those days he and his friends shared fantastic meals in his bungalow. Most of them would contribute something. A bottle of wine, a cauliflower, some imported delicacies – French cheese, Italian olives.

It was always a grand feast. And his friends were due any time, and there was nothing. No food.

For a moment he froze. The situation was clear. There were only two options. Either he would go down and stick a sign on the door:

'RESTAURANT CLOSED FOR THE DAY. SEE YA TOMORROW' and continue dancing with her, or go quickly to the kitchen to cook some food.

What was his decision?

He saw himself smiling at the thought: today his food was going to be very good, very juicy. And in a moment he was in the kitchen chopping spinach.

Since then, he has often asked himself how he could have done such a thing. Remember, she had all the colours of his love. She was what he had been looking for! That was the moment he had been waiting for all his life. And then? In his days of solitude, he often wondered what possessed him to let her leave his life like that. The answer still eludes him.

Does it mean that cooking means more than anything else to him? More than even making love to the woman of his dreams?

Perhaps. Perhaps it just happened that way on that day. Her vision still haunts him.

He still remembers what he cooked that day! He cooked cannelloni di spinaci e mozzarella.

Beloved Osho,

When the old road has come to its end and the new path is not seen yet...

When the past has no more meaning and the new dawn is still far away...

When everything looks old and futile and the new has not arisen yet...

When I know what I am not and I don't know who I am...

When there is no hope, not even for a new hope...

Beloved master, is this the dark night of the soul? Will I see the dawn?

Sarjano, it seems you have come to the point of the China Wall that we were looking for. Just have a good laugh and jump! The past is finished; there is no meaning in it. According to you, you have understood what is false, so there is no question of clinging to it; you don't have anything to lose. Why not have a good laugh and jump?

It never happens the way you are asking. You remain intellectual. You are saying the darkness has gone but the light has not come. Now what am I supposed to do? It can't happen in the very nature of things. The moment you understand the false as false, instantly you know what is real. These two things don't happen separately. There is not a gap of time, they happen together. Here you understand what is false, and immediately, instantly, you know what is real. How can you understand the false as false if you don't understand the real as real? Without the understanding of the real you cannot call anything false.

So your question may look very relevant – it is not. I will read it so you can see.

"When the old road has come to its end and the new path is not seen yet..."

Then what are you seeing? That's just what I was saying: have a laugh and jump. The old road is finished and the new you cannot see. Certainly there must be a valley. Just say, "Giddup!" and take a jump! It does not need an answer, it needs a little courage. But I say to you, in the very nature of things it does not happen. "When the old road ends..." *That is where the new road begins. The end of the old is the beginning of the new. They are not two separate things; there is not a gap between the two.*

If there had been a gap, then it would have been impossible to find the new, because you would need something to join the old to the new. What will you call it? Old or new? A bridge, a road, you will need something to make them join – what will you call it? If you call it old, then when you were saying the old is finished, it was not finished. If you call it new, you have already found it, you just move on. No, there is no gap ever. In existence there are not gaps; everything is continuous.

Do you know when you became young and your childhood ended? Can you remember the day, the date, the hour, the minute, the second? Everything is continuous. Do you know the day you will become old? Will you be able to mark it on the calendar? "Today I am becoming old. Youth is finished. Now begins old age." You never know. Things are continuous. Yes, one day you realize that you are old now. But it is not the moment when you become old. You don't become old in a single moment. It is a process. It goes so slowly without making any noise.

If you see that "the old road has come to its end and the new path is not seen yet..." *I cannot concede that. If the old is seen as ending, that is the beginning of the new. Move on it.*

"When the past has no more meaning and the new dawn is still far away..." *It does not happen. You are asking a very intellectual question, but existence has no obligation to fit with your intellectual categories. Existence goes on its own way. You have to fit with it. If the past has no more meaning, you have become new. The dawn has come; the birds must have started singing, the flowers must be opening, the sun is rising.*

Have you ever seen a gap between the night and the day? When the night ends the day begins; when the day ends the night begins – immediately. There is no gap at all. If there had been a gap there would have been immense difficulty how to jump it. The day has ended, you are standing there and the night has not begun. Now how to jump? Where to go? Nature does not leave anything incomplete.

You say, "When everything looks old and futile and the new has not arisen yet…" *How then can it look old and futile? With what are you going to compare it? When you say everything looks meaningless, it implies that you have a certain understanding of meaning. You know what meaningfulness is. Only in comparison to meaning can you say that something looks meaningless.*

Only in comparison to life can something look like death. If you don't know anything about life, you cannot describe somebody as dead. These categories are combined. They are two sides of the same coin.

But you go on and on: "When I know that I am not and I don't know who I am… When there is no hope, not even for a new hope… Is this the dark night of the soul? Will I see the dawn?" *It is nothing so great as you are making it. The dark night of the soul is experienced only by very great mystics. It is not, Sarjano, spaghetti! The dark night of the soul means you have come close to the dawn. The darker becomes the night, the closer is the dawn. The dark night of the soul is a moment of celebration because the dawn is not far away. If the dark night has come, then the dawn is implied in it. It is bound to come, in fact it has come. It is not separable from the dark night.*

But you have a habit, Sarjano, of complaining. This whole question is nothing but grumbling, complaining, that you have done everything that was needed. The old is finished, the false is dropped, the dark night of the soul has come, and nothing is happening. You remind me of Moses.

Moses is standing facing the Red Sea. Behind him in the distance, clouds of dust rise from Pharaoh's army, hot in pursuit. Suddenly with a mighty roar, the waters part, opening an escape.

Moses looks ahead at the wet roadway and the cliffs of water on either side. He lifts his face to the sky and murmurs, "Tell me something, God, how come I always have to go first?"

Such a great miracle is happening and he is not going to thank God. He complains about why it always happens that he has to go first.

If all that you are saying is really happening, be thankful. If the old has ended, you will see the new. If everything has become meaningless, you will find authentic meaning. If the dark night of the soul has arrived, dance, rejoice, the dawn is not very far away.

But always be grateful.

Prince Edward, the Queen of England's youngest son, meets one of Kaddafi's daughters at a party and they fall in love. Edward tells his mother that they want to be married, which puts the Queen into a dilemma. On one hand she is pleased, because it will dispel all the rumors about Prince Edward's homosexuality, but on the other hand, to have any allegiance with Libya will annoy Ronald Reagan considerably. Her motherly instincts get the better of her and she consents to the marriage. But, still not trusting the girl's motives, the Queen instructs James Bond to spy on the young couple. The next morning Bond reports back to the Queen.

"What happened, Double-O-Seven?" she asks.

"Well," says Bond, "first she said to him, 'I offer you my honor,' then he said to her, 'I honor your offer.'"

"So what happened next?" asks the Queen excitedly.

"Well," says Bond, "after that it was ON her, OFF her, OFF her, ON her, all night long!"

What you need, Sarjano, is a good laugh and just jump. If the old road has ended, jump. You will be on the new road. Certainly you cannot be on the old road. If everything has become meaningless that is a great freedom. It means the very effort of trying to find meaning in things is an exercise in utter futility. Life has significance but no meaning. Meaning is a mind trip. Significance is a great love affair of the heart.

And Sarjano, you are not potentially a man of the head. You are potentially a man of the heart. But everything is topsy-turvy in you, upside down. You have not realized a simple fact about yourself, that you are a man, not of logic, but of love. Drop all intellectual bullshit. Get deeper into your heart and you will be able to see the new light, the new path, the new dawn. They are here, but your eyes are closed. The head is blind. Only the heart has eyes.

But it is strange that almost every culture of the world, every society, and every civilization that has up to now pretended to exist, they all say love is blind – without exception. But I want you to be absolutely clear about it.

Only love has eyes. Logic is blind.

But all these societies wanted you to be fixed in the head and forget all about heart, because heart is not much use in the marketplace. What is needed there is head, what is needed there is cunningness, cleverness, what is needed there is reason. Love is not needed at all in the world that we have created. That's why it is ugly and miserable. Without love man cannot get rid of misery, despair, anguish. He is bound to suffer. Only love is the savior, the redeemer.

Just get down from your ladder a little towards the heart. The heart is exactly in the middle between your head and your being. Once you are down in the heart, you will have a totally different vision of things. And then I can tell you one step more. From the heart to the being is a very relaxed, silent, peaceful journey with no hindrances. But from the head there is no direct way to the being.

And society has played a tremendously criminal trick on every human being. They have cut the heart completely away from you. This is the strategy so that you cannot reach to your being. You can reach to the being only via the heart. And heart has been ignored by your education, by your religion, by everybody. It has been forced into darkness.

So you are hung up in the head and you cannot go anywhere. You can only go on making questions, intellectual gymnastics; but it is all meaningless, futile. Rather than questioning, you should start moving towards the heart. That is the true rebelliousness, love revolting against logic. And then from love to being is a very simple, very joyful way. It is a garden path full of roses.

Looking at your question, all that I can feel, Sarjano, is that you are not supposed to be an intellectual, a heady person. You are not. I have seen your tears and I have seen your laughter and I know that you are misplaced. It is within your hands to revive your heart which has been repressed and drop your head which is not your destiny. It is nobody's destiny. The destiny is to realize the being, and the being can be realized only via the heart. Unless you know and learn the art of love, unless you are sensitive and creative, unless you forget all Aristotelian logic, you will never reach to your being.

And your being is the place where sat-chit-anand – *truth, consciousness, bliss – are waiting for you. Just a small effort from head to heart, then there is no effort needed at all. Effortlessly you will slowly sink from your heart into the being.*

This reminds me that all the Eastern mystics have been saying that no effort is needed to find yourself, because they were all from the very beginning trained to be in the heart. The modern mind, particularly the Western mind, finds it difficult to understand that you can achieve anything without effort. Some effort has to be made. The reason for this problem is that the modern man is head-oriented and the people who were talking about effortless let-go were heart-oriented. The situation has changed.

That's why the modern man finds it difficult to understand the mystics of the East. There is a certain gap that has arisen. They were talking in the language of the heart, you are listening in the language of the head, and there is no communication between head and heart.

Moving from the head to the heart is the first step of any authentic meditation. And the second step you don't have to take. It happens on its own accord. And there are only two steps. One you have to make, that is from head to heart. And the other happens spontaneously on its own accord. You simply relax and you will find yourself slipping deeper and deeper, and one day suddenly, all is achieved. All that was missing has become available. The whole is yours. The whole mystery is yours.

Sat Chit Anand, Ch 28, Q 2

In those days another event happened to his surprise and disconcert and that was that Osho had him called by Neelam, his new Indian secretary, who told him with a huge smile that Osho had expressed the desire that a room in the ashram should be given to Sarjano. She said that the room would be in Krishna House, one of the five buildings of the ashram, and as soon as the room had been refurbished he could finally come and live inside the Commune!

He wasn't happy at all about this, because he very much liked to stay where he was living, in a little house that he had found by the river, and also because he knew that living in the ashram he would have to renounce forever all his old and dear habits, such as playing poker all night long, for example, or to fuck shouting on the roof with one of his girlfriends, or to invite all his friends to some sumptuous dinner he would cook… all in all he had absolutely no desire to move from where he was, but how could he say all this to Osho?

The simple fact is that he would never have dared to say no to his Master, not even if he would have sent him to the moon, then what to say when he was offering a room to be closer to him?

He didn't say anything in that moment and accepted even Neelam's invitation to go and see his new room, and to find out when it would be ready. The room was very spacious and beautiful, and he thought that thousands of sannyasins would have been ultra-happy for such an offer, but he couldn't see the positive side of it; he was simply annoyed, sad, and with a great sense of impotence about this unexpected gift, to which he simply couldn't say no.

The room was going to be ready in a couple of weeks, and during this time everybody saw him going around with a face becoming more and more dark and depressed, because he absolutely didn't know how to disentangle himself from this situation, neither how he could say no to Osho.

After having seen him moving around with such a face as if he were waiting for his death sentence, one day Neelam called him into her office and asked for an explanation about his horrible mood, and about his perennially angry face, and all this since the very day she had told him of Osho's invitation. He decided to tell her the whole truth, saying that he was very happy where he was staying and that he had no desire whatsoever to suffer all the rhythms and restrictions of living inside the ashram, that he liked to have fun and make noise with his friends, until late, and all in all if he were going to accept this room, it would be only because he was absolutely incapable of saying no to his Master.

Neelam listened to him in silence and didn't say a word, but as soon as it was possible she reported all of their conversation to Osho, who simply started laughing and then proceeded to dictate a short message to her to be read to Sarjano.

The message was:

Beloved Sarjano, I had heard that you are broke and that you are having some financial difficulties, and I thought that you may be having some problems in paying the rent of the house where you live; hence I've told Neelam to prepare a room for you in the ashram. But if you are happy where you are, then you don't have to accept it forcibly, just to please me!

You can stay happily in your house and enjoy it with all my blessings, because there will be certainly someone else who will be very happy to have it!

"Give it to someone else then!" he shouted in great release, and he left dancing, like someone finally free from an enormous burden.

***

CHAPTER 13

Short Trip To Italy, Back To The Ashram And Meeting Mai

And finally the day of his departure came; his visa was expiring in a few days, and furthermore all his money was running out, hence he had to go to Italy for at least a month to apply for a new visa and some old money, and then come back. He was calling it "old money" because he was always making the money he needed in the same old way for more than ten years: he was a very good friend of a few Italian pop stars, people like Battiato, de Andre', Gianna Nannini, all names that probably mean nothing to you, but in Italy they were among those on the very top of the chart.

At least once a year he would go visit them at their homes; each one of them was in some enchanting place or other in the countryside, where no photographers or journalists had ever been allowed. He would stay there for a couple of days, first making some juicy interview, then shooting a few dozen rolls of film, eating the good food generously offered to him. Then upon return to Milan he would give all the pictures to his photo agency, sell the interviews personally to some glossy magazines with whom he had previously arranged his articles, and at the end of his monthly effort he would have managed to raise at least 20 million of the old lire, which was then more or less the equivalent of 15,000 US dollars, the money that he needed to live in Pune like a king for at least another year…and now he was ready to leave Italy.

When he arrived at the ashram, he immediately found out about two nice surprises: the first was that while he was away, Osho had asked for when Sarjano would return to have a place for himself, a restaurant organized by himself only, run by him without anybody's interference, where he could cook all the food that he liked, and in his own way!

Osho seemed tired like him about all the complaints that he was always hearing about Sarjano in the kitchen, always about the same passion, for his determination to give always his best and most of all to respect the timing, to the point when his crew was slowing down a bit and lunch was at risk of being late, he would start shouting in his loudest baritone: "Vamo…vamo…vamo VAAAAAAAAAAAMM MMOOOOOOOOOOOOOOOOOO!"

Yes, that long, and he was expressing it with such a volume that it was probably heard ten blocks away!

Beloved Master,

Ten years ago I came to your feet and found that unknowingly I was already there. Have I ever been somewhere else in my life or in any life? Isn't it that this thirst of ours has created your smile to show us how existence smiles?

Beloved Master, I don't know what the question is or if I have any more questions for they are quenched day after day by your love and my gratitude. But then why did I say to myself, jump now? And yet, I look back once more to my passion and to its old songs and dreams.

Oh beloved Master, can you really promise me that passion is always transformed into compassion?

My god! Sarjano... Has everybody gone mad? You are also in the same trouble...!

But your passion is different. It has nothing to do with ordinary, blind natural forces. Your passion is what has brought you to me, which even makes you feel that perhaps you have always been here, or even in other lives too.

You are asking, "Isn't it that this thirst of ours has created your smile to show us how existence smiles?

"Beloved Master, I don't know what the question is..."

There is no need to know what the question is. Just know the answer....

This silence is the answer.

This love is the answer.

This feeling of a thirst being quenched is the answer.

Who cares about the question?

The whole of humanity can be divided into two categories: the majority has questions, and the minority has answers. It is very rare to find a person who has both – I have never come across any person, living or dead. By the time a person reaches to the answer, questions disappear. Questions are just like darkness: when you reach to the light, they disappear – not that they are solved, they simply dissolve.

In this quenching of the thirst, day after day, certainly a love and a gratitude arises which says to you, "Jump now." But the old, the past, is heavy. To drop it, even though it is meaningless, needs a lion's heart, because you have identified yourself for long, too long, with things which you are not. And now suddenly, you have to drop all those identities of many lives.

It is not only difficult for you, it is difficult for everybody. But howsoever difficult it may be, it is not impossible. If it has not been impossible for me, why should it be impossible for you? If hundreds of mystics around the world have been able to drop the whole past and have never looked back, you are also capable of the same courage – you have just not tried it.

But you go on looking back. You say, "And yet I look back once more…" *How many times have you looked back, and how many more times are you going to look, again and again,* "just once more"?

The past that has been is no longer there, and that which is, is herenow. You need to jump without hesitation. A slight hesitation, a split second's hesitation, and you have missed it.

But you say, "And yet I look back once more to my passion and to its old songs and dreams.

"Oh Beloved Master, can you really promise me that passion is always transformed into compassion?"

I have described clearly: if your love is hiding lust, it cannot be transformed into compassion; there is no way. But if you have really loved, without even your becoming aware, one day you will find your love has become more and more lovingness, your passion has become more and more compassion. Just the right seed is needed and the roses are going to blossom. But learn to forget and forgive the past.

The present has greater dreams and greater mysteries to open their doors for you; you will not be a loser. The past is gone already; you cannot do anything about it. And if you have dreamed in the past, and if you have sung and danced in the past, what prevents you from singing and dancing in the present? If those songs of the past, and the dances and the love affairs of the past, are preventing it then they are not your friends. They are your enemies; they are unnecessary luggage. Drop them without thinking even for a single moment to drop or not to drop. Just drop them – the present is the only reality.

If you can make the present your only reality too, you will have greater dreams and greater dances and greater passions – and greater love. And then, certainly, a man who lives in the present is capable of moving from love to compassion, from passion to compassion, without difficulty and without effort.

In fact, it is not right to say that he is capable, the right thing will be to say that it happens on its own accord. You just be in the present. It is such a fire that it burns all that is rubbish in you. And it is such an opening that you cannot exhaust the songs and the dances. And once you know real diamonds, you will forget automatically those old stones that you used to think were diamonds.

To cling to the past is dangerous because it does not allow you to be in the present, and all that existence has is in the present. The past is only memory and the future is only imagination.

The present is the only reality.

All that I mean by meditation is to be in the present – no past, no future. Just let this moment be all, and you have come in contact with the heart of the universe. Great will be the blessings, and unknown treasures will be open to you. And things which are unsayable will be heard by you, will be lived by you.

Now, something religious…

One day while on holiday in Italy, Hymie Goldberg finds himself traveling in a train compartment with Pope the Polack, Mother Teresa and a beautiful young orphan girl. Suddenly the train enters a tunnel and the compartment is plunged into darkness. Then everyone hears the sound of a kiss, followed by a slap across the face. When the train leaves the tunnel, everyone looks at each other in stony silence.

Mother Teresa thinks to herself, "One of these filthy guys kissed my orphan, but she, being a good girl, slapped him."

The girl thinks to herself, "One of these guys tried to kiss me, but in the dark kissed Mother Teresa instead, and she of course slapped him."

Pope the Polack thinks, "That Jewish jerk kissed the girl and she slapped me instead – the bitch!"

And Hymie thinks to himself, "I hope there is another tunnel soon so I can kiss my hand and slap that Polack idiot again!"

Om Shantih Shantih Shantih, Ch 9, Q 2

Beloved Osho,

Lately you have been showering such unbearable and overwhelming friendliness on us, that it drives me totally bananas.

I get an uncontainable urge to stand up and cuddle you.

How do you manage to be both such a friend and such a master to us? Isn't a master supposed to stand aloof and cool, like a Buddha?

Why does all this intimacy, even so delightful, scare me so much?

Will I forget the moon, bite your finger, and take you for granted once more?

This is from the private secretary of Niskriya, Sarjano.

Sarjano, nobody can drive you bananas; you are a born banana. And you are saying, "I get an uncontainable urge to stand up and cuddle you."

Whenever such an urge arises, just stand up and cuddle Niskriya. He pays you!

You are asking me, "How do you manage to be both such a friend and such a master to us?" *A master is not a master if he is not a friend too. But vice versa is not true. A disciple is a disciple and cannot claim friendship to the master, for a simple reason: because the disciple has to rise to the heights – only then he can cuddle the master.*

I have given you a substitute. He is not a master, he is a simple human being and he would love being cuddled.

A master is always a friend, but his friendship has a totally different fragrance. It is less friendship and more friendliness. Its intrinsic part is compassion. He loves you because he cannot do anything else. He wants to share his experience because he can see you are searching for it, you are thirsty for it. He makes his springs of purest water available to you. He enjoys and feels grateful if you receive his gifts of love, of friendliness, of truth. But rarely have you come across such a master, because the old style was for the master to be very serious and to keep a distance. To allow intimacy, to allow friendliness…he was afraid that his truth and his finding might be lost in the crowd.

I am a beginning and an end: the beginning of a new kind of master and an end of the old style of masters. Certainly I am not like Gautam Buddha; I have left him twenty-five centuries back. If I am just like Gautam Buddha, that means consciousness has not evolved higher than where Gautam Buddha left it.

I say unto you, consciousness has grown higher, reached bigger peaks, deeper depths than Gautam Buddha.

Gautam Buddha is a prototype of all the old masters. The disciple has to be kept far away. He has to learn discipline, respect, obedience. In a certain way it was a spiritual slavery.

I don't want you to be my slaves and I don't want you to obey me. I want simply that you should understand me; and if my experience is authentic and your intelligence is able to understand it, you will follow it on your own accord.

It is not obedience. I am not telling you to do something, I am telling you to simply understand and then follow your understanding wherever it leads. I am happy whatever you become; just remain truthful and sincere to your own being.

The old master asked, "Be sincere towards me, be authentic towards me, be obedient towards me." I simply cannot do such harm to you, particularly to those whom I love.

I want you to be sincere to your own truth.

Yes, I can show you the path, how to find yourself. But I cannot order you; this is not an army. But the old world of masters and disciples was almost just like an army: everything had to be according to the rule the master had given. And centuries have passed and the rule remains and people go on following it without any understanding. They cannot even answer why they are doing it – just because it is written in the scriptures, because great masters have said it.

But times change; circumstances change. Moreover, no two individuals are the same; hence no rule can be applicable to all the individuals, century after century. In fact no rule can be applicable to you all even in this moment; there is no question of centuries. Even in this moment you are all separate individuals like beautiful pillars of a temple – supporting the same roof, but the pillars have a distance; they have their own unique individuality.

You are all here to seek and search the truth of your being – that is the roof of the temple. And you are all like the pillars – but every pillar has to be himself. It may support the same roof, but it is not going to be a replica of another pillar. He has to be his own, original self.

I am saying this to you so you remember that I don't belong to the old category of masters, and there is no category to which I can belong. Neither do I want any of you to be imitative. Life is not a dance when you are just an imitation. It is a dance when you are yourself.

I am not like anybody – Gautam Buddha or Lao Tzu or Chuang Tzu. I love these people; I love them because they were unique. But I am myself and I love my uniqueness just as I love their uniqueness.

Your question is significant when you ask, "Why does all this intimacy, even so delightful, scare me so much?"

It is very simple, Sarjano. Love is the most dangerous thing in the world, because love dissolves you just like a dewdrop disappearing in the ocean. It does not kill you, but it certainly makes you so big, so huge, that you cannot think in the old terms as when you were just a dewdrop, sitting on the lotus leaf.

The lotus leaf...just a little breeze and the dewdrop starts slipping towards the ocean. You can understand the fear of the dewdrop. The dewdrop can see the ocean and knows perfectly well that within a minute it will be gone.

Intimacy and love are the most dangerous things, because they dissolve your personality, your ego, your I-ness. They give you authentic reality, but they take away all that is false and not intrinsic to your existence.

It is a kind of death. Every great love is a death and a resurrection.

You are saying, "Will I forget the moon, bite your finger and take you for granted once more?"

Sarjano, if you have seen me, if you have loved me, you cannot forget the moon. And as far as biting the finger, Niskriya is available – for all the cannibals who are here, bite Niskriya. I really mean it!

And Sarjano, you can never take me for granted. It is impossible for love, it is impossible for trust – and I know your heart and I know you have loved me. It is because of that love that such a question has arisen in you.

Now, Sarjano, it is time for prayer.

In fact it is always time for prayer. Even when we are talking seriously, and everybody is listening very seriously, it is time for prayer.

Deep down a laughter is gathering like a raincloud; soon it will be showering. And the time has come.

Gorgeous Gloria, after an examination, phones her doctor and asks, "Doctor, would you see if by any chance I left my panties in your office?"

The doctor looks in the examination room, returns to the phone and tells her, "I'm afraid they are not here."

"Sorry to trouble you, Doctor," replies Gloria, "I will try the dentist."

Three guys are sitting in the pub one evening, talking about their dogs.

The first guy, a car salesman, says,

"My dog is incredible; I have trained him as my assistant. Watch this!"

He whistles, and his dog jumps up and races out of the door. Five minutes later, he is back. In his mouth are all the papers, signed and sealed, of a brand new Cadillac car he has just sold. The salesman pulls out a box of biscuits and gives one to his dog.

"That's nothing," says the next guy, a doctor. Just then, there is a screech of brakes and a crash of metal outside the pub. The doctor whistles and his dog jumps up and races out of the door.

Within five minutes the dog has bandaged up all the casualties, called an ambulance and comes running back into the pub. So the doctor gives his dog a biscuit.

"That's nothing," says the third guy, a lawyer. He gives a whistle and his dog jumps up, eats all the biscuits, screws the other two dogs and then goes out to lunch.

Kowalski goes into the ice cream parlor and orders a chocolate ice cream.

"I'm sorry, sir," says the clerk, "but we are out of chocolate."

"Oh," says Kowalski, "in that case I will take some chocolate."

"No, no, sir," says the clerk, "you don't understand. We have run out of chocolate."

"Oh," says Kowalski, "then, just give me some chocolate."

The clerk looks hard at Kowalski and says, "Okay! Spell, 'van', as in vanilla."

Kowalski spells V-A-N.

"All right," says the clerk, "now spell 'straw', as in strawberry."

Kowalski spells straw.

"Good!" says the clerk, "now, spell 'fuck' as in chocolate."

Kowalski looks puzzled and says, "But there is no fuck in chocolate."

"Aha!" shouts the clerk, "that's what I have been trying to tell you!"

YAA-HOO! The Mystic Rose, Ch 1, Q 2

Beloved Osho,

Last time I left Poona to go West, you told me "Help my people there." I'm going to the West now, in spite of the fact that the last time I didn't help your people there.

When I came here fourteen months ago, I promised myself that I would never leave you before I die. Now here I am with my greasy suitcase pointed to Italy, and still I don't know who your people there are, nor how I can help them.

Beloved Master, I really don't know what to say to your people in Italy. Do you think a smile will do? I would like to bring with me a little taste of this silence.

Can you help me?

Sarjano, you still think you are alive? According to your promise, you died long ago!

But there are many dead people going here and there. And you are telling me that last time when you went, you did not help my people there. You are a very compassionate man!

Last time at least you were alive. This time, please don't help anybody. The best will be for you first to clean your greasy suitcase. And what is the need to go to Italy? The whole of Italy is coming here! I don't understand at all. If you want to help Italians, you will find more Italians here than you will find in Italy.

Just the other day somebody told me that Lufthansa, the airline, announced while passing over Poona towards Australia that "We are passing over the house of Bhagwan Shree Rajneesh." Now this is unprecedented, this new announcement. You pass over the Kremlin or the White House or the Taj Mahal – but to announce a poor man's house, who has nothing but a few dirty jokes to tell you...

And where are you going? If you have decided already and you are not going to change your mind, then I will tell you a few jokes. Tell my people. The problem is how to decide who my people are. There are different kinds of my people: a few are my friends and most of them are my enemies. So whoever you help, you are helping my people. I have simply two categories – right, Niskriya?

The God Thor is getting bored sitting around Valhalla drinking mead all the time, so he comes down to earth for some fun. He meets Gorgeous Gloria in Las Vegas and they soon go to bed together.

They stay there for three days and three nights in a row. On the fourth morning as he is leaving, he decides to tell Gloria how she has been honored.

"My dear," he announces, "I am Thor."

"You are Thor," says Gloria, "I am thor, too – I can't even pith!"

Sarjano, you won't last in Italy long. You will be coming back on the next plane; you won't have much time. So I will give you one more joke to keep as a spare.

After ten years in the army, the men are sent for a medical check. The soldiers strip off their clothes and enter the doctor's office one by one.

The doctor puts his stethoscope on the first man's chest and says, "Sophia Loren." The man's heart beats quickly. "Boom! Boom! Boom!"

"Raquel Welch," says the doctor. "Boom! Boom! Boom!"

"Your wife," says the doctor. "Boom."

"Perfectly normal," announces the doctor. "Go and stand over there."

The next man is examined in the same way. "Marilyn Monroe," says the doctor. "Boom! Boom! Boom!"

"Your wife." Complete silence.

"Good," says the doctor. "Go and stand with the other man."

The next man comes for the examination.

"Sophia Loren," says the doctor. "Boom…boom…boom…"

"Brigitte Bardot," tries the doctor. "Boom…boom…boom…"

"Your wife," says the doctor. "…boom."

"Strange," says the doctor. But still you are quite normal. Anyway, go and stand with the other men:"Boom! Boom! Boom! Boom!"

YAA-HOO! The Mystic Rose, Ch 2, Q 3

[…] Everything moves, only the mirror remains.

That mirror is you.

Realizing it is the greatest experience of life.

And those who have not realized this mystic rose have not lived at all. They simply pretended to live, carrying their suitcases…I told Sarjano, "Clean the grease from your suitcase." And the second thing I have not told him, I thought he would understand himself, was that he should open the suitcase and give the things back to the people to whom they belong. I was thinking he would understand. But now, anybody who is missing anything can go to Sarjano, before he leaves for Italy. Of course the things will be a little greasy, but something is better than nothing. My suspicion is that even the suitcase is not his own. And he is here, sitting…

YAA-HOO! The Mystic Rose, Ch 3, Q 2, Excerpt

[Osho repeats part of a sannyasin's question]
"I feel mean."

Very good! So who is telling you not to feel? Feel mean, perfectly mean! And here, my people will enjoy it. "This fellow is going...he is perfectly mean. Just avoid him!" But there are people even greater than you think, meaner than you can believe. Have you seen Sarjano? The day I told him to open the suitcase and give back all the things in the suitcase to the people they belong to, he disappeared! He said, "Now it is too much." He will come back – and I can assure you, when he comes back, open his suitcase and see: it will be empty. He always comes, fills his suitcase, and goes away. And just after three or four days, he will be back.

So, don't you feel in any way that you are the only mean person. There are greater fellows and they are all respectable. I love Sarjano, he is very articulate.

YAA-HOO! The Mystic Rose, Ch 8, Q 3, Excerpt

[...] Sardar Gurudayal Singh is driving down M.G. Road one day in a brand new Maruti car. His friend, Sarjano, stops him and says, "Hey-a Sardarji, where did-a you get that brand-a new car?"

"Well," replies Sardar Gurudayal Singh, "I was going for a spin to Mulshi Lake on my old Yezdi motorbike, when I saw this sexy American girl, Ma Papaya Pineapple, stranded by the side of the road in this car. So I stopped and fixed the car for her."

"Far out-a," says Sarjano. "Then what happened?"

"Well," continues Sardar Gurudayal Singh, "Ma Papaya Pineapple looks at me in a very sexy way, nudges me in the belly and says, 'Thanks man, I'm really grateful. I will give you anything you want!'

"So naturally," adds Sardarji, "I took the Maruti!"

Zen: The Quantum Leap From Mind to No-Mind, Ch 11, Q 1, Excerpt

[...] Sarjano goes to see Dr. Azima in the medical center. "Doctor," says Sarjano, "I think-a I got-a flying crabs!"

Azima is amazed and takes a test. Sarjano anxiously awaits the results. He is dismayed to see Azima come back with a sad look on his face. "I am-a sorry, Sarjano," says Azima, "but I have-a some good news and-a some bad news."

"Give-a me the good news," replies Sarjano.

"The good-a news," says Azima, "is-a that those flying crabs you-a had, turned out to be-a fruit flies."

"Great-a!" cries Sarjano, "and what about the bad news?"

"I am sorry," says Azima, "but the bad-a news is, your banana is-a dead!"

Zen: The Quantum Leap From Mind to No-Mind, Ch 15, Q 1, Excerpt

[…] Sarjano goes into the medical center and asks Dr. Azima for some condoms.

"These-a are the best-a ones," says Azima, handing him a packet.

But Sarjano interrupts him and says, "Don't-a worry – the cheapest will-a do."

So Azima gives him the cheapest and Sarjano pays. Then he immediately opens the pack, pulls out a condom, unrolls it, throws it on the floor and begins to stamp on it with his foot.

"What-a the hell are you-a doing?" cries Azima.

"Don't-a stop me," says Sarjano. "This is-a exactly the way I-a gave up smoking!"

Zen: The Solitary Bird, Cuckoo of the Forest, Ch 1, Excerpt

[…] Milarepa, Devageet and Sarjano find themselves sitting outside Pythagoras Clinic waiting to see Doctor Azima.

"What are you guys here for?" asks Devageet.

"It's-a my prick," admits Sarjano, nervously. "It has turned bright-a orange!"

"What?" exclaim Milarepa and Devageet together. "That is what I'm here for," says Milarepa. "And me too!" exclaims Devageet.

So the three swamis enter the clinic together.

Undressing, Milarepa and Devageet expose their bright orange machinery, and Sarjano unrolls his sausage.

"My God!" says Azima. "That is amazing!" And he starts to make his examinations.

"How is your sex-a life?" asks Azima. "Do you make-a love once a night?"

The three swamis look at each other and shake their heads in silence.

"Well-a, how-a about twice a week?" continues Azima.

"There was a time…" reflects Milarepa. Devageet and Sarjano nod quietly.

"Well-a, how about twice a month-a?" asks Azima.

"I wish!" says Devageet, dreamily.

"Once a month?" suggests Azima. There is another silence.

"Well, that's okay then!" says Azima. "Don't be worried. It is just-a rust!"

The Miracle, Ch 5, Q 1, Excerpt

So, one day he was called to the main office, where he was literally ordered to stop shouting in this inhuman manner. "You need to cool down, Sarjano, because your shouting is scaring everybody, and it's time you stop this and start to contain yourself a little!"

The woman who had asked him to cool down with such severe authority was one of his occasional lovers, who seemed to enjoy his shouting in the night when they were making love very much, hence he answered: "You never seem disturbed by my shouting! If you ask me the same thing tonight, while we are making love, then I will certainly cool down immediately… because you don't understand that it is always THE SAME energy, and if you like this kind of energy when we are making love, you'll have to be ready to suffer it even when I work, it is so simple! Or, I can cool down as you have requested, but then I will do the same when we make love too – if this is your wish!"

The woman let him go without a word, and from that day on she no longer bothered him with these stupid requests, thank GOOOOOOOOOOOOOOOOOOODDDD!

Anyway, this story seemed to have become a serious problem in the whole Commune, and it had certainly arrived to Osho's ears, which made him decide that henceforth Sarjano should have his own place, where he could work, cook, shout with his friends as much as he liked. The place already existed, and it was beautiful and located in a green garden where people used to go to smoke a cigarette in peace, since it was the only permitted smoking area in the entire ashram. From now on it would be called 'Osho Café' and host all of Sarjano's creations.

He gathered in no time a heterogenic crew, made up mostly by old friends who were no longer surprised by his sudden shouting, then he placed around 30 tables under the trees, then a little more than one hundreds chairs, and asked to have a professional oven for his pizza, and he was ready to start!

'Osho Café' became immediately an elegant (and costly) alternative to the ashram canteen, which was serving more or less the same food every evening; but now whoever had some money to spend would come to his place to eat ravioli, vegetarian lasagna, gnocchi, cannelloni stuffed with mushrooms and cheese, and all those creations that he could never have made in the canteen's kitchen, because it would have been impossible to make it for so many people.

[…] On a trip to Rome, Sarjano is driving down the street in Jayesh's bright red Ferrari at about a hundred and fifty miles an hour.

Suddenly, from a side street, the Pope-mobile pulls out in front of him. With no time for Sarjano to hit the brakes, there is a colossal collision.

The next thing they know, Pope the Polack and Sarjano are watching their souls departing the earth together. Of course, there is a bureaucratic, computerized mix- up on the way to Heaven, and as a result, Sarjano is sent to the Pearly Gates, while Pope the Polack is sent to Hell.

The Polack Pope, obviously pissed off that he is in the wrong place, soon convinces those in charge that there has been a mistake. And in the blink of an eye, he is transported to the Pearly Gates. As he walks into Heaven, he meets Sarjano just coming out.

"I'm really sorry about this," says the Pope, bending to kiss the Gates, "but I have waited all my life to kneel at the feet of the Blessed Virgin Mary, the purest virgin who has ever lived."

Sarjano flashes a bright smile at the Polack Pope.

"Sorry, Father," he says, buttoning his pants, "But you are-a too late!"

The Original Man, Ch 9, Q 1, Excerpt

The second surprise that he found after his return was a young Japanese woman who was visiting Pune for the first time. He had noticed her from the very first day, because this young woman had the longest hair that he had ever seen in his life, and was moving around regularly alone, with that long, long hair that was almost touching the ground.

Days passed by, and every time he saw her she was always alone, and after one month he had never seen this mysterious beauty talking with anyone – not for a single moment! Normally he would have approached her instantly, because that's what he was usually doing with anyone he liked, but he was a little intimidated at the idea to get closer to her – maybe she was not speaking English at all, maybe she was mute – and he was very uncomfortable with this situation, until one day fate came unexpectedly to his help.

That faithful day he was requested to take some pictures of a dance group for the ashram's magazine, which was called 'Osho Times' and was published in seven different languages. So he went in the room where the group was happening, carrying all his photo-equipment, and there amongst the participants he saw to his great surprise the mysterious Japanese girl! While he was taking pictures she couldn't see him, because in that moment everybody was having a blindfold on their eyes, and had to dance without seeing anything and without to be seen either, in order to be absolutely free to express themselves without any judgment.

He shot as many pictures as he could, clicking ad infinitum on this magic figure that was dancing wildly with her long hair flying in the air like huge, black wings, and then he left, after having asked the group leader when the group would be over. He got to know in this way that the group was ending after three days, and he decided instantly on that day to be at the gate waiting for her.

Standing at the door to the room where the group had finished, three days later, once he saw the Japanese marvel he went closer to her and told her, smiling: "Sorry to disturb you, my name is Sarjano, and I am one of the ashram's photographers. I have been asked to take some pictures of this dance group, so three days ago I was here with my cameras and have taken a lot of pictures of you while you were dancing, but you haven't seen me because you were wearing a blindfold like everybody else. Anyway, the pictures are very beautiful and if you like it I can show them to you right now, because I have them here in my bag."

The girl, who had stopped for a minute to listen to this stranger, started to walk away in silence, without even looking at him or saying a single word.

He was not the type to give up so easily, hence he ran after her and said: "Listen, if you don't want to look at your pictures here, in the middle of the road, I can show them to you tonight, after the discourse. We can meet at the Gateless Gate, and I'll take you to the Blue Diamond to celebrate the end of the group in style!"

"I have chosen this hotel because it is very close by, and because these days they have a real Japanese chef as guest of honor and they are serving sushi, that some Japanese friends have assured me to be very good: what do you say?"

The girl looked into his eyes for a long moment; then she nodded imperceptibly with her head, without saying a word, and went away.

At 9 p.m. he was outside the ashram's gate waiting for her, trembling and shaking like a kid at his first date, because this woman was really intimidating him to the max with her mysterious behavior… shit, she hadn't even said her name and up to now he didn't even know the sound of her voice!

When she arrived, she started simply walking silently next to him towards the Blue Diamond, which was at the time the most luxurious hotel in all of Pune, and featured a couple of restaurants that weren't bad at all.

They entered, sat at an isolated table and started looking at the menu. "Now I will finally hear her speak…" he was saying within himself, but the girl simply placed a finger upon the dish she had chosen from the menu, which was the special of the day, and left him to the task of ordering for both.

While waiting for the food, he gathered some courage and asked her:

"What is your name?"

"Prem Mai," she answered softly – but at least he had heard her voice!

So he asked again: "And do you know the meaning of your name?"

"Garden of Love…" she whispered, without adding another word.

Meanwhile the food had arrived, and they started eating in total silence; at the end he paid for the bill and they walked out together. At that point it was far past ten, and he didn't think it would be safe for a woman to walk home alone in the night, hence he offered to escort her home.

They walked just for five minutes, naturally in silence, then she stopped in front of a three storey building and with her finger she indicated the first floor: "There, I live there." she said matter of fact."

He said, with enormous surprise, "Look how strange life can be! This is almost incredible, or perhaps is a sign of the destiny, saying that we were bound to meet one day, because I live here too, on the third floor, and I've been here for over one year! I wonder only how we have never met before, not even on the stairs!"

They started climbing up the stairs, slowly slowly, and once they had arrived in front of her door, he asked if she would like to come up to his apartment for a cup of tea. He told her that he had a vast variety of herbal teas, including Japanese bancha tea and if she would be willing to enjoy it… She made her usual little nod of assent that he knew already too well, and followed him for two more flights of stairs.

While they were drinking their herbal tea, he stood up from the chair where he was sitting, and went to sit on the sofa next to her without saying a word, and as soon as he saw her putting down her cup, he took her hand and held it in silence. With those minimal movements that he had learned during his experiences with 'The Living Theatre' in the glorious sixties, he started to get closer to her, with almost imperceptible movements, until he was in contact with her.

She had a very light and ethereal smell he had never experienced in his life, and a very soft skin at the first touch, pleasantly deprived of any trace of hair. After ten minutes of absolute immobility, he placed his arm with immense tenderness around her shoulders, then slowly slowly the other one, and finally, as if she were a newborn baby, he pulled her towards him with infinite sweetness and hugged her. In all this he could see that she was simply repeating every one of his gestures, which made it absolutely clear that this was the first time in her life that she was hugging a man!

They stayed in this position, tenderly hugging for more than one hour, without saying a single word – an absolute record, he was thinking, since he had probably never stayed a full hour without talking in his entire life. Then suddenly she stood up, and the next minute she was gone without saying a single word!

"But what the hell have I done now?" he said loudly to himself. "Why has she left like this?" He sat there with his head in his hands, thinking about this strange behavior, when after just five minutes he heard the bell ringing. He went to open, and saw her there in front of him with a few bags full of clothes, a large suitcase, and a few dresses still fixed to their hangers thrown over her shoulders.

"I'm coming to live here with you," she said, without adding anything else. He would never have expected something like this, and he was simply astonished, so he whispered to her – not to ruin that perfect moment: "It is very beautiful what you are doing, and I feel deeply honored. I could just throw myself at your feet right now, if I didn't know that it would embarrass you too much!"

Meanwhile she opened her small purse from where she pulled out an airline ticket and gave it to him, saying simply, but with a great unsuspected determination: "This is my return ticket to Japan, and I want you to destroy it."

He took the ticket in a flash and ripped it in hundreds of pieces, which was very likely the equivalent of a marriage declaration, and from that moment on he found himself married to a woman he only knew the name of and nothing else! From that moment onwards, they represented the strangest couple in the world, the most absurd, the most incredible and paradoxical, the one composed by two perfect opposites, facing each other like two totally unknown worlds, but who managed to live together for more than ten years, without ever even one argument, a fight, a complaint – NOTHING!

He was so overwhelmed by the astronomical enormity of this event that he decided instantly this to be a divine experiment, wanted by God in person, who was having fun putting together the two most polar opposites living on this planet, an Alpha and an Omega, just to see how they will manage it!

He felt tremendously grateful for having been chosen to be part of this experiment, and was already considering this meeting being the most important event of his entire life (besides the ones with Osho, naturally!) and he couldn't stop to marvel about it at every day passing. Since everything was flowing smoothly among them in spite of their macroscopic differences, he came soon to this simple and definitive conclusion, which could be expressed as: "Don't break my balls anymore with your supposed great differences!"

To explain it a little better: the differences between a Hebrew and a Palestinian are NOTHING, if we compare them to the differences existing between them. The differences existing between a Pakistani and an Indian are NOTHING compared to the differences existing between these two creatures. The differences between blacks and whites are NOTHING, if we compare them to the differences that they were enjoying every day a little more!

To make it short, all those people which have been waging wars for centuries about such trivial differences could as well fuck off en masse, because they were simply ridiculous with their so-called 'differences'. This conclusion brought him tremendous strength, and for this he was grateful to his silent partner, because he knew that this 'information' would enter sooner or later into the core of the collective unconscious of the planet; hence he was feeling like a kind of herald of the 'new era'.

You probably won't believe it, and perhaps you are going to give him a skeptical smile in return, but the truth is that the greatest realizations of the planet do not need to be transmitted verbally; they don't need any words to propagate themselves, because they travel with another type of 'information wavelength', much more subtle and penetrating.

There is a little story he always loved to narrate, and that he found absolutely enlightening in this regard.

Some years ago, a group of zoologists were observing a very strange phenomenon happening among the monkeys of the island of Sumatra. They had discovered that a group of monkeys was mastering – God knows how – a simple trick: they had found out that if they climb a tree with a stone weighing about a couple of kilos and then drop it on top of a coconut on the ground, the stone would break the shell, making it thus much easier to take out the pulp of the fruit and eat it. But the strangest thing was that just after a few weeks later, ALL the monkeys of the island knew and were using this simple trick, and without having ever met to exchange this information!

As if this was not enough, these scientists realized that after a few months even the monkeys of the nearest islands had learned the trick, and without ever getting in direct communication with the monkeys that had created it! Now, are you starting to realize how it works?

Once the 'information' has been established on the planet, it starts to travel by itself, irrespective of the fact that those who had created it were propagating it or not. The so-called 'author' could as well be dead, or have decided to live in a cave for the rest of his life, and it would make no difference at all, because the information would spread anyhow in its own rhythm and according to its timing. Believe it or not, this is the story, and I hope that something has entered your skull!

He was therefore calling what was happening to him and Mai THE GREAT EXPERIMENT, and he was absolutely proud for having been chosen to represent it.

***

CHAPTER 14

Two Opposites Meet And The Last Zen Stick

Monsoon arrived shortly after with its romantic rains and our two lovers started to have long walks in the pouring rain, having a hot shower after reaching home and then jumping on the bed to cuddle and hug each other.

Mai meanwhile had not changed her behavior by one iota, and she was speaking just a little less than strictly necessary, and sometimes even less than that! They spent three or four monsoon months like this, during which the only articulate sentence he would hear from her was a beautiful expression that she had borrowed from Osho; but she seemed totally unaware of this, because she had made it spontaneously her own now: "I want to live like a bird, leaving no traces in the sky…"

Too bad that the person who had said these words first was one that had fought all his life in order to leave a trace, if not in the sky, at least on our consciousness, while Mai was more and more careless about the surrounding world. Sometimes she would not utter a single word for days and days, to the point that his friends meeting her for the first time would invariably whisper into his ear, asking "Is your friend mute?"

"No, no," – he would answer invariably. "It is just that she is not interested in all the bullshit that we usually say to each other!"

By now his closest friends began referring to them jokingly – but not really – as 'San-jano and Suor Mai'!

According to him everybody was wondering how something like this was possible, how such a powerful and energetic character like him could ever live with a woman who at first sight looked almost like a corpse or something like that!

Deep down he liked all this curiosity that was surrounding them, and the anxious look of his friends who seemed waiting to see how this incredible story would end up; but at the same time they were all very surprised and even admiring them, because their love affair was continuing without any sign of tiredness, or any contrast, or incomprehension, and they looked full of respect and sincere admiration at him for managing to live such a paradox, the one of two polar diametrically opposed that finally met.

Our two pigeons – one white and the other black – were living in halcyon until one day they decided to go for their first trip together, since Osho had another crisis due to his 'American poisoning' and was not coming out for his daily discourse.

They decided to go to Bangalore – first because they had heard it was a very beautiful city, and secondly because it was home to a certain U.G. Krishnamurti. Even though he was not claiming any relation with the famous J. Krishnamurti, he had the reputation of being a big saint. While in Pune, some friend had given him a book of U.G. called *Mind is a Myth* which was a collection of his discourses that he had found extremely interesting, to say the least, and now he wanted to meet the author and perhaps have an interview with him, which he could sell to some New Age magazine.

Once they arrived in Bangalore and found a little cozy hotel where to stay, he asked the taxi driver if by any chance he knew the address of this philosopher. The taxi-driver obviously did, so the next morning they asked him to take them to U.G.'s house.

When they arrived there, the guy was sitting in the garden having his morning tea; he recognized him instantly because he had seen his picture on the book cover, hence they went close to him and bowed in a respectful namaste. Then he told him straight away that they had not come to ask any question, and that in fact they would not ask him anything at all, but they wanted only to spend a couple of days with him, eating together, sitting in silence in his beautiful garden, sharing some chats among friends – to which U.G. responded with a big smile on his face. Then he thanked them openly for not having come to his house to give him shit with some stupid pseudo-spiritual questions as it was normally happening, and that he was very happy to have two foreign friends around for a couple of days.

He had wisely decided – or at least this was his intention – to stay away from the terrific hits that this sagacious mystic was distributing to his left and to his right with pitiless and surgical fierceness, but he managed unfortunately only until the day of their departure!

During the three days spent with U.G., eating his food, or cooking for him some Italian delicacy which he appreciated very much, he was careful of not asking him anything, and neither did Mai. He had a lot of fun watching the hordes of pilgrims coming from all over the world with their 'significant' questions, to which they usually received answers so ruthless in their simple and brutal truth that most of them slunk away with their tails between their legs, in a disconcerted silence and with the darkest of faces!

After three days he had gathered enough material to write an eventual article, hence he decided that at this point all that he needed were a couple of pictures; so a few hours before leaving he asked him simply: "Can I take some pictures of you?"

It was the first and most innocent question that he had made in three days, but at these words U.G. looked at him as if he were looking at a piece of shit, then he let go a long and painful sigh, as if he had been waiting just for this all the time – which is the opportunity of hitting him with one of his terrific sticks. Looking at him almost in disgust he said, "Would you ask a flower, a bird in the sky, a star, if you can make a picture of them?"

This simple answer – and yet so truthful – left him speechless for a moment, then he started mumbling some timid excuse: "Well, I have asked you because one never knows – you may not like to be photographed and…"

The severe face of U.G. Krishnamurti was enough to stop any more of these risible excuses, and while he kept on explaining his reasons, U.G. was looking at him in silence, with an expression more and more incredulous, disconcerted and vaguely nauseated!

He took a few shots anyway, and after a couple of hours they left for Pune, where he forgot soon all about this story, because he had certainly recognized the enlightenment of this guy, but for sure he didn't need another Master or another guidance, hence he knew that he would never see U.G. again.

Who didn't forget happened to be just U.G., who died only a few years ago; before his death in 2008 he was approached by a group of German sannyasins that had just completed a book about him, and they had come to Bangalore only to ask him if he had a couple of pictures of himself that could be used on the cover of their book.

U.G. simply smiled, saying that he never had a picture of himself during his entire life but if they knew Sarjano they could ask him, "Because Sarjano has taken some beautiful pictures of me nearly twenty years ago – you know Sarjano, don't you? You have just to find out where he lives now and you can ask him, and you will be certainly happy with what you see!"

These German sannyasins knew well that at the time he was living in Goa, where he had opened an Italian Restaurant called *My Place* in a huge garden, and they went immediately to visit him. When they told him the whole story, and the words of U.G. about his pictures, he almost couldn't believe how that could be: this U.G., after having treated him – well, deservingly – in such a rude manner, was still remembering that twenty years ago he had been photographed by him!

His German friends liked the pictures very much and offered to buy a few of them, leaving him one thousand euros for the disturbance. Talk about the beauty of having some enlightened friend!

Anyway, after having sold these pictures, they returned to Pune the next day, where they found out that Osho would resume his discourses that same evening, although he didn't know what kind of surprise his Master had prepared for him…

During his first discourse after his long absence, Osho was saying at a certain point:

> *[…] There is no competitiveness, there is no condemnation. Disciples move from one teacher to another teacher with their permission – and there is no hierarchy. Gautam Buddha is not higher than Mahakashyapa, and Mahakashyapa is not higher than Bodhidharma. The very word 'hierarchy' comes from the idea of the inferior and the superior.*
>
> *The world according to the Buddhas is divided into two kinds of Buddhas: a few are sleeping, and a few are awake – not much of a difference. One who is asleep today may*

wake up tomorrow. And one never knows – one who is awake today may fall asleep tomorrow. In this miraculous existence everything is possible.

It will be difficult for your reason to accept that a Buddha can become again unenlightened, but I know many Buddhas who are sitting here unenlightened. And many times they come to the very verge of becoming enlightened, and immediately turn away, being afraid that, "Who knows? If you go one step more, you may never come back" – and your girlfriend is waiting outside!

Sarjano has gone somewhere for a few days. I asked Neelam, "I don't see Sarjano…?" She informed me that she had asked Sarjano and Sarjano said, "If I am not missing him, why is he missing me?"

Sarjano, you may not miss me; I miss you. I am my *kind of a Buddha. I miss people – and even people like Sarjano! Everybody was happy when he was gone….*

The Zen Manifesto: Freedom From Oneself, Ch 3, Excerpt

As soon as he arrived at home he wrote him a personal letter to explain what had really happened, which was, since he was not speaking, he and Mai had decided to have a little trip to Bangalore and to meet this U.G. Krishnamurti.

The next day Osho brought out the subject during his discourse, taking the chance to give him THE LAST hit of his life, and of course the most astronomical and ferocious of all!

The Last Zen Stick

The last gift of his Master before he died:

[…] Before I answer your questions, I have to talk about a letter by Sarjano.

The other night I talked about him. He has written a very beautiful and loving letter, but as you know Sarjano, he is lying. I have no objection to it; if you are lying, lie beautifully and totally. A life without lies will be very boring.

When I told you the remark Sarjano made to Neelam: "If I don't miss him, why does he miss me?" – he was not right, he was not true. He has been missing – he may not be aware of it.

Many of you are not aware of what you are missing. Many of you are not aware of what you have forgotten. But his case can be taken as an example.

He told Neelam, "I am not coming to the discourses because they are too long. I am watching the sky, sitting on my balcony."

Do you think the sky is smaller than my discourses?

And Sarjano was not on the balcony either. He was not even in Poona. I keep myself perfectly aware of where you are. Looking at Sarjano's eyes the other day, I saw that he has been with U.G. Krishnamurti. And not only has he been with U.G. Krishnamurti, he has been taking other people there too.

There is nothing wrong in it, only one thing has to be remembered: when you are fragile in your growth, people like U.G. Krishnamurti can destroy you. These people have missed their life, and now they are living in frustration. And in frustration people start behaving like women. They start breaking things, throwing things. That's what U.G. Krishnamurti is doing.

But let him do what he wants to do. It is none of the business of anybody else to come in the way when he is throwing a disk. It is his disk. Why should you get unnecessary wounds? They are not your own.

It is a misery to say to you that many of you are carrying wounds of others, miseries of others, tragedies of others.

Have you ever looked at a simple fact, that you don't have to be miserable – it is by choice?

And if you, Sarjano, were going to U.G. Krishnamurti, you should have told Neelam without lying that you "are watching the sky". Now, what has happened to the sky? The sky is still there, the balcony is still there, and what are you doing here? And particularly for you, I am going to make the discourse long. I care for my people.

Today he has written a letter in which he feels afraid that, "Perhaps the ghost of Rajneeshpuram will take possession of this commune also." Sarjano, it is not you speaking, it is U.G. Krishnamurti. He has never lived in a commune.

A commune gives certain responsibilities and certain freedoms. A commune is not necessarily destructive of the individual. In fact, that is the very purpose of the commune: to preserve the individual, his integrity.

A commune is not an organization, but when thousands of people are involved, somebody has to cook, and somebody has to watch on the door, and somebody has to do small things. There are people who start thinking that even doing these things is destroying their freedom. This is sheer nonsense.

A certain responsibility is not against freedom; in fact, freedom can only exist with responsible people. Somebody has to take care of the gardens, otherwise there will be no flowers.

Sarjano's trouble may be the trouble of a few other sannyasins. It has to be made clear that a commune is not dictatorial, but it is not democratic either. It gives respect to the individual. With the respect it gives the responsibility also, that you have to be aware not to trespass on anybody, and that you have to contribute to the commune.

If you are taking from the well of the commune, you have to contribute something – whatever you can do.

When you are working with friends there should be no discussion about anything, only dialogues. There should be no need to impose anything on anybody. When intelligent people are there, they can see the reason themselves. They are not to be forced.

But there are a few people who think licentiousness is freedom.

Sarjano, that is your attitude.

Licentiousness is not freedom.

We are sitting here – nobody is forcing you to be silent. It is according to your intelligence that you are silent, and this gives your individuality a tremendous grace.

One of my attorneys in America was puzzled. He was not a sannyasin, and he was employed just because he was an authority of law, a dean of the faculty of law in a California university. He must have seen students his whole life, but he had never seen a master.

So he took me aside one day, and asked, "I am puzzled. Even when the magistrate comes in, it has to be announced that 'The magistrate is coming: you all stand up.' But when you come, nobody announces it. Your people are there – we can understand why they stand up. But my puzzle is that I myself feel like standing. And when I look at the people standing, only fifty percent are sannyasins; fifty percent are other people."

As sannyasins started standing, others were too, unknowingly, without any awareness – they found themselves also standing. They may not have been in favor of me – their agreement or disagreement is not the question.

Your silence is not democratic – you have not been asked to vote to be silent. It is not dictatorial – you have not been told that you have to be silent. This is the beauty and dignity of your silence: it is arising out of you. It is not imposed from outside; it is coming from within. And when something comes from within, it has a beauty and a grace, and a tremendous aliveness. This is not the silence of a graveyard; this is the silence of a garden. It is not dead; it is throbbing with life.

Sarjano, Zen teaches revolution in a graceful way. In the name of revolution much ugliness has happened in the world. Zen wants you to understand the implications of the inner revolution, and you have to go on your own way. Zen simply makes it clear that there is nothing to be found, that there is no truth which is hidden – it is only your eyes which are closed.

Do you see the shift? All other mystery schools in the world have been teaching that the truth is hidden. If it is only a way of saying it, it can be forgiven. But the reality is, truth is not hidden. Truth is all over the place, only our eyes are closed.

And when you are going through an operation, you have to behave. Don't think that asking a certain behavior of you is necessarily slavery. Freedom can exist only according to a certain behavior pattern which you have accepted consciously, knowing all its implications.

When "yes" comes from your own being, then only is it true. If it comes out of fear, it is untrue. If it comes out of greed, it is not true. When it comes only out of understanding, without fear, without greed, without punishment, then you act according to your inner truth.

It is a miracle that thousands of people can live here without any conflict, without any fight, without any violence. The whole world can live with such peace and silence if freedom is not misunderstood as licentiousness.

Freedom is a greater responsibility; it gives you dignity and pride. It makes you aware that you are living in a meaningful way. There is no other meaning to be found.

When I said to you yesterday there is no meaning in life, there is no ultimate goal, you can misunderstand me. What I was really saying is that there is no meaning in life; hence you are free to create it. There is no goal in life, no fixed fatality; then your hands are free to paint, to sculpt, to love, to live. But now you have to depend only on one thing, and that is your own inner light.

Zen is the awakening of the inner light. And in that awakening, all moralities follow on their own accord.

People have asked me, "Zen looks beautiful, but where is the morality?" Because all the religions of the world teach you morality, they have created an idea that unless a morality is taught, forced, disciplined, you are going to be immoral. Your immorality is taken for granted.

The truth is different. If you simply awaken into your consciousness and act according to that awareness, your life is going to be moral, virtuous. Without being dragged by religions, forced by people, without creating any guilt, Zen gives you a tremendous freedom. But the freedom is as great as is your responsibility – if you drop responsibility you also drop your freedom.

Most of the people in the world have lived in slavery because of a simple psychological fact: slavery is cozy. Freedom is an open sky; slavery is the security of the cage. The bird in the cage need not worry about food, need not worry about enemies, need not worry about changes of seasons, but he has sold his freedom for all this security.

Zen's effort is to take you out of your cages. Those cages have beautiful names: Christianity, Hinduism, Jainism, Buddhism. The effort of Zen is, it does not matter what kind and what shape of cage you are living in, but don't live in a cage. And the whole universe is available to you. It has not to be searched for, it is already there throbbing in your heart. Just be more conscious of your interiority, and you will start growing up.

Very few people grow up; most people only grow old. Growing up makes one a Buddha. And the lowest has the potential to become the Buddha. But never become a Buddhist – that is a cage. Never belong to any organization. Never belong to any system of belief or morality. Just belong only to your own freedom – and freedom certainly brings immense responsibility. For everything you do you are responsible. There is nobody else to take the responsibility. That's why people have agreed to believe in all kinds of lies.

God is a lie, but it helps people to make him responsible. He made the world: if he has made us the way we are, he is responsible. They have believed in prophets, in messiahs, just to give them their responsibility. And all your messiahs, your Christs, your Krishnas, ask you only one thing: "Believe in me and I will take care of your spiritual life."

There are millions of Christians, and they believe in Jesus and they believe in God, but their spirituality has not blossomed. Nor has it blossomed in other religions. Something is fundamentally wrong. Zen makes it a point to make you aware of that wrong. Giving up responsibility felt good – the burden is gone. But with the responsibility gone, your freedom has also disappeared. And a man who doesn't know freedom knows nothing of life, knows nothing of love, knows nothing of creativity, knows nothing of this immense universe.

When I say there is no meaning, I mean you have to create meaning. It is not there ready-made, on sale. When I say there is no goal, I simply mean you have to learn to live without goals. A man lives only to the point, to the depth, who has no goals, no sources, who is alone in this vast universe without any guidance.

All scriptures are unholy, because they all pretend to be your guidance, your guides. But you don't need guides. You need awareness – and every guide will want you to be blind. It is easier for the guide if people are blind, because they don't ask questions, they don't create doubt. They are ready to be slaves if security is given to them, and that's what all religions are giving you: security in afterlife, security in heaven.

Just the other day I was watching a film about Jesus – and I love the man. Unless I love anybody, I don't criticize him; I don't feel he is worth criticizing. Watching the film, there were a few points....

In one part, a rich man, a young man who had just inherited almost an empire, came to Jesus and asked him, "I would love to follow you, but what are the conditions?"

Jesus said to him, "The first thing to do is, go and distribute all that you possess to the poor."

The man said, "All?"

Jesus said, "Yes. Give everything and come to me."

The man was standing; he hesitated, and a giggle went through the crowd. And as the rich man disappeared into the crowd to hide his face, Jesus made his famous statement: "A camel may pass through the eye of the needle, but a rich man cannot pass through the gates of God."

In this way, poverty has been praised. And when you praise poverty you destroy the art of creating wealth, the art of creating more comforts, and you console the poor in his misery and in his poverty. And the man, the young man who has come, you ask too much of him too early. A master should not be in a hurry. He has just inherited an empire, and you ask him to distribute all!

And he asked, "All? Do you mean all?"

If Jesus had said to him, "Distribute a part of it," and as he would have come closer, "Distribute a little more," as he would have become more intimate and more understanding , his whole empire would have been distributed. It is Jesus who is preventing him. He has come and he is ready, but asking too much when the time is not ripe shows a hurriedness.

I would not have asked him for anything. If he had come, he would have been welcome; and, by and by, you would have helped him to disperse his empire.

In fact, before a person becomes alert and aware, you should not ask such impossible things. But all the religions have been asking impossible, unnatural things. That man must have gone with a guilt, with a feeling of inferiority that he did not have the guts. Now you have created a wound in him. Who is going to heal him?

People have looked at Jesus as if he is a healer. I say unto you, he has created more wounds in humanity than any other man. But those wounds are very psychological; they are not on your body, they are on your mind. And all the religions have done that.

All the religions have condemned women because they have the body of a woman. Nobody has bothered that without a woman's body there would be no possibility of procreation. Even the so-called God had to use a woman. Strange! Why did he have to make poor Mary pregnant? And both were condemned: the husband, the wife. The name of Jesus' father is not mentioned much at all. But as I was watching the whole story, he seems to have been far more human, far more understanding than even your God. God at least could have managed nine months; there was no need to create this scandal of Jesus not being the son of his own father. The same God gives the commandment: "You should not commit adultery" – and he himself commits it. Jesus is the proof of God's adultery.

But these fictions are consoling – a God who comes when it is needed. Strange – that he was needed in Judea, in Israel, and he was not needed anywhere else. And Judea is a small place, nothing beautiful about it. God chooses a poor carpenter's wife – and he is thought to be omnipotent. He knows all. So he must have known that this boy was going to be crucified at the age of thirty-three.

Knowing all this, still all the religions have been condemning women. And all their tirthankaras, *and all their* avataras, *incarnations, all are born of women. And still, the mother of all your god men is condemned. In the trinity of Christianity there is no place for the woman. In fact, around the world the woman has been treated as if she is just a commodity to be used.*

But why have women accepted it? For the same reason you have accepted other kinds of slaveries – security: the husband will take care. Ancient Indian scriptures say, "When a woman is a child, the father should take care; when a woman is young, the husband should take care; when a woman is old, the son should take care." But because of this security and care, you are destroying the woman's freedom. And the woman has agreed, just as other people have agreed, to all kinds of slavery. The reason simply is their consciousness is missing.

The whole effort of Zen is to bring you to your own consciousness. And then there is no need of any scripture, and there is no need of any guide. You have your own light and you can live accordingly – intensely, joyfully, dancingly. But people go on trying to find some guide.

For what has Sarjano been going to U.G. Krishnamurti? Perhaps he may give him the truth.

Nobody can give you the truth.

Truth is already enshrined in you.

You have to discover it.

The Zen Manifesto: Freedom From Oneself, Ch 4, Excerpt

In spite of all this slamming from the Master, there was still somebody around who believed in him, who trusted him – and not just 'somebody' but a great therapist called Vasumati.

This one Vasumati was famous for her therapeutic groups devoted to couples (hopefully in a crisis!) – so much so that her group was called simply 'Couples' or sometimes 'Relationships'.

This woman in her late thirties had also the habit to come for lunch to his house where he was preparing a succulent meal for all his friends every day, and slowly slowly they had become best friends, to the point that often she would confess to him everything about her delusions and pains regarding her own relationships with men.

To say it all, she was not very lucky with men, who often abused her and were very insensitive; but instead of consoling her he was always there to explain that it was mostly her responsibility in all these stories, and she was always listening to his advice with great interest and receptivity, until one day, after one year of intense sharing, she came to him with this incredible proposal:

"Listen Sarjano, it is more than one year that I come here searching for some consolation about my miserable love stories, and I have realized at my expenses what a great intuition you manage to have about the 'couple dynamics'.

"These days I'm preparing a new group for couples which will be called 'Co-dependency', because speaking with you I have come to understand three things. The first is that man wants to be independent, the second is that woman wants to be dependent, and the third is that both these ambitions are stupid – because for a relationship to work there can be no independency nor dependency but only co-dependency; otherwise everything goes to hell!

"Since you have been my inspiration and my guide in this process of understanding, I want to ask you to be my partner in the creation of this group and then lead it with me! I think we can make a great team, me and you, almost perfect: what do you say?"

"Well, it is quite a big proposal that you are offering, it is not a joke!" he answered. "I have to think about it, because I may like to play the therapist at home, between some ravioli and some lasagna, but you are asking me to become a professional, and mostly to work with a celebrity like you, while I'm totally unknown in this field!"

"C'mon, Sarjano, you must be aware that everybody knows you in the Commune, and I'm sure that this experiment will be accepted with curiosity and sympathy by the whole ashram!"

"Maybe you are right, but I prefer to write to Osho and ask him what he thinks about this, because it is not a decision that I want to take on my own, and I'm sure that he will give me the right guidance."

After these last words they parted with the promise that as soon Osho would reply he in turn would inform her immediately.

That day he wrote a loving letter to his Master, explaining to him in detail what kind of proposal he had just received, and Osho's answer came in less than twenty-four hours; but it was not a little written answer as usual but an invitation to meet Neelam, his personal secretary, straight away!

He went immediately to her office, and he was even a little worried, because he couldn't understand what she possibly had to tell him, in order to invite him to her office.

There he discovered that not only had Neelam invited him, but now she was closing the door and locking it so that nobody could hear what she had to tell him.

Once he had sat down in a chair and relaxed, Neelam brought out a little note, telling him that these words had been dictated by Osho, one by one, to make sure that there was not going to be any misunderstanding about it, and now she was going to read him the Master's message:

> *Beloved Sarjano, I want to tell you that I'm absolutely happy for all that you are doing in the kitchen, and also I want you to know how much I love your pictures, so I would like to invite you to stay with that, and nothing else. I want you to put all your passion and all your creativity in these two things, and nothing else.*
>
> *And, more than everything, I want to tell you clearly that I don't want you to hang out with those therapists!*

It happened also that when saying "those therapists" Neelam made a gesture with her hands, as to chase away a mosquito or some other molesting insect, the gesture known in Italy as 'scio, scio'!

In that moment he pretended to be incredulous, but he was just pretending because in fact he knew Osho very well and he could easily imagine him while doing this Neapolitan 'scio, scio' – dirty mosquito.

The fact was that he wanted to see it again, just to be sure to have understood correctly, hence he said, "C'mon, Neelam, I can't believe that Osho said just that, and in this way too!"

"I'm sorry to disappoint you, Sarjano, but this is exactly what he said:

I don't want you to hang out with those therapists!

And in saying so she made again that 'pussa via' with her left hand, trying to imitate Osho's gesture.

He had no intention to let go or give up, because he wanted to see the whole scene one more time, to be sure he would never forget it; hence he told Neelam for the third time, "C'mon, do you really want me to believe that Osho made such vulgar gesture with his hands?"

"As you like, Sarjano, because this is exactly what Osho did." And she showed again that gesture, saying that this was it, and now he could go back to his kitchen and make his pizzas!

"A brilliant career destroyed even before to start!" he was thinking, giggling in his heart, where he would keep forever the memory of Osho's guidance to his best cook!

Naturally, he never said a word about it to Vasumati. He just waited until she came again for lunch, and then told her that Osho had begged him to stay in the kitchen, that the Commune's kitchen needed him.

Then finally came the moment when they had to think about their visas again, without which they couldn't stay in India any longer. Usually his friends were going to Kathmandu for this incumbency, or to Sri Lanka, from where they could come back after two weeks with a new visa valid for one year, but he thought that this could be a good occasion to show Italy to his beloved. He asked her if she was ready to go to Rome with him to apply for a new visa, telling her that his mom was living alone in that city, hence they could stay in her house without having to end up in some hotel, and that mom would be very happy to meet her and get to know his new girlfriend.

She made her usual nod of assent without saying a word; they bought two tickets and started getting ready to leave. They had a return ticket valid for two weeks, so it was going to be a short holiday, but two days before their departure he received a fax from Alberto, his old friend living in Trastevere in the same building as his mom, informing him that his mother had disappeared and was not to be found anywhere! He answered that by pure chance he was heading to Rome in just a couple of days and so he would find out himself what was happening.

The next day he got another fax, in which it was explained how his mom had gone on the street in search of her little cat, and in her search she got lost and was incapable of finding her way home, until after a while she was spotted by a patrolling police car. The policemen had noticed this old woman roaming around with no direction, and since she couldn't even say to these policemen where she was living, they had brought her to S. Maria della Pieta, the biggest hospital of that area.

In Alberto's fax it was further lined out that his mother looked to him a little out of her brain lately, because she was getting lost even when she was going shopping close to her house, that she was too often inconclusive and disarticulated while speaking, and all her neighbors were a little worried about her.

"I'm coming!" he wrote as an answer, and the next day he flew to Italy with his mysterious Japanese. Once they arrived at Rome airport they grabbed the first taxi available and went straight to his mom's house where they found the door strangely open and entered to find the most revolting spectacle in front of them!

There were cat shits and pees all over and the smell was simply unbearable, hence he pulled up his sleeves and started to throw away everything in sight: bed sheets, blankets, even some mattresses, besides obviously all the carpets spread around the house. Mai helped him by filling a bucket with water to which she added some disinfectant and then started washing the floor until it was shiny.

After several hours the house was clean and neat and he decided to go to the hospital to see his mom. After a five minute bus ride they reached S. Maria and after a quick search found his mother lying on a bed, restless and nagging as usual. As soon as his mother saw him she didn't waste any time in greeting or hugging her only son but started immediately to complain loudly, in her typical Neapolitan style: "Ah, you are here, finally! Who in hell has brought me here I don't know, but now you'll take me home – right, Cicci? I want to go home!"

"Let me sign some papers and then I'll take you home. Don't worry; now you can relax, Mom. I am here with you."

He signed those few papers; then he called a taxi that took them all home within a few minutes. While in the car, his mother was trying to have some conversation with Mai, who obviously couldn't understand a word and therefore was not answering at all. After a few minutes his mom asked him, "Cicci, who is this girl here?"

"She is my new Japanese girlfriend," he answered quietly.

"But she doesn't understand a word! I'm speaking to her and she doesn't even answer!"

"Mom, I've told you that she is Japanese, and naturally she doesn't speak our language."

"Whatt-a Japanese and Japanese, Cicci? I'm telling you, she doesn't understand nothing!"

They arrived at home, where even his mother was surprised by how clean and shining the house was. It was a big apartment for a woman living alone, because there were four bedrooms, plus a living room, a huge kitchen. His mother had been living there for the past twenty years, because her rent was fixed by law; besides the fact that she had to walk up three flights of stairs, she was paying the equivalent of only thirty dollars a month, which in a central area like Trastevere was really nothing; hence she never wanted to move from there.

Sometimes, in order to get some extra money, she would rent a room to some of his friends when they were transiting in Rome; therefore he had been giving his mom's address to anyone who needed to stay in the capital for some time, and this way his mother had always some company, plus a little money for paying the rent.

Once they settled down, he started analyzing the condition of his mom because he wanted to understand if she possibly had Alzheimers or something like that, but he couldn't understand anything besides the fact that his mother seemed totally insane and had lost any logical sense.

While dinner time was approaching, for example, his mom had asked him for some money to go shopping in order to prepare something to eat; so he took some money out of his pocket and placed it on the table in front of her and asked, indicating the different notes one by one, "And this – how much money is it?"

"I don't know," said his mother.

"And these coins?" he asked further.

"I don't know," she answered again.

"Mom, if you can't even recognize the money, how can you go for shopping?"

"But what do you want? Give me this money so I can go buy some food, because I'm hungry!"

He decided to accompany his mom just to avoid further troubles, so all the three of them went out together to buy some bread, some spaghetti and all the necessary food items to make a sauce, plus a lot of fruit and some vegetables for a good soup.

He paid himself, so that his mother wouldn't have to confront the complexity of money, and after half of an hour he was in the kitchen cooking for everybody. He was cooking his master soup, the same soup that Shunyo, one of Osho's caretakers, used to define as "This is not a soup, it is a blessing!"

But then, during a moment that he had distanced himself from the pot, his mother stepped in and, God knows why, put a handful of soap powder in his little creation! Perhaps she had mistaken it for salt, but the result was that he got immediately very angry, and he could have strangled her for this, and while he was trying desperately to control himself Mai appeared suddenly behind him whispering: "Remember that you can always laugh…"

These words – of an incredible wisdom – managed to cool him down completely, because in fact it was true, since his soup was making soap bubbles and naturally one can certainly laugh at it, rather than getting pissed off in such a way!

He would be forever grateful to Mai for the help that she gave him during those critical days. He decided that the next day he would bring his mom to a specialist, to find out exactly what was afflicting her.

After a long series of examinations, the response was just what he had feared: his mother had Alzheimers – and not only since a few months, but at least since a few years, and it was a miracle how she had managed so far living alone. At this point he decided that he just couldn't abandon his mother in this condition and go back to Pune, but he had first to find a decent solution for her problem, and he had only two weeks to find it.

He visited all the institutes of the area, including the asylum for retired people in Trastevere, which seemed to him to be a very dignified place, quite clean and full of old chaps playing billiards all day and vivacious old women who were spending their time knitting or embroidering something or other. It was all in all a very cozy place with a truly human fragrance; hence he told his mom about the place that he had just seen and asked her if she wouldn't prefer to stay in this asylum, rather than living alone in this large flat.

His mother looked at him in anger, shocked by such a proposal; and even if she was sixty-eight by then, she told him vehemently and with a great contempt, "Are you crazy or what? What do you have in your brain? I don't want to live amongst old people – do you understand?"

He thought that it would be useless to explain to her that she was of the same age as those people; he felt that his mom wouldn't understand, and probably she was still feeling like a little girl, hence she needed to be treated as such!

Near the house, just behind the square S. Maria in Trastevere, there was a laudable institute, called S. Egidio, which had become a meeting point and source of assistance for all those young migrants coming to Rome in search of a job, mostly from North Africa, people from Morocco, Algeria or from Tunisia, so one day he decided to have a look at this place, because he thought that maybe there he could find the solution to his problem, and miraculously he did find it!

Amongst a group of Moroccans there was a nice young couple, just married, and with her showing already the first signs of an incumbent pregnancy he thought immediately that they were good people, clean, gentle and with a clear loving attitude, so he made them the following proposal: "Guys, I have a mother that lives nearby totally alone, in a big apartment with four bedrooms. My mother has Alzheimers now and she can no longer live alone. She needs someone to assist her, otherwise she is at risk of hurting herself or creating some trouble; hence I thought that you might like to move out from the barracks and come live in a nice apartment in the center of the city – of which you can occupy half – in exchange of taking care of my mother as one member of your family. Moreover I can see that your lady is pregnant, hence she is going to stay at home most of the time, and it will be just like having another little daughter to take care of. Nothing extraordinary or difficult; on the contrary, it is going to be very, very simple! Then, when your kid will grow up, I'm sure that he will start to play with my mom, because she is really in a childlike space, and from her side I can guarantee you that she will enjoy playing with your kid very much.

"So what do you say about my proposal?"

The Moroccan couple could hardly believe in such an offer, and as they were visibly very happy about this unexpected opportunity they all decided to go straight away together to give the good news to his mother.

His mom received them with a smile, and offered even one of her habitual coffees which she still remembered how to prepare since it was her favorite drink, and he finally imparted the latest news. "Mom, in two days I'll go back to India, but you don't have to worry, because these nice Moroccan friends are going to stay here with you: they will prepare your food, make your bed, they will keep the house clean, they will go shopping, and they will take care of all your necessities – isn't this beautiful?"

"Whaaaat… what did you say?" erupted his mother angrily. "Do you want to leave these two dirty Negros in my house? Get lost!"

He turned immediately towards the poor Moroccans, who obviously were totally shocked at his Mom's words, and he whispered in their ears: "Oh my God, she is having another of her terrible attacks! Poor her; she has even started having a delirious attack; she must be suffering so much in this moment!"

He knew well that this was not the case at all, because his mother had just spoken in a rare moment of lucidity, and she could have been even more racist, but naturally he continued with the scene of the poor woman overwhelmed by delirium tremens, just to avoid disconcerting or offending those two nice people.

Anyway, it seemed to everybody that the issue was closed like this, at least for the moment, and there wasn't much to say anymore. Hence the couple left a little sad, and he was forced to postpone his departure, because he just didn't have the stomach to abandon his mother in such a situation.

In the afternoon he took Mai for a walk by the near river, and after they had walked in silence for one hour, he told her simply, "I can't leave with you the day after tomorrow. I must stay here until I find a decent solution to my mom's problem, hence you'll have to go back to Pune alone; but you don't have to worry, because I don't think you'll have to wait for too long before my arrival – at most a couple of months."

She looked at him in silence for an eternity, with a totally incredulous face in front of this perspective, then she said only a few words: "I'm staying here with you." And that was it!

Three months passed, Christmas was arriving, but no solutions seemed to appear on the horizon, and he was more and more depressed about the whole situation, knowing well that without the silent and loving support of Mai he would have already freaked out or have become mad.

As if all this were not enough, he got a call one day from a Milanese girlfriend who said with a voice broken by tears: "Have you heard the latest news from Pune?" And not hearing him answer, she proceeded to tell him that Osho had left his body the day before!

To say that this was like a tree trunk in his face or a fist in his stomach would have been an understatement, because this was the most devastating news that anyone could have given to him.

During the last few years he often had this recurrent nightmare: he dreamt that he had left Pune for a few days, and in his absence Osho was dying. As soon as he would get to know about it, he would try to get back to Pune immediately, because he wouldn't want to miss that moment for anything in the world; but in one way or another he was not capable to go back to the ashram, and would consequently fall into deep anguish… and then he would wake up and realize that it was only a bad dream and that he was still in his bed in Pune! This kind of nightmare had visited him at least half a dozen of times in the last year, and now it was happening for real!

He decided that he had to inform Mai straight away; hence he invited her for the usual walk by the river, which seemed to have become the place of their confessions. They walked in silence for a couple of hours, then sat down by the river and he told her, "Yesterday Osho left his body. If you like I can go now to the travel agency and get you a ticket to fly out tonight, so that tomorrow you can be in Pune and you can at least take part in the celebrations which are bound to be happening."

She sat in silence for another five minutes; then she said very softly only two words: "No need." And that was it.

They went back home in silence and they never spoke again on the subject, but returned to their task of caretakers of this old woman with Alzheimers.

Months passed, and not only was there no solution in sight but the condition of his mother was getting more and more aggravating, to the point that she was often incapable of recognizing even her friends who were coming to visit her, even less Mai for that matter, so much so that sometimes she would ask, "Cicci, but who is this woman?" To which he would respond patiently that she was his new Japanese girlfriend, and that he had told her already a thousand times!

His mother would shake her head, and then conclude, "Cicci, I speak to her and she never answers, what-a Japanese are you talking about? She doesn't understand a thing, let me tell you!"

Meanwhile Mai had learned mysteriously and with an unsuspected sense of humor how to answer to his mom: "Cicci, she understands, she understands" – and in perfect Neapolitan dialect!

Unfortunately, the situation of his mother was becoming worse by the day; so much so that now she was forgetting even to smoke! His mother had been a chain smoking addict for over forty years, and she could have smoked two packets of Alfa a day, because they were the cheapest cigarettes on sale, and now she was reduced to the extent of forgetting even her old habit.

She was glued to the television all day though, and whenever she saw somebody smoking she would immediately remember 'something' and run towards him, shouting, "Cicci, give me this thing, give me…" And meanwhile she was making some gestures with her hands, or bringing her right hand to her mouth as if she were smoking, keeping on repeating, "And give me this thing – but where are you keeping it?"

He understood very well what his mother was trying to convey, but he was always pretending that he didn't understand, saying to her, "Mom, if you don't tell me what you want, how can I give it to you?" To which his mother would start looking at him in anger, saying, "Fuck off ! Go away!" – because somewhere and somehow she knew that she was being teased, but after five minutes she would totally forget the whole story.

Since he began noticing that by now she was incapable of distinguishing the good from the bad, and more important black from white, he decided that the time had come to invite the Moroccan couple again; he asked them to come his mom's flat the next day, telling them that it would be nice if they could bring some little sweet or some patisserie for his mom, because this would put her in a better mood!

The next day the couple rang the doorbell and he went to open and invite them into the kitchen to sit near his mother while he was making coffee, because Lucia had forgotten how to do it – or perhaps she had forgotten that she used to like coffee more than anything else.

While his mom was devouring all the little desserts brought by our Moroccan friends he started once more to tell her that in a couple of days he would go back to India, but she didn't need to worry, because these two nice people would stay with her and take care of her needs.

It was truly the same movie as six months before, with the only difference that the woman now had a huge belly, and his mother, rather than freaking out like the first time, had gone towards the couple as if she wanted to hug them, but then limited herself to grab the arms of both, saying, "How beautiful! So you are staying here with me, Cicci? Yes, yes, stay both here and then we can eat these sweets every day. How happy I am that you are going to stay with me!"

Done!

Now he knew to have found the best of solutions for his mother. And in fact this couple took care of her for more than five years, till the day of her death, which they mourned twice: first of all because a dear one, almost part of the family, had died, and secondly because the landlord threw them out immediately, since he didn't want to leave his beautiful apartment in the hands of two poor Moroccans when moreover he could rent it out for much more money.

Anyway, at that point he didn't know if he had any desire to go back to Pune, because Osho was dead, and he was sure that the ashram would become in no time a kind of church, or one of those institutions rich only in rituals but poor in substance and depth; he was quite hesitant about what to do next. During the last three months he had received hundreds of letters and phone calls from his friends who were begging him to come back, because the ashram – according to them – had never been so beautiful and so alive, and it seemed that Osho really had kept his promise, when he was saying:

[…] I will be dissolved in my people…

Everybody asked him in their own way to come and see by himself if the Commune had become an even better place, more joyous and more celebrative after the Master's death; so in the end, after having exchanged a few words together, they decided to leave with the next flight available. In reality even Mai wasn't sure if she wanted to return to the ashram, because she was also pessimistic about its future, and she was almost sure that from now on its beauty, its purity, its immense source of positive energy would have disappeared by and by; and she was afraid to lose that marvelous intimacy that had been establishing itself between them during the last six months, an intimacy made only of long silences, and therefore immensely precious.

He told her that they would go there just to have a look, and if they would like it they'd stay; otherwise they could always come back to Italy, or go somewhere else to start a new life.

They left three days later, with the Moroccan couple already having moved into the apartment and hugging him warmly and thanking him profusely. They guaranteed him he didn't need to worry about anything, because his mom was in good hands and they would take care of her as if she were a member of their family.

With these assurances in their hearts they managed finally to leave, and the next day they were already at the ashram's gate where they got a reception as if the king and the queen had just came back!

His friends were all happy about his return, because also the Osho Café had been closed down in his absence, and now everybody was hoping to be able to again eat his ravioli, or his famous presenta, and he was greeted with great festivity and a surprise that his friends invited them instantly to share the enormous bungalow that they had just rented right behind the ashram! They told them that they had kept two rooms free on purpose, one for him and the other for Mai, and they wanted to bring them immediately to see this marvel of a house.

The bungalow was really beautiful; it was built on two floors, had two huge terraces, and was surrounded by a beautiful garden full of flowers. The kitchen was spacious, so he decided to accept their offer, and after having asked Mai if it was okay with her, they instantly took possession of their new home.

A few days after arrival, he decided not to waste any more time and to start reactivating the Osho Café as soon as possible, because he was thinking about his poor friends deprived of his food for over six months, and he really couldn't wait to see them salivating over his Eggplants Parmesan!

After one week the place was inaugurated with the crème de la crème of the Commune who had come to check out the new restaurant and to see him too, besides enjoying those huge slices of pizza that he had made for the occasion in enormous quantity.

He had broken his own record for the event, and had prepared 150 large trays of pizza, each serving twelve pieces, totaling 1,800 portions; at the end it turned out not to be enough, because they were soon totally finished, while people were still coming in en masse!

The ashram had indeed become even more beautiful during their absence and had become much larger too, since they had bought a huge piece of land next door where they were building some pyramids in black marble, apparently on Osho's suggestion, who had asked that some pyramids should be created as a perfect space for meditation, because they would help us tremendously to enter in a meditative space.

Alas the place was no longer called 'Osho Ashram', but now 'Osho Commune International', which appeared to him like a deep betrayal.

The place had really changed a lot during those six months, yet he felt he was breathing in a different atmosphere, much more responsible and creative, because by now everybody knew that their growth depended only on themselves, and there was no longer the Master's guidance; hence each one of them would have to grow up alone.

The mood in those days seemed to confirm truly the most beautiful heritage of Osho, the feeling was just as if Osho were still there among them, purely dissolved in his people, and his presence and his love were palpable wherever he would go, and for a few years he was living in paradise. Naturally there were people who had absorbed Osho more, and those who had imbibed him less, but all in all everybody seemed to be moving with much more love and meditativeness than in the past.

One of the people that he liked the most at that time was Anubuddha, a Californian Rebalancer who had spent the last two years giving a massage to Osho every day.

Anubuddha was already a great body worker on his own, and a real talent in his field, a great innovator, becoming in fact one of those who created the Rebalancing method. However, the simple fact of giving a session to Osho every day for over two years had certainly added a new depth to his work, a touch even more magical and sensitive, transforming him into what he firmly believed him to be – the best body worker in the world.

The beauty and the uniqueness of this place, plus the incontrovertible fact that it was producing not only the best therapists in the world but the best body workers too, was easily explainable with the simple fact that in the Commune massage artists of every kind were gathering, from those practicing Rolfing to the experts in Postural Integration, the followers of the Alexander Method, those who loved Ayurvedic massage... But the new circumstance was that all these people were not living in their reclusive field or in the ivory tower of their single expertise, but were sharing continuously technical information, input, a variety of methods about what they were doing, with all the others, giving thus life to an immense network of information and knowhow never been seen before on the planet. In this unique way of sharing everyone was gathering the best points from other people's techniques, and ending up with their own super method.

Rebalancing, for instance, which nowadays has become famous all over the world, was born by almost spontaneous germination from a small group of artists that had deliberately decided to put together all their techniques just to see what would come out of it. What came out was naturally the most complete, integrated, effective method of massage ever seen on the planet 'The Rebalancing'!

The same was happening in the field of therapy, where those who were practicing Gestalt were sharing information with those playing with Encounter, which from their side were mixing with those practicing the Primal, and at the end each one of them came to know all the methods circulating in the world of therapy. Therefore, do not marvel that he keeps on repeating that Pune ashram has created simply the best therapists and the best body workers in the world, because it is a fact that can be explained very easily and rationally.

With Anubuddha he had become best friends, because this sublime artist used to come every day to eat at his house, together with his eternal companion Anasha. After lunch they would invariably go to the terrace and sit naked inside a huge bathtub in the sun and smoke a little joint. After that, they regularly talked about religion and spirituality, giving birth every day (after their little smoke…) to what Anubuddha defined as 'our spiritual speculation', insisting continuously that he should start collecting these conversations and make a book out of it!

It had happened that out of the enthusiasm of having such a big house just close to the ashram and with a huge garden, he started cooking a delicious lunch every day for his friends who were coming in more and more numbers, participating in the event by bringing some imported delicacies. There was always someone offering a piece of Parmesan cheese, a can of olives or capers, or some of those precious dried mushrooms that Italians call porcini, so he always ended up having the best of ingredients to prepare a succulent meal. And finally, before they went home again, all those who wished to do so placed a little monetary contribution in a little box prominently exposed in the kitchen for this eventuality.

It was clear to everybody that if on the next morning he would find some money in the little box, he would go shopping and then cook for about twenty people, otherwise there would be no food at all – simple! He did suspect that the money he found there was always given by the same five or six most regular visitors, but it didn't matter to him; he didn't care a bit to know who was putting money in the magic box and who never did, because for him it was enough that the money necessary for the shopping would be there, and that made him happy, irrespective of who in particular had left the money.

To make you understand better how the whole game was functioning, it suffices to say that everybody was free to come to have lunch at any day they wished, and also free to leave some money or not, since there was no control about that, and this simple method selected the people according to their love, their spontaneity and their self-acceptance. For example, there were people coming every day, like Anubuddha and his girlfriend, there were people coming a couple of times a week (less trust in existence!), there were people coming only once a week. And those who came once a month revealed, according to him, very little trust and a poor image about themselves, because these people were basically afraid of 'disturbing' if they were to come too often!

There was this Niskriya for example, Osho's cameraman, called Stonehead by the Master. He came only a couple of times for lunch, and the second time, after having eaten like a pig, went close to him and told him, lowering his voice to a whisper, "Can I talk to you for a minute?"

"Sure, please go ahead," he answered.

"Well, I would like to talk to you privately, if you don't mind," said our Stonehead.

"Sorry, there is nothing 'private' in my life," he answered simply. "You can talk freely here."

Lowering his voice even more, Niskriya told him that these lunches he was offering to everybody must cost him a fortune, and he wanted to know how he could contribute to it from his part – perhaps by giving him some money."

He answered, raising his voice so that everybody could hear him, "There is Stonehead here who wants to contribute to our lunches, but he is speaking very quietly because he feels ashamed! I want to tell him to relax about it, to come here more often and to make himself comfortable, until one day he will understand by himself what to do for these nice gatherings to continue."

And that's how our Stonehead started to come nearly every day, to enjoy one meal after another! After a few months Stonehead had become so comfortable that he forgot completely about his desire to help and started even a little flirt with one of the girls living in the house.

One morning before going shopping he went to open the magic box and discovered in horror that there was nothing in it, not even one rupee! He didn't get upset though but limited himself to place an impromptu sign at the door which said "Restaurant closed because of absence of funds"! That day he obviously didn't prepare anything to eat, but the girl who had been flirting with Niskriya went to his home to say goodbye to him because she knew he was leaving for Germany the same day.

Once she arrived there, Niskriya asked her how come she wasn't at Sarjano's place for lunch; she told him about the sign stuck to his door, telling him that for today there was no lunch at all. Listening to this, Niskriya became suddenly very serious; then he took pen and paper, wrote a quick note, placed his message inside a huge envelope, went into his bedroom for a minute and came back with the envelope much more heavy and hermetically closed, saying, "Please give this letter to Sarjano because I'm about to leave and I have to be at the airport within an hour, so I cannot bring it myself; but you have to assure me that as soon that I'm gone you'll give this to Sarjano."

She told him that he could relax completely about it, telling him that she was going immediately back home and would give Sarjano his message straight away; he didn't need to be worry about it. When the letter finally reached into his hands, he opened it and read the little note inside on which was simply written: "I'm sorry Sarjano." – and nothing else.

The envelope seemed to contain something else, so he put his hand inside and found ten notes of one thousand rupees each, which explained his message better and also the way that he had chosen to apologize!

The very next day he placed another sign at the door which said: "Come back friends, the funds have arrived – Hallelujah!"

This was more or less the atmosphere in that house which continued to offer his delicious meals for at least five years in a row, to the joy of all the participants of these fiestas.

However, there was something which was disturbing him very much in all this sharing, and this was the fact that none of his friends who were therapists or meditation leaders could not simply consider his cooking for what it was, nothing less than his meditation, and they kept on coming into the kitchen to disturb him with the excuse of bringing him some flowers, or to hug him or anything. In fact he would have liked to be totally alone while he was cooking, and he had even put up a sign at the entrance of the kitchen that simply said, "Meditation in progress – please do not disturb!" But nobody was giving a shit about it and people continued to enter freely as if there weren't any meditation going on there.

One day he even tried to explain it to one therapist who had entered bringing some flowers with him and was sent to hell on the spot, with the explanation that if he were giving a session to a patient, would he have liked somebody to enter the room and stop him just to give him some flowers? So, why was he coming in the kitchen to break his balls like this, and interrupting his work while he was cooking?

No matter how many times and with how many different metaphors he tried to explain that cooking was truly his meditation, the fact remained that nobody would listen, with the only exception of Anubuddha, who was always waiting for after lunch to have their usual half hour of 'spiritual speculations'.

In the afternoon he was naturally at the Osho Café to prepare his marvelous dinners for about 150 – 200 people every night, then at 9 p.m. he would be there again to serve his food and collect everybody's compliments.

Once in a while he would organize some musical events too, with people like Prem Joshua or Devakant, two great musicians who were coming to play just in exchange for a sumptuous dinner. Yet according to him the Osho Café was missing a daily entertainment, hence he decided that the time had come to invent something new and possibly provocative, as was his style.

What he invented can be summarized by a huge poster that was made for the event by a painter, giving the instructions for the new game, which was called:

"THE CHEAPEST GURU IN THE WORLD"

(With only one rupee you can have an answer to any of your problems!)

INSTRUCTIONS FOR CORRECT USE:

1) The visitor shall sit in front of the Guru.
2) He may place a coin in the container opposite.
3) He will look into the Guru's eyes and will formulate his question.
4) He will get his answer.
5) He will leave in silence and make space for the next visitor.

Then, in capital letters, marked one by one, there was the last paragraph, which read:

"FOR NO REASON WHATSOEVER,
FOR NO AMOUNT OF MONEY,
IN NO CIRCUMSTANCE
WILL THE GURU GIVE ANOTHER ANSWER!"

He had to prepare the performance very well at first, because he wanted to have an assistant – which he found in the massive figure of Dhyanesh, our Indian boss of the guards, who dressed up like a classic Indian for the occasion, with turban and sandals incurved at the bottom; then he needed a big hammer, a stick of the same dimension, and finally a mirror of discrete proportion.

The stick and hammer were made by him, using simply some blocks of Styrofoam and carving out the shapes and painting both in brown color to make them look as if they were of solid wood. The stick in particular was a little masterpiece of hyperrealism because it seemed absolutely real and totally threatening.

On the night chosen for his first performance, he wore a white long robe which made him look like a real guru, and then he sat waiting with the faithful Dhyanesh by his side, carrying in his hand a big apple made of plastic which had a section missing. If someone would put a coin on the missing chunk, a worm would come out to grab the coin and slip it inside the apple.

After a while there were hundreds of people reading carefully the instructions, until a Neapolitan friend came forward to ask the first question, which was a masterpiece of pseudo-mystical inquiry with big words meaning nothing, and seemed to have been posed only out of the desire to embarrass him and see how he could answer to such an intricate and elaborate question.

The question was more or less: "When the kundalini energy rises and moves from the first chakra to the second, and then to the third, where does it meet with the prana and how can it reach the seventh chakra with all this weight?" – and so on, with a series of bullshits one after the other, to formulate a question full of intricate symbols, posed with the only intent of confusing him.

He was well prepared for this kind of question, and in fact the hammer and the stick were there just for such questions, so much so that he had established a little sequence of conventional signs with Dhyanesh: if he would raise one finger in the air, his corpulent and threatening assistant would grab the hammer and throw a quick hit on the head of the unfortunate questioner.

If he would raise two fingers, it meant calling a stick, this too suddenly and abruptly, with a whack on the head of the one who had asked for it!

If finally he would raise three fingers, his assistant would have to pick up the mirror next to him and place it in front of the guy who had requested an answer.

After that crypto-mystical question, he slowly raised one finger, to which Dhyanesh let go a terrific hit on the head of the poor Neapolitan who – before realizing that the hammer was totally innocuous – got scared like hell and his face went white by all this terror!

After that he closed his eyes and reclined in his big chair of a little guru, while the guy, after recovering from the shock and all the people laughing around him, didn't seem to have any intention to vacate his seat, expecting perhaps some words after the hit. When he opened his eyes again and saw him still there, he started to raise slowly his finger in the air, saying, "Would you like another answer? The first wasn't enough?"

The guy ran away in a flash, leaving the seat to a beautiful girl that looked as if she had found a way to tease him a little, and in fact she said, "I have a serious problem: I have lost my dog and I cannot find it anywhere. Can you help me?"

The technique that he had planned to use for this game was that whatever question he would have been asked, even the most stupid like this one for example, he would have answered as if it were the most important question of his life, giving it an absolute dignity and an answer adequate to this dignity.

He looked into the girl's eyes for a long moment, and then he told her: "This is a false problem. Actually it is not a problem at all, in the sense that you don't have any dog and you never had, because you simply can't possess an animal, because the dog belongs to himself and it cannot be otherwise!

"You can call him 'your dog', if you wish so, but it will make no difference, because what matters are his feelings and not your useless definitions. The dog can be your friend, he can even be faithful to you his whole life, but it will never belong to you, he will never be 'your dog'. Hence you can relax and begin to understand the nature of animals, rather than going around asking these stupid questions and thinking that this creature could be 'your dog'!"

The girl was quite in shock and totally surprised about the funny and light wisdom that she had received, and instantly, without thinking for a second, she wanted to pose another, hopefully more serious, question. But the game was over for her, as per the instructions that didn't include a second question. Greatly disappointed, she left.

Nearly every person coming forward was playing light and jokingly with their question, but after receiving the answer, nearly everybody had the sense of having wasted a chance, and at this point they wanted to ask a 'real question' – but it was too late, alas, even if there were people ready to offer one thousand rupees in order to ask another, more pertinent question!

Then came a young guy with a face full of pimples, sat in front of him saying that he too had a big problem: "I can't find a girlfriend," he said, trying to hold his laughter. To which our mini -guru raised three fingers in the air, with the result that the faithful Dhyanesh placed instantly the big mirror in front of his face so that this guy could look at himself a little better, and this was his answer. Everybody started laughing; the guy looked confusedly in the mirror for a moment, and then sneaked away amongst people's laughter!

The performance went on for a couple of hours, with the people more and more amused, until his Indian assistant announced that the next will be the last question for the evening. Everybody started to look around to find out who would be the last victim, when the Neapolitan guy who had the first hit with the hammer came back in front of him, saying he wanted to be the one to ask the last question.

Our guru didn't even want to hear about it, but the guy was very stubborn and on top everybody around was sympathizing with him, shouting that it would be right if he could have the last answer, since with his previous question all he got was just a big hit on his head!

It had become very late at that point, and it was about time to close the Osho Café, hence our Guru nodded in condescendence with his head, and authorized the Neapolitan to ask his second question, to which this guy came to kneel in front of him and asked him in all seriousness, "Sarjano, why do you make a fool of yourself like this?"

Our guru looked at him in silence for quite some time with authentic compassion, because he was thinking that this poor guy was really asking for trouble if he had reduced himself to ask something of this kind. Then he answered him with all the depth that he managed to gather: "Yes, my dear friend, what you say is really true. I'm making a fool of myself tonight, and do you know why? Because you are all, you more than anyone else, so serious, but so deadly serious, that it is only out of sheer compassion from my side to offer you a reason to smile, at least once in your miserable life!

"I know that I'm making a fool of myself, but I do it only very occasionally, and I'm doing it totally CONSCIOUSLY, in absolute awareness, just to give you a good laugh, while you are keeping on making a fool of yourself every day, practically at every instant of your life, and you do it without even realizing it, in total UNAWARENESS.

"This is the only difference existing between me and you – that I make a fool of myself consciously and you make a fool of yourself much more, but totally UNCONSCIOUSLY, without even knowing that you behave like a fool all the time!"

Needless to say, everybody cracked up laughing, while our Neapolitan hero was probably repenting to have insisted so much for asking the last question!

What else could he write to describe the light and funny climate of those days?

Well, the most important thing was the arrival of his son Amore, who had just completed his Lyceum and had expressed to his mother the desire to spend some time with his dad, because he hadn't been living with him since a long time. So Silvia had bought him a ticket and helped him to leave for Pune. As the reader will recall, Amore had changed his name to Marco when he was six years old because he had been relentlessly teased about his name by his class mates.

When he arrived at the ashram, everybody wanted to know Sarjano's son, and he was introducing him every day to dozens of people, until one day they met some friends that had been living in Sicily when he was still a little child, and they said that as far as they could remember his name was Amore, so they asked him how come that he had changed his name. His son started to look here and there, supremely embarrassed, until he met the eyes of two beautiful teenagers that were there following the whole scene, and had started whispering to each other, "Have you heard, that guy is called Amore: what a beautiful name!" Then, addressing him they asked, "Who has given you such a beautiful name?"

Amore realized immediately that in this place he no longer needed to be ashamed of his name, but on the contrary he would gain a lot of points with the girls, so he proudly reclaimed his original name and accepted finally to be called Amore!

He found for him a nice room in the big bungalow where he was living with Mai and with the very Marco which had been the inspiration of his choice of name; he had been his best friend in the old Sicilian commune where he spent his childhood. However, a sort of serious problem arose shortly after he moved in, because Amore enjoyed being in that house so much that he would come out only for a couple of hours in the evening to help him at the Osho Café; otherwise he was staying all day at home to chat with his father's friends, to play poker for hours with Marco and two more rascals, or to play furious table tennis in the garage with a Chilean guy who had taught him his favorite mantra: "Vamo…vamo… vamo….VAAAAAAAAMMMOOOOOOOOOOO" – that had created so many problems in the Commune. This Chilean was using this mantra especially when he was playing doubles with another Chilean against the father and the son, without counting a holy spirit that would make him and his son win all the games they played against the two Chileans.

His son had so much fun at home that he was barely going to the ashram, plus there were his famous lunches with a variety of teenagers that had started coming with their moms to visit, only to flirt secretly with Amore, who was enjoying all these attentions very much, even if everybody was referring to him as 'Sarjano's son'. But anyway, time would give him revenge because in a couple of years it was he who was to be known everywhere as 'the father of Amore'!

The relationship between him and Amore couldn't have been more beautiful, more loving, more mature, because he had discovered that even after more than ten years they hadn't been living together, his son still considered him the most beautiful father in the world and more than a father he considered him his very best friend. He often said that Sarjano was certainly the best father in the world, but he would have preferred him not being his father, because in this way they could have been even better friends!

The respect, the admiration, the love that his son had for him were definitely making him worthy of his name, and in fact this obvious punch line was in everybody's mouth: "Your son Amore is really an amore!"

He was an 'amore' too, in his own way, and it was only out of his love that after six months of this life he decided to throw his son out of the house and let him do something for his life, that little scoundrel! With this he wanted to say that it would have been much better if his son would detach himself a little from that house and maybe start going to the Commune more often, where he could meet people, socialize, do something, meditate, and on top could study some of the arts that were offered, do something creative in his life, maybe giving massages, for example.

Anubuddha, the best rival in table tennis that his son had found amongst his friends, had invited him many times to sign up for the next Rebalancing training, because he truly believed that Amore had first of all two beautiful hands with very good energy, and that he was also full of that love which his name was inspiring. He therefore thought that Amore could be a body worker of great talent, and one day he told him all this with such passion that Amore couldn't refuse his invitation, and within three months he was transformed into a fabulous Rebalancer.

Amore, thrown out from home out of love, found immediately a sweet little home with a garden, and started naturally to go to the Commune every day, and even though he never managed to be initiated into sannyas by Osho, he ended up becoming a real sannyasin, much more authentic than certain types of guys with the holy medallion around their necks!

Months went by, and his life with Mai was proceeding more and more beautifully, but the day when they had to start taking care of their visas was quickly approaching. Mai from her side had decided to go to Japan to apply for her visa and combine this occasion to visit her parents which she hadn't seen for over two years; so she flew East, promising to be back after one month.

He really didn't know where to go for his stupid visa (after all he had been in India nearly twenty years, hence they could have given him some sort of 'honorary citizenship'!) until he got a message from Silvia saying that she didn't like the idea that Amore had to travel alone all the way back to Rome, adding that if he would come to Italy with him, she would reimburse him for the return ticket. He decided to accept her invitation and flew to Rome with his son.

Silvia was naturally at the airport with her car waiting for them and was really happy to see her two men together in one go. They arrived at her beautiful little villa in Monteverde, one of the most exclusive areas of Rome, when he realized immediately that her lover, Satyamo, wasn't there anymore. So he asked to Silvia what had happened, to which she replied in short, "We can talk about it another time, because now I'm just too happy to see both of you here!"

Days passed by, and Silvia showed no signs about reimbursing his ticket, hence he decided to move in order to make some quick money, simply repeating his usual pilgrimage: he would go to Milo in Sicily to meet Battiato, then to Sardinia to visit De Andre, and finally to Siena to see Gianna Nannini, all three of which at that time were not only his best friends but the most famous Italian pop stars.

When he had finished his pleasant job and had scored at least twenty million of the old lire, he thought that the time had come to go back to Pune. He called Silvia on the phone to tell her that he had finished all his work, and that most likely he would fly back from Milano. Silvia seemed very disappointed by the news and begged him to fly from Rome where he could spend a week or two with her, and also she hadn't had time to tell him what happened with Satyamo. And she insisted such much that he simply answered, "If you want to see me, first you have to pay for the camel!" – which was an expression used often while playing poker.

She understood the metaphor instantly and began apologizing profusely that she hadn't given him the money for his ticket yet, as she had promised when he was in Pune, but he cooled her down telling her that he would arrive by train the next day, and asked her to come to the station to pick him up with her car.

Once he was out of the station, he saw immediately Silvia's car parked in front with the engine on; he jumped in with his entire luggage and they headed towards home. Even during this short trip Silvia was continuously apologizing about the money issue, and continued even when they arrived home and she rushed to open a drawer, pulled out a bunch of money and started to count it under his nose: "One hundred thousand, two hundred thousand, three hundred thousand…" and so on, until reaching one million lire.

He took the money in his hands and asked her, "Is this my money?"

"Sure," said Silvia. "This is your money."

"It is mine and I can do whatever I want with it?"

"But sure! This is your money and you can do anything you want with it."

At that point he took a lighter from his pocket and he simply burned the whole million lire, with Silvia at first screaming with despair and then almost fainting on the spot!

"See, Silvia, this is just to tell you that I don't care a bit about money, because what matters is how much you care." But at the same time he was thinking that these little "lessons" were becoming a little too expensive for his meager finances, but for Silvia, who he had always loved very much, he would have done this and even more!

Hearing his mother crying, Amore ran to see what was happening, and when he saw him with the last fragments of burned notes in his hands, he understood instantly what had just happened and commented, "Wouldn't it have been better if you had given this money to me who still doesn't have a ticket to go back to Pune?"

Amore in fact was trying in his own way to find the money for a return ticket and he had given massages to Silvia's girlfriends at 50,000 lire per session, but he still didn't have the amount necessary. At this point his mother, who seemed to have learned the lesson, told him that he didn't need to worry about his ticket, because she would pay happily for it. Ten days later she took them both to the airport and saw them flying away.

The day before their departure, Silvia finally decided to tell him what had happened between her and Satyamo. She explained that her man practically had left for good six months ago, saying that he was tired to be treated like a stray dog; since that day he had completely disappeared and he had never written or phoned.

Silvia was crying while narrating this story, but he had no intentions whatsoever to console her, and he left her in the shit that she had created for herself, deciding that more than consolations she needed someone who would tell her the truth, and she had just found that!

"See, Silvia, you have been with Satyamo for more than ten years, and what have you been doing during all this time? You were complaining day in day out about the fact that he didn't have any job, and basically wasn't making any money, so you were compelled to support him totally and to take care of all his needs."

Satyamo was a very creative person and he even had been trying to work in Rome as an actor, but he was too good for that. Then he put together a salsa band with some friends, later he directed our little theatrical masterpiece *Faggots*, plus he was even going to play for some parties or at marriages to make some money.

He went on, "In all this time what have you been doing? You were constantly lamenting that he was doing nothing, while in reality this poor guy was always doing something – maybe just composing some song or writing a few lyrics, but you have such respect for money, and such little respect for the people who love you, that you were continuously asking, 'But when are you leaving? When are you going to find a decent job?'

"Now he has finally gone, perhaps in search of a job, and you are here crying because Satyamo has followed your advice and has gone forever! You have no right to cry now, besides over your insensitivity, because you have been asking for it: you have been telling him to leave so many times that at the end he has taken your words for real. Now accept your responsibility, look inside of you, and the next time that you are close with a man like this, don't treat him again in this way, please!"

He never got to know if Silvia had understood, but even years later he saw her crying because Satyamo had abandoned her. Sometimes it is very difficult to understand certain people!

***

CHAPTER 15

The End Of A Dream

After seven years (could it be the famous seven year itch?) since the Master had left the body, slowly slowly, but inexorably, the newly christened Osho Resort became just this: a luxurious resort for pained souls in search of a quick spiritual fix.

Now just for simply entering (former ashramites like him excluded, thank God!) it wasn't the 50 rupees as during the time when Osho was alive, but 500 rupees net, which meant that the cost of entrance had been raised ten times over ten years!

Since there was nothing in all of India which had increased to such an extent, we may be able to understand why he was more and more disgusted by the entire story.

Instead of new prayers or new chants, every day new rules were popping up and the place, besides becoming more and more expensive, seemed to become even more and more political, because it had become filled with little gangs trying to acquire more and more power, and they were always fighting amongst themselves.

The undisputed Boss of the most powerful gang, the one who was taking all the most important decisions (like to remove Osho's portraits from everywhere) was one Michael O'Byrne, aka Jayesh, who had arrived at the Ranch – what a strange coincidence! – just after the first visit of the FBI to the Commune!

In those days there was a rumour going around everywhere, whispering that this guy was a CIA agent and that he had been infiltrated there by his bosses to have a first look at the Ranch's activities. This guy had managed with a perfect strategy and refined seduction to get in no time very close to the Master, choosing after a few days to operate with a very simple game, which consisted in seducing Hasya, Osho's new secretary and become her boyfriend.

Since she was living in the room attached to the one of the Master, he, as the servant cavalier of the Secretary, ended up meeting Osho several times a day.

His escalation continued undisturbed even in Pune, where he dropped the mature secretary to engage himself with Vivek, who had been Osho's caretaker for the past thirty years.

He wouldn't ever believe that these events were casual, because this Jayesh was a really handsome and fascinating man, and anyone could have seen that he knew how to deal with women and how to manipulate them, hence what was his need to start a relationship with a woman much older than he, since he could have had nearly any of the young women at his disposal?

He had always had the suspicion that there was some dirty design, a subtle plan behind this story and behind this strange fiancée business, but after all it was none of his business and he stopped thinking about it.

He could never have imagined that the place of his rebirth and of his spiritual growth could ever be lowered to such an extent, and he was totally appalled by it, with the result that he was continuously talking with his friends about the degrade of the Commune, saying that it was necessary to do something to save the ashram from further degradation; however, nobody seemed to give a shit about it and they would hardly respond to his desperate invocations, or at least this was his impression.

One faithful day, he had just finished eating at the Resort's canteen, he was approached by the musicians who used to play in the evening during the darshan with the Master – on video of course! These musicians looked around as if to make sure nobody was listening, then they told him abruptly: "We have heard that you want to shout about the truth in Buddha Hall, one of these evenings..." – and then, without even waiting for his answer, they said: "There is no need for you to shout, because we have all decided to give you our microphone! Well, we are not going to put it in your hand, but if you sit near us, like you have been doing hundreds of times, once we finish playing we are going to leave the microphone on the floor near you, so you can take it and say clearly and loudly what you need to say, because moreover, the guy at the mixer is in accordance with us, and he will not switch off the power as he usually does in that moment, hence the microphone will be still functioning!"

He could hardly believe his luck, and he asked them if they were joking or they wanted to tease him, but the musicians told him that they had never been more serious in their life, and that he had simply to inform them when he wanted to pull it off.

"Why waste time at all? I'm going to do it directly tonight!" – he proposed with all his enthusiasm: "Tonight is okay with you guys?" The musicians agreed, hence all he had to do was go home to get ready for the big event.

You have to realize that in the entire history of the ashram – or whatever they were calling it now – the evening function had never been disturbed by anybody, neither had there been someone reading a proclamation during the ceremony. Hence this event was going to be very likely a great shock for nearly everybody, and it would have had some serious repercussions. Probably they would kick him out from the Commune forever, but he didn't care a bit, because he was considering the place dead and buried, and he wasn't the type of person to entertain himself with corpses or distant memories.

Once he arrived at home, he had a good shower, put on the white robe that Osho had presented him with twenty years ago, and sat in meditation with closed eyes for a few hours. After his long meditation, he got up very slowly, grabbed a pen and a piece of paper and wrote his little proclamation, which had to last no more than 45 seconds, because this was precisely the interval between the end of the music and the video discourse to start.

Once he had written his little poem and had controlled the timing to be exactly 45 seconds, he went back to his meditation, because he wanted to arrive in front of the microphone totally clean, relaxed, with no anger inside, neither feeling negative, yet his meditation was interrupted just one hour later by the ring of the doorbell.

He went to open and saw in front of him Radha, a sort of Neapolitan derelict who used to pretend to be his best friend, and behaved with him like an older sister, as she knew that he was originally Neapolitan like her, and she thought that she was supposed to protect him from his intemperance and troublemaker attitude.

This poor woman had been informed by the musicians about what was cooking for that evening, and she had come only to try dissuading him from doing such a thing. She asked, "But who is asking you to speak out? What are you gaining out of it?"

He would have loved to explain to her that not everybody was doing things in order to gain something as she had always done… as this Radha belonged to that special category of second-rate therapists – simple pretenders that didn't have any original ideas in their mind but simply assembled as best as they could four or five techniques that they had learned here and there, giving it some great name, like 'Love and Meditation', improvising as therapists, and even making a lot of money out of it. He decided not to answer, but asked her to leave immediately because he was meditating.

After Radha had gone, he went back in search of his silence, and once he found it, he deepened into it for another hour, until he felt finally ready for his impossible mission.

He entered the Resort wearing Osho's robe and went to sit near the musicians as planned. They twinkled to him saying that they had placed some friends around him, in order to slow down the eventual arrival of the guards who would certainly try to stop him, in order to give him those 45 seconds that he needed to read his inspired little poem.

The function started as usual at 7p.m. with the musicians spreading their sweet music and the people around them swaying softly following its rhythm, and as soon they stopped playing and they had left the microphone on the floor, he grabbed it in a second and started to read very quietly and lovingly:

"BELOVED FRIENDS,

MA YOGA NEELAM, OSHO'S SECRETARY FOR INDIA, HAS BEEN FORCED TO RESIGN DUE TO POLITICAL PRESSURE FROM JAYESH, CHAIRMAN OF THE INNER CIRCLE.

NEELAM HAS ALWAYS BEEN OSHO'S AMBASSADOR OF THE HEART AND AS JAYESH IS DISREGARDING OSHO'S GUIDELINES FOR THE INNER CIRCLE, WE THE PEOPLE WHO SUPPORT OSHO'S VISION, ASK HIM TO RESIGN HIS POSITION.

WE ASK THAT NEELAM BECOMES THE CHAIRWOMAN OF THE INNER CIRCLE.

WE ARE NOT HERE FOR POWER POLITICS; WE ARE HERE FOR MEDITATION, LOVE AND CELEBRATION.

THIS ANNOUNCEMENT IS IN SUPPORT OF THE NEW MAN WHO REJECTS POLITICS AND EMBRACES LIFE, LOVE, MEDITATION AND LAUGHTER.

LET US CELEBRATE NOW THE NEW MAN AND THE NEW WOMAN!"

Miraculously he managed to finish his reading, and just in the moment when he was uttering his very last word, two huge guards arrived, pushing and puffing amongst the friends trying to slow them down, grabbing him under his arms like a bag of potatoes and carried him away.

While the guards were doing their dirty job, the people who had witnessed the whole scene were shouting: "Leave him alone! Bring him back, what are you doing?!" It was useless, because the two gorillas carried him for 50 meters to the gate, where they threw him out without any compliments!

During the night there was an incredible traffic of messages, phone calls, visits from people who wanted to know what was going on, because they were all worried for him, and he was quite happy to see all this solidarity showered upon him, until at dawn he managed finally to go to sleep.

The next morning he decided to pass by the Resort to check out the atmosphere and to verify if his prediction had been right or not, because somehow he was sure that the guards at the gate would have an order of not letting Sarjano inside the premises. But he was wrong, because when he reached the gate and pretended to enter the two Indian guards greeted him as usual and were about to let him through without a problem.

He stopped in front of the gate and asked them jokingly: "Do you even let rebels like Sarjano enter? They haven't told you to prevent me from entering yet?" The two guards burst out laughing and told him that they hadn't received any message about it, and even if the order to stop him would arrive, they would let him enter anyway!

Once he had satisfied his curiosity he decided not to return for a couple of days, because he was afraid that everybody would gather around him to ask more details about the whole story, so he moved towards the German Bakery to have a cappuccino in peace.

After one hour he was still there chatting with some friends – he had nothing to do, hence he could stay all day at the bar drinking with his friends – when he saw two of the ladies working for the Big Boss Jayesh running towards the Bakery. The two ladies were looking just for him, and once in front of him, they proceeded to tell him emphatically that there was some trouble going on, and that he was requested to go to the Resort with them immediately!

He asked what was happening and why all this agitation, to which the alert functionaries told him that some people had seen him in front of the Resort's gate just one hour ago, speaking with the guards, and then leaving without entering, and they had concluded that the guards wouldn't let him enter!

They added further that the news of Sarjano having been banned from the Resort had spread like a wild fire amongst all the sannyasins and there were already people going to the main office to complain, or even asking to meet Jayesh in person to enquire and ask what the hell was happening.

In view of all this commotion, the Boss had sent them in search of Sarjano, to convince him to come to the Resort for at least half an hour, just enough to be seen by everybody, so that everybody could see that he hadn't been kicked out as the rumors were saying.

He started laughing at the thought that until a few hours before, he was sure that they would have thrown him out like a stray dog, and now they were asking him to come back and to show up… and they were even begging him to do that! He decided to comply with the request of the two anxious ambassadors and went for a walk inside the Resort, with the result that he was seen by everybody and calm finally returned among the orange-people.

They had found however, their own method to punish him in a very cruel way, because the very next day he was called to the main office and he was brought in the presence of the Personal Secretary of the Boss, who informed him plainly and without blinking that from that moment he could no longer work in the Commune, that Osho Café had been closed for good, and from now on he was no longer supposed to translate Osho's books anymore, and even less so writing for the Osho Times, especially for the Italian edition, which had the long tradition of publishing an article written by him in every issue since many, many years!

He immediately went to the Italian Osho Times office to see if the girls who were running it had already received the news, and saw both of them crying at their desks. They told him in tears that just half an hour before Shunyo had been there to tell them that from today on Sarjano couldn't write anything for their paper anymore!

This Shunyo, besides been in charge of the entire publications related to Osho, was one of his dearest friends, but the two girls told him that even when they informed her that Sarjano was a pillar of the Italian Osho Times, she became aggressive and said that these were the orders and they weren't supposed to be discussed!

So they allowed him to enter the Resort, but they had cut him off from every communication, any creativity, in one word from all the activities that he had embraced in the Commune.

He thought about that poor Shunyo who he had fed for years, since she was the girlfriend of Marco, his Roman friend who had followed him to Pune over ten years ago and with whom he was sharing his house, this poor Shunyo that used to say sitting in front of his soup: "This is not a soup, it is a blessing!"

'What people have to do in order to live or just to survive…' he was telling to himself bitterly.

Naturally now, wherever he would go, people were asking continuously about this story and what he wanted to do next and so on and since he was getting tired of all this blah blah he decided at a certain point to propose to Mai to go together to Goa for a couple of weeks; and the same evening they were already on the night bus that would take them to the ocean.

At that time all sannyasins going to Goa ended up inevitably in Candolim, a long strip of beach extended from Calangute to Fort Aguada, where one could find a couple of resorts (not in Pune style!), very sweet and civilized because they had been hosting these sannyasins for thirty years and had slowly learned the most elementary hygienic norms, and even to cook in 'western style'.

He knew that even too well, because every time he landed at Dona Florina's, his favorite little resort, she would ask him to teach to her servants how to make lasagna, or the famous 'Spaghetti on the Rocks' (with sea-food), or the 'Eggplants Parmesan' or other Italian specialties.

They spent a dreamlike month with Dona Florina, eating fish every day, taking long walks at dawn along the ocean, enjoying the multicolored sunsets of Goa, and forgetting all about the mess they had left behind them.

When they finally came back to Pune it was about the end of March, and he felt immediately something in the air that he didn't like at all, like a presage of some scandal on the way, and as usual his feelings were right and his intuition revealed itself correct.

Walking around the Resort he noticed that more than half of the population had left for the West, because the so called high season was over, and the place looked much emptier, without even his best friends around. After having returned since just a couple of days, he was informed by some viscid functionary that he was expected to go to the main office for some communication of extreme importance.

"Here we are!" – he said to himself, expecting the worst; and the worst certainly came, because in the vast saloon of the Central Office the entire staff of renegades at the order of Jayesh had assembled in full. They looked like a kind of modern version of The Holy Inquisition of medieval memory, and their faces were promising trouble, for they were all very serious and they didn't waste any time in telling him what a delinquent he was.

The first person to speak against him was Zareen, an Indian woman that had always sworn to love him immensely, but in that moment she started simply to make a long list of his misbehaviors, and how all this was defaming the good name of the Resort.

What hasn't been told so far is that the very next day after his exploit in Buddha Hall, there was a big article in the local newspapers – without anybody understanding how it was possible, and a week later the weekly magazine India Today, perhaps the most respected political magazine in India, had sent a female reporter to write a long story about the latest events at the Osho Resort.

This woman had been searching for him, and got his narration of his own version about all that was happening in the Resort, and published it later in a massive article. As if this was not enough, a journalist friend had asked him if he wanted to write a short story about his experience for The Indian Express about his experiences, and the response was a long story called "Three Dictators Sitting in an Ivory Tower are Destroying the Commune".

In fact, all these bureaucrats had more than one reason to be angry at him, hence to make it shorter he told them simply: "Listen guys, I don't like to waste my time unnecessarily, hence just tell me what you want from me now, and let's finish this story!"

There was a long, embarrassed silence, because all these people had been his close friends, at least in the past, and many of them were even habitué at his homely lunches, until a viscid little Indian, who was working as an accountant for the Big Boss told him in all seriousness: "We want you to give back your entry pass."

"Is that all?" – he replied with great coolness, throwing at the same time his pass in the face of that idiot!

Then he looked one by one at every member of this 'Religious Tribunal' and said his final words: "I just want to tell you that you are going to regret this decision bitterly.

"Fare you well, my friends!"

And within one minute he left his old ashram forever, and from that moment on he would not enter anymore.

And at that point finally the strategy of these bureaucrats became clear to him: they didn't kick him out immediately, because they understood that to throw him out just after his proclamation would have stirred tremendous agitation, a popular protest never seen before, hence what did they do? They waited a couple of months until the commotion had cooled down and the majority of old sannyasins had left for the end of the season to kick him out unopposed like a dirty dog. But for sure this was not going to be the end of it!

If he couldn't enter the Resort anymore, nothing was preventing him from walking in front of it, and in fact every morning he would walk in that direction to meet his friends who would talk with him about the whole story, suggesting even some way or some excuse how he could come back in the Resort. "We are sure that if you utter some public apologies, they will let you enter again."

Inevitably he would answer, "I will apologize for sure if I had something to apologize for, but the plain fact is that in my opinion I have nothing to excuse myself for: what can I do?"

Then he liked to tease the two Indian guards who had said a few months before that if he were banned they would let him enter anyhow, so he would stand in front of the gate intoning a sort of litany: "Indian bolo-bolo…very cheap… Indian bolo-bolo…" with the result of exposing their contradiction very clearly, even though he knew that they had no choice, because if they would let him in, they would have been thrown out too.

Anyway, he wasn't in the mood to give up and leave just like this, hence he decided to return for a while to his street warrior attitude and start creating some disturbance for these bureaucrats.

The first thing he did was a huge poster with this message written on it:

"STOP BANNING OSHO'S PEOPLE"

While the other side read: "TRUTH WILL WIN"

With these two posters sandwiched over his shoulders he placed himself in front of the Resort's gate, to be admired by all the passers-by and to attract people to stop and talk about the whole issue.

Not satisfied with this, he produced also a small flyer that was written by Osho in person! It was in fact nothing else than an answer that Osho had given him to a question on the subject of punishment, that seemed truly written for this occasion.

On top Bapu, the Sufi mystic from Hyderabad, had sent him a message which read: "I'm with you, Osho is with you, but please don't get attached to stones!"

And that's when he decided to leave Pune for good and start a new life…

What remains of a dream…

Since that faithful day he never entered the Resort again, neither did he visit any other Osho Center, nor did he hang out with sannyasins or take part in any meditation. For that matter, he never listened to any of Osho's discourses or read any book or lecture whatsoever… and it's up to you to guess why!

There was no space for memories in him, neither nostalgia, nor any sense of loss… he was utterly empty, and filled only with gratitude.

He knew that Osho was smiling at all this, and at most he would have giggled:

"Well done, Sarjano!"

These people could even delete His name from the planet, but they would never be capable of erasing it from his heart, from his very soul, where Osho will abide forever and ever.

That is in fact the only thing that remains of a dream: an immense gratitude. And in the words of Vandana, one of the few sannyasins who were still in contact with him and sent him a message called "What Remains" it simply says:

"You are so beautiful Sarjano!
This is no longer hero worship,
just recognition and acknowledgement!
You are a one-off incarnation of an extraordinarily wild
and beautiful being,
who has dance-partnered existence,
without restraint for more than 65 years,
and existence is delighted with the partnership…"
Or, I can just whisper my final song:
"What can I say…
What can I say…
I love you!"

***

Osho's samadhi

Wanting to stay in India, and with no desire to return to the West, Sarjano moved to Goa, where on the insistence from his many friends, (a very warm insistence!) he opened an Italian Restaurant called *My Place,* described by *The Times of India* as *"My Place* is not only the best Italian Restaurant in all of Goa, but perhaps in all India…"

Feel free to visit it, any time, because the newly renamed restaurant *Buon Appetito* is just Sarjano's mirror: it is open every day, including during the monsoon and in 11 years has never closed, not even for one day!

Sarjano, Goa 2014